The Origins of Irish Convict Transportation to New South Wales

The Origins of Irish Convict Transportation to New South Wales

Bob Reece
Associate Professor in History
Murdoch University
Western Australia

First published 2001 by
PALGRAVE
Houndmills, Basingstoke, Hampshire RG21 6XS and
175 Fifth Avenue, New York, N. Y. 10010
Companies and representatives throughout the world

PALGRAVE is the new global academic imprint of
St. Martin's Press LLC Scholarly and Reference Division and
Palgrave Publishers Ltd (formerly Macmillan Press Ltd).

Outside North America
ISBN 0–333–58458–9 hardback
ISBN 0–333–58459–7 paperback

In North America
ISBN 0–312–23211–X hardback

This book is printed on paper suitable for recycling and
made from fully managed and sustained forest sources.

A catalogue record for this book is available
from the British Library.

Library of Congress Cataloging-in-Publication Data
Reece, Bob, 1940–
    The origins of Irish convict transportation to New South Wales / Bob
    Reece.
      p. cm.
    Includes bibliographical references and index.
    ISBN 0–312–23211–X (cloth)
      1. Penal colonies—Australia—New South Wales—History. 2. Prisoners,
    Transportation of—Australia—New South Wales—History. 3. Prisoners-
    -Ireland—History. 4. Irish—Australia—New South Wales—History. 5.
    New South Wales—Emigration and immigration—History.

    HV8950.N6 R44 2000
    364.6'8—dc21
                                                    00–027250

10   9   8   7   6   5   4   3   2   1
10   09 08 07 06 05 04 03 02 01

Printed in Great Britain by Antony Rowe Ltd, Chippenham, Wiltshire

Contents

List of Illustrations and Maps   ix

List of Abbreviations   xii

Acknowledgements   xiii

Introduction   xv

1 Irish Transportation before 1783   1
Virginia   1
'To be Barbadoes'   2
White slaves   5
Self-transports   8
Ireland's transportation laws   11
The Irish system   12
'A parcel of likely men'   15
Irish critics of transportation   18
The Hard Labour Act   21
Military recruitment   23

2 Crime in Late Eighteenth-Century Ireland   26
Organised criminals   28
'Prince of Pickpockets'   34
The Sall Dubb Club   38
Prostitution   39
Rural Crime   41

3 Prisons and Punishment   45
The New Prison   45
Kilmainham   53
Black-dog Prison and the Marshalseas   55
Sir Jeremiah Fitzpatrick   56
County gaols   57
'The fatal board'   59
'Detain not the excruciated soul'   62
Larry   63

4   The Revival of Trans-Atlantic Transportation   **66**
'Servants is the word'   67
Nova Scotia   71
Africa   73
Cape Breton Island   74
'Worse than the haunts of wild beasts'   76
Alternatives to transportation   77

5   Emigration, Runaways and Returnees   **81**
'Emigrating madness'   81
'This traffic in human flesh'   85
Runaways   87
Returnees   89
Frederick Lambert   92
'Father' Fay   93

6   The Revival of Irish Transportation   **98**
The *Nancy*   101
The *Anne-Mary*   104
'A load of serpents'   110
The *Dragon*   112
The *Dispatch*   115
The *Chance*   116
'A present to the Congress'   118
'A gentle Remonstrance'   123

7   Irish Anticipations of Botany Bay   **125**
The Police Bill   125
The Botany Bay announcement   129
'Such acute beings'   131
'The Mixture and probable cross of Breeds'   133
Satirical anticipations   137
Pressure on the gaols   142
'Petticoat miners'   144
'The most wretched footing'   146

8   The Voyages of 1788: New London and Cape Breton   **150**
'Quite transported'   152
'A Suit of T-- and F-------'   153
The *Providence*   155

Main à Dieu Harbour 158
Governor Macarmick 160

9 **The Newfoundland Voyage** 166
Talamh an Eisc 168
'Great disorders' 170
The Winter house 172
'The Goal Disorder' 173
'The most outrageous Set of People that ever lived' 174
Prince William Henry 176
The Ferryland 'riots' 179
'Such a Banditti' 182
'The best Shoplifter in Ireland' 183
'Cruising' in Newfoundland 184
The *Elizabeth and Clare* 187

10 **The Newfoundland Convict Crisis** 191
'Scurvy and the Flux' 194
'A national indignity' 195
The Regency crisis 197
'This ill-advised step' 200
'Neither colony nor plantation' 201
'A loop hole' 204

11 **The Barbuda Affair** 208
'A great gainer or loser' 208
Barbuda 210
'A great uneasiness and alarm' 211
'Such an amazing expence' 216
'This horrible abuse in Ireland' 217

12 **Crisis in the Gaols** 220
The Newgate riot 222
Kilmainham 226
Penitentiary houses 228

13 **Irish Transportation to New South Wales** 231
The transportation debate 232
The new Act 234
'I was in hopes' 235
'Of an incorrigible description' 241

The convicts of the *Queen*   242
'A sailing party'   248
'A desert corner of the earth'   249
'Clear the way till I mount my *landau*'   252
'An epitome of Botany Bay'   254

14   The *Queen* Transport   **256**
Camden, Calvert and King   258
'The most dreadfull instance of Cruelty'   260
Lieut. Blow   264
'Sailed, *Queen*'   265

15   Irish Transportation 1792–1795   **267**
Henry-Gore Sankey   268
The penitentiary option   271

*Appendix   I   Expenditure on Irish Convict Transportation,
1787–89*   274

Appendix   II   The Newfoundland Shipment, 1789   275

*Appendix   III   Virginian Legislation Prohibiting the Landing of
Convicts, 1788*   282

Appendix   IV   Documents Relating to the Barbuda Voyage, 1789   283

Appendix   V   Reports from the Botany Bay Parliament   288

*Appendix   VI   Documents Relating to the Voyage of the Queen,
April 1791*   292

Notes   304

Bibliography   348

Index   361

List of Illustrations and Maps

Illustrations

1 Convict assignment warrant, Virginia, c. 1760s   13

2 English cartoon of aristocratic convicts arriving in America.   18
   Detail from *Political Electricity: or, an Historical & Prophetical
   Print in the Year 1770. Bute and Wilkes invent. Veridicus &
   Junius fect.* By courtesy, Prints and Photographs Division,
   Library of Congress (LC–USZ62–45564)

3 William Eden, Lord Auckland. From *The Journal and*   19
   Correspondence of Lord Auckland ..., 2 vols, London:
   Richard Bentley, 1861 (frontispiece).

4 A Dublin Watchman. A Dublin Newspaper Seller.   29
   From *The Dublin Cries: or a Representation of the various
   Cries and Callings throughout the Streets, Lanes and Allies
   of the City and Liberties of Dublin*, printed by G. Powell,
   in Green–Street, opposite New Prison, and sold by
   D. Carpenter in Newry.

5 'Barrington Picking the Pocket of J. Brown, Esq. of   35
   Brandford'. Also illustrated are Barrington's tools of
   trade. From: *Memoirs of George Barrington, containing every
   Remarkable Circumstance, etc.*, London, 1790

6 'A Prospect of the Parliament House, in College Green   40
   Dublin'. College Green and Dame Street were a favourite
   haunt of prostitutes in the 1780s.

7 The New Prison (Newgate). From Robert Pool and   48
   John Cash, *Views of the Remarkable Public Buildings
   Monuments, and other Edifices in the City of Dublin* .... Dublin:
   Dublin Society, 1780.

8 Tholsel, Skinner's Row, Dublin, c. 1791. Many of the   49
   convicts transported in the 1780s were tried here.

9 Sir Jeremiah Fitzpatrick, Inspector–General of Prisons.   58
   Portrait in oils by W. Barnard, after S. Drummond.
   By courtesy, National Gallery of Ireland.

10 The Governor's House, Halifax, Nova Scotia. By courtesy, 72
National Archives of Canada (C2482)

11 'Landing from an Emigrant Ship' By courtesy, Prints 84
and Photographs Division, Library of Congress
(LC–USZ62–32284)

12 Late eighteenth-century brig of the kind used by Irish 102
contractors in the trans–Atlantic convict trade.
From J.F. Millar, *A Handbook on the Founding of Australia* ...,
Williamsburg [Va.]: Thirteen Colonies Press, 1988.
By courtesy, J.F. Millar

13 'Potomac Company President, George Washington, 109
overseeing the construction of the canal at Great Falls,
Virginia'. Negro slaves were found to be more reliable than
Irish indentured workers. Artist's impression. By courtesy,
Hagley Museum and Library, Wilmington, Delaware

14 Advertisements in the *Maryland Journal and Baltimore* 114
Advertiser in February and April 1788 for runaway Irish
servants

15 The Earl of Dunmore, Governor of the Bahamas, 1786–97. 120
From a full length oils portrait by Sir Joshua Reynolds,
1756, in the National Portrait Gallery, London. By courtesy,
Prints and Photographs Division, Library of Congress
(LC–USZ62–1002)

16 Advertisement for the *Chance* in the *Maryland Journal and* 122
Baltimore Advertiser, 1 February 1788

17 '*The first* Parliament *of* Botany Bay in *High Debate*'. 140
Anonymous etching in the style of Thomas Rowlandson,
from *Walker's Hibernian Magazine*, December 1786,
opp. p. 685

18 St John's, Newfoundland, 1780s. The ship is an English 171
man-on-war of the kind that brought Vice-Admiral
Milbanke to Newfoundland. By courtesy, Paul O'Neill

19 HMS *Pegasus* at the entrance to St John's harbour, 1786. 177
By courtesy, National Archives of Canada (C2539)

20 John Fitzgibbon, Earl of Clare. From *Walker's Hibernian* 196
Magazine

21   Poolbeg Fort, Dublin Bay, where the   206
     Newfoundland convicts were landed in January 1791.
     Etching by J. and H.S. Storer, after J. Sadler

22   'View near St John's Antigua'. Government House is on   213
     the left and in the centre is the parish church robbed by
     the Irish convicts. From John Luffman, *A Brief Account of
     the Island of Antigua, Together with the Customs and Manners
     of its Inhabitants ...*, London, 1789

23   'Cutting The Sugar Cane'. The sugar planters of the   215
     Leewards used negro slaves in the 1780s and had no
     interest in white workers. *Ibid.*

24   John Fane, Earl of Westmorland. It was during   237
     Westmorland's Lord Lieutenancy that the transportation
     of Irish convicts to New South Wales was finally agreed
     upon by the Home Office. From *Walker's Hibernian
     Magazine*

25   Petition to Lord Lieutenant Westmorland on behalf of   246
     Eyre Jackson of Co. Galway, 13 April 1790. By courtesy,
     National Archives of Ireland (PPC, f. 25.)

26   No image of the *Queen* survives, but this drawing of a   257
     c. 1770 New York–built merchantman, the *London*,
     provides some idea of what she would have looked like.
     Drawing by M.A. Edson, Jr. from J.F. Millar, *Early American
     Ships*, Williamsburg [Va.]: Thirteen Colonies Press, 1986.
     By courtesy, J.F. Millar

27   Letter from an anonymous convict to Captain Alexander   261
     Hood of HMS *Hebe*, Cove of Cork, 5 April 1791.
     By courtesy, National Maritime Museum, Greenwich
     (MKH/9, MS68/099)

Maps

The Bahamas   xix
Leeward Islands   xix
North America   xx

List of Abbreviations

ADM	Admiralty records, Public Record Office, Kew, London
AONSW	Archives Office of New South Wales, Sydney
BL	British Library
BT	Board of Trade records, Public Record Office, Kew, London
CO	Colonial Office records, Public Record Office, Kew, London
CSP (CS)	*Calendar of State Papers (Colonial Series)*
DNB	*Dictionary of National Biography*
FO	Foreign Office records, Public Record Office, Kew, London
HO	Home Office records, Public Record Office, Kew, London
HRA	*Historical Records of Australia*, series i
HRNSW	*Historical Records of New South Wales*
JHC	*Journal of the House of Commons*
JIHC	*Journal of the Irish House of Commons*
LC	Library of Congress, Washington, D.C.
ML	Mitchell Library, Sydney
NAI	National Archives of Ireland, Dublin
NAW	National Archives, Washington, D.C.
NLI	National Library of Ireland, Dublin
NMM	National Maritime Museum, Greenwich, London
PANL	Provincial Archives of Newfoundland and Labrador, St John's, Newfoundland
PANS	Public Archives of Nova Scotia, Halifax
PC	Privy Council records, Public Record Office, Kew, London
PP	Parliamentary Papers (Great Britain)
PPC	Prisoners' Petitions and Correspondence, National Archives of Ireland
PRO	Public Record Office, Kew, London
T	Treasury records, Public Record Office, Kew, London

Acknowledgements

This book has been a long time in the making and it would be imposs-ible to list all those who have given me assistance. However, I would like to express my particular gratitude to my friends Gearoid Kilgallen, Pat and Detta Connole, Michael, Aileen and Ivan O'Brien, Fred and Terese Wood and Danny Cusack who helped in various ways during my research trips to Ireland. Similarly, my visit to Newfoundland and Cape Breton Island was facilitated by Heather Reeves, Geoff Farmer, John and Maire Mannion, Danny Vickers, Hans Rollman, Sean Cadigan, Richard McKinnon and Ken Donovan. In Washington, my friends Phillip and Pat Thomas offered their inimitable hospitality when I was working in the Library of Congress. Research assistance was provided by Ruan O'Donnell, Danny Cusack, Beth Leslie, Perry McIntyre, Gillian Hughes, Tony Horton, Allen Robertson and Alex Costley; the costs involved in the project were met largely by a grant from the Australian Research Council, supplemented by the Canadian government's academic enrichment scheme and Murdoch University. Michael Durey, Alan Shaw and Don Baker read the manuscript in draft, while Brian McGinn generously shared with me his vast and detailed knowledge of the Irish in North America and the Caribbean. His con-tribution to the book was truly invaluable. Finally, I want to acknowl-edge Lesley, Laura, Anna and Owen Reece for their loving support and forbearance in the face of extended absences from home.

Fremantle   BOB REECE
August 2000

For Hazel Kathleen Reece (née St John)
and her Irish forbears

Introduction

When the first Irish convict transport to New South Wales, the *Queen*, anchored at Sydney Cove on 26 September 1791, more than a dozen of the 148 men and women on board were veterans of a renewed but short-lived phase of trans-Atlantic transportation following the end of the American Revolutionary War.[1]

This useful system had led to the despatch of about 36,000 British and 13,000 Irish male and female convicts across the Atlantic between 1717 and 1776, mostly in the guise of indentured servants. Trans-Atlantic transportation was inexpensive and benefited British and Irish shipping and trading interests as well as ridding both countries of their incorrigible criminals. It also provided an important source of labour for the American colonies. When peace was negotiated with the Americans in 1782, both Dublin and London hoped that the system could be re-established and subsequently attempted to do so.

Patriotic American opposition to the renewed trade meant that alternative destinations had to be found, first by the British in Honduras and subsequently by the Irish in the West Indies and Canada. The disastrous outcomes of the first Irish shipments, together with the continuing rise in urban crime and the chronic insecurity of Dublin's overcrowded gaols, meant that by mid-1785 the Irish authorities had serious problems on their hands.

It might be said that if there had been no Botany Bay, the Irish authorities would have needed to create something of the kind themselves. However, Ireland was in the difficult position of having numerous convicts of its own but (apart from the improbable site of Dalkey Island in Dublin Bay) no places of its own to send them. It was entirely dependent on access to His Britannic Majesty King George III's remaining 'plantations' or colonies in the Americas in order to dispose of them. As in Britain, a penitentiary system was regarded as a desirable but long-term and expensive alternative.

The debate amongst Australian historians over the reasons for the choice of Botany Bay as Britain's first penal settlement – between the proponents of political expediency on the one hand and strategic and commercial advantage on the other – has generally overlooked the significance of Ireland's problems.[2] The debate has ignored Ireland's urgent need to find a dumping place for its convicts after 1783. It has also ignored Ireland's elimination of the United States, the Canadian settlements and the West Indies as practical alternatives to a British penal colony in west Africa or New South Wales. Irish efforts to resume trans-Atlantic transportation helped to ensure that Botany Bay was the only remaining choice for the Pitt government in August 1786. The Irish story provides an important new perspective on a debate which historians such as David Mackay believe to be moribund.[3]

In his most recent examination of the circumstances of the Botany Bay decision, Alan Frost has made no reference to Irish transportation.[4] Although his work has challenged the earlier picture of overcrowded and disease-infested hulks, a disorganised First Fleet and generally rushed and haphazard decision-making in relation to Botany Bay, it is the Irish situation that provides the best evidence of a 'dumping' policy. And from 1791 it was the British government which tardily implemented that policy on the Irish government's behalf.

Eris O'Brien,[5] A.G.L. Shaw[6] and W. Oldham[7] all noted that Ireland had its own separate system of transportation until the end of 1790. They also pointed out that the first arrangements to send Irish convicts to Botany Bay were initiated by the British government after ultimately disastrous attempts by the Irish authorities to resume the convict trade to North America and the Caribbean. Oldham,[8] Ekirch[9] and more particularly Gillen,[10] described the three abortive shipments of British convicts to Baltimore and Honduras between 1783 and 1785 which led the British government to abandon trans-Atlantic transportation until the 1820s. O'Brien,[11] Oldham[12] and more particularly Martin[13] and Reece,[14] described the shipment of Irish convicts sent to Newfoundland in July 1789 and its dramatic consequences. Nevertheless, the significance of these fiascos has not been fully appreciated.

Nor has Irish trans-Atlantic transportation aroused the interest of Irish historians. Apart from the early work by Fr Aubrey Gwynn,[15] Fr Joseph J. Williams[16] and John Blake[17] on the Irish sent to Barbados during the mid-seventeenth century, there is only Audrey Lockhart's useful survey of the Irish indentured labour trade to the American colonies in the eighteenth century.[18] Lockhart's work built on the research of the American colonial historian, A.E. Smith,[19] which has in turn been followed by A.R. Ekirch's detailed examination of British and Irish trans-Atlantic transportation before the Revolutionary War.[20] As yet, there are no specific studies of Irish convicts in Pennsylvania, Virginia and Maryland where most were sent.

Transportation as a social and political issue in Ireland in the late eighteenth century has also been largely ignored. However, R.B. McDowell noted the Anglo-Irish political crisis of December 1789 brought about by the return of the convicts shipped earlier that year to Newfoundland.[21] This has been discussed in more detail recently by Ann Kavanaugh in her political biography of John Fitzgibbon, Earl of Clare.[22] Oliver MacDonagh's work on Sir Jeremiah Fitzpatrick[23] has added to our knowledge of Irish penal reform and Brian Henry has dealt with transportation in the context of Irish crime and punishment.[24] However, the full history of Irish trans-Atlantic transportation during that period and the circumstances of the subsequent switch to Botany Bay have not been properly explored.

The present account makes it clear that whether or not the Pitt government had long-term strategic and commercial plans or hopes for Botany Bay, the Irish authorities regarded it as an expensive but secure dumping place for 'incorrigible' criminals. Until the end of 1790, however, the Home Office's reluctance to find space for Irish convicts in the transports sent to Botany Bay left Dublin castle with no alternative but to continue shipping them off to the Americas.

Although there is no direct documentary evidence that the Botany Bay decision was made by the Pitt government in response to Irish as well as British domestic pressures, strong Irish interest in any new scheme for disposing of convicts had been made very clear to the Home Office from as early as May 1785. After the Botany Bay decision was revealed in late 1786, a series of British viceroys and their senior officials at Dublin Castle repeatedly pressed the Home Office for permission to participate in the projected scheme.

Nor did the Irish authorities have any interest in Botany Bay other than as a convenient place to dump convicts. Ireland's traditional trading links were with continental Europe, North America and the Caribbean and it possessed no mercantile interest in New South Wales, the Pacific islands or the Far East. The merchant princes who dominated Dublin Corporation and traditionally made the arrangements for convict transportation had a vested interest in maintaining the trans-Atlantic trade. Indeed, they were still trying to revive it as late as 1792.

It is not sufficient to say, as Shaw did, that 'in 1790, *naturally enough* [my emphasis], New South Wales was fixed on' as a destination for Irish convicts.[25] This book looks at why and how that change was made and what it reveals about Anglo-Irish relations during the turbulent era of 'Grattan's Parliament' and the uneasy relationship of Britain and Ireland with the newly emergent United States in the aftermath of the Revolutionary War.

In order to do this, it has been necessary to survey briefly the earlier history of Irish convict transportation to the Caribbean and North America and the increase in crime in late-eighteenth-century Ireland which made its revival seem so essential to contemporaries. Transportation is placed in the context of Irish crime and punishment, focusing on Dublin, which accounted for the great majority of those men and women who were either sentenced to transportation or whose capital sentences were commuted. Considerable attention is paid to the overcrowded and insecure condition of the prisons, particularly Newgate and Kilmainham in Dublin, which had reached crisis point by 1784.

Transportation is also presented in the context of renewed Irish emigration to and trade with the United States in the immediate post-1783 period. In Maryland and Virginia, rebellious and runaway Irish servants helped to strengthen opposition to the admission of convicts. And in Ireland, the renewed criminal exploits of numerous convict *returnees* from North America and the West Indies led to demands for a more remote dumping place.

The tragi-comic story of the nine shipments of Irish convicts sent to the Americas between 1784 and 1789 is told in detail here for the first time, revealing the problems they caused for gaolers, captains, agents and colonial governors as well as the sometimes horrendous experiences they suffered themselves. These shipments constitute an almost forgotten but by no means insignificant part of what is now being called the 'Irish *diaspora*' or 'scattering' of the late eighteenth century.[26]

Finally, new information is revealed about the circumstances surrounding the departure of the *Queen* transport from the Cove of Cork for New South Wales in April 1791 and the origins of those 'acute beings' who survived the voyage and subsequently formed the nucleus of Australia's founding Irish population. The fact that some were veterans of earlier trans-Atlantic transportation serves to symbolise the historical links between Ireland, North America and the settlement of New South Wales.

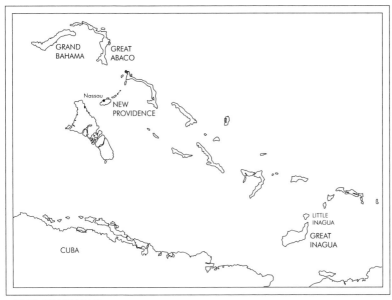

THE BAHAMAS

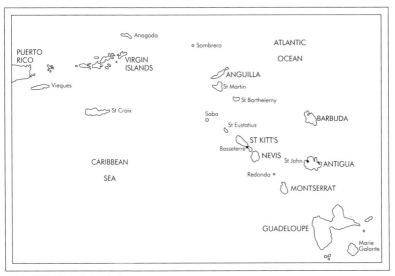

LEEWARD ISLANDS

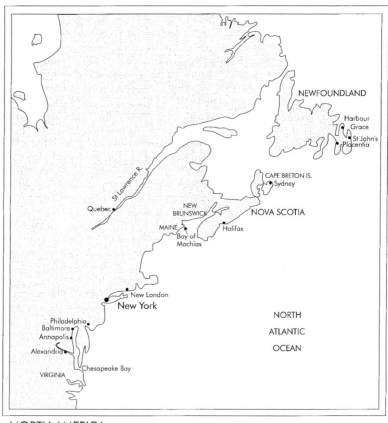

NEWFOUNDLAND

Harbour
Grace
St John's
Placentia

CAPE BRETON IS.
Sydney

St Lawrence R.

NEW
BRUNSWICK   NOVA SCOTIA

Quebec

MAINE

Bay of   Halifax
Machias

New London
New York   NORTH

Philadelphia   ATLANTIC
Baltimore
Annapolis   OCEAN

Alexandria

Chesapeake Bay

VIRGINIA

NORTH AMERICA

1
Irish Transportation before 1783

Ireland, like England, had a long history of exporting its 'vagabonds' and criminals to the West Indies and North America. When the onset of the advent of the Revolutionary War in early 1776 made it no longer possible to transport English convicts to Pennsylvania, Maryland, Virginia and other America colonies, it also interrupted the Irish trans-Atlantic convict trade which began with political exiles to Barbados in the mid-seventeenth century and had been systematically pursued by sending criminals to the American colonies from the 1720s. Viewed more broadly, this was part of the transmigration of British and Irish labourers to North America and the West Indies which began in the early seventeenth centiury.

Virginia

The transportation of Irish undesirables to the Americas was suggested as early as 1607 when King James I was advised that seven or eight thousand *kerns* or swordsmen, 'descended from Horseboyes, Idle persons and unlawfull propigations', should be sent to the new English colony of Virginia.[1] Sixteen years later, a similar proposal was made by Sir Arthur Bourgchier in his *Advertisements for Ireland* when he suggested that 'if Virginia or some other of the newly discovered lands in the west were filled with them, it could not but serve and raise the country much, and relieve and advance them withal'.[2] In the meantime, it had also been proposed that the traditional Irish landowners dispossessed by the Chichester plantation in Wexford be sent to Virginia as an alternative to imprisonment.[3]

Virginia was a logical destination because the colony had a strong Irish connection from the outset: many of the members of the Virginia

Company had Irish interests, southern Irish ports supplied the colony with cattle and goats, and Irish stockings clad the settlers' legs. By 1621 when one of the suppliers of cattle, Daniel Gookin of Cork, settled at Newport News, there was a direct immigration link which he used to import numbers of young Irish contract labourers for sale to the settlers for about £8 per head.[4] However, it was not until 1653 that Virginia received its first Irish 'Tories' or political outlaws.[5]

Thousands of Irish indentured labourers were directly recruited in Ireland for Barbados, colonised in 1627, and the principal island of the Leewards group, St Christopher (better known as St Kitt's), which was colonised jointly with the French in 1624.[6] By 1634, Catholic Irish reportedly rejected by the Virginians had established themselves on Montserrat in the Leewards.[7] Montserrat and nearby Antigua also drew settlers from St Kitt's when Governor Sir Thomas Warner expelled Irish Catholics to relieve religious tensions on the overcrowded island.[8]

So many Irish servants arrived in the West Indies during the 1630s that after rebellion broke out in Ireland in 1641 the Assembly of Barbados, fearing that they would join the Spanish or French, enacted legislation prohibiting the landing of any more. However, the insatiable demand for plantation labour meant that the practice continued and the law became obsolete.[9] Carl and Roberta Bridenbaugh have estimated that in 1650 the Irish constituted more than half the entire population of the British West Indies, easily outnumbering the English.[10]

'To be Barbadoes'

There is no clear evidence that the English government's Virginia schemes were ever implemented but in the wake of Oliver Cromwell's invasion of Ireland in late 1649, rebel soldiers, 'tories', a handful of Roman Catholic priests,[11] and 'vagabonds' of both sexes were transported by Bristol sugar merchants to Barbados and sold to the sugar planters there as indentured servants.[12] If the rebels sent earlier to the Continent are included, the total number transported during the whole of the period from 1641 to 1660 may have been as high as 50,000, although there is no way of computing this accurately. It is even more difficult to estimate how many were sent to Barbados and other parts of the West Indies between 1649 and 1655, but there were probably some thousands.[13] According to a planters' petition, Barbados received 12,000 prisoners of war and 'many thousands of other persons' during those years.[14]

As far as can be established, the first instance in Ireland of transportation for political purposes was in November 1649 when captured followers of Oliver French of Galway who could not be exchanged for English prisoners were to be sent to Barbados if merchants would take them. And after the sacking of Drogheda in September 1649, the handful of spared defenders were ordered by Cromwell to be sent there.[15] Scots and English prisoners of war had been transported earlier on the order of Parliament after the battle of Preston in Scotland and the capture of Colchester.

No Irish prisoners were recorded as being sent to Barbados during the following two years, but in the summer of 1652 after the clearing of Catholic Irish from Waterford, Cromwell's Council of State for Ireland issued at least three orders for the shipping of Irish rebel prisoners to Barbados.[16] So common was transportation from Ireland during the early Commonwealth period that 'to be Barbadoes' was a common expression.[17]

The physician-general of Cromwell's army of occupation and Ireland's first demographer, Sir William Petty, estimated that between October 1641 and October 1652

> There were transported of them [Irish rebels] into *Spain, Flanders, France*, 34,000 Soldiers; and of Boys, Women, Priests, &C no less than 6,000 more, where not half are returned.[18]

The Catholic nationalist historian, J.P. Prendergast, in his *Cromwellian Settlement of Ireland* (1865) chose to interpret the latter part of this statement as signifying that the 6,000 'Boys, Women, Priests, &C.' were transported to Barbados,[19] although the context clearly indicates that they were sent to the Continent with the soldiers.

In order to enforce the clearance of Catholic Irish from land to be made available for Protestant settlers, the Second Parliament of the Protectorate enacted legislation in June 1657 providing that those who failed to transplant themselves to Connaught or Clare within six months would be charged with high treason and 'sent into America or some other parts beyond the Seas ...'.[20] However, the rate of transportation seems to have been already in decline by 1655.

In addition to the removal of political prisoners, Cromwell's commissioners-general for Ireland had ordered in May 1653 that the English statutes authorising the exile of 'rogues, vagrants, sturdy beggars, idle and disorderly persons' should henceforth also hold force in Ireland.[21] That Irish exiles were landed in New England as well as the West Indies during this period can be deduced from the Act of the General Court of Massachusetts of 29 October 1654 prohibiting the practice and imposing a heavy fine on offenders.[22] The English Parliament was also petitioned 'to prevent the importation of the Irish papists and convicts that are yearly powr'd upon us, and to make provision against the growth of this pernicious evil'.[23]

Similar laws applying to all convicts were enacted by the legislature of Maryland in 1670[24] and by Virginia in 1671 after political offenders attempted to organise a rebellion there some years earlier. The Virginia order was confirmed in England through the influence of Lord Arlington and extended to all the American colonies, effectively diverting transportation to the West Indies for some decades.[25] Nevertheless, the English authorities were not to be deterred. In October 1697 the Council of Trade and Plantations told the Lords Justices that 'the unwillingness to receive convicts in other places [in America] is more or less according to the different circumstances of each place, and may vary according to the time in respect of war and peace, and always according to the quality and circumstances of the convicts themselves'.[26]

The informal arrangements for transportation to New England and to Barbados and other West Indian plantations during the Cromwellian period were inevitably abused by Bristol merchant-captains anxious to make a profit by selling exiles to the planters as indentured servants and not too particular about how they obtained their passengers through the use of 'spirits' or agents. It was never true (as Prendergast asserted) that 'Ireland must have exhibited scenes in every part like the slave hunts in Africa'.[27] However, there are at least three documents for the period 1654–7 which reflect the authorities' concern that some of those put on board ships in Dublin for Barbados were 'not comprehended as vagrants or idlers'.[28]

So serious was the abuse of the system that on 4 March 1657 the commissioners-general of Ireland decreed that all existing orders granting permission to transport vagrants were null and void and that henceforth, idle persons would be prosecuted 'according to the usual proceedings of justice'.[29] Nor was the practice limited to Ireland – 'spiriting' to Virginia was recorded in England as early as 1644 and twenty years later it was causing 'tumults' in the streets of London where mob pressure forced individuals into exile. When regulation proved ineffectual, the death penalty was introduced in 1670 for failure to register the transportation of a servant.[30]

By far the most notorious effort to transplant the Irish to the West Indies was in late 1655 when the Major-General of the Forces in

Ireland, Lord Henry Cromwell, indicated his willingness to arrange a shipment of 2,000 Catholic boys and girls from Galway and Kinsale to populate and provide labour for the newly-acquired English colony of Jamaica.[31] 'We could well spare them', Cromwell wrote to Secretary Thurloe in London, 'and they might be of use to you; and who knows but it might be a means of making them Englishmen – I mean, Christians?'[32] While there is no conclusive evidence that this and other recorded schemes of Irish transportation came to fruition, the existence of significant Irish populations in late-seventeenth-century Jamaica and Barbados, together with St Kitt's, Antigua and Montserrat, indicate that some did. According to the report of a returned Irish missionary priest in July 1669, there were then about 8,000 Irish in Barbados and 4,000 more in the other West Indian plantations.[33]

In addition, the rapid growth from the mid-seventeenth century of Ireland's exports of salted provisions to Barbados, the Leewards and Jamaica and its imports of sugar and rum had led to the establishment of a number of Irish Protestant and Catholic merchant houses there.[34] By 1680, southern Ireland was providing half of the food imports of the British West Indies.[35]

White slaves

The brisk demand for indentured labour in Barbados during the mid-seventeenth century is made clear in a description by F. Barrington, an Englishman who paid a visit there in 1655:

> The custom of all merchants trading thither is to bring as many men and women as they can. No sooner doth a ship come to an anchor but presently the islanders go aboard inquiring what servants they can buy. If they are above seventeen years of age, they serve but four years, according to the law of the island; but if under seventeen, then [it is] left to the discretion of the merchant as he can agree with the planter. These servants planteth, weedeth, and manuereth the ground, all by hand.[36]

The purchase price for a landed indentured worker in the 1650s was about 1,500 pounds of sugar, which provided a profitable back-loading for the Bristol merchant-captains.[37]

According to Richard Ligon, an early historian of Barbados, the island's sugar planters did not even treat their indentured servants as well as they did their negro slaves:

> The slaves and their posterity, being subject to their Masters for ever, are kept and preserved with greater care than the servants, who are theirs but for five years, according to the law of the Island. So for that time, the servants have the worser lives, for they are put to very hard labour, ill lodging, and their dyet [is] very sleight.[38]

John Scott, an English visitor to Barbados in about 1667, saw Irish servants and freemen working together with slaves in the fields 'without stockings' in the 'scorching sun'. He reported that they were 'derided by the negroes, and branded with the Epithet of "white slaves"'.[39]

Although there was a minor rebellion by 'Irish Servants and Negroes' in Barbados in 1655,[40] for the most part the English planters managed to keep the two groups of workers separate and mutually antagonistic. More significant was Governor Daniel Searle's anxiety about the loyalty of the Irish when he learnt of war with Spain in September 1657.[41] Two months later, Searle vigorously objected to receiving eighty-seven 'Irish rogues' (presumably exiles) on the grounds that they were unsuited to militia duty as well as plantation labour.[42] Most of the Irish servants on Barbados and St Kitt's at that time were described as having been transported for treason.[43] Ten years later, Searle's successor, Governor William Willoughby, complained that Irish servants made up at least half of the 4,000-strong militia of Barbados. He expressed a strong preference for 'the downe right Scott, who I am certaine will fight without a Crucifix abouyt his neck'.[44]

Although the Irish had arrived in thousands in Barbados and the Leewards between 1649 and 1660, their numbers were considerably reduced thereafter. According to Jonathan Atkins, Governor of Barbados 1674–80, the settlers 'grew weary of them, for they proved commonly *very Idle*, and they do find by Experience they can keep three Blacks, who work better and cheaper than one White Man'.[45]

Changing political conditions in Europe focused attention once again on the loyalty of the Irish. With the declaration of war between France and England in 1666, Irish indentured servants and freemen of the English part of St Kitt's plundered their masters' estates and burnt their buildings before joining the French. In a crucial battle in May 1668 they were said to have inflicted more losses than did the French. According to an English witness forced to flee to the nearby island of Nevis:

> the Irish in the Reare (allwaies a bloody and perfidious people to the English Protestant Interest) with Comand near 100 deepe ... fired

Vollyes into the ffront and killed more (then ye Enimy) of our owne fforces.[46]

At Montserrat, the majority Irish population rebelled in January 1667 and, acting in concert with a French invasion force of 1,200, held the island until June.[47]

The Treaty of Breda restored their part of St Kitt's to the English in 1667, but there was a further rising by 130 armed Irishmen in support of the French in February 1689 after news was received that William of Orange had become King of England.[48] The English planters' estates were again plundered and the French seized the English part of the island once more.[49] On Nevis, the resident Irish were disarmed and packed off to Jamaica 'lest they should serve us they did St Christopher's'.[50] And on Montserrat, where almost 800 Irish outnumbered 300 English, they were described by Sir Christopher Codrington in July 1689 as 'of late ... turbulent and rebellious'.[51]

The natural legacy of all this was a strong prejudice on the part of the English planters and authorities of Barbados and the Leewards against the reception of any more Irish servants.[52] Indeed, their suspected involvement in a slave revolt in Barbados in 1692 led to a total ban by the planters there.[53] Restrictive laws specifically relating to the Catholic Irish were also passed by the legislatures of Nevis and Montserrat.[54] At the same time, the change to a sugar monoculture by the end of the seventeenth century meant that white indentured servants were largely replaced by black slaves and many of the Irish freedmen moved voluntarily from Barbados and the Leewards to Jamaica. This movement was also encouraged by Jamaica's 'deficiency law' of 1676 which required planters to keep one white worker for every ten slaves[55] and earlier legislation restricting the direct importation of convicts.[56]

Nevertheless, there were still enough Irishmen left in the Leewards for them to help the French attack St Kitt's once more in 1706 and to inflict serious damage on Nevis. An English official on Nevis in early 1723 described them as

most obstinate and perverse in their Nature and Manners; Inveterately disaffected to His Majesties Government; and that person has been esteemed the most Couragious amongst them, who rejects everything proposed by their Governours; This Temper they have been remarkable for ever since the Revolution.[57]

Emigration of indentured servants from Ireland to Jamaica continued during the late seventeenth and early eighteenth centuries, but by the 1730s the Protestant colonists there were agitating to stem the flow. In November 1731, Governor Robert Hunter asked the Board of Trade in London to reverse the recent repeal of legislation favouring Protestants as it 'may be be of some [assistance] in deterring at least the native Irish Papists, of which our Servants and Lower Rank of People chiefly consists, from pouring in upon us in such Sholes [*sic*], as they have done of late years, they are a lazy useless sort of people, who come cheap and serve for deficiencys, and their hearts are not with us ...'.[58]

After 1725, the Dublin newspapers ceased to carry advertisements seeking servants in the West Indies and by 1750 only skilled tradesmen from Cork and other Irish trading ports were being employed.[59] In the meantime, however, the export of Irish indentured servants, including convicts, to Philadelphia, Maryland and Virginia had been in full swing in response to the growing demand for labour in those colonies.

Self-transports

After the Restoration, the authorities in Ireland also followed the English custom of allowing certain classes of criminals to go into voluntary exile overseas. There are very few records for this period and most of the information that survives is contained in the judicial papers of James Butler, first Duke of Ormonde, who was Lord Lieutenant and Lord Chief Justice of Ireland from 1662. These indicate that he and his brother judges were empowered to exercise the Royal Mercy by allowing convicted prisoners and informers to take themselves out of Ireland after a substantial bond was deposited against their return. Barbados appears to have been the destination normally stipulated, no doubt because the provisions export trade from southern Ireland meant that shipping was easily available. However, Newfoundland and other ports in North America were also prescribed and even the more traditional destinations of France and Flanders were sometimes mentioned by judges as fulfilling the conditions of exile.

Rice Havard was tried by Sir William Aston of the Court of King's Bench at Dublin Castle on 26 May 1669 and found guilty of breaking and entering the house of Alderman John Preston and stealing pewter and other goods to the value of £20. Emphasising that Havard was a young man, that it was his first offence, and that most of the goods had been returned and he seemed truly penitent, Preston petitioned the judge to allow him to be transported to the West Indies. Agreeing to this, Aston ordered

> that if any merchant or other person with sufficient security will give bond to the Clerke of the Counsell, to His Majesty's use, of one thousand pounds sterling, with condition that the said Rice Havard shall, within fifteen dayes after he shall be delivered out of the prison wherein hee doth now remaine, shipp himselfe in some shippe or other vessell bound for some part of the West Indyes and shall not come on shore until hee shall bee landed there, nor returne from thence into this kingdom without lycence from the Chiefe Governor or Governors here for the time being to be in writing first obtained, upon certifycate of the said Clerke of the Councell of giveing such bond as aforesaid, the Sheriffe, or gaoler under whose charge the said Rice Havard doth remaine, shal sett him at liberty and deliver him to such merchant or other person or persons as shall engage for him to the purpose aforesaid.[60]

It seems that this early judicial order of transportation could be made as a merciful commutation of execution for a capital offence, but it amounted to a form of exile secured by a financial bond and arranged and paid for by the prisoner himself. In the case of Rice Havard, who was obviously a well-connected young man, Richard Cannaday (Kennedy) and another Dublin merchant offered the necessary security against his return.

Nor would Henry More O'Neile, gentleman, of Co. Louth, have experienced much difficulty in finding people to vouch for him and to act as guarantor. He had been found guilty at the Dundalk assizes in February 1668 of the 'felonious assaulting and robbing of one Gawen Tippin ... in the King's highway' five years earlier. The following March he was also found guilty of the 'felonious breaking of His majesty's gaole at Atherdee [Ardee] ...' after being imprisoned for the earlier offence.[61]

The granting of mercy was not necessarily determined by the class or status of the convicted person, however. A poor woman, Margaret Litle, was only required by Aston to have £100 deposited before being set at liberty and putting herself on board a ship 'bound for the Newfoundland, Barbadoes, or some port in America ...'. She had been found guilty and sentenced to death in January 1667 for the theft of £3.18s. and some linen from a baker in Pimlico, Dublin, but had been reprieved by Aston 'uppon consideration of her ingenious confession and the passionate sorrow she exprest ...'.[62]

A similar order had been made by Ormonde himself in 1667 concerning a 'poore boy', twelve-year-old Nicholas Commerford, who had been convicted for theft and sentenced to death at the Kilkenny assizes in March 1665, but respited at each subsequent assizes on account of his 'minor age'. Petitioning for him to be allowed to go to Barbados, the Mayor of Kilkenny, Peter Goodwin, told Ormonde that 'he was prompted thereunto by others, being a very simple and innnocent boy, and [I] doe think him to be an object of his Majesties mercy, hopeing thereby that he may be a better man'.[63] In this case, Ormonde required the same surety of £100 before Commerford could be allowed to ship himself to Barbados.

In another case, three men from Co. Meath appealed to Ormonde against their conviction for theft on what they described as false evidence supplied by relatives of some 'notorious malefactors' whom they had earlier assisted in bringing to justice. Believing that they now possessed 'no hope of liveing quietly amongst their countrymen', they sought a pardon. Ormonde accordingly ordered that after supplying a surety of £300 they 'shall ship themselves aboard some vessel bound for the Barbadoes, or some other part of America, Flanders, or France ...'.[64]

Transportation could also be a means of removing known criminals who had not been convicted of any offence. In May 1667, Ormonde was petitioned by the justices of the peace for Co. Meath concerning a number of prisoners who had earlier confessed to 'severall felloneys' but had then denied them and been acquitted for lack of evidence. Citing 'the evil consequences of such notorious and known robbers to be sett at liberty will tend to the further distruction of the country', the justices asked Ormonde to order the prisoners' transportation to Barbados. Responding to this, Ormonde instructed that they be allowed to ship themselves there on receipt of a surety of £300.[65]

Although there is no definite evidence that exile was still being used as a means of exporting dangerous Papists by this time, there was an instance in 1669 of a 'Dominican fryer', Keane Carroll, being allowed to delay his departure from Ireland because of ill health. Carroll's original offence was not stated, but an extension of time before he removed himself 'beyond sea' was granted by the judge on condition 'that he shall at all times behave himselfe inoffensively and as becometh a loyal subject, without acting contrary to the laws or statutes of this land ...'.[66] The only instance in the Ormonde papers of a petitioner who might have stood to gain from the exile of those to whom mercy was extended was John Archer, mariner, who petitioned in February 1669 that two capitally condemned prisoners in Dublin's Newgate prison be reprieved and transported to Jamaica in his ship.[67]

During the eighteenth century, the convention of voluntary transportation was maintained by Irish as well as English judges and magistrates who sometimes agreed not to sentence a convicted prisoner on condition that he took himself into exile for a specified number of years and put up a bond against his premature return. These 'self-transports' were then free to choose their own ship to America and could not be bought or sold on arrival there.[68] The notorious Frederick Lambert, whose extraordinary career is discussed below, was one such case.

Ireland's transportation laws

From the early eighteenth century, transportation to the Americas was formally instituted within the Irish criminal justice system as a regular means of dealing with lesser offenders. Beginning as a form of conditional pardon for capital offences, it was subsequently prescribed in a number of statutes as a penalty in its own right. Following the British legislation of 1703, the original Irish legislation of 1704 (*2 Anne, c. 12*) authorised transportation to 'some part of her Majesty's plantations beyond the seas' as a reprieve for the death penalty for those convicted of stealing less than two cows or ten sheep, of felony worth not less than 20s., or of harbouring robbers, tories and *rapparees* (outlaws).[69] The sheriffs of each county were responsible for delivering them to merchants willing to ship them off on condition of providing a £20 bond and producing within eighteen months an official certificate which indicated that they had been landed in the Americas. This was supplemented by an Act of 1707 (*6 Anne, c. 11*) which ordered that 'all loose, idle vagrants and such as pretend to be Irish gentlemen [tories]' should be kept in gaol until they could be pressed into the Navy or sent to the American plantations.[70]

A further Act of 1719 (*6 Geo. I, c. 12*), based on the key British legislation of 1718, reinforced the 1704 Act by providing 'for the better and more effectual apprehending and transporting felons and others ...'.[71] Another of 1721 made return from transportation a capital offence (*8 Geo. I, c. 9*).[72] More importantly, an Act of 1726 (*12 Geo. I, c. 8*) strengthened that of 1719 by authorising the payment of a fixed subsidy to merchants and establishing a formal procedure for the listing and delivery of convicted prisoners from the gaols and the levying of funds by the courts to pay for their transportation.[73] It also provided for the execution of convicts who refused to sign the articles of transportation, which effectively preserved the old principle of voluntary exile. In the same legislation, bigamy and smuggling were made transportable offences. Another Act of 1730 (*3 Geo. II, c. 4*) added forgery and perjury to the list and set the sum of £6 for each convict to be transported – £1 for the sheriff's expenses and £5 for the merchant's.[74]

Following the legislation of 1707 covering vagrancy, the 'Vagabond Act' of 1735 (*9 Geo. II, c. 6*) empowered the judges and magistrates of Dublin to order transportation as a punishment. The Act prescribed seven years' transportation for 'all loose, idle vagrants' and 'all loose persons of infamous lives and characters' of the city and county.[75] Altogether, 'vagabonds' accounted for a much higher percentage of Irish than English transportees. As in England, however, prisoners were normally give terms of seven or fourteen years, with only a few sentenced to life.[76]

Until the new Police Act of 1786 (*26 Geo. III, c. 6*) replaced them, these were the statutes which underpinned transportation as a punishment in Ireland.[77]

The Irish system

As a result of the Dublin Four Courts fire of 1922, most of the records relating to the administration of Irish transportation for the period up to 1836 were destroyed and not a great deal is known about how it operated. Apart from the Dublin newspapers, which normally reported the business of quarterly assizes and the despatch of convict transports from Dublin, the main source of detailed information on the trans-Atlantic trade up until 1775 is a report made to the Irish House of Commons in February 1743.[78] From this detailed document, which looked at the six years of operation since the 1735 legislation, it can be seen that transportation was essentially a decentralised arrangement under which local government authorities bore the responsibility (and their rate-payers the cost) of holding in prison and then shipping off offenders who had either been sentenced to transportation or whose capital sentence had been commuted to the lesser punishment.

It was only in Dublin that the numbers of convicts to be transported warranted the chartering and provisioning of a special ship or ships each year, which was the customary responsibility of Dublin Corporation and hence its Lord Mayor. Indeed, it was an important perquisite of office and one which the aldermen were loath to relinquish when responsibility for shipping arrangements was notionally assumed by the British authorities in late 1790.[79] Elsewhere in Ireland, town corporations arranged with ship-owners and captains engaged in the trans-Atlantic trade for the removal of those under sentence of transportation after each quarterly assizes.

A convention had developed as early as 1739 whereby the Lord Mayor of Dublin and the mayors or chief magistrates of other ports of departure witnessed blank indenture papers for transportees either in prison or on board ship, enabling the master of the vessel to sell them as indentured servants in Philadelphia, Maryland or Virginia where their labour was most in demand. Without an indenture paper they would not be transported by any captain as their labour could not be sold. In practice, the document served the same effective purpose as the traditional undertaking to go into voluntary exile.

The term of indenture was fixed at seven years, regardless of the length of the actual sentence recorded. And as an indentured servant possessing useful skills could be sold for as much as £20 in Philadelphia, Baltimore or George-Town, shipping convicts to America was a profitable business. Indeed, it was so profitable that when rival groups of merchants petitioned the Irish Parliament for the contract in 1739, the rate of payment for transportation was halved by law to £3 per head.[80]

The arrangement also suited the convicts by making it possible for them to pass themselves off as ordinary free labourers, tens of thousands of whom indentured themselves to ships' captains at Irish

I N Purfuance and by Virtue of Acts of Parliament, made and provided for the more effectual Tranfportation of Felons to his Majefty's Plantations in America, I do hereby affign unto

a Convict within the faid Statutes, to ferve him, his Heirs or Affigns, for the Term of feven Years, commencing the
being the Day of the Ship
Arrival in VIRGINIA.

1 Convict assignment warrant, Virginia, c. 1760s.

ports in return for their passage to America during the decades before 1776. Those convicts who had the means were even able to purchase indulgences on the voyage and their liberty on their arrival in America.

That the signing of indentures was an essential part of the Irish system of transportation can be seen from a dramatic incident in Limerick in about 1774, recalled some years later by the *Freeman's Journal*:

> A ship being ordered to Limerick for the purpose of taking in transports for America, Mr. Dodgeworth, one of the Sheriffs, brought a fellow of the name of Daly, as a transmit under sentence of transportable felony. On lodging him in Limerick gaol, the villain told Mr. Dodgeworth that he begged to whisper him some important information, which stooping to receive, the inhuman ruffian made an attempt to cut the throat of the Sheriff with a razor; but by a sudden exertion, the latter turned his neck, and the other succeeded only so far in his attempt, as to lay his cheek open in a dreadful manner; under the wound of which the Sheriff remained ill for some months. In the mean time, the felon refused signing any indenture, until the Mayor of Limerick took the summary mode of ordering him to the cart's tail and whipt through the city; which he bore until he was supposed to have received little short of one thousand lashes before he would sign his name.[81]

The master of the vessel which took Daly to America duly sold him to a planter of Annapolis, Maryland, and he subsequently received a captain's commission in the Revolutionary Army. Another Irish convict, Samuel Grandall from Ulster, took a leading part in the riots at Rhode Island over the Stamp Act.[82]

Transportation was a punishment frequently resorted to by judges and magistrates in the Irish courts from the 1720s to the 1770s. According to Ekirch, who has provided the most comprehensive account of British transportation to America before the Revolutionary War, more than 13,000 Irish men and women (about 227 a year) were sent to the American colonies between 1718 and 1775, which would account for about one-quarter of all the convicts from the British Isles during those years.[83]

Although there are no official statistics for the whole period, Lockhart's analysis of the Irish House of Commons report of 1743 reveals that 937, or almost half, of the 1,920 convicts recorded as having been sent off from Ireland during the previous six years had been sentenced in the province of Leinster (which included the city of Dublin), 542 from

Munster, 296 from Ulster and 145 from Connaught.[84] Of the 990 whose offences are recorded, 531 were banished as 'vagabonds' and 459 were sentenced to transportation for felonies, principally grand larceny.[85] On the basis of these figures, a high proportion seem likely to have been Roman Catholics, many of them from Dublin where the laws against vagrancy and larceny were most frequently applied.

Most of the convicts were shipped from George's Quay and Rogerson's Quay on Dublin's river Liffey,[86] but Limerick, Galway, Cork and Waterford were also ports of embarkation for smaller batches. In Dublin, the crowd which gathered on these occasions was invariably sympathetic to the exiles and there are numerous newspaper accounts from the time of attempts to rescue them as they were carried in open carts from prison to the quays.[87]

The 1743 report revealed a number of weaknesses in the transportation system: records were inadequate; the full amount of appropriation money had not always been paid to merchants; and captains had sometimes landed convicts in other parts of Britain or Europe instead of the Americas. Accordingly, legislation passed by the Irish Parliament in 1744 prescribed the death penalty for merchants who broke the terms of their contracts.[88]

One continuing feature of the Irish system was that a prisoner sentenced to transportation did not begin to serve his term until he was physically removed by ship from the kingdom.[89] This was also the practice in Britain until the new enabling legislation of 1784 provided that the term of transportation ran from the date of sentencing.[90] The Irish system worked well enough when numbers were small and the shipping arrangements were in the hands of local authorities who had every interest in disposing of prisoners quickly because of the cost of maintaining them in gaol. However, during the period after 1783 when numbers sentenced to transportation increased sharply, the system was centralised in Dublin and delays in shipping meant that some prisoners remained incarcerated in overcrowded and unhealthy conditions in the city's two gaols for as long as three and even five years before they could be removed. The bitter resentment inevitably arising from this was to be a major cause of the epidemic of prison unrest between 1784 and 1795.

'A parcel of likely men'

No separate study has been made of Irish convicts in the American colonies, probably because most of them when they arrived were virtually indistinguishable from the large body of Irish indentured servants –

perhaps as many as 165,000 – who went to America before 1775.[91] From the early 1720s, Philadelphia was a favourite destination for Irish ships' captains transporting convicts as it was the centre of the indentured servant trade.[92] Although little documentation survives, there is a captain's record of a 'parcel' of twenty Irish convicts being sold as indentured servants in Philadelphia in 1740 for between £9.10s. and £13.10s.[93] In order to avoid special import taxes levied by the legislature to deter the trade, captains in earlier years had landed them at New Jersey and along the Delaware estuary to make their own way to Pennsylvania.[94]

One of the Irish entrepreneurs active in Philadelphia and closely involved in the servant trade was George Bryan. Eldest son of a prominent Presbyterian Dublin merchant, he had spent some time at St Kitt's before becoming established in a business partnership with James Wallace in Philadelphia in 1752.[95] Both he and his father's firm, Samuel and William Bryan, owned a number of ships on the Dublin–Philadelphia run[96] which were used to import indentured servants. On 6 August 1752, for example, the *Pennsylvania Gazette* advertised the arrival from Ireland of the *Sarah and Rebecca* with 'a parcel of likely men and women servants, among who [are] tradesmen of different sorts, whose times are to be disposed of by Wallace and Bryan …'.

The custom of landing convicts as indentured servants was widely practised by Irish and English captains but did not always go unnoticed. In 1737 a Maryland newspaper reported 'an arrant cheat detected' when a vessel arrived at Annapolis with sixty-six indentures signed by the Lord Mayor of Dublin and twenty-two wigs 'being evidently brought for no other use than to give a respectable appearance to the convicts when they should go ashore'.[97] In another instance in 1748, the captain of a vessel from Belfast bribed his crew not to reveal the real identity of two women convicts who were skilled in spinning so that they could be sold profitably as servants in Boston.[98]

Ekirch suggests that of the 25,000 Irish immigrants arriving in Pennsylvania from the 1720s until the Revolution, 'at least several thousand were Irish'.[99] Restrictions progressively imposed by the Pennsylvania Assembly limited the influx for some years before they were overturned by the Crown. In the meantime, however, many Irish and English convicts were landed in the Chesapeake colonies of Maryland and Virginia where unskilled field labour was needed and indentured servants were to make up something like one quarter of the population by 1775. The planters there were not so concerned about their servants' origins, particularly if they were young and vigorous.[100] Convicts were often preferred in Virginia because the seven-year term of their indenture was two years more than the longest term for free immigrants and they did not have to be paid 'freedom dues' at the end of their service.[101]

As their identity as convicts was largely obscured, it is necessary to look at the more general American perceptions of Irish servants to assess their impact. However, Irish convicts are said to have contributed to the reputation of Irish servants in Pennsylvania as 'troublesome characters'.[102] And according to one authority on indentured labour in eighteenth-century Maryland, the predominantly Roman Catholic Irish servants 'were regarded as undesirable for religious and racial reasons ...' as well as for their known or suspected convict background.[103] Significantly, the Attorney-General of Virginia was granted a raise in salary in 1732 due to the increase in work from burglaries and thefts committed by convicts.[104] In New Jersey there were frequent newspaper reports of Irish convicts committing offences and breaking gaol.[105] Irish names figured prominently in newspaper advertisements for runaway servants in Pennsylvania, Maryland and Virginia. They also had a reputation for rebelliousness which was boosted by their organisation of the 'red string plot' in Georgia in 1735, one of the two failed servant insurrections of the period.[106]

Although Irish convicts were not singled out for particular attention by Benjamin Franklin and John Dickinson, the two most outspoken American critics of transportation before the Revolution, they had no doubt contributed to the general reputation of transportees as being responsible both for increased crime and the spread of disease. When Franklin wrote angrily in 1751 that 'the emptying their jails into our settlements is an insult and contempt, the cruellest that ever one people offered another, and would not be equal'd even by emptying their jakes [latrines] on our tables',[107] he was living in Philadelphia whose large population of Irish servants included many convicts.

Despite these criticisms and the energetic efforts of legislators and magistrates, the labour value of Irish as well as English convicts and their cheapness in relation to newly imported African slaves meant that they continued to be in demand.[108] The high proportion of slaves in the two Chesapeake colonies led the authorities there to see convicts as a destabilising force. However, the availability of profitable back-loading in tobacco in particular and continuing demand for indentured servants from planters and other employers determined that Maryland and Virginia remained the most popular destinations for Irish and English shippers until the late 1760s. The vast majority of convicts transported between 1718 and 1775 were sent to Maryland.

2 English cartoon of aristocratic convicts arriving in America.

Although the convict trade had been taxed or otherwise impeded by legislation in South Carolina as early as 1712, in Virginia in 1722 and 1755 and in Pennsylvania in 1722, 1729 and 1743, most of these efforts were blocked by the British Crown.[109] In Maryland in 1751 the Baltimore magistrates attempted to insist that employers purchasing convict servants should deposit a £50 bond against their good behaviour, but this was overruled by the Provincial Court.[110] A further attempt in 1754 to levy a tax of 20s. on every convict brought into Maryland was also quashed by the Crown.[111] However, a temporary English resident, William Eddis, wrote from Annnapolis, Maryland, in September 1770 that the Virginians had 'inflicted very severe penalties' on the masters of vessels introducing convicts and that consequently Maryland was 'the only province into which convicts can be freely imported'.[112] Nevertheless, the last shipment of British convicts to America before the Revolution was put ashore at the James River in April 1776.[113]

Irish critics of transportation

Transportation from Ireland during the late-eighteenth century did not produce anything like the debate that it aroused in Britain where it

3 William Eden, Lord Auckland.

was portrayed by commentators either as an inadequate or unnecessarily harsh punishment or as a waste of human resources.[114] William Eden (later Lord Auckland), for example, had complained in his influential *Principles of Penal Law* (1771) that transportation was 'often beneficial to the criminal, and always injurious to the community'.[115] Nor did he think that it should be prescribed for 'offences by no means so heinous in their nature, as to require the extirpation of the criminal from the society of his fellow-citizens'.[116] As the architect of the 1776 Hulks Act and the 1779 Penitentiary Act of the British Parliament when he was under-secretary to Lord North, he was determined not only to make hard labour an alternative to transportation for less serious offenders,[117] but to make it the property of the state rather than of private merchants, captains and employers.[118]

Eden does not appear to have taken much interest in penal reform during his later stint as Government Secretary to Lord Lieutenant Carlisle at Dublin Castle between 1780 and 1782, being more concerned with commercial matters. However, there were those in Ireland who believed as he did that transportation was not a matter of ridding the country of its human pests but of depriving it of potentially valuable labour. In a sharp commentary on social conditions, the anonymous author of a 1765 pamphlet entitled *Animadversions on the Street Robberies in Dublin ...* had described the perceived increase of crime in the city as a serious threat to the economic life of the city. Reviewing the events of the previous two years, this unofficial spokesman of the merchant class painted a grim picture of a metropolis virtually besieged by desperate criminals:

> The extraordinary distresses which have fallen upon this city, during the course of the two last winters, have been felt very sensibly by the inhabitants: they arose to such a degree, as made the internal commerce of the city languish: the higher sort were attacked in their carriages, plundered and abused, and put in fear and danger of their lives. The trader, after the close of day, was afraid to stir out of his house, on the necessary matters of his calling; the shop-keeper, with reluctance, kept his shop open: the journeyman, in dread, carried home his work, to receive payment due for his week's labour; old men, young women, servants, and children, were alike the prey of these rapacious villains.[119]

The author complained of the long delays in the legal system which resulted in criminals being 'dismissed for want of evidence'. His suggested solution was to replace the old custom of parish watchmen with a centralised system of policing by which guards would be stationed on a daily basis, supplemented by 'flying parties to patrole every where, to see that all was well in the several quarters, and that all duty was properly performed'.

Significantly, he did not see hanging as an effective deterrent:

> Neither law, admonition or the most dreadful examples, make the least impression upon these unhappy men: for they have been

known, on carrying on[e] of their own gang from the gibbit [*sic*] to the grave, to lay down the corps [*sic*], and commit a robbery by the way.

Unlike others of his class, however, he did not regard transportation as a solution. The previous two years had seen 189 convicts shipped off to the American plantations, but with no observable effect on the rate of crime. More to the point, this exodus of mostly young men represented 'a deplorable loss to a trading city'.

The Police Act of 1778, which undertook a partial reform of Dublin's antiquated and ineffectual system of parish watchmen,[120] was a tardy response to the central thrust of *Animadversions*. The hard labour legislation of the previous year, to be discussed below, was both a response to the criticism of transportation and a means of dealing with what was believed to be its only temporary suspension.

The Hard Labour Act

The imminent outbreak of the Revolutionary War meant that British and Irish transportation to North America was brought to a halt in early 1776.[121] Both governments quickly took measures to deal with what they saw at that point as only a temporary problem: the British Parliament passing Eden's Hulks Act in 1776 (*16 George III, c. 43*),[122] which had to be renewed each year, and the Irish Parliament enacting similar legislation in 1778 (*17 & 18 Geo. III, c. 9*), which allowed magistrates and judges to order hard labour on port works for a term of from three to ten years as a substitute for transportation. The Irish legislation was initially valid for two years but was subsequently extended until 1785.[123]

The preamble of the Irish Act made it very clear that although the American War had made trans-Atlantic transportation 'inconvenient' for the time being, it also accepted Eden's view that the use of convict labour for public purposes was both economical and potentially reformatory:

Whereas the transportation of convicts to his Majesty's colonies and plantations in America ... is found to be attended with various inconveniences, particularly by depriving this kingdom of many subjects, whose labour might be useful to the community, and who by proper care and correction might be reclaimed from their evil courses: and whereas until some other effectual provisions in the place of transportation to his Majesty's colonies and plantations in America can be framed, such convicts (being males) might be employed with benefit to the publick in the raising sand, soil, and gravel from and cleansing the river Anna Liffey in the harbour of Dublin, or any other service for the benefit of the navigation of the said river and harbour eastwards of Essex-bridge, or in any other service after directed ... or being female might be kept to labour of a less severe kind within this kingdom.[124]

The intention of what became known as the *Hard Labour Act* was that all suitable male prisoners sentenced according to its provisions would be brought down to Dublin, but that women and 'weak or aged males' were to be employed in houses of correction supported by the grand juries in the counties where they were convicted. Hard labour on the Liffey was to be carried out under the supervision of overseers appointed at sessions of justices of the peace; refusal to work could be punished by whipping. At the end of his term, the prisoner was entitled to receive clothing and 'not less than forty shillings or more'; the term could even be shortened if he showed signs of reformation. However, there was no clear indication in the legislation of how the system was to be administered and there was no mention of hulks or other accommodation for the prisoners.

In practice, no effort was made by the Irish government or by Dublin Corporation to ensure that hulks were commissioned, overseers appointed by justices of the peace and port works carried out. Indeed, apart from the despatch of some women and boys to the city Bridewell, no special provision was made for the numerous prisoners sentenced to hard labour between 1777 and 1785. As the Irish penal historian J.P. Starr has pointed out, the Hard Labour Act did not provide for any system of inspection and had no effect when prisoners sentenced in this way were committed to Newgate where there were no facilities for labour. This itself was contrary to the Act, which stipulated that those condemned to hard labour should be held separately from petty offenders.[125]

Why Ireland did not attempt to emulate Britain's hulk system is not revealed in contemporary documents, although it probably had to do with the fact that responsibility for the administration of the Act was not set out clearly in the legislation. Furthermore, no Parliamentary vote was made for its implementation and Dublin Corporation would no doubt have been unwilling to raise the additional revenue needed. In the meantime, the operation of Britain's hulk system on the Thames and at Portsmouth and Plymouth was making it clear that the cost of operation was by no means fully compensated for by the value of the labour obtained.

The reality was that most prisoners sentenced to hard labour at Ireland's quarterly assizes were put into Newgate with everyone else, placing increasing pressure on the prison system. Many had to be released before the expiry of their sentences to make way for others newly convicted.[126] However, prisoners were still being sentenced to hard labour in early 1783[127] and the Act seems to have remained in force until 1786 when it was effectively replaced by the transportation provisions of the new Police Act.[128]

The outcome, according to a Dublin sheriff who gave evidence before the Parliamentary committee on gaols in 1783, was that

> persons sentenced to hard labour crowd the gaols, and there being no means of employing them, become a nuisance and additional expence to the public, endangering the health of the prisoners, debauching and corrupting their morals, to a pitch of depravity scarcely credible.[129]

The committee was also told that women and young boys committed under the Act to the Bridewell at Smithfield were not allowed fire, candles, blankets or straw and that any profit from their labour went to the gaoler's wife.[130]

Military recruitment

Apart from questions of undefined responsibility and cost, the major disincentive to implementing the Hard Labour Act was no doubt the relative ease with which young male prisoners could be 'pressed' into the Royal Navy and the East India Company's forces during the course of the American War.[131] During the late 1770s and early 1780s, Dublin Corporation ordered the periodical 'sweeping' from the streets of known vagabonds. They were then held on board the *Lovely Nancy* tender in the Liffey, together with the convicted criminals who had opted for service until they could be removed by transports to their place of duty. In January 1783, the *Hibernian Journal* hoped that the government would once again resort to the system of rounding up vagrants and handing them over to the East India Company.[132]

The end of hostilities with the Americans meant that this convenient arrangement came to an end for the time being. When it was announced in February 1783 that the most recent collection of vagabonds and undesirables was to be released in Dublin after being held for only a short time, the *Freeman's Journal* expressed considerable anxiety at the prospect:

> The discharge, a day or two hence ... of above two hundred fellows ... and among whom were many known vagabonds who have been in prison, fills the town in general with alarm. It is hoped the spirited officiations, which took place last winter among the principal inhabitants of several parishes of this metropolis, will again be speedily revived, in order to keep a good look-out for many of those dissolute gentry, that have been dismissed so suddenly, and so unexpectedly.[133]

Two of those due to be released were Reilly and Burgess (described as 'notorious offenders') who had agreed with eight others from Newgate to serve in the East Indies but were discharged at Gravesend in London when hostilities ceased.[134] Reilly, who had been one of the first prisoners to break out of Newgate in 1781, had avoided recapture for three years. On one occasion he

> was playing Chess and carousing in Plunket-Street, in Consequence of which two Peace Officers went there and apprehended him, but in leading him through that Street, a riotous mob assembled, principally Women, who rescued this daring Offender, cut and abused the Officers, and once more enabled this Villain to continue his Depredations on the Public.[135]

Similar feelings were expressed by the *Freeman's Journal* in early 1783 about the repatriation of other ne'er-do-wells who had been pressed into the Royal Navy during the war and had seen service in foreign parts:

> It is highly incumbent on the citizens of Dublin, at this time, to guard against thieves and house-breakers, as the number of idle and disorderly vagrants which were dispersed on ship-board, in consequence of the war, will be every day returning home, [and] after spending what little they bring with them, will resort to their old practices of plundering the public.[136]

News of the anticipated landing of 200 disabled soldiers from England in early May caused further apprehension that they would 'shortly be followed by many thousands of unprovided Men, who, in a year of such Scarcity, and Stagnation of Trade, must turn loose in Banditties [*sic*] on the Public, at a time that it is already evident our Police was never known so lax, nor Robberies so frequent'.[137]

In addition to the threat posed by returning soldiers and seamen, the generally unhappy economic situation in Ireland at the time provided a fundamental problem. Indeed, the working classes of Dublin's Liberties district had been suffering from the effects of economic decline for some years. In particular, weavers, stocking-makers and ribbon-makers were hard hit both by British imports and by technological change. In January 1783, Lord Mayor Thomas Greene distributed aid to the poor who it was believed might otherwise have perished.[138] According to the *Hibernian Journal* in April, thousands of the unemployed were roaming the Liberties and descending on the nearby countryside in search of sustenance:

> the Manufacturers [workers] form Parties to go into the neighbouring Villages, particularly along the canal, where, on entering the Houses, they warn the Country-People to be under no Apprehensions – that they only want Food to eat, and having obtained that, no Violence should be offered.[139]

In February 1784, Lord Lieutenant Rutland was so moved by the plight of the Dublin poor that he asked the British Treasury for £3,000 to spend on relief measures. Two months later, he requested a further £3,600 to provide work for weavers who would otherwise become destitute.[140] However, working-class agitation against imported manufactures developed into serious civil unrest during the summer. By August, Rutland was seriously concerned about the maintenance of law and order in the city.

It was these factors, together with the rapid increase in Dublin's population and wealth and the proliferation of opportunities to plunder its affluent upper classes and those who supplied their needs, which helped to create what was seen to be a crime wave and a threat to public order in the city of Dublin from the early 1780s. As in London and other British cities, the ensuing 'moral panic' of the propertied classes helped to bring about the renewal of transportation as the only perceived solution.

2
Crime in Late Eighteenth-Century Ireland

My dear Polly,

I am down at last. I now must die, prepare a Holland shirt for your poor Jack, which shall be the last, tell Harry to send a decent oak coffin, and to pay you the balance of the last tattler, it is worth 15 shiners. Tom owes me twelve pieces of our last collection at Bray. I behaved generous to him, and never stagged, therefore I hope he will pay you. My friend, at Harold's Cross, holds a cup, two watches and six copper-plate papers of mine – I would advise you to marry him, in order to partake of the BIT, he will never see you want whilst there is powder and shot – I bequeath unto him (as a token of my regard for him, and in order the better to support you) my pair of trusty BULL DOGS, who never failed BARKING in cases of necessity. Do not grieve, I MAY see you again, if the NECK CLOTH misses. Adieu, my sweetheart,

– your's,

J.K[eena]n[1]

John Keenan was hanged with two other men at Gallows-hill, Kilmainham, on 21 July 1784. According to a newspaper report of the event, they all 'behaved with the decency becoming their situation', and Keenan 'with remarkable signs of contrition'.[2] A young man, probably in his late 20s, he was nevertheless a veteran highwayman who had been capitally convicted on no less than six previous occasions but had escaped hanging by making (or perhaps pretending to make) 'discoveries' to the authorities about other crimes in which he had been involved. He had also endeared himself to the authorities by acting as hangman at Newgate on at least one occasion.[3] This time, however, he had been found guilty at the Commission of Oyer and Terminer of robbing a military officer, Capt. Withers, in Long-lane in the heart of Dublin the previous January. And Judge Robinson evidently decided to make an example of what the *Hibernian Journal* called 'the most notorious offender that has for a long time since fallen victim to justice'.[4]

Three weeks before his trial, Keenan and another prisoner had been discovered by Gaoler John McKinley[5] cutting through the bars of their cell in old Kilmainham gaol with a saw made from a clock spring in a frame, together with oil and sulphuric acid.[6] Asked by Robinson after his conviction if he had anything to say before sentence was passed on him, he replied 'nothing, but that he was determined, after his death, to haunt his prosecutors, and McKinley ... in order to revenge their conduct towards him'.[7]

Keenan's letter, addressed to his wife in Kevin-street, was found in his cell at Kilmainham after his execution and was published by the *Hibernian Journal*, not so much for its poignant message as for its examples of criminal argot. These would have been a curiosity for upper-class Dubliners who seldom ventured into the seamier areas of the city. At the same time, the final despatch of a highwayman was a source of relief at a time when there was an epidemic of armed robberies. Nor were the plunderers any respecters of persons. In October 1785, for example, Lord Sudley and Lady Hatton were held up in their carriage at the gate of Phoenix Park, the resort of Dublin's aristocracy, and robbed by four 'excellently mounted' men dressed in long cloaks and armed with pistols and sabres.[8]

Throughout the 1780s, the Dublin newspapers carried detailed accounts of crimes reported to have been committed in or near the city. There was also a comprehensive coverage of the Co. Dublin and Dublin City quarter sessions where magistrates presided and the Commission of Oyer and Terminer where more serious crimes were heard by judges. Quarterly assizes in the various county centres throughout Ireland were reported more fitfully. Before the new Police Act of 1786, both pro-government and anti-government newspapers highlighted urban crime in order to press the case for police reforms. After the implementation of the Act in September 1786, 'opposition prints' like the *Hibernian Journal* and the *Dublin Evening Post* continued their detailed coverage. Now, however, it was part of their campaign to discredit the new, centralised police system which they represented as strengthening the authority of Dublin Castle and diminishing the sovereignty of the Irish Parliament.

For these diverse reasons, the exploits of Dublin's criminals probably received more newspaper coverage than those of any other European city of the period. What emerged from the comprehensive chronicling of Dublin crime and the somewhat repetitive discussions of possible solutions during the 1780s was the problem of finding an appropriate and effective form of punishment for theft and robbery. Transportation remained the only alternative to hanging at one extreme and whipping and branding at the other.

Organised criminals

While it is problematic to speak of a 'criminal class' in Dublin in the 1780s, it is clear that there were many people for whom crime was the principal source of livelihood and whose language and ethos reflected their membership of a vigorous criminal sub-culture. Although Dublin did not have a Daniel Defoe or a Hogarth to record their way of life, enough survives from the newspapers of the day and from oral tradition to suggest that the city had its hard core of professional criminals.

As well as the gangs of highwaymen, footpads and house-breakers who preyed on the city and its surrounding villages and hamlets as John Keenan and his mates had done, there were organised groups of shop-lifters who 'worked' the main business streets of Dublin and Belfast. One of the best-known of these criminal 'corps' was captained by a man known as 'Mocatasaney' and controlled by clearly set rules and orders. When seven members of this gang of 80 were caught in Belfast in December 1784, their *modus operandi* was described in detail in the newspapers:

> they frequent all the market towns for thirty or forty miles round, divide their spoil in common, and defray individual expences of prosecutions etc. from the general fund. No less than 40 of the the gang have been in and about the town for five or six years past, and an uncommon number of petty robberies have been committed by them in that time. On the market days particularly they are very industrious; they generally go in squads into shops, and have always a receiver behind backs to move off with the loose things which the others may find means to hand over – females are chiefly agents upon these occasions,their long cloaks being admirably calculated to conceal the booty. Rolls of tobacco, and bundles of made-up teas, dye-stuff etc. in grocers shops frequently fall into the hands of these pirates; and stockings, handkerchiefs, etc. in woollen-drapers; a whole piece of frieze was taken away from a shop on the quay last Friday evening.[9]

Another well-known shop-lifting gang in Dublin used women as decoys while their male associates plundered everything within reach. Warning the public of their exploits, the *Hibernian Journal* even provided a helpful description of the two women involved:

> One of them is a thin, young looking woman, full eyes, snaggle teeth, and speaks with a brogue – the other [is] elderly, squat and rough-faced, and both remarkably well dressed.[10]

In Dublin during the 1780s there were constant newspaper reports of gangs like these who used various techniques to distract the hapless shopkeeper while the loot was either concealed beneath capacious clothing or passed back to an accomplice at the door.

There were also accounts of gangs of 'sharpers' or tricksters who practised a variety of ruses, ranging from the ordering of goods without paying for them to the time-honoured trick of 'ring dropping'.[11] In January 1790, *Walker's Hibernian Magazine* described a versatile English gang then in town:

> Dublin, at the moment, swarms with a flight of English sharpers – adepts in the mysteries of their profession, and general professors in

NINE o'Clock ! Nine o'Clock ! paſt Nine o'Clock, and a dark cloudy Night.

4   A Dublin Watchman

BLOODY News, laſt Night's Packet, bloody News.—Here's the Monthly Magazines, and all the neweſt Publications

A Dublin Newspaper Seller

the art of shop-lifting, pocket-picking, ring-dropping, swindling, and coining. They assume all shapes and appearances – clergymen, farmers, horse jockies, agents, riders, and are strait or deformed, young or old, lame or otherwise, just as occasion suits. Many of these fellows are old, and notorious offenders on the Bristol and London *paves* – they generally *cruise*, as they term it, in gangs of three and four, dispersed at convenient distance, and within call ... in order to facilitate the escape of each other when detected.[12]

In January 1784 the *Hibernian Journal* described the ruse employed by a teenage thief to deceive a shop assistant:

Wednesday morning last a silver smith[,] an inhabitant of Dame street, was robbed of a considerable quantity of old plate in the following manner – a Boy, tutored for the purpose, with a leather satchel on his shoulder and cleanly dressed, stole unperceived into the shop, and hastily proceeded to the Drawer where the plate was deposited, removed it to his bag, immediately after which he was seen by an attendant of the place, but having supposed from his youth and genteel appearance to be at Hide-and-seek from some of his juvenile companions, and confirming this idea by crying out 'cuckoo' when noticed, he was suffered to depart without suspicion; soon after a discovery was made too late, however, for the recovery of the articles.[13]

Another young boy 'to all appearance no more than nine or ten years old' perfected a system of robbing the post which sometimes produced worthwhile results:

By fixing a little tar in the holes for the reception of letters at the Post-office, in order to prevent them from sliding down – his hand being small, he could easily put it in, and watching his opportunity, he took out what letters happened to adhere to the tar. Amongst others, it seems, was the letter which contained the 100£ note.[14]

Gangs of young boys specialised in the use of a diamond or special knife to remove a pane of glass from a jeweller's window and steal the valuables on display.[15]

In many cases, experienced criminals took on 'apprentices' in the tradition of the notorious English thief-master, Jonathan Wild, betraying them to the police when it suited their purpose. One such Fagin-like figure, a man called Broderick, was committed to Newgate in May 1783 in the belief of his being 'not only the Tutor of several unhappy Youths, but finally the means of their being apprehended ...'.[16]

In October 1788 the *Freeman's Journal* reported that the training of young thieves was being conducted on a systematic basis:

> There are a number of young villains, from eight or nine to about fourteen years of age, who generally assemble at the fall of the evening at Christ-church-yard, where at night time they are joined by vagabonds of more advanced years, by whose directions they proceed on different parties through the city, for the purpose of picking pockets, and filching whatever may lie conveniently within their reach on the counters of such shops as they find with doors left open, and perhaps carelessly attended by the owners.[17]

The attraction of shop-lifting and picking pockets was that goods thus obtained could be used to raise ready cash from one of the city's scores of pawnbroking establishments. It was not necessary for a person pawning items to provide their name and address; consequently, they could not be traced when stolen goods were located by the owner in a pawnshop. Nor was it always easy for shopkeepers or owners to positively identify the stolen goods as their own when it consisted (as it commonly did) of such items as cloth, garments, stockings, handkerchiefs or hats. Despite the introduction of new regulations under the Pawnbroking Act of 1786,[18] complaints about pawnbrokers continued even after further legislation was enacted in 1788.[19] More valuable items such as watches, rings and silver buckles could be used as stakes at the gambling-houses in Smock-alley, where shuffle-board was a popular game.

Burglary was also extremely common in Dublin, with young boys being used to enter windows and pass out goods.[20] Independent teenage robbers also employed various stratagems to enter unlocked dwellings. This was the ingenious system employed by sixteen-year-old John Egan, who was caught stealing plate from a house in Capel-street in late August 1783:

> he has a Bird tied with a String, with which he amuses Himself through the Streets, and when he sees a Hall-door, or Parlour-window open, he takes care to suffer the Bird to fly in and from his genteel Appearance the Passengers conclude he has no other Object in view than the Recovery of his Bird. By this Artifice he has com-

mitted more Depredations on the inhabitants of St. Mary's and St. Thomas' parish forsome weeks past than any Offender double his Age has done for years.[21]

One of the most active gangs of burglars was led by Hugh McGowran, better known as 'Morning Star' because of his nocturnal habits, who was arrested in September 1787 after a long career and sentenced to seven years' transportation for house robbery.[22] If the jury had not reduced the value of the goods stolen by him to 4s. 9d., below the 5s. specified in the statute, the judge would have been bound to sentence him to death.

The systematic theft of door-knockers, coal-vault stoppers,[23] iron railings and lead from house roofs was very common as there was a brisk market in these metals. Although it had been made a felony punishable by seven years' transportation in 1732 and was to become a capital offence in 1787,[24] detection was difficult and proceeds were good. In October 1787 thieves blasted away the massive lead coat of arms of the city adorning the facade of the Tholsel, the old customs house in Skinner's-row which served as Dublin's magistrates' court and town hall.[25] The Grecian temple of Marino built by Lord Charlemont on his Co. Meath estate was stripped of 1,500 pounds of lead and even Dublin Castle ballroom lost part of its roof.[26] Perhaps the most sensational theft of the decade took place in March 1788 when a gang broke into the Rotunda, the favourite gathering place of Dublin's social elite at the top of Sackville-street, and 'completely gutted' the fine organ of all its lead pipes.[27]

Not even the lead casings of buried coffins were safe from plunder. In one bizarre instance in September 1783, a woman was arrested after taking a parcel of lead to a dealer in Fishamble-street: 'On his opening the parcel, he observed his own Mark, and the inscription of his wife's Coffin, who was interred in St Mary's Church about Seven Years ago'.[28] The woman subsequently gave information against the parish gravedigger who had been her regular supplier. Coffin-stealing and body-snatching were common in parish graveyards.[29] And dog-stealing was practised in Dublin on a scale which anticipated Jaroslav Hasek's descriptions of early twentieth century Prague.[30]

Dublin's textile industry also offered easy opportunities for theft from the laying out of newly-treated cloth in bleaching-grounds in various parts of the city.[31] The plundering of cloth from these locations, as well as from the newly-extended Linen Hall, became such a problem that special legislation was passed to make it a capital offence.[32]

A frequently reported crime in the late 1780s was the 'stripping' of children.[33] The practice was for an older woman to entice a well-dressed young girl into a back lane with a promise of sweets or money and then to remove all her clothing for sale to a pawnbroker or one of the used clothes dealers in Plunket-street.[34] The *Dublin Chronicle* described one such incident in October 1788:

> The cries of a child, about six years old, yesterday, in one of the old houses near the end of Lazer's-hill, having engaged the attention of some persons passing by, they found a fine little girl stripped almost stark naked with some gingerbread in her hand, which she said was given to her by a woman, who took away her clothes to be washed. She proved to be the daughter of a very respectable tradesman on George's-quay and had been inveigled for the purpose.[35]

From time to time, Dublin was plagued by an unpleasant fraternity calling themselves the *Pinkindindies*, 'so-called from the habit of stabbing or *pinking* with small swords unfortunate females and then robbing them of their clothes and their property'.[36] In December 1784 the *Hibernian Journal* reported the return to town of this gang. Seven of its members had forced their way into a house in Mecklenburgh-street, cutting and abusing the three women there before tying them up and plundering their apartment.[37]

Even after the introduction of the new police system in September 1786, large groups of young *buckeens* continued to flout public order in the streets of Dublin by indiscriminately attacking passers-by or committing other nuisances. The *Hibernian Journal* reported a particulary obnoxious example of this anti-social behaviour in October 1786:

> A few nights ago a number of young men, lovers of fun, planted themselves at the corner of Charles-street, Mary-street, and Mary's-lane, armed with tin or pewter squirts, and syringed every person who came by, with a liquid too gross to be mentioned. An old Scotch officer, on sharing these odoriferous favours, turned about and instantly knocked down the syringical engineer, who had the assurance to call for the interposition of the Police guard.[38]

Later that month, there was a more serious report of riot and outrage at night in the streets:

a number of armed buckeens and unfledg'd rioters have paraded thro' Parliament-street. Essex-street, Capel-street, Ormond-Quay, and other parts of the city, abusing and ill-treating almost every person that came in their way, and endeavouring to force into houses, where their behaviour is so gross and brutal, that it would disgrace even an uncivilized Indian.[39]

'Prince of Pickpockets'

The gentle art of 'diving' or picking pockets was highly developed in Dublin where large gatherings of people congregated in public buildings such as the Royal Exchange, the Linen Hall and the new Customs House, or at theatres and assembly rooms. Book auctions, church services, the drawing of the national lottery and even public executions also provided favourable conditions.[40] For example, at the hanging of a veteran street robber called George Wilde, better known as 'Ree-raw', on Kilmainham's Gallows-hill on 8 October 1787, a ten-year-old boy picked a gentleman's gold watch.[41] Another pickpocket caught in the act at the Four Courts in July 1788 was found to have garnered no less than twenty-five handkerchiefs and a silver snuff box in a morning's work.[42]

Whole gangs of pickpockets converged on busy city thoroughfares where detection was difficult. In October 1783 the *Hibernian Journal* complained:

> At present, even by Day-light, it is impossible to pass the crowded Streets, without losing a Handkerchief, or some other loose Article in the Pocket. These thefts are committed by little Boys, who push into Crowds, and where there are Stoppages, particularly High-street, Skinner-row, and the corner of Castle-steet, where these Depredations have been committed with great Success for some Days past. The apparent Instance [*sic*] of the young Rogues screen them from Suspicion; and even were they examined, no Part of the Plunder can be found upon them, as they have constant Attendants who make off with the Prize. On Saturday evening a Gentleman detected a Boy not more than eight years old, who with great dexterity had deprived him of his Handkerchief and Gloves; he instantly seized him, and with great difficulty compelled him to confess the Robbery, and that a Woman had made off with the Booty.[43]

One of the best-known Dublin pickpockets aand burglars was a man called Brazil Fox. After many attempts to secure him, he was eventually

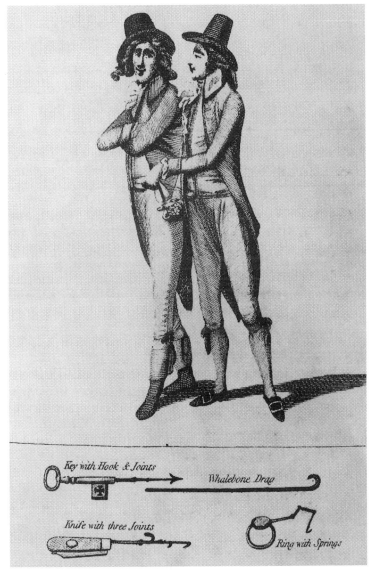

Key with Hook & Joints

Whalebone Drag

Knife with three Joints

Ring with Springs

5 'Barrington Picking the Pocket of J. Brown, Esq. of Brandford'. Also illustrated are Barrington's tools of trade.

committed to Newgate in April 1783 for robbing a house in Meath-street.[44] However, by far the most celebrated professional thief in both Dublin and London during the 1780s was George Barrington, popularly known as the 'The Prince of Pickpockets', who operated with his cosmopolitan gang of accomplices between the two capitals until his eventual conviction at London's Newgate in September 1790 and subsequent transportation to New South Wales.[45] During his heyday, Barrington's visits to Dublin were extensively reported in the press, his reputed exploits in both cities always being newsworthy both for their daring and their scale.

Born at Maynooth in June 1755 and educated in Dublin, Barrington had run away from school in May 1771 because of a fight with another boy, taking with him the schoolmaster's money and his sister's gold watch. After some experience as an apothecary's clerk, he joined a troupe of strolling actors led by an Englishman, John Price, who had fled to Ireland to avoid transportation to America. He demonstrated some talent on the stage: according to his colleagues, he 'had a speaking eye, an expressive countenance, a tolerable theatrical figure, a very pompous enunciation, and a most retentive memory'.[46] However, he quickly became more interested in the business of picking pockets in which Price and the others instructed him. Lack of income during the lay-off season meant that thieving was a useful sideline for some actors. For Barrington, however, it became a profession which he practised with total commitment and masterly skill, using his knowledge of surgical instruments to develop his own ingenious tools of trade.[47]

Barrington was described in the Dublin newspapers of late 1784 as having recently escaped conviction and heading a 'numerous gang' which met nightly at a notorious gaming-house on the corner of Crane-lane and Essex-street.[48] His return to Dublin in February 1788 gave the *Freeman's Journal* an opportunity to remark on his now-legendary skills:

> By various accounts, the *noted* and *famous* BARRINGTON, is lately arrived in this city: doubtless he intends honouring some of our crowded churches, the law courts, *Promenade*, Theatre, and other public places, to keep in practice his unrivalled *sleight of hand*.[49]

Other reports followed, notably one in early 1789 when he arrived with a group including the well-known Jewish 'bruiser' or prize-fighter from London, Daniel Mendoza.[50] The practice was that when Mendoza staged one of his popular exhibitions of the art of pugilism, Barrington and his minions relieved members of the crowd of their their purses and valuables. The most noteworthy and daring exploit attributed to Barrington was carried out during his last visit to Dublin in early

1790.[51] It was reported that at a charity sermon at St Mary's Church in north Dublin, the purses and pockets of no fewer than thirty members of the congregation were taken by 'the Archpickpocket'. Amongst the victims was Lady Charlemont, who was said to have lost no less than twenty guineas.[52]

Reporting Barrington's seventeenth arrest and confinement in London's Newgate in September of that year, Dublin's *Morning Post* suggested that despite his earlier successes in avoiding prosecution, this time his situation was 'rather critical'. During all his visits to Dublin he had never been caught. Furthermore, one of his local accomplices, a receiver of stolen goods at Coal-quay, had apparently made enough money from the business put his way to bail Mendoza and any others of the gang who were unlucky enough to be committed for trial, 'and afterwards enable them to buy off all evidence'.[53] Barrington's partner on his last visit to Dublin was a young American *protége* called Redmond or Hubert, who had recently distinguished himself in London by defrauding the profligate young Duke of York of a large sum of money.[54] Redmond was acquitted in the Dublin Recorder's court in March on a charge of picking pockets, but was subsequently convicted for stealing a pair of silk stockings and sentenced to seven years' transportation.[55] However, he was 'sprung' from Newgate a month later with the assistance of a prison messenger, Matthew Nulty, who was later convicted for his part in the escape and transported on the *Queen* to New South Wales to serve seven years.[56]

It is one of history's ironies that when Barrington himself was finally despatched to New South Wales on the *Albemarle* in January 1791, he should subsequently have achieved the position of chief constable of Parramatta and hob-nob with General Joseph Holt of 1798 fame. Perhaps he also met up again with Mat Nulty, who had paid a high price for assisting his friend Redmond to escape from Newgate. It is a tribute to the power of Barrington's legend that he was long credited with writing and reciting a prologue at the opening of Sydney's first theatre in 1796.[57] The lines in question were certainly in keeping with his character and his style:

> From distant climes, o'er widespread seas we come,
> Though not with much eclat or beat of drum,
> True patriots all, for, be it understood,
> We left our country for our country's good;
> No private views disgrac'd our generous zeal,
> What urg'd our travels, was our country's weal.[58]

The Sall Dubb club

Some places in Dublin were well known as 'thieves' kitchens', or the social meeting places of the city's more dedicated criminals. A new establishment of this kind which was noted in late 1786 was the small beer tavern in Phoenix-street kept by Sarah Conolly, better known as 'Sall Dubb', where the *Freeman's Journal* advised officers of the newly-reformed police to pay a call:

> There is a weekly club held there on Monday nights, when all those children of industry, termed scamps, divers, siles, ruffs, sneaks and badgers, as well as the knights of the post and their fair dulcineas resort:- If the Sheriffs and the Commissioners of Police would now favour the President of this club with their company, and take a friendly pipe and a tankard of Thompson [ale], it might be productive of benefit to the community.[59]

In the inner city, notably the area around Newgate itself, there were numerous dram-houses, gaming-shops and 'night-houses' or brothels which remained open all night for a largely criminal clientele. Copper-alley was a laneway notorious for dens of this kind.[60] It was in this vicinity, too, that well-organised gangs of coiners went about their work in backrooms and cellars. In November 1784, for example, Sheriff Jenkin discovered such a factory where a group had been at work for some time.[61]

In late 1784, some parts of the city were regarded as virtual no-go areas after dark because of the proliferation of armed robbers. North Earl and Great-George's streets and their vicinity were so badly infested with footpads that 'Ladies there are prohibited from making nighly visits to each other, as none of them will venture out after nightfall ...'.[62] It was even said that robbers used nearby Mount Eccles as a rendezvous 'whence they dispatch scouts to watch the different avenues ...'.[63] Inadequate street lighting in the form of oil lamps facilitated the operations of footpads and thieves. Lamps in the major streets were put out by 12 p.m. or 1 a.m. and whole areas of the Liberties were scarcely lit at all.[64] Furthermore, expensive lamp glasses were frequently stolen or smashed by 'inebriated gentlemen' on their way home.[65] In December 1786 a well-organised strike by Dublin's lamplighters kept the whole city in darkness for a week. Nevertheless, it had been claimed that after new municipal legislation in 1784 Dublin was 'the best lighted capital in Europe'.[66]

Prostitution

Prostitution was not in itself a crime during this era, but prostitutes often robbed their customers or were involved in picking pockets and shop-lifting as a further source of income.[67] It is difficult to estimate how many women and girls were 'on the town' in Dublin in the 1780s but a newspaper writer's description of the city centre in 1783 suggests that they were very numerous:

> Dame-street is as much crowded with prostitutes every night as ever it was, who, attended by their bullies, render it unsafe for a peaceable citizen to walk through it after nine o'clock.[68]

There were also complaints about women street-singers

> who go about Day and Night singing obscene and low Ballads, to the great detriment and painful conclusion of decent Company, especially in Courts and Alleys, where the polluted stuff is distinctly heard in whatever part of a House a Company happens to be.[69]

The new Police Act of April 1786 gave constables the power to take 'night-walkers' and any others 'loitering about without visible means of support' before a justice of the peace who could then commit them under the Vagabond Act if they failed to produce a surety for their good behaviour.[70] However, the situation had not changed significantly by September 1787 when it was observed in the *Freeman's Journal* that 'the swarm of these shameless and abandoned women that nightly prowl through the streets of this metropolis is really become a most intolerable nuisance ...'.[71] The only step that the Dublin Corporation authorities had taken to alleviate the nuisance was to make available the city Bridewell at Smithfield and the House of Industry in Channel-row for the reception of vagrants of both sexes. Even then, the only punishment that could be inflicted on the women was cutting off their hair. Nor was the House of Industry a very secure holding place: forty women escaped in November 1786 by making a hole in the wall.[72] In fact, there was little that police and magistrates could do to control 'night-walking' beyond committing the women temporarily to these institutions.[73] When twenty-one prostitutes were rounded up and brought before the Dublin City quarter sessions at the Tholsel on 11 October 1788, they were immediately released. The Recorder 'in a very learned charge, expatiated on the liberty of the subject, and the cruelty of confining persons in prison, without sufficient charge ...'.[74]

By early 1791, the *Morning Post* was alleging that the newly-reformed police were usurping the role of pimps by taxing prostitutes' nightly takings and throwing them into the cells if they refused to pay up:

> There is scarcely a police watch-house throughout the city that does not every night realize some of the most *knowing* schemes of the Beggar's Opera. The *Macheaths, Filcher, Mats O' the Mint, Nimming Neds, Loekits* and *Peachums* of Gay's comedy, were all novices compared with the Police Constables and their scarecrow gangs; with the difference that instead of sharing the plunder of the night with the *Polly Peachums* and *Jenny Divers* who fall into their clutches, they first pick the pockets of the unfortunate wanderers, and then furnish them with the dungeons for refusing tribute.[75]

Frustration at the inability of the authorities to control prostitution ultimately led to public attacks on prostitutes and the burning of brothels.[76]

6 'A Prospect of the Parliament House, in College Green Dublin'. College Green and Dame Street were a favourite haunt of prostitutes in the 1780s.

Rural crime

Not surprisingly, the Dublin newspapers did not pay so much attention to crime in the countryside, although they could hardly ignore the agrarian outrages which were rampant in the south of Ireland. During the 1780s, the province of Munster was plagued by well-organised rural gangs known as 'Whiteboys' and 'Rightboys' who pursued a brutal and unrelenting campaign against land agents, tithe-farmers and others who were seen to threaten the interests of poor tenant farmers and landless labourers. Much of this agrarian terrorism was intended to serve as a deterrent, as with the horrendous example made of a former tithe-farmer of Co. Kilkenny in December 1784:

> These nocturnal reformers a few days ago proceeded to the house of Mr. John Mason, a very honest, industrious man, near Ferragh, who was the tythe-farmer, but at present out of that employment, they broke open his house, dragged him out of his bed, and placed him naked on horseback, and after carrying him five or six miles, most barbarously and inhumanly cut off his ears, and in this bleeding and mangled condition buried him in a grave they had prepared, leaving only his head and mouth uncovered. They robbed him of his fire-arms, and many other articles of value.[77]

The perpetrators of crimes of this kind were seldom caught and prosecuted because of the difficulty of obtaining witnesses other than the victims themselves and their relatives. Consequently, most of the prisoners convicted at Ireland's rural quarterly assizes during the 1780s had been committed on charges of highway robbery, common theft, animal-stealing or serious assault.

Much of the non-agrarian crime arose from the various parish fairs marking saints' feasts days, which offered easy pickings for professional thieves following the circuit in the summer season. An example was reported in Co. Kildare in July 1783:

> On Monday a number of notorious thieves attended the yearly fair on the Curragh; a greater scene of confusion cannot be conceived than they created in about half an hour; not a being who kept a stand but suffered more or less; one missed 95 yards of frize [*sic*], another 50 yards of ratteen, and so on from one end of the fair to the other. Two suspicious looking fellows were taken into custody,

but after a long examination were suffered to depart, as nothing could be proved against them. A number of the gang are supposed to be the villains who lately arrived from England, as many who spoke the accent were observed in the crowd, but disappeared in a short time.[78]

Fairs also provide opportunities for faction-fighting and other expressions of the violence which seems to have been endemic to the Irish countryside and often resulted in prosecutions for murder or serious assault.

It was not an infrequent occurrence for armed gangs to attack the houses of the well-to-do, beating their occupants into submission and plundering everything of value that could be carried off. One such attack on the house of Theobald Wolfe Tone's father near Bodenstown in Co. Kildare in late 1786 was widely reported in the Dublin press:

The following daring robbery was committed on Thursday the 19th of October, instant, between the hours of ten and eleven at night. The house of Mr. Tone, of Blackhall, in the county of Kildare, was broke open by six or seven armed ruffians, disguised by cloth tied over their faces, who bound the family, and after abusing and cutting Mr. Tone with a knife, carried off the following articles: a carbine, a brass-hilted regimental sword, silver tea tongs, table and tea spoons, a shagreen cased watch, three large silver medals, two plain gold rings and garnet hoop, a twenty, a ten, and five guinea bank note, two guineas and a half in gold, and twenty-three shillings in silver, bills on Dublin, and other securities, to the value of £400, with several articles of wearing apparel: Before the villains went off they wantonly broke the china, a large looking-glass, and almost every article of furniture in the house.[79]

One of the best-known of these groups which operated in Co. Fermanagh until it was broken up in December 1790 was 'Peeble's gang'.[80]

As there were no systematic crime statistics for the 1780s in Ireland, we have to depend on contemporary newspaper reports, making allowances for the biases which these sometimes reflected. The return for the year 1790 made by Sir Jeremiah Fitzpatrick to the Committee on Police Business of the Irish House of Commons in April 1791[81] provides a comprehensive listing of the crimes successfully prosecuted throughout Ireland but without indicating their distribution. Of the

784 men and women found guilty out of 2,963 tried, he made the following classifications:

Murder – hanged 22; fined and confined 19; Pleaded pardon 3; burned in the hand and confined 19

Coining – hanged 1; fined and confined 1; held to bail 1

Forgery – fined and confined 1; pilloried and transported 1; confined 2

Burglary – hanged 24; transported 12

Robbery – hanged 25; transported 4; burned in the hand 1

Rapes and Running Away With Women – hanged 6; confined 4

Felony – hanged 17; transported 110; whipped and confined 9; confined 30; whipped 34; burned in the hand and confined 27; fined and confined 11; pilloried 1

Horse-Stealing – hanged 4; transported 1

Cow-Stealing – hanged 3; transported 3; burned in the hand 1

Sheep-Stealing – hanged 1; transported 4; burned in the hand and confined 2; confined 1; held to bail 1

Pickpockets – fined 6*d*. 1

Frauds and Swindling – whipped and confined 3; fined and confined 1; pilloried and confined 4; fined 2; whipped 2; transported 1; confined 5

Receiving Stolen Goods – whipped 1; fined 1; fined and confined 1; confined and pilloried 2

Forcible Possession – confined 1; transported 2

Rescue – fined 17; fined and confined 15; confined 1

Misdemeanors – fined and confined 16; whipped 6; fined 23; confined and whipped 10; confined and burned in the hand 4

False Imprisonment – fined and confined 1

Vagabonds – transported 2; transported unless bail given 3; held to bail 1

Perjury – pilloried 1; pilloried and transported 2; pilloried and confined 3; fined and confined 1; judgement arrested 1

Riots – whipped and confined 10; fined and confined 9; whipped 2; fined and held to bail 6

Combinations – whipped and confined 5; fined 5

Assaults – fined and confined 73; confined 5; fined 83; whipped and confined 4

Burglary, robbery and felony accounted for most of the more serious offences with no less than 142 offenders being sentenced outright to transportation. Already, however, the pattern of criminality was being coloured by the political and religious conflicts which were to mark this bloody decade. Noting the increase in the number of murders over the previous year, Fitzpatrick remarked that 'the cause is the religious riots in the North of Ireland, which so long disgraced this quarter of the kingdom'. [82]

3
Prisons and Punishment

It was no doubt the overcrowded and insecure situation of Dublin's two main gaols, together with the inefficacy of hanging as a deterrent, which provided the main incentives for the resumption of transportation in late 1784. During that year there were a number of escape attempts and in subsequent years these almost amounted to an epidemic. Although official records relating to the criminal justice system and to transportation have not survived, a series of parliamentary committee reports in the 1780s and 1790s provide ample evidence of prison conditions.

The New Prison

By the end of July 1784, the New Prison, or Newgate as it was more generally known, was estimated to be holding as many as three hundred prisoners, almost twice as many as its London namesake.[1] Some had been there for as long as three years.[2] The main reason for the chronic overcrowding was that prisoners, including women, who had been sentenced under the 1777 Act to hard labour as an alternative to transportation had not been provided with any work and were simply sent to join everyone else at Newgate. As the *Hibernian Journal* pointed out,

> the time which should be allotted to labour, is, in conjunction with their numerous visitors, spent in plotting mischief, as well against the public at large, as their keepers.[3]

As we shall see, it was not until June 1790 that Dublin Corporation adopted the recommendation of the then Inspector-General of Prisons,

Sir Jeremiah Fitzpatrick, by converting part of the Bridewell at Smithfield into a penitentiary for the purposes of 'useful labour'.[4] In the meantime, chronic overcrowding at Newgate was the normal state of affairs.

Another threat to the security of Newgate was the use of the front of the prison for hangings. In late 1782, public executions for Dublin City were transferred from the old site at the Baggot-street corner of St Stephen's Green to recently-completed Newgate where there was greater security against the crowd seizing the body, and (according to old Dublin custom) depositing it on the doorstep of the prosecutor. At first, executions at Newgate depended on the crude system of a plank projecting from one of the first-floor windows – an innovation attributed to the Marquis of Buckingham who had given particular instructions for the exemplary hanging of a prisoner convicted under the amended 'Chalking Act' of 1778.[5] However, in early 1783 a 'tremendous apparatus' consisting of an iron platform or scaffold suspended from four pulleys was attached to the front of the prison.[6] Known as the 'new drop' or 'iron maiden' and based on a design introduced by McKinley at Kilmainham earlier that year, it had the capacity to deal with two victims at a time.

Not only did the relocation of public hangings attract huge crowds to an already congested part of the city on execution days, but it seems to have provided a further stimulus to the prisoners to rise up against their gaolers. In almost every case of a reported riot or break-out at Newgate or Kilmainham during the 1780s, an execution had taken place within the previous twenty-four hours or was due the following day.

The problems at Newgate[7] could also be traced to the location of the building, its design and the inferior supervision, workmanship and materials employed in its construction. Built at Little-green, an open space north of the river and to the west of Capel-street, it was near the site of old New Gate, an ancient towered pile at the top of Thomas-street which had been medieval Dublin's western gate and part of its protective wall. Since 1485 it had served as the town prison with a long history of appalling conditions and ill-treatment of prisoners.

Following a 1767 parliamentary inquiry into gaols which found that old New Gate was 'in a very ruinous condition', holding 170 prisoners rather than the 80 for which it was designed, Dublin Corporation decided to build a new prison nearby. The foundation stone for the building was laid in October 1773, but it was not until September 1780 that the first prisoners were moved there from old New Gate.[8] The latter was used as a repository for prostitutes until January 1782 when Dublin Corporation finally decided that it 'should be immediately pulled down, the same being a nuisance ...'.[9]

Completed in 1780, Newgate, or 'the New Prison' as it was then known, was located in a low-lying and badly drained area of densely inhabited streets and alleys which hemmed it in and made any expansion impossible. Indeed, the 170 feet by 127 feet site chosen for the prison was so restricted that there was insufficient space for a perimeter wall to be built. Little-green was also the location of both the corn market and the root and potato market of Dublin, which meant that the area reeked with the stench of rotting vegetables.[10] Ironically, it was surrounded by one of the main concentrations of criminal activity in Dublin, particularly Cutpurse-row, Dirty-lane and other notorious alleys leading off Francis-street where prostitutes and thieves lived in a maze of tumble-down dwellings and where gambling-houses, brothels and drinking-shops flourished.

The design for the New Prison had been produced for a competition in 1773 by a reputable English architect, Thomas Cooley, who had earlier designed Dublin's Royal Exchange.[11] Reviewing it in their *Views of the Most Remarkable Public Buildimgs, Monuments, and Other Edifices in ... Dublin*, Robert Pool and John Cash wrote that, on the whole, the design of the gaol was 'superior to those hitherto erected in this kingdom'.[12] It was their belief that Cooley had benefited from reading the treatise by prison reformer John Howard, which had been published in 1776.[13] They were impressed by the measures taken to prevent gaol fever by allocating each prisoner a separate cell. In addition to the ninety-seven cells, there were 'transport-rooms' for those sentenced to transportation, cells for the condemned, and apartments for more well-to-do prisoners together with the gaoler's own apartments. There was also a large common hall and two courtyards or exercise yards. Nevertheless, Pool and Cash believed that the stairways were too narrow to allow free circulation of air and both the chapel and the infirmary should have been situated on the ground floor.

Built at a total cost of £18,000, Newgate was supported by an initial grant from Parliament of £2,000, most of the remaining £16,000 having to be found by Dublin Corporation from its rate-payers.[14] It was only when a serious 'epidemical disorder' believed to have originated from old New Gate 'destroyed many very worthy Persons' and threatened the whole city in 1776 that MPs responded to a petition for more funds to complete the building.[15] Howard, who had then been making

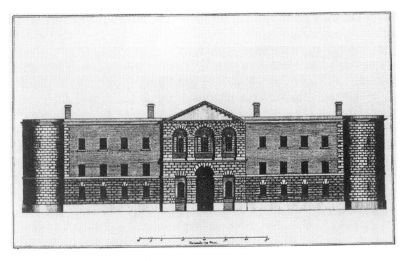

7 The New Prison (Newgate)

his first visit to Ireland, predicted the outbreak after visiting the old prison in March that year.[16]

The façade of Newgate, with its four drum towers executed in Wicklow granite, was intended to resemble the Bastille in Paris and was superficially impressive. In the words of Maurice Craig, Dublin's architectural historian, it was 'a powerful piece of terroristic architecture'.[17] However, the walls had not been 'cramped' or properly laid, being 'composed generally of small stones and bad mortar without bond', and it was not difficult for prisoners to make holes in them.[18] Within three years of its opening, Dublin Corporation had to authorise the expenditure of £1,000 for repairs to the structure.[19] Like other public buildings of the time, Newgate was a notorious example of wholesale 'jobbing' and peculation and there were frequent complaints about its continuing cost. In February 1787, for example, the *Freeman's Journal* protested that although £26,000 had already been spent on its construction, 'every day calls for fresh repairs and accommodations, for which the citizens of Dublin labour under the heavy burden of accumulated taxes'.[20] A few days after a mass escape in July 1790, it described Newgate as 'one of the most inconvenient unsafe gaols that ever was erected' with walls that were barely nine inches thick.[21]

Finally, there was the serious problem of mismanagement. Howard, who had been optimistic while Newgate was being built, was totally disillusioned. In June 1782, a little more than a year after its comple-

8 Tholsel, Skinner's Row, Dublin, c. 1791. Many of the convicts transported in the 1780s were tried here.

tion and first intake, he told the Irish House of Commons committee on gaols and prisons that he found it 'in every Respect the very Reverse of every Idea he can form to himself of a perfect and well-regulated Gaol'.[22] Morals were 'totally neglected', men and women being mixed together. There was no provision for hard labour for women or for religious services. The sick and dying lay on the stone floors 'destitute of every Assistance'. Describing the prison as 'dirty beyond Description', he predicted an outbreak of gaol fever during the next winter. Accompanying him to the prison to see for themselves, the committee found Newgate just as he had told them. Ventilation was poor, no medical attention was provided and three or four prisoners were employed as turnkeys. Debtors and a number of boys between the ages of nine and sixteen gaoled for petty offences were 'mixed indiscriminately with the most hardened Felons and Malefactors...'. Henry Roe, who had been appointed Gaoler at the outset, had not been near the prison for five months because of illness.

When the committee called upon the High Sheriffs of the city to account for the situation, it was surprised to find that the latter had no jurisdiction. Dublin Corporation was not charged with overall responsibility, which was theoretically borne by the grand juries elected every three months. Consequently no one was responsible for enforcing all the worthy reforms enacted by the Irish Parliament during the period from 1778 until 1787, despite members' continuing efforts to pin down the Corporation whose Charter made it politically unassailable.[23]

In May 1785, Sir Jeremiah Fitzpatrick's evidence before the same committee of the House of Commons indicated that the situation had deteriorated even further:

> The women's apartments are so crowded, and full of smoke, that they are insupportable. They are confined in the apartments, in consequence of the work going on in the yard, which is neglected; as not a stone was laid for fifteen days past. The apartments, or rather cells, are shocking, stinking, ill-contrived places. [There is] Neither hospital, kitchen, or wash-house. The men's courtyards, half-covered with water, as the sewers are stopped (by means of the workmen). Four fellows under sentence of death, with small boys of not more than twelve years old, in the common yard, are a melancholy spectacle. The goal [is] crowded, and in consequence of the passages to the sewers not being properly secured, the goaler is alarmed, and from the necessity he is under to prevent the possibility of escape, he cannot give the unfortunate prisoners the indulgence he seems well disposed to do.[24]

The continuing problem was that effective responsibility for the prison's management remained in the hands of the Gaoler, whose position was subject to annual renewal but very little scrutiny. The only conditions attached to his appointment by Dublin Corporation were that he should 'constantly reside' at Newgate and that he should enter into a bond of £2,000 from which the Corporation would be indemnified in case of any escape.[25] The appointment and payment of turnkeys was a matter for him to arrange. Consequently, he relied on prisoners' fees payable on their acquittal, together with rents and payments for various indulgences, to supplement his annual stipend of £120 from the Corporation. He also received rent from prisoners occupying separate cells and enjoyed 'the exclusive right to supply the prisoners with various necessities until 1785, when such practices were forbidden unless under written orders from the Inspector of Prisons or from a doctor'.[26] The abolition in 1784 of discharge fees for those acquitted meant that he became even more dependent on illicit revenue.

From 1785 until January 1789 the Newgate Gaoler was George Roe, who succeeded his father to the position after serving as his deputy for some years. Successfully resisting the different prison reforms attempted by Parliament from 1778, he exploited to the utmost the various sources of revenue which Newgate made possible. However, it had never been difficult for prisoners and turnkeys to subvert the rules of the gaol, including the importation and consumption of alcohol. According to one account:

> Whiskey is put into a bladder, and a string being let down from one of the holes made to admit light and air into the rooms, is tied to the neck of the bladder, and drawn up. Thus the prisoners obtain what quantity they please, through the assistance of those who visit them, and the public houses opposite the gaol are all furnished with the abovementioned conveniences.[27]

Indeed, even when the supply of alcohol was expressly forbidden in 1785, Deputy Gaoler Walsh leased one of these public houses in order to maintain what must have been a profitable business. The turnkeys also supplemented their meagre wages by performing various useful services for the prisoners. Many of the escapes and attempted escapes made during the 1780s must have depended on their co-operation.

Some idea of the physical arrangements in Newgate can be gathered from this detailed description based on an official report of 1808. Clearly, the reforms commencing with the legislation of 1778 had had little effect:

> In the front are the guard-room, gaoler's apartments, hospital, common room, chapel &c. and in the other sides of the quadrangle are the cells, which are universally 12 feet by 8, injudiciously disposed, badly ventilated, those in the upper stories accessible by narrow staircases, and all opening off corridores [*sic*] only three feet four inches wide. The interior area, totally insufficient to admit of proper and separate courts for the sundry classes of prisoners, is divided into two nearly equal parts by a passage for persons who visit the prisoners, with whom they can converse through grated apertures in the walls on either side. The part on the south, 61 feet by 56, and of which the centre was in 1808 occupied by an offensive necessary [latrine] without a sewer, formed a court-yard for all the male prisoners under criminal charges of every description, who were crowded together from the number of 8 to 13 persons in the same cell: off this opened their only common hall, 20 feet by 117, and here consequently the tried and the untried, those charged with

felonies, and with petty offences, and even persons under sentence of death, were all indiscriminately mingled, without any attempt at classification. The northern part of the area is divided into two yards, one 54 feet by 43, off which are the cells for prisoners of a better description; the other only 54 feet by 17, for females, where there was, in 1808, the same mixture of prisoners as in the male side; the untried and the convicted promiscuously herded together, and in general from 10 to 14 women of all descriptions in a cell 12 feet by 8. The hospital, 20 feet by 17, was injudiciously situated, ill contrived, ill ventilated, and destitute of hot and cold baths. The chapel, situated in an upper story, was accessible with difficulty by narrow winding stairs; and there was no room set apart for the chaplain, in which he could hold private communication with a prisoner under any circumstances.[28]

Most prisoners were accommodated in the common halls, only those with money being able to afford private cells.

The insecurity of Newgate became clear within a few years of its completion. In late July 1783, George Roe narrowly foiled an attempt by a number of capitally-convicted prisoners to escape.[29] And a year later, when as many as 250 prisoners were confined, a number 'charged with the most atrocious robberies and crimes' sawed off their irons, broke into one of the prison's towers and had made a hole almost big enough for a passage to freedom before they were detected.[30] A week later, sixteen prisoners sawed off their irons and escaped through the prison 'necessary' or latrine and into the sewer which connected with an underground watercourse called the Bradogue Water flowing into the river Liffey at Ormond Quay. Some were recovered when George Roe, who lived on the premises, discovered what had happened. A guard was also mounted on all the gratings and latrines in Pill-lane, Fisher's Lane and other streets which marked the progress of the watercourse to the Liffey in order to intercept the remainder.[31] A fifteen-year-old boy who had managed to escape was recaptured a few days later when he tried to steal some silver spoons.[32] Another two men were subsequently discovered in a public-house in Thomas-street.[33]

Roe was subsequently fined the substantial sum of £500 by Justice Robinson for his negligence in allowing the prisoners to escape,[34] but nothing was done to improve the security of Newgate. As we shall see, there was an attempted mass break-out by women prisoners under sentence of transportation in August 1784. In February 1791 in an exploit which would have gratified Houdini, two 'noted robbers' called Neal and McLaughlin

> who were but a few days ago apprehended, and who were confined
> in the inside dungeon of the gaol, double bolted and neck-yoked,
> found means, in the most wonderful and unprecedented manner
> ever recorded in the Annals of Newgate, to effect their escape.[35]

Commenting in January 1786 on a rash of recent escapes and escape attempts, the *Hibernian Journal* had concluded that Newgate 'must want some very essential part of strength suitable to such a place'.[36] It suggested the Bastille system where prisoners were lodged in high-arched rooms with square towers housing a permanent guard.

As we shall see, a plan to ensure better security was drawn up by Dublin Corporation in September 1790 after a further rash of escapes, but once again nothing eventuated and continuing escape attempts meant that a military guard had to be posted permanently outside the prison.

Kilmainham

'There is not so weak or so ill-contrived a gaol perhaps in this Kingdom as that of the county of Dublin, and it is hoped that a new one will be built on a proper construction and site', the *Freeman's Journal* remarked in June 1784.[37] Occupying a low-lying site near the River Camac, the gaol was by then in ramshackle condition, its foundations weakened by frequent flooding.[38]

A few months earlier, about seventeen prisoners had managed to saw off their shackles and knock down the under-gaoler when he came to lock them up at dusk. When they found the upper hatches closed, they set fire to the doors of their cells and threw broken bottles at the military guards when they arrived.[39] In a more recent incident already noted, Gaoler McKinley had discovered John Keenan and Edward Doyle cutting the bars of their cell.[40]

Although McKinley managed to secure Keenan and Doyle, it was only 'as well as the wretched jail he keeps would admit of'.[41] At that time, the gaol's four small underground cells were accommodating sixty-four prisoners, with no discrimination between grades of crime and no segregation of the sexes. Security at Kilmainham was made almost impossible by narrow grated windows, known as 'giggers', which gave on to the street and enabled prisoners to obtain food, liquor and gaol-breaking instruments from visitors at virtually any time.

The open gratings also allowed those stronger inmates who mono-polised access to them to become 'a terror to all passing by, who will not relieve them'.[42] In October 1784, some prisoners called out to a passing baker to sell them a loaf of bread, which he had to cut up and push through the grille. 'When putting his hand pretty far in, it was secured by a noose of a rope held fast, while, with horrid imprecations, he was threatened to have it cut off, if he had made the least noise, and demanding his money'.[43] A passing philanthropist wishing to present half-pence to the prisoners was treated in the same way in July 1787.[44]

In the wake of the attempted break-out in early 1784, the Grand Jury of Co. Dublin finally agreed to Sir Edward Newenham's long-standing request that a plan be prepared for a new and larger county gaol and this was authorised by an Act of Parliament in March 1786. In its pre-amble, the Act referred to Kilmainham as being 'situated in a low and unhealthy place and unable to contain and keep securely the number of persons committed to it'.[45]

Work had actually begun in late 1785 by Capt. William Jones to a design produced by John Traile and modified by John Howard, who visited Dublin on a number of occasions before his death in 1790 to supervise its progress.[46] Directed as it was by 'intelligent and public-spirited gentlemen', the project brought an enthusiastic response from the *Hibernian Journal* in June 1785:

> we may hope this prison will serve as a model for all those that are shortly to be improved and rebuilt in the several parts of this kingdom, whose present state is in general so execrable, that the recital of a late report thereon would grate the feelings of even obdurate minds.[47]

Two years later, the *Freeman's Journal* believed that Jones' 'independency of fortune' meant that it would 'not be made a base job of, like that of the Marshalseas, Newgate, etc'.[48] In consultation with the Grand Jury and no doubt Traile, Howard subsequently modified the design to provide a separate cell for each prisoner and proper security for the increasing number of prisoners awaiting transportation.[49] The final design was said to have been influenced by Howard's knowledge of Reading Gaol.[50]

The new Kilmainham was not to be completed until August 1796, however, and in the meantime overcrowding at the old county gaol was at crisis point. For the most part, Kilmainham housed prisoners awaiting trial or sentence at the Co. Dublin quarter sessions, but at times it had to take the overflow from Newgate as well. In March 1786, when McKinley was away at the assizes, fourteen prisoners, one of them the 'noted street robber Ferrally', picked a hole in the wall beneath the gratings used by visitors and escaped. On this occasion, some women had spent the day at the gratings to distract the guards' attention from the feverish work going on inside and were later able to screen the men from observation as they emerged from the hole.[51]

Some indication of conditions within the prison can be gathered from John Howard's report of his third visit to Dublin in 1787 when he found the prisoners 'all drunk at 11 a.m.'. On a later visit he prevented a fire from starting amongst the straw in which the prisoners were lying.[52]

Black-dog Prison and the Marshalseas

Although the aptly named Black-dog Prison and the four Marshalseas or debtors' prisons did not accommodate prisoners sentenced to hard labour or transportation, their deplorable state was symptomatic of the general prison system. Situated next to Dublin's principal meat-market, Black-dog Prison housed petty offenders and sometimes returnees from transportation in conditions which were nothing less than atrocious.[53] Describing it as an 'intolerable nuisance' and calling on the authorities to do something quickly, the *Hibernian Journal* in July 1784 referred to the 'heaps of ordure always lying about' which made the situation of the inmates 'truly deplorable'.[54] In December that year they were evacuated so that it could be demolished.[55]

The Four Courts Marshalsea was visited in December 1783 by the gaols and prisons committee which

> found the common Halls below, and several Rooms above, so filthy and crowded with Men, Women and Children, that it appeared to them extraordinary how they supported Life with any Degree of Comfort, the Sick and Healthy were indiscriminately mixed in the same Room.[56]

In early January 1787 when the police entered the City Marshalsea to arrest and convey to Newgate two sisters who had grievously assaulted a fellow prisoner, the other prisoners broke open the doors and tore down the walls for bricks to throw at them. As a consequence, one prisoner was killed and the gaol was left 'a scene of destruction which can be scarcely conceived or imagined'.[57] A further visit by the gaols and prisons committee of the House of Commons to the Four Courts Marshalsea in March found that 'the Prison appears a Scene of Disorder, Irregularity, and Intoxication'.[58]

The commitment in May of fourteen more debtors to the City Marshalsea, 'where there was not a vacant corner before', led the *Hibernian Journal* to express concern about the likelihood of disease breaking out there with the advent of warmer weather and to compare their situation with that of criminals sentenced to transportation:

> thus many persons of reputation and advantage to the community, must fall sacrifice to contagion, whilst hundreds of felons of every description of infamy are daily transporting to a land of health and liberty. Pray whose [life] is most eligible, that of the felon or poor debtor?[59]

Later that month the Lord Chief Justice, Lord Earlsfort, who had just completed a tour of inspection of the city's gaols, told the Dublin Grand Jury that there was an urgent need for reform, the horrors of some being 'shocking to humanity'. The City Marshalsea was 'an hovel dreadful to imagination, a number of persons huddled together without even a little straw to lie on, surrounded by noisome stenches ... yet even this was nothing when compared to the state of the Bridewell'.[60] Situated in an old malt-house in James-street, Smithfield, the city Bridewell was the repository for vagabonds and prostitutes without visible means of support who were 'swept' from the streets from time to time on the orders of the city's sheriffs and magistrates. Under the terms of the Vagabond Act, they could be transported if they offered no sign of reformation.

Sir Jeremiah Fitzpatrick

Appointed Inspector-General of Prisons by the Duke of Rutland in May 1786 under the terms of the new Police Act of that year, Sir Jeremiah Fitzpatrick set about the truly Herculean task of reforming prison conditions in Ireland.[61] A medical doctor with a particular interest in prison diseases, he had published an influential pamphlet entitled *An Essay on Gaol-Abuses and on the Means of Redressing Them ...* in 1784[62] and was regarded as Ireland's leading authority on the subject. Influenced by the writings of Cesare Beccaria, William Eden, John

Howard and Jeremy Bentham, Fitzpatrick also had a good comparative knowledge of prisons and their health problems in Europe and the West Indies. On his initiative, legislation for the better governance of prisons was passed by the Irish Parliament in 1787, resulting in the building of a number of new prisons around the country under his personal supervision.[63] However, all this had little impact on prison management in Dublin itself which was beyond his direct control. Fitzpatrick was a zealous and energetic man, but he was dealing with institutions which remained under the jealous and penny-pinching control of Dublin Corporation and other local government bodies throughout Ireland.

It was not until after Peter Holmes' gaols and prisons committee's damning report to the House of Commons in March 1788 and Howard's observation that he had never seen gaols worse than in Ireland, that Fitzpatrick's continuing indictments of Newgate resulted in George Roe's dismissal by Dublin Corporation and the appointment of an Inspector of Gaols for Dublin itself.[64] Despite this, one basic problem remained unsolved. An Act of 1778 (*17 & 18 Geo. III, c. 28*) had authorised justices of the peace to ensure that gaol conditions were satisfactory and to provide beds, blankets and straw from funds made available by the Grand Juries.[65] However, the latter were always slow to make payment and the gaolers would not make these provisions at their own cost. Consequently, the aims of the legislation continued to be thwarted.

County gaols

The only comprehensive descriptions of county gaols in Ireland were made by John Howard in his published accounts of 1784 and 1791[66] and by Fitzpatrick in his annual reports to the Irish Parliament between 1786 and 1793. In his evidence given to a committee of the House of Commons in July 1793, his last year in office, the Inspector-General provided a general indication of the situation which prevailed throughout the country before the prison reforms of 1784–7:

> the greatest cruelties were practised by Gaolers, Marshalsea-keepers, and by Keepers of Sponging-houses, in most parts of this Kingdom. That Extortion was almost constantly practised, Intoxication encouraged, Rapes, Robberies, and even Murders, were committed within Prisons with Impunity. That the Filth and Confined Air, particularly in the damp underground Cells and Dungeons, bad,

9 Sir Jeremiah Fitzpatrick, Inspector-General of Prisons. Beside him are the plans for New Kilmainham.

scanty, and unwholesome Food, often without Straw, and most frequently without Covering, laying on the Damp Clay Floor and
loaded with Irons ... gave rise to the most fatal Diseases, scarcely
known at this day to exist.[67]

Thanks to Fitzpatrick's zealous building programme which commenced immediately after his appointment in 1786, there were thirteen new county gaols completed by 1793, eight more were under
construction and others were undergoing improvements. 'There are
more jails at present building for malefactors in this kingdom ... than
any person living can recollect any former period', the *Hibernian
Journal* remarked approvingly in August 1788. However, it also had to
admit that 'from the multiplicity of transgressions ... they were never
more necessary than now'.[68]

In the meantime, break-outs were becoming extremely common. In
late December 1782 a number of prisoners, including the notorious 'Jack-
a-boy', escaped from Cork's North Gaol. In April, May and August 1783
there were attempts at Carlow, Clonmel and Kilkenny respectively.[69] On
3 January 1784, eleven prisoners under sentence of death escaped from
Monaghan gaol[70] and another from Tralee gaol in May.[71] In June a noted
horse thief who had earlier escaped from Maryborough (Portlaoise) gaol
was detected with another prisoner attempting to break through the wall
of the gaol at Mullingar.[72] In September of the same year, four prisoners,
including one under sentence of transportation, escaped from Sligo gaol[73]
and in October nine prisoners escaped from the gaol at Galway.[74] In late
November when the escape of a group of felons was foiled at Tralee, they
were found to have files, aquafortis, a musket and a 'strong party' waiting
to assist them in the town.[75] In February 1785, five more prisoners
escaped from Monaghan gaol[76] and two men armed with pistols attacked
Dungarvan gaol in Co. Waterford, releasing five prisoners and shooting
one of the guards.[77] In May, three men escaped from Carlow gaol and a
break-out at Galway by two suspected murderers was only narrowly prevented.[78] There was yet another attempted escape at Mullingar in
August[79] and in November, thirteen prisoners broke out of the gaol at
Naas, Co. Kildare.[80]

'The fatal board'

Although there were almost as many capital offences on the statute
books in Ireland in the 1780s as there were in England, including the
amended 'Chalking Act' of 1778 which provided for execution and

dissection within forty-eight hours of conviction and sentence,[81] there was also a recognition in some quarters that the harsh penal code was not an effective deterrent against crime. Indeed, the number of public executions in Dublin had increased sharply from seven in 1780 to seventeen in 1783 and twenty-two in 1784 without having any significant effect on the crime rate.[82]

Executions were frequently counter-productive in the feelings they aroused towards authority. The *Hibernian Journal* described in harrowing detail the hanging in front of Newgate on 9 August 1783 of two men and a youth who had been convicted of 'robbing and cutting' a gentleman near Booterstown on the outskirts of Dublin:

> Egan came first forward, and in a very audible Voice declared his life had been sworn away, but that he heartily forgave his Persecutor. Woods next stepped out on the fatal board, but did not Speak. When the little Boy, Short, appeared, so universal and loud a Shriek from the immense Multitude who attended the Execution, was never before heard. To see such a Child, as it were, about to be executed, so small in Stature, and so very youthful in his Appearance, that no person could think him more than thirteen or fourteen Years of Age, was extremely shocking.[83]

Noting before the event that Short was to be the youngest boy ever to suffer death for a robbery, the newspaper reflected on the possible reasons for Ireland's and England's high rates of execution by comparison with other civilized countries:

> Unfortunately for these kingdoms, Society is every year robbed by the Gallows of more Members, than all the rest of Europe put together. We are a more wicked People, or we have a worse Police, than the rest of the World.[84]

Preferring to accept the latter explanation, the *Hibernian Journal* believed that 'the human slaughter' of that month (two other men had been hanged at Newgate on 2 August and two at Kilmainham on 6 August) suggested the need for a new Bill to reform the police.[85]

After the execution of Keenan and his companions at Kilmainham in July 1784, the *Hibernian Journal* remarked on the dubious efficacy of capital punishment as an antidote to crime:

The frequency of execution of our criminals, we are sorry to observe, instead of deterring others from the prosecution of the wicked practices that have brought these wretches to such an ignominious and untimely end, seems to stimulate their hardened companions to further acts of outrage and villainy.[86]

As an example of this, the newspaper described the recent attack by a gang on a Dublin doctor in Exchequer-street.

In December 1784, after another rash of executions at Newgate, the *Hibernian Journal* concluded that neither imprisonment nor execution had any deterrent effect:

Fatal and reiterated experience has proved, that the infliction of imprisonment has no other effect than confirming the delinquents in stronger habits of vice and wickedness, [and] that the practice of executing criminals at the front of the gaol has familiarized the ideas of the unhappy culprits to death, and that the example intended by the law loses its terror, shame and effect.[87]

As if to reinforce this view, in March 1785 a seventeen-year-old boy sentenced to death for a number of robberies 'laughed heartily, and all the way to the new gaol, he, and his unhappy [*sic*] companion in the carriage, were in a constant roar of merriment, to the amazement of every spectator'.[88] There was another report in June that year of a highway robbery committed by the brother of a man called Meaghan who had been hanged for street robbery the same morning. According to *Walker's Hibernian Magazine*, 'This incorrigible villain had just stepped out of the house where his brother lay waking when he committed the ... robbery'.[89]

The entertainment value of public executions must have greatly detracted from the dread effect intended. It was common practice in Dublin as well as in London for the fabricated 'last speeches' of condemned prisoners to be either printed and sold as broadsheets or (more commonly in Dublin) declaimed by ballad singers and other street performers. In November 1788 a writer in the *Freeman's Journal* complained bitterly that 'a number of vagabonds were crying out, in all quarters of the town, the last speech [*sic*] of Rev. Patrick Fay and Maria Lewellin even under the window of the New-prison'.[90] He believed that this 'shocking custom', which he thought was practised nowhere else in Europe, should be banned by the magistrates 'as even a convict in the serious meditation of making his best peace with Heaven, must feel himself haunted by a lying anticipation of his last sentiments'.[91]

'Detain not the excruciated soul'

Perhaps the most counter-productive aspect of hanging was that it was often done so badly, transforming what was intended to be an exemplary tragedy into grim farce and arousing a spirit of revenge rather than a respect for the law and its instruments. Dublin's Jack Ketch might well have heeded William Eden's advice that 'Solemnity indeed is requisite, for the sake of example, but let not death be drawn into "lingering sufferance"; detain not the excruciated soul upon the verge of eternity'.[92] Although the new 'machine of execution' introduced by McKinley at Kilmainham in January 1783 and adopted at Newgate in the same month[93] should have made for greater efficiency, the hangman's poor handiwork still resulted in horrendous suffering by some victims. On 2 August 1783, Christopher Burgess and Patrick Godfrey were hanged in front of Newgate by means of the new device before an enormous crowd. Burgess' execution was efficient enough but Godfrey's was badly bungled by the 'trotler' (throttler or hangman), producing what *Walker's Hibernian Magazine* called 'a scene of torment, agonizing beyond expression':

> The rope having slipped the usual place, through the negligence of the executioner, he was suspended by the chin and the back of his head, and seemed to avail himself of the accident for about seven minutes, by remaining motionless; but not being able to endure the pain longer, he began to plunge, struggle, and groan in a dreadful manner. He at length clung to the body of his wretched companion and put his legs about him. He continued clinging in this manner about seventeen minutes, when the rope being slackened, and his strength wearing out, he relinquished his hold, made many other desperate struggles, and at the end of twenty -five minutes relaxed his limbs to the pressure of death ... The feelings of above 10,000 spectators, during this shocking conflict, must be better conceived than described.[94]

Feelings also ran high on other occasions when it was revealed that an earlier victim had been innocent of the crime for which he had been hanged. This information usually emerged in the form of a confession made by another condemned prisoner at the gallows. Before being hanged at Kilmainham in September 1792, for example, John Cunningham confessed to a robbery a year earlier for which the returnee John Dalton had been arrested.[95] Indeed, executions were sometimes a more efficient means of eliciting the truth from criminals than the courts.

Last-minute reprieves might be arranged if such confessions or 'discoveries' were expected or new evidence had been received, although these did not always arrive in time. This was the case at Kilmainham's Gallows-hill on 20 March 1784 when a letter of reprieve was delivered just after Hugh Feeny and John Murphy had been 'turned off'. They were immediately cut down from the gallows but, as the *Hibernian Journal* reported, 'the lamp of life being extinguished, every effort used for their recovery proved ineffectual'.[96] No doubt this had included a 'snig in de jugler' (cutting a vein), a long-established method of making the blood flow again and thus reviving life.

Sometimes the late reprieve was contrived to shock its beneficiary into reforming his ways. The *Freeman's Journal* in July 1790 reported the case of Garrat Kirwin (George Kirwan), 29, who had already been shaved and prepared for execution at Kilmainham when His Majesty's most gracious pardon on condition of transportation was delivered. 'It is hoped', the newspaper remarked, 'that he may hereafter become a useful member in some other country, having here experienced all the terrors, though he escaped the actual pains of death'.[97] Kirwan was to be one of the first Irish convicts to be shipped to Botany Bay the following April.

Traditionally, the hangman had been the principal object of the assembled mob's almost ritualised wrath, sometimes wearing a grotesque mask to conceal his identity and a wooden bowl under his shirt for protection against the inevitable missiles.[98] However, with the abolition of the traditional procession from the prison to the gallows and the transfer of executions from St Stephen's Green to the front of Newgate in 1782, a military guard had to be provided.

Larry

Dublin's robust criminal sub-culture offered its own idiosyncratic evidence of the inefficacy of hanging as a deterrent. Written by a Waterford-town clothier in the 'Newgate Cant' or 'Slang Style' used by John Keenan and his associates and employing the black humour of their trade, 'De Night Before Larry Was Stretch'd' reputedly celebrated the bungled execution of Frederick Lambert at Newgate in October

1788.[99] This, together with 'Luke Caffrey's Kilmainham Minit [Minuet]', 'Luke Caffrey's Ghost' and 'Mrs Coffey', were well-known Dublin hanging ballads of the period which must have been sung at many a wake in the dram-shops of Copper-alley and Dirty-lane after an execution. The first verse of 'Larry' celebrated the comradely support traditionally extended to the condemned prisoner in Newgate:

> De night before Larry was stretch'd,
> De boys all ped him a visit;
> A bit in their sacks too dey fetch'd –
> Dey sweated deir duds till dey ris it.
> For Larry was ever de lad
> When a boy was condemn'd to de squeezer
> To pawn all de togs dat he had,
> To help his poor friend to a sneezer
> And warm his gob 'fore he died.[100]

There was also a convention that condemned prisoners spent their last night drinking and gambling the proceeds of the sale of their bodies for dissection. According to the report of Lambert's final hours before he was due to be executed on 30 October 1788, 'so little concerned was he, that he played cards on his own coffin'. And when an order from the Lord Lieutenant arrived from Dublin Castle the next morning granting mercy, he received the news without registering any emotion. 'There are few beings, thank Heaven, in humanity', observed *Walker's Hibernian Magazine*, 'who have arrived to such a degree of hardihood'.[101]

For professional criminals like John Keenan, hanging was a risk made acceptable by the slender chance of being caught under the ineffectual system of policing in operation until September 1786. Even if a robber or burglar was unlucky enough to be seized, there was always the possibility of intimidating the prosecutor, buying off witnesses, or purchasing liberty from the authorities by making 'discoveries', as Keenan had so often done before. When all else failed, there was the stoic gallows philosophy of 'Larry' to fall back upon:

> 'Dough sure it's de best way to die –
> De devil a better livin'!
> For sure, when the gallows is high,
> Your journey is shorter to heaven!

But what harasses Larry de most,
And makes his poor soul melancholy,
Is to tink of de time dat his ghost
Will come in a sheet to sweet Molly!
O! sure it will kill her alive!'[102]

4
The Revival of Trans-Atlantic Transportation

By the end of 1782 it seems to have been assumed by the London and Dublin governments that transportation to North America, which had lapsed for almost ten years because of the war, would be re-established on the old footing. As the Beauchamp Committee was to observe wistfully three years later, 'the old System of Transporting to *America* answered every good purpose which could be expected from it'.[1] Although a number of American provincial assemblies had threatened to pass laws preventing its resumption, none had actually done so and there was a renewed demand for indentured labour in Pennsylvania, Maryland and Virginia.[2]

In December 1782 the London merchant and shipping contractor, Duncan Campbell, who had monopolised the sending of British convicts to Maryland and Virginia before the war, and another contractor, William Hamilton, were asked by Lord North to provide estimates of the cost of transporting 250 male prisoners to America.[3] Although Campbell began to receive convicts on board the *Censor* hulk on the Thames in early 1783 with a view to their transportation to America, what subsequently happened to them is not clear.[4]

Meanwhile the English-born Baltimore merchant, George Salmon, was writing enthusiastically to London merchant and shipping contractor, George Moore, about the possibility of renewing the convict trade.[5] When he was informed by North in mid-July that Moore was willing to ship off immediately 150 'healthy and able-bodied convicts' to Maryland and Virginia at no expense to the government beyond the fees payable to the clerks of assizes and the gaolers,[6] King George III gave his warm approval in the often-quoted remark that:

Undoubtedly the Americans cannot expect nor ever will receive any favour from Me, but the permitting them to obtain Men unworthy to remain on this Island I shall certainly consent to.[7]

Entrepreneurs, politicians and officials responded quickly to the opportunity to renew commercial relations with America. Long before the formal peace treaty was signed in Paris in September 1783, both the Irish and the British governments had passed legislation designed to facilitate trade with the Americans. And convict transportation, after all, had been an important part of that trade. The renewed demand for labour was expected to overcome the problem of being represented by Benjamin Franklin and other patriotic American critics as dumping unwanted social refuse on the shores of the infant republic. However, when Moore heard a rumour a few days after making his offer to Lord North that the Continental Congress had resolved not to receive convicts, he told him that if by any chance his shipment could not be landed in any part of the United States, he would 'land them at Nova Scotia', but at the cost of 3 guineas per head.[8] As this was still cheaper than William Hamilton's tender, the King told North that it should be accepted.[9]

'Servants is the word'

In late July, with North's personal encouragement and the promise of a payment of £500, Moore despatched 143 convicts on the *George* (Captain Thomas Pamp) to Baltimore, Maryland, for sale by Salmon as indentured servants. In April of that year, Salmon had written to Moore suggesting that convicts could be readily and profitably be disposed of in Baltimore:

> I don't know anything [that] would bring more money here than a parcel of Servants or Convicts which was formerly a good business. They would readily be admitted here notwithstanding former laws and I think they could be got by you and sent at little expence [*sic*].[10]

In a subsequent letter in October, by which time the first shipment was expected to arrive any day in Baltimore, Salmon again reassured Moore that there was little chance of arousing local opposition:

> Depend upon it[,] they will most assuredly be admitted. I have got the opinion this day from my Lawyer and he says there can be no

obstruction to their being sold. The Governor's Council are Gentlemen whom I am well acquainted with, so that I have both Law and interest to back me. You may therefore make yourself perfectly easy on that head, as I would be far from leading you into a Scrape.[11]

In late November, by which time he had been informed by Moore that a mutiny on board the *George* had delayed its sailing, Salmon was still keen for more consignments of convicts to be sent to Baltimore as long as careful precautions were taken:

They must all be cleard out with you for Halifax. Should you mention this place the [illeg.] would be taken here by a Law soon passed to prevent their being imported. At present no such Law is in being and if we only act with proper caution the business might be carried on for a great length of time without any person suspecting. Servants is the word and they may be imported every day of the year.[12]

In late December, when the *George* had not appeared and he was beginning to worry for the safety of his shipment, Salmon nevertheless continued to press Moore to make a contract with the Home Office for the regular despatch of convicts to Baltimore:

Altho' the Congress have made this State the place of their residence and that they are within 30 miles of this town, yet don't be alarmed on that account – they can't enact a single Law and as to our own House [of] Assembly I am sure they never will have reason to pass one without we act in too glaring a manner which there is no necessity for. On the whole you may depend upon my information and that I never will lead you into a Scrape.[13]

Probably in response to Salmon's advice, Moore had changed the name of the ship he had chartered from the *Swift* to the *George*, and announced its destination as Nova Scotia. After the mutiny off the Kent coast on 29 August, which enabled 48 of the 143 convicts on board to escape, the ship had to return to port and did not sail again for Baltimore until October. Its eventual arrival there on Christmas Eve meant that Salmon had great trouble disposing of all of the convicts as indentured servants. Not only had a heavy fall of snow made it difficult for would-be purchasers to come to town, but most of the local demand for labour had already been met by the arrival of the *Olive Branch* with 180 indentured Irish servants just six weeks earlier. Consequently, he had to be content with rather less than the thirty guineas per head that he had confidently anticipated. At the same time, he had to meet the substantial cost of keeping the unsold convicts on board ship and under guard in the iced-up harbour for several weeks.

Following information received in a letter from Matthew Ridley, a principal of the rival merchant firm of Pringle and Ridley of Baltimore who had been tipped off by American Foreign Secretary John Jay in Paris about Salmon and Moore's scheme, Governor William Paca had already forewarned the Maryland General Assembly on 2 December of 'a Fraudulent Plan which British Subjects are adopting to introduce British and Irish Convicts into the United States'.[14] Although this outraged the legislators, they were reassured by the accompanying news that a mutiny had prevented the shipment from going ahead. When the arrival of the *George* with the remaining convicts on board was made known in Annapolis on Christmas Day, Salmon seemed bound to suffer the wrath of the Assembly, although he was saved its full force by the ship's delay and the Christmas adjournment on 26 December.

Before the Assembly met again in April, Salmon was able to use seasonal gifts of cheese and porter to his legislator friends to ensure that there was no further agitation for a law forbidding the landing of convicts. In the meantime, however, he had to head off the other shipments which had already been arranged by Moore. Before he could inform the London merchant of the difficulties he had encountered with the first consignment and to beg him not to send any more for the time being, the latter had despatched the *Mercury* to Baltimore in April 1784 with 179 convicts on board, again announcing that the vessel was bound for Nova Scotia. Once more there was a mutiny which resulted in the escape of about 100 convicts and delayed the ship's arrival. This time, however, neither Baltimore nor any other American port would permit the remaining 86 convicts on board to be landed. Nor were they made welcome at Bay Settlement, Honduras (Belize), when Moore's two agents tried to land them there and were only disposed of after great difficulty and expense.[15]

A further shipment by Moore on the *Fair American* of twenty-nine convicts, together with an unknown number of indentured negroes, to Honduras was also rejected by the Baymen (white settlers) in December 1785, despite a clear instruction from Evan Nepean to the

Bay Settlement Superintendent, Col. Despard, that every assistance was to be given to Moore's agent for their disposal.[16] They were then taken off in the direction of the Mosquito Shore (Nicaragua) where another British settlement had been established. What happened to them ultimately is not known, although Moore suffered a serious loss on the voyage.[17]

Lord Sydney, Home Secretary in the new ministry formed by William Pitt, had clearly intended that further shipments of convicts should be sent to Honduras in view (as he admitted in October 1784) of 'the greater difficulty I see in disposing of these people in any other place in the possession of His Majesty's Subjects'.[18] However, news of the hostile reception given by the Baymen to the *Mercury* and the *Fair American* eventually forced him to abandon this plan. On 6 February 1786 he wrote to Lieut.-Governor Clarke of Jamaica:

> It is necessary I should now inform you, for the satisfaction of the [Honduras] settlers, that upon a further consideration, a decision has taken place against the prosecution of the measure: indeed in the present situation of affairs in those parts, I am satisfied, from what has passed here on the subject, that it might be productive of much mischief.[19]

The Jamaica legislature had already passed a law prohibiting the importation of white indentured labour, which made it impossible to send convicts there.

Thus it was that no further attempts were made to send British convicts to North America or the Caribbean before the decision was reached by William Pitt and his ministers by 18 August 1786 to establish a penal settlement at Botany Bay. By this time, it was also clear that plans to send more convicts to serve in the west African garrisons of the Africa Company and to establish convict settlements at Lemain Island in the Gambia River and Das Voltas Bay (Namibia) could not be proceeded with.[20] However, Cabinet had still been considering Canada and the West Indies two months before the Botany Bay decision[21] and in December there were newspaper reports that it might send capital offenders to Africa 'to be slaves for life'.[22] Even as late as May 1790, when the Second Fleet of British convicts was already nearing the New South Wales coast, the Home Office was not prepared to countenance another West Indian colony enacting legislation which would expressly forbid the transporting of convicts there.[23] This was an option to be exercised once again in the despatch of convicts to Bermuda in 1824 to work in the dockyards there.[24]

Nova Scotia

The British authorities hoped that if the Americans did refuse to take convicts again, one of the remaining British settlements in the Caribbean or North America might provide a practical alternative. Lord North had authorised the evacuation of American Loyalists to Abaco in the Bahamas in December 1782 but the rapid influx of refugees taxed the resources of the small island where land had also to be purchased from the owners. Nova Scotia, which was also authorised by North as a Loyalist sanctuary, recommended itself because of its greater size and the availability of large tracts of Crown land which convicts could help to develop.

It was no doubt with this contingency in mind that North wrote to Governor John Parr of Nova Scotia in August 1783 telling him that arrangements had been made with George Moore to send 'One Hundred, and Fifty Felons' there and requesting him to allow them to be landed and disposed of 'as hath been usual on former occasions'.[25] It was a form of insurance against the possibility of Moore's shipment being rejected at Baltimore and other American ports. At the same time, Nova Scotia could be announced as the ship's official destination in order to conceal the real one from the American authorities.

Parr's response to this news is not recorded, but it would certainly have been unfavourable. Nor is there any evidence to support Sydney's assertion that convicts had been sent to Nova Scotia 'on former occasions', except for a notorious French expedition led by Troilus de Mescouez, Marquis de la Roche, in 1518 which had left forty-eight hapless prisoners to fend for themselves on Sable Island for five years.[26] In the event, as we have seen, Salmon was able to dispose of Moore's shipment at Baltimore – although not without some difficulty.

Nova Scotia had been suggested to North's government as a destination for convicts as early as 1778 by members of the House of Commons committee appointed to examine the operation of the Hulks Act.[27] However, Duncan Campbell told the committee in the following year that 'none of the remaining British North American colonies were suitable for transportation on the old system. ...'[28] Instead, Nova Scotia was flooded from early 1783 by thousands of American Loyalist refugees, including freed and bonded slaves, Governor Parr being instructed to assist with grants of land and provisions for the needy. By October 1783, 20,000 had arrived from New York and many were facing a bleak first winter on the island.

10 The Governor's House, Halifax, Nova Scotia.

Less than a year after North's dispatch to Parr, a surprise arrival from London gave the governor an opportunity to express his vehement opposition to convicts. In August 1784, the transport *Sally* arrived unannounced in Halifax harbour with about 260 Loyalists from London, most of them blacks and all 'destitute of clothing and provisions'.[29] Formerly serving in the Royal Navy during the American War, they had been stranded in London where thirty-six were subsequently prosecuted for theft and held in the city Bridewell.[30] In response to an approach to Lord Sydney by London's Lord Mayor, Robert Peckham,[31] they were packed off to Nova Scotia with scant regard for their welfare. Although not transported in the legal sense, the fact that a number were criminal offenders gave them the *de facto* status of convicts.

No less than thirty-nine of the Loyalist refugees on board the *Sally* were lost during the passage from an outbreak of yellow fever and another twelve died within a few days of the ship's arrival at Halifax.[32] Having ordered the setting up tents on an isolated beach to feed and shelter the survivors, Parr told Sydney that he was 'much at a loss how to provide for them … not knowing whether as Refugees, or in what Capacity I am to receive them'.[33] This, together with the arrival just a few weeks earlier of a shipment of 260 black Loyalists from St Augustine in the West Indies (described by Parr as the 'poorest and most distress'd of all beings without a shilling, almost naked, and destitute of every necessity of life'[34]), placed an enormous strain on the struggling settlement. In October, Parr wrote privately to Evan Nepean at the Home Office, begging him not to allow the same thing to happen again:

> I can not let this opportunity slip without requesting you to use your good offices, in preventing the Lord Mayor of London from sending here any more of the Canallie [*sic*] of the City, or sweepings of Jails, as he lately did in the Sally Transport, by an application to Lord Sydney. They are unwelcome Guests to Infant Settlements.[35]

That there was a subsequent shipment of English convicts to Nova Scotia is suggested by the nineteenth-century historian of the island, Beamish Murdoch, who recorded that on 1 November 1784 'Some convicts were brought here [Port Roseway], but the governor [Parr] refused to land them'.[36] However, there is no reference to the incident in Parr's correspondence with the Home Office or in any other contemporary record. Nor does their reported date of arrival correspond with any of the known British and Irish trans-Atlantic convict shipments for the post-war period, unless it was the shipment which the shipping contractor William Hurford had apparently agreed in early 1783 to take to America but whose outcome is still shrouded in mystery.[37]

Parr had not protested in vain. When Nepean was asked by the Beauchamp Committee in May 1785 'Whether there is any plan for sending Convicts to *Cape Breton*, or any of the *British* Settlements in *America*?', he replied that 'there have been strong Representations made against it from *Nova Scotia* – That he believes there are very few Settlers in *Cape Breton*, and that he has heard of no Plan for sending them to *Canada*'.[38] It was no doubt with Parr's plea in mind that the government also decided in late 1786 to send the next shipment of black Loyalists to Sierra Leone.[39]

Africa

Some English judges were sentencing prisoners to transportation to Africa in early 1782 in the belief that the hulks were counter-productive and that transportation would be resumed to Cape Coast Castle and other Africa Company forts in West Africa. However, a year later they were specifying America as the destination instead.[40] There was no discussion in the Dublin newspapers during the first half of 1783 about the renewal of transportation and no reports of any prisoners being sentenced to exile until July 1784 when two soldiers found guilty at a court-martial for repeated desertion and theft were said to have been sentenced to be transported to Africa.[41] In the following month, John Connor was found guilty at the Drogheda assizes of 'boarding a sloop on the North Quay, and attempting to rob the captain', for which he was sentenced to be transported for seven years but with no destination prescribed.[42] At the same assizes, a man called Lucas received a similar sentence for robbing a woman of a silver watch and other articles.[43]

While Irish judges and magistrates obviously believed by mid-1784 that transportation would soon be renewed and were sentencing prisoners accordingly, there was a good deal of speculation as to where those under sentence would be despatched. In August 1783, for example, the *Hibernian Journal* published a report that a treaty was being negotiated between the governments of Britain and Algeria by which the latter would undertake to

> receive all Convicts transported to Salee or Mogador, from Great Britain and Ireland, and retain them in slavery for a certain term of Years, or during Life, in Consideration of the annual Present of Warlike Stores, &c being increased One-third.[44]

Nothing came of this idea, which echoed William Eden's earlier suggestion that 'the more enormous offenders' should be sent to Tunis or Algiers to make possible the freeing of Christian slaves held there.[45] Nor, as far as is known, was official consideration ever given to the despatch of Irish convicts as military conscripts to Africa. However, in August 1783 the *Dublin Evening Post* published a letter from a resident of Cape Breton Island saying that since the Irish government was disinclined to put into effect the provisions for hard labour in the 1777 Act, that transportation should be resumed – not to the American ports but to Cape Breton. Indeed, he believed that the coal and iron mine owners there were so anxious for bonded labour that they would 'cheerfully pay the cost of their transportation'.[46] The *Hibernian Journal* subsequently noted in January 1784 that the North administration had itself been considering a scheme to transport convicts to Cape Breton to work in the coal and iron mines. The idea was expected to be taken up again and the necessary arrangements made, as it was 'no party matter'.[47]

Cape Breton Island

Cape Breton Island to the north of Nova Scotia was not officially opened up for settlement until later in 1784 when Thomas Townshend was promoted to the peerage as Lord Sydney and at the same time appointed Home Secretary with responsibility for the colonies. Cape Breton was thenceforth separated from the government of Nova Scotia to form a separate province and Major F.W. des Barres was appointed as its first Lieut.-Governor in July. Arriving at Cape Breton in November, he selected a small peninsula on the north coast as the site for his capital and named it Sydney after his benefactor. A month earlier, three vessels carrying about 150 'Associate Loyalists' had arrived under the direction of Abraham Cuyler, the former Mayor of Albany, New York, who had successfully petitioned the British government for permission to settle at Cape Breton. Cuyler was subsequently to become the colony's Government Secretary and Registrar and a permanent thorn in the flesh for the unfortunate governors appointed there.

After the site of Sydney had been cleared and surveyed, barracks were built for the 33rd Regiment despatched there from Halifax and a start was made on houses for des Barres and his senior officials. In the meantime they 'had long to reside in shanties of the meanest description'.[48] In an interesting parallel with what was to happen some years later at Sydney, New South Wales, the infant settlement was at one point in fear of destruction by the local Micmac Indians who sought revenge after one of their number was killed by a ship's captain. The crisis was only resolved when des Barres used negotiations with the Indians as an opportunity to call in a brig of war from Halifax which promptly dispersed them with its guns.[49]

Hundreds more Loyalist settlers had arrived at Sydney in 1785 after the initial influx of 1783–84 and there were serious problems with provisions, the winter of 1785–86 being particularly arduous. When Governor des Barres was summarily recalled by Lord Sydney after protracted disputes with the senior officers of the military garrison and the government of Nova Scotia over the control of supplies, he was replaced in October 1787 by Lieut.-Colonel William Macarmick.

That conditions at Sydney did not improve very much under Macarmick's regime is clear from the account given by an officer of the 42nd Highland Regiment who arrived there in June 1789. In August he wrote to a friend or relative in Britain:

> What the Island of Cape Breton may prove, fifty years or a century hence I am not qualified to determine, but I venture to say that Sydney can never prove of any essential service to the Empire, as its harbour is impenetrably shut up with Ice and inaccessible to the whole world for at least seven months of the year; I am also informed that the soil is but indifferent as well as the Timber …

What they dignify with the name of a town consists of about 50 Hovels and stands twelve miles from the Entrance of Spanish Bay, upon a very fine river which extends a considerable way up the Country. There appear here and there a few attempts to form settlements but as far as I can judge they do not seem likely to succeed. In Sydney itself there is not the smallest trace of Industry as the Inhabitants live by selling Rum to the soldiers, and were they to be withdrawn (which God Almighty soon grant) it would be instantly deserted ... I have passed a great part of my life in America and been in many unpleasant and disagreeable situations but I do declare without exaggeration that I think Sydney far the worst.[50]

'Worse than the haunts of wild beasts'

In early September 1783, the *Hibernian Journal* published a letter calling on MPs to bring in a Bill enabling transportation to Canada and Nova Scotia 'as well as to the African and East Indian settlements'. Pointing out that 'to the Scandal of the City' the 1777 Act had never been enforced, the anonymous correspondent complained that

in Consequence, Hundreds of Rogues have been discharged from Prison ... and suffered to continue their Enormities on the public, until the Commission of more capital Offences has consigned them to the Gallows.[51]

In addition to the renewal of transportation, the correspondent called for the more effective policing of the city by establishing 'four or five Military Patroles' to replace the 'wretched bands of Watchmen, scattered up and down, [who] do no more service than so many old Women, but on the contrary associate with Rogues and with Prostitutes to rob the honest'.[52]

The next issue of the newspaper carried an advertisement calling on the inhabitants of St Mary's Parish 'for their own, and the public safety', to form new parish associations. It was

a matter of notoriety, that Capel-street, and all the Avenues leading thereto, are infested every Night with Swarms of Vagabonds and Prostitutes, who produce innumerable scenes of robbery, violence, Obscenity, and Disorder. This, indeed, every Parish in Dublin should be the more urged to do, from the Consideration of the many Thousands of the Idle and Profligate (formerly employed in the war) poured into the Metropolis, in consequence of the peace. If some Expedient of this kind is not immediately adopted, the ensuing Winter will render Dublin worse than the haunts of Wild Beasts, to its Inhabitants.[53]

As we shall see, agitation of this kind eventually resulted in Ireland's new Police Act of March 1786 with its provisions for the reform of the police under a new centralised system, controls over prostitution and drinking and the broadening of the definition of where convicts could be transported.

Alternatives to transportation

Although the renewal of trans-Atlantic transportation had been mooted in Ireland since the end of 1783, there was by no means general support for the idea amongst those concerned with the problem of crime. In January 1783 and again in September 1784 there was some correspondence in the *Hibernian Journal* about the need to change the criminal laws.[54] It was subsequently reported that following the recent precedent in Britain, some members of the Irish Parliament proposed to bring in a Bill to reform the penal code:

> Felony, in which are included several crimes of different sorts, to be atoned for in a more rational and profitable way, than death, which, to a hardened wretch, has little or no terror: but the idea of living in misery, and becoming a spectacle of permanent infamy for years, must sensibly affect minds, which, long and variegated scenes of guilt may have rendered callous to every other feeling.[55]

By what means a prisoner might become 'a spectacle of permanent infamy' the writer failed to make clear, although the emphasis on 'rational and profitable' suggests that he may have been thinking of the penitentiary system which was then being advocated by John Howard, Jeremy Bentham and other reformers in Britain and was already embodied in William Eden's Penitentiary Act of 1779. Within the next few years, which saw Howard make a second visit to Dublin, this idea was to gain considerable support in Irish circles. Nevertheless, the cost was regarded as prohibitive.

As an alternative, the *Hibernian Journal* recommended in January 1785 that prisoners be assigned to the East India Company's service as they had been a few years earlier. Not only would this save government the cost of getting rid of them, it argued, but it would serve Britain's wider economic interests from which Ireland, too, could benefit:

> When it is considered that the source of national wealth is principally the East, that the chief hope of discharging an immediate national debt is from that quarter, and that a fresh war is apprehended by Mr. Hastings, it is ridding ourselves of an evil, and serving Great Britain, to hand our delinquents over to the East India Company.[56]

When it became generally known in early 1785 that the Pitt government had fixed on the island of Lemain, 150 miles up the Gambia River in north-west Africa, as a new destination for British convicts,[57] concern was expressed in Ireland as well as Britain about its extreme unhealthiness. The *Hibernian Journal* called for 'a mode of punishment much more agreeable to the dictates of humanity, and at the same time perfectly consistent with sound policy and public utility'.[58] It suggested the improvement of the port of Dublin 'and other national objects of a similar kind' which required the intensive use of labour:

> Thus, such miscreants, who may now be considered as the very entrails of humanity, might be rendered serviceable to society in their particular department; and Government would be entirely exculpated from the charge of diverting those unhappy persons to the almost inevitable destruction of a climate so very unfriendly to [a] European constitution.[59]

The proposal in 1785 for the construction of a new harbour and promenade at Dalkey in Dublin Bay also gave rise to suggestions then and in subsequent years that convict labour could be used for the public benefit. According to a correspondent to the *Hibernian Journal* in June 1787, this would mean

> converting the island of Dalkey to a receptacle, where convicts hitherto cast for transportation may be kept as constant labour for life, or for a certain time, according to the enormity of their crimes.[60]

More considered discussions of crime and punishment were rare in Ireland but in its issue for February 1786 *Walker's Hibernian Magazine* published a short essay which assessed the options. Although

'Thoughts on Criminals' was contributed anonymously, it echoed the ideas of William Eden, whose 1784 'Discourse on Banishment' was probably in circulation before its publication as the Preface to his *History of New Holland ...* in 1787.[61] Indeed, it may well have been written by him. Rejecting hanging because of its inequitable application to crimes 'very different in degree' and its ineffectiveness as a deterrent, the author also believed that the most recent of these 'legal massacres' (five convicted prisoners had been executed at Kilmainham on 18 February) showed it to be actually counter-productive:

> We have lately had a melancholy image, where malefactors have advanced in troops to death, and where, advancing with the spirit, and apparently with the piety, of martyrs, they have seemed objects of envy rather than spectacles of horror.[62]

While the transportation of convicts to America had produced useful reformation, the hulk system in Britain had only served 'to teach and learn iniquity'. Nor had the drafting of British convicts to Cape Coast Castle in Africa as garrison troops been a success: 'they go to mutiny ... and to provoke to murder'. Instead, a wise government should use the severity of justice to promote 'the greatest moral and political good' by means of enforced labour:

> In criminal cases of an inferior nature, such punishments might be inflicted as would tend to reform the convict, and make his labour serviceable to his country. Public works and public roads would afford a sufficient employment, and such an establishment might be made as would induce the criminal to perform his duty for the charms and for the rewards of virtue. By such means many might be saved who now suffer an ignominious and an early death; and many might be so much purified in the furnace of adversity, as to become the ornaments of that society of which they formerly been the bane.

A similar recommendation was made by the *Freeman's Journal* a year later in relation to younger offenders for whom there was no 'intermediate place of correction'. Instead, they were sent to Newgate 'to be perfected in vice, from an association with the very out-casts of society'.[63]

Nevertheless, the Irish Parliament was even less willing at this point than its British counterpart to undertake the responsibilities that such a system demanded: the provisions of the Hard Labour Act were not being put into effect and no serious thought was given by the government to a House of Correction for juveniles until 1790. Trans-Atlantic transportation continued to offer the simplest and cheapest solution, despite the risk of antagonising American patriots.

Reports of the mutinies on the *George* and the *Mercury* and the ultimate disposal of their remaining convicts were duly reprinted from the London press by the Dublin newspapers, so that when the Irish authorities made it clear in October 1784 that transportation was about to be resumed there was already an awareness that America might be a problematical destination. Nevertheless, no legislation had as yet been passed by Maryland or any of the other American provincial assemblies expressly forbidding the importation of convicts and Lord Mayor Thomas Greene no doubt believed that it was worth taking the chance of sending off another shipment to one of the American ports.[64]

5
Emigration, Runaways and Returnees

Another development which made the disposal of Irish convicts in the United States increasingly prolematical after the end of the war was the renewed flow of Irish free emigrants to Baltimore and Philadelphia and the rapid glutting of the labour market there. Added to this was the generally unfavourable reputation of Irish indentured servants, convicts or otherwise, before the war and the renewed problem of Irish runaways. For the Irish government, there was the vexing problem of 'returnees', transported convicts who managed to make their way back to Ireland.

The peace released a tide of Irish free emigration and exports which had been banked up for seven years. According to contemporary Irish estimates, Irish emigration to the American colonies had been running at about 5,000 a year until 1775.[1] The export of linen cloth, provisions and porter had also been a good business for Irish merchants and one which they were keen to resume.[2] At the same time, they were anxious to arrange the importation of flaxseed, tobacco, wheat, rum and other commodities as highly profitable back-loading. Two vessels were entered for exports to Philadelphia in early February[3] and in March the Dublin newspapers were happy to report the consignment there and to Baltimore of cloth and earthenware as well as the traditional pork, beef, beer and butter.[4] Less enthusiastically, they remarked on the 'rage for emigration' which was already gripping the Irish populace.

'Emigrating madness'

As early as February 1783, the *Freeman's Journal* expressed alarm at 'the sort of emigrating madness' afflicting the working classes of Dublin:

> Tradesmen of all descriptions imagine mountains of gold may be made on the other side of the Atlantic; but ... the case ... [is] totally otherwise. The Americans want the common necessities of life, and could less be expected after such an unequal and destructive war? where shirtless and shoeless regiments have fought their scanty cloaths [sic] into the remaining tatters. The real fact seems to be, that if those who are so fond of emigrating give the Americans breathing time, to heal their wounds and form their constitution, it may be found a profitable country, but at the present, HOME carries so evident a preference, that the infatuation of ignorance alone could excite an emigration.[5]

Nor was emigration fever restricted to the capital. The *Freeman's Journal* reported that ships were being got ready in the north of Ireland as well:

> The passenger trade to America is likely to commence with all its former vigour, and drain this country of its most useful and industrious inhabitants. Ships are already put up on this ruinous traffick from all the northern ports, and it is thought will be crowded with the number prepared to emigrate to the regions of liberty.[6]

There was even a report that several hundred families in Co. Monaghan and Co. Meath, oppressed by the particularly extortionate tenant system practised there, had decided to emigrate to Philadelphia *en masse*.[7]

The large number of emigrants on board the first ships to Philadelphia and Baltimore alarmed the Dublin newspapers. 'The spirit of Emigration is more prevalent than was at first imagined', commented the *Hibernian Journal* in March, 'and ... more passengers offer at the Ports of Cork, Belfast, Waterford and Dublin than can be accommodated in the Vessels sailing for America'.[8] Two more ships sailed for Virginia and Philadelphia in April, bringing the number of emigrants during the first few months since the peace to 500.[9] By July, it was being reported that the demand for berths had reached the point where cabin passengers were being charged as much as thirty guineas and steerage passengers fifteen guineas, all having to provide their own rations for the voyage. A poor harvest the previous year and the consequent high cost of food, together with the sharp decline in exports to England following the peace, had combined to make emigration to the United States appear more attractive than ever.

One of the first Dublin merchant firms to take advantage of the peace were Arthur Bryan and his nephew George Bryan of St John's Quay. Owners of a number of ships including the Finnish-built and double-decked brigantine, *Duke of Leinster*, of 255 tons they had strong connections with Philadelphia and were active in the indentured servant and general export and import trade for twenty years before the beginning of the war.[10] They also had connections with St Kitt's in the Leewards where Arthur's brother, George Bryan Senior, had spent some time before establishing himself in Philadelphia in 1752, and with Antigua where Arthur's nephew, Edward, was a merchant.

Remarking that 'the Rage for Emigration seems to be increasing to an alarming degree', the *Hibernian Journal* suggested in May the establishment of a fund to support skilled artisans and 'lower Orders of Workmen' whose emigration would have a deleterious effect on Irish manufacturing.[11] It even called for an immediate sitting of the Irish Parliament 'to obviate the many ill Consequences of national Depopulation'.[12]

Before the end of 1783 there were reports in the Dublin newspapers of fraudulent schemes being practised by merchants and shipping agents who had the most to gain from emigration. Men and boys who could not find the money for their passages to American ports were obliged to sign blank indenture papers and were sometimes held in 'secure houses' until embarkation. In September, a Dublin apprentice boy was reported to have been kidnapped and put on board a ship bound for Philadelphia.[13] Calling upon the government to stop this 'abominable species of Traffic', the *Hibernian Journal* warned would-be emigrants that by signing indentures they gave ships' captains

> a power of selling them as miserable Slaves in the American Plantations, where they are treated more like Wild Brutes than Fellow Creatures, and from whence, if they attempt to escape, and are caught, they are almost whipped to Death, and very often hung up to terrify others from following their Example.[14]

At the same time, the newspaper reported with satisfaction that some of the artisans who had gone to America in the first ships had already written letters home

> expressive of a sincere repentance of the precipitate Folly, in running from Ireland to a Country of Distraction and Want, were every Man who is not possessed of ready Money is treated with

Insult and Contempt, as a subject of the British Crown. The Markets are so over-stocked, that Articles are sold cheaper than they can be manufactured; in so much that none but Carpenters and Bricklayers could get any Sort of Employment, and even the wages of the Former did no amount to Half a Crown per Day.[15]

A Belfast man recently arrived in Philadelphia wrote: 'Nobody would ever come out here that cannot pay their Passage, and have something to begin in the World with'.[16]

The absence of controls on these first post-war emigrant ships was highlighted by an incident on board the *Liberty* in 1783 when indentured male servants broke down the bulk head separating them from the women. The 'mutinous riot' was only put down after one of them had been killed.[17] Another Dublin newspaper report in late 1784 calculated to quell the enthusiasm of would-be emigrants was that some of the Irish already gone to America had been sold as indentured servants to former black slaves.[18] Graphic descriptions of the exploits of bloodthirsty Indians were also intended as a deterrent.[19]

LANDING FROM AN EMIGRANT SHIP.

11 'Landing from an Emigrant Ship'.

Stories like these in the Dublin newspapers must eventually have had a dampening effect. The flow of emigration took between 600 and 800 Irish men and women to Baltimore in 1783 and 1784 and as many as 5,000 to Philadelphia in the last months of 1784.[20] By the end of 1786, it was estimated that as many as 11,000 Irish people had emigrated to the United States since the peace.[21] However, the exodus declined dramatically in 1785 and was not revived until 1789[22] when the demand for labour had picked up once more.

Although the outward flow was already diminishing in 1785, measures were taken by the Irish government that year to discourage emigration. The Seduction of Artisans Bill was passed by the Irish Parliament early that year, making it a criminal offence to contract with or persuade 'artificers' or skilled workers to emigrate[23] and there were subsequently a number of well-publicised prosecutions in Dublin, resulting in one imprisonment and a heavy fine of £500.[24] However, these were not until June 1788 when the flow of emigration had begun to pick up again. Similar legislation was also passed by the British government, together with an act which made it illegal to transport emigrants on British ships as a form of debt servitude. According to D.W. Galenson, this would explain why the post-war indenture system in America relied more on Irish and German immigrants than before.[25]

'This traffic in human flesh'

From his office in Philadelphia, the British Consul Phineas Bond reported to the Board of Trade in London on the abuses being practised at American ports on redemptioners and indentured servants from Ireland, Britain and Germany. In November 1787 he described to the Trade Secretary, the Marquis of Carmarthen (subsequently the Duke of Leeds), 'this traffic in human flesh':

> I have ... often, heretofore, been witness of the severity experienced by redemptioners and indented servants brought hither from different parts of Europe; numbers crowded in small ships – provisions scarce and bad and the treatment oppressive and cruel.[26]

Redemptioners, who had agreed to work for a set time in order to repay the cost of their passage from their wages, were frequently given no opportunity to obtain employment on arrival and were thus reduced to the plight of 'common indented servants', being sold off for a term of years:

It too often happens ... that the merchants and masters of ships, with a view to clearing their vessels immediately and to save the expenses of maintaining their unfortunate passengers deprive them of the hope of being redeemed by abridging this limited time, and before their friends can receive intimation of their arrival and inter-pose their relief, they are frequently hurried in droves, under the custody of severe and brutal drivers, (for these are [the] terms) into the back country to be disposed of as servants. I was lately an eye-witness of a scene which interested me exceedingly, but I could administer little more than pity ... for, in me, any interposition might have been construed as an endeavour to discourage the spirit of migration in which the consequence of the United States is so essentially involved, as one means of increasing population.[27]

Reports of this kind published in the Dublin and Cork newspapers certainly helped to slow down Irish and British emigration to the United States between 1785 and 1788. Bond observed to Carmarthen in November 1788 that the 'spirit of migration has of late years remit-ted exceedingly'. However, numbers continued to arrive, especially from Ireland, 'and the phantoms of freedom and happiness under the new Constitution may tempt greater numbers to follow the example'.[28] Indeed, according to Bond's later figures, 5,213 Irish immigrants, mostly indentured servants and redemptioners, came to the United States in 1789 alone. One ship, the *Nancy* of only 131 tons, was reported to have carried no less than 300 passengers from Londonderry to Philadelphia. Others carrying German immigrants packed in as many as 800.[29]

Conditions on board such grossly overcrowded vessels can only be imagined. Indeed, they may well have been worse than those endured on some of the Irish convict ships across the Atlantic. In one instance in late 1790, a Philadelphia-based society for the encouragement of Irish immigration managed to prosecute the master of a Londonderry vesel whose passengers had been reduced to short rations for most of the voyage.[30]

In 1788 and again in 1789, Bond outlined to the Duke of Leeds his plan to discourage emigration from Ireland and Britain by regulating the ships engaged in the indentured servants trade and making it less profitable.[31] Writing in August 1789, Bond told him that during the previous few weeks, the *Conyngham*, *Havannah* and *St James* had arrived in the Delaware River from Ireland with a total of 442 emig-rants on board. Other shiploads of Irish had come to Baltimore.

According to Bond, the emigrants on board the *St James* 'generally appear reputable and above the common class and have brought property with them'. Unlike the German Palatine immigrants, most of whom were indentured servants, the 240 Irish landed at Baltimore that year had paid their passages.[32]

Bond told Leeds that his regulatory scheme would 'soon check a trade very oppressive to a number of valuable people, and very destructive to the interests of both kingdoms by draining them of many useful and laborious inhabitants ...'.[33] Writing to Leeds again in January 1790, Bond told him that he was convinced that further inducements would be held out 'to draw a large body of people from Ireland' during the following summer and that these would be successful 'if difficulties be not immediately thrown in the way'.[34]

Despite these repeated attempts to interest his minister and patron, Bond's suggested scheme was not taken up and the tide of emigration from Ireland continued to flow. The only development which at all inhibited overall trade between Ireland and America was the British government's proclamation of 25 June 1788 which forbade the importation into Britain of American wheat. This had a serious impact on the hinterland of Baltimore where wheat was a staple crop and reduced the potential of back-loading of cargo from Irish ports.

However, tea and tobacco continued to be highly profitable, particularly (Bond believed) since most of it was 'run' to Ireland to avoid paying duty and subsequently taken to Britain. In 1784 and 1785, a total of almost 10,000 hogsheads of tobacco had been cleared for Ireland from Philadelphia alone.[35] In May 1787 Bond observed that some of the tobacco bound for Londonderry on the *Penelope* had been 'cut up in quarters and bound up in ropes, ready to sling on horses when they should be landed on the Irish coast'.[36]

Runaways

As we have seen, Irish convicts, together with redemptioners and indentured servants, had achieved a certain reputation during the decades before 1775 which can only have militated against the acceptance of renewed Irish convict transportation to America. When the *Duke of Leinster* arrived at Baltimore from Dublin on 6 November 1783 with almost one hundred redemptioners on board, the merchant firm of Stewart and Plunket to whom they had been consigned advertised them in the *Maryland Gazette, or Baltimore General Advertiser* for ten guineas a head.[37] Within a week, however, the agents were offering a reward for the return of seven of the men who had absconded from the ship even before their passages were redeemed by their employer-purchasers.[38]

Within a few months, some of the employers who had paid their ten guineas to Stewart and Plunket were advertising for the return of their runaway Irish servants. On 12 March 1784, James Giles of Baltimore sought the return of Edward Joyce, 'about thirty years of age, has a down look, and black curled hair, has been used to drive a coach ...', who was last seen at the stage office in Baltimore and was supposed to have made off with the Irish servant of Mr Murphy, bookseller. When he absconded, Joyce was said to be wearing 'a green shag jacket, and sundry clothes tied up in a handkerchief'.[39] William Murphy duly advertised on 26 March for the return of Richard Lewis, 'of a ruddy complexion, short black hair, part of which is come out, owing to sickness, between fourteen and fifteen years of age, nearly five feet high ...'. Lewis was last seen wearing 'a bearskin greatcoat, a buff coat, nearly new, with gilt buttons, black corded breeches, with steel knee buckles in them, white cotton stockings, new shoes, with brass buckles ...'.[40]

A Philadelphia bookseller, William Pritchard, brought an appropriately literary touch to his advertisement in the same newspaper in February 1786 for a runaway called O'Neil, at the same time providing an exemplary caricature of the Irish servant type:

A CAUTION to the PUBLIC
A SWINDLER

This honest caution friends receive,
Which now to you we freely give,
To guard against the wiles and wits
Of cunning knaves, and swindler's tricks;
Imported swindlers grow so fast,
They'll surely make us wise at last.
A true description here you'll trace,
Of Teague the swindler's matchless face;
A strong Hibernian, full bred brogue,
Distinguishes the artful rogue.
Devoid of ev'ry manly grace,
With native impudence of face;
Some five feet high the hero stalks,
But rather shuffles when he walks.

A full grown paunch projects before,
Enough to fill a common door.
His hair long-bobb'd his shoulders grace,
Of dandy dun adorns his face;
Well-rigg'd, the rogue, from top to toe,
His tailors to their sorrow know;
Deck'd out with every jemmy thing,
The rascal sports a swindled ring,
A nice cut onyx, neatly set,
While new silk hose his legs bedeck.
Now of the lining of his head to speak,
Its [sic] cram'd with Latin and with Greek;
Quite fluff'd with academic rule,
Late teacher of a Latin school.
But why should we his name conceal?
The swindling scoundrel is O'NEIL.
Beware then friends, nor trust the rogue,
You'll know him by his native brogue.
And if discovery can be made,
So that the law may catch the blade,
A good reward will then be paid,
          By H.G. & W.P.[41]

Returnees

While runaway servants caused problems for their employers in Maryland, Virginia and Philadelphia, those transported convicts who managed to return to their homeland were seen as a menace to Irish society at large. Indeed, the return from North America after 1785 of numbers of transported criminals was one of the reasons why the Irish authorities and Dublin's newspapers were so enthusiastic about the Botany Bay scheme when it was revealed in late 1786. However, when it seemed unlikely after a year of waiting that the Irish government would be allowed to participate, the problem of returnees began to loom almost as large as the state of the prisons. As the *Hibernian Journal* put it in September 1787:

The transports from this kingdom not having been sent to Botany Bay, but landed in Nova Scotia, must certainly give a degree of life and spirit to the *gentleman marauders* remaining, as they are not cut out *for ever* from the hope of seeing their friends in this country. The run is not as long as to New-York, and we may reasonably expect to see, by every returning vessel, gentlemen of the *pad* and the *highway* returning from the new world, and going over the *old ground* in Ireland.[42]

The *Freeman's Journal* believed that until all returnees were hanged, there would be 'no end to the constant robbing':

Those experienced villains, hardened in iniquity, are prompt to head any gang; and knowing every avenue of escape, it cannot be a surprize that so few of them are detected.[43]

Indeed, the Dublin newspapers from early 1787 onwards carried frequent reports of the exploits of notorious returnees who were described as once again practising their old trades as house-breakers, shop-lifters, pick-pockets, highwaymen and the like. As we have seen, it was not difficult for convicts to bribe the captain of a transport to put them ashore on the Irish coast en route for North America. Nor was it difficult once in America, where they were not constrained by prison or chain, for convict runaways to buy or work a passage home. Some were wealthy enough to purchase their freedom on arrival. Then there were the convicts of the *Dispatch* who escaped to France in May 1787 after the mutiny on board. No doubt they were the subject of this somewhat romanticised story published in the *Freeman's Journal* in October 1788:

The son of a noted constable had returned about twelve months since from the vessel in which he was sent off for transportation – he now walks publicly through the streets and, no doubt, is going on with his old trade of getting what he can from the public. He, with many others, extricated themselves from their irons, and were put ashore near Cork, and each was allowed to bring a young girl along with him.[44]

One of the most notorious returnees to be apprehended was William Hacket who was finally hanged at Gallows-hill, Kilmainham, on 28 April 1787 after being convicted of burglary. Two years earlier, he had been reprieved literally at the last minute at the same gallows on condition of accepting transportation for life, 'from which, however, he thought proper to return in a short time, and by following his old wicked course, brought on the unhappy fate he has suffered'.[45] Another veteran Dublin robber, Hugh McGowran ('Morning Star'), whom we have already noticed, had recently returned from transportation and was suspected of a highway robbery committed in September 1787. He was captured together with Obigal Davis, another returnee, by Newgate Gaoler, George Roe, early the following month.[46] In December, Timothy Mahony and four other returnees were recognised and apprehended at the Royal Exchange in Dublin.[47]

In January 1788, the *Hibernian Journal* reported that a 'noted robber' called Moran was following his old trade in Co. Kildare after the vessel transporting him had been stranded and he and his comrades were set at liberty.[48] There was also the case of that 'most atrocious and daring offender' Anthony Molloy who made an arrangement with Captain Debenham of the *Providence* in October 1788 so that instead of being landed with the other convicts at Cape Breton Island, Nova Scotia, he was reported in January 1789 to be 'openly walking the streets of Dublin at liberty'.[49] Molloy had been convicted for the theft of £100 worth of silver plate from an auction-room in Anglesea-street, Dublin, the proceeds of which enabled him not only to purchase a suite of two apartments for himself at Newgate and to 'cut a genteel figure amongst the cargo of rogues sent out', but to 'bribe off the destination of his sentence'.[50]

When Molloy was finally captured by the constables in Francis-street, Dublin, in early April 1789, he was found to have on him two pistols, some keys, and 'a paper containing directions for coining'.[51] However, as he was being taken by wherry from the North Wall to the awaiting ship on 13 June, he jumped overboard and managed to escape in a boat which was there for the purpose.[52]

Two other well-known offenders, John Cunningham and a man called Ellis, who had recently returned for transportation,[53] were thought to belong to a gang of robbers preying on pedestrians on the outskirts of Dublin. When Ellis was recognised by the police in Francis-street in July 1789, he managed to knock down no less than six of them single-handed. Although reinforcements arrived in the form of Sheriff Tweedy and a sergeant's guard, the assembled mob pelted them with stones and Ellis was able to make his escape.[54]

In early 1790 the *Hibernian Journal* expressed satisfaction at the final capture of the two men and hoped that an example would be made of them so that others like them would be obliged to return to the countryside.[55] However, Cunningham was one of the forty prisoners who escaped from Newgate through the sewers on 20 July[56] and although he was recaptured and served a six months sentence, he then joined a gang in the Liberties which included another returnee, William Dalton. He was subsequently hanged at Kilmainham on 12 September 1792 with the leader of the gang, George Robinson, and another of its members after being convicted of taking part in the armed robbery of a house in Cork-street during which the owner was shot dead.[57]

A year later there were reported to be more than twenty returnees walking the streets of Dublin and the *Morning Post* wondered at their audacity: 'It is strange that wretches who have obtained the boon of life on condition of transportation should stake it, worse than act of the die, at hazard; and some of them will eventually fall under the unhappy predicament'.[58] Relief was expressed at the capture in September 1790 of a returnee called Laurence Lynch, *alias* James McHugh, *alias* William Reily, *alias* Reardon who had broken out of Maryborough (Portlaoise) gaol a few weeks earlier and was believed to be the principal of a particularly industrious gang of counterfeiters.[59]

In one extraordinary incident in January 1791, a young woman confronted by an armed man at the second lock of the Grand Canal managed to grab his cocked pistol and shoot him through the head while he was exchanging her silver buckles for his own. This 'desperate, able looking villain' by the name of Thompson was subsequently discovered to have returned from transportation about three years earlier 'and ever since had been marauding the public'. As evidence of this, a search of his clothing revealed twelve guineas and two bank notes.[60]

Nor was the problem of returnees confined to Dublin and its environs. In February 1790 the *Morning Post* reported an incident in Co. Meath in which a gang of about forty alleged returnees attacked the house of a Mr Dillon, and when driven off by his servants 'departed ... uttering horrid oaths against his life, and the destruction of his family'.[61]

There is no indication that any of the Newfoundland returnees of January 1790 escaped from Newgate and committed further crimes. However, William Dalton, who went to Barbuda on the *Duke of Leinster* in November 1789, somehow managed to return to Dublin and to his old habits. After becoming involved with Robinson's gang, he was arrested by Police Inspector William Shea in October 1791 for robbing the Earl of Clanwilliam of a gold watch, gold seals and a purse containing a five-guinea note.[62]

Frederick Lambert

Perhaps the most notorious returnee of the late 1780s was Frederick Lambert. Originating from a respectable family in Wexford where his father had been a city councillor, Lambert had first been convicted for taking part in a robbery in Dublin's Pill-lane. Sentenced to death at the Commission of Oyer and Terminer in July 1783, he avoided the penalty by agreeing to transport himself for life. Apprehended after returning from transportation, he had been committed for that capital offence and put on trial in June 1788.[63] When the judge accepted his plea that he had been shipwrecked on the way to his destination, his sentence was once again commuted to transportation.

While awaiting the next shipment in Newgate in August 1788, Lambert became involved in a dispute with a fellow prisoner, Francis Bathurst, who had been gaoled for throwing a child out of a three-storey window. When Bathurst declined a challenge to fight on the grounds of Lambert's infirmity, the latter drew a razor from his pocket and ripped open Bathurst's stomach before he could be restrained by three other prisoners. The prison surgeon dressed the wound, the sight of which so horrified the Church of Ireland chaplain, the Revd Mr Gamble, that he fainted on the spot and had to be carried downstairs to the main yard.[64] Somehow surviving the terrible attack, Bathurst subsequently had Lambert convicted under the Chalking Act and he was finally (but inexpertly) hanged in front of Newgate on 30 October 1788.[65] We have already noted that Lambert was the likely inspiration of that famous hanging ballad, 'De Night Before Larry Was Stretch'd'.

'Father' Fay

Another celebrated returnee (or rather, escapee, because he is not known to have ever returned to Ireland) was 'Father' Patrick Fay (or Fahy). Convicted at the Tholsel quarter sessions in September 1788 on several counts of forging a receipt for £13.18s.9$\frac{1}{2}$d,[66] Fay had managed through the influence of well-placed friends in Dublin to delay his transportation for nine months. In his own petition to the Lord Lieutenant seeking a pardon, he pointed out that it would have been easy for him to have escaped while awaiting trial – indeed, it was his absolute belief in his innocence that had caused him to seek trial. However, he had not thought that a capital felony could be heard at a quarter sessions and advice from eminent counsel had supported this view. Furthermore, the prosecutor (complainant) in the case, Patrick Fullam, had subsequently made a declaration of his innocence.[67] Fay's main argument, however, was that as a man of considerable property and with five motherless children ranging from twelve to three years, he was hardly likely to have sacrificed his life and their welfare for the relatively insignificant sum of money involved.

Indeed, it seems likely that the forgery charge had been used as a device to get Fay out of the way. A former Roman Catholic priest, he had publicly recanted his faith and become a priest of the Church of Ireland. Purchasing the Readership or chaplaincy of the Royal Hospital at Kilmainham, but 'on a faulty title', he eventually lost his place there because of alleged misbehaviour. He had subsequently practised as a 'couple-beggar' or marriage celebrant, keeping an 'open house for the marriage of persons of all ages, ranks and descriptions'. He was said to have married as many as six couples a day for as much as a guinea a time. This lucrative practice virtually came to an end when the Archbishop of Dublin, Robert Fowler, regarding him as a 'disgrace to religion, and a nuisance to society', had him disqualified after long and expensive litigation.[68]

Fay had also been sentenced to six months' imprisonment at the Commission of Oyer and Terminer in Dublin in November 1786 for 'assaulting and cutting in a most dangerous manner' a certain Bridget Duffy and was fortunate to have been let off by Chief Justice Lord Earlsfort on a promise of good behaviour and the payment of compensation to his victim.[69] The following April he was involved in an incident which suggested that there was nothing of the effete cleric about him. Before a huge crowd gathered in a field near the Circular-road, Phibbsborough, he took part in a wrestling match with a 'chair-man' (sedan-chair bearer) for a gallon of whiskey. In the outcome, as the *Freeman's Journal* put it, 'this *lopped-off* branch of ... [the Church] obtained the victory'.[70]

Some measure of Fay's reputation in more polite circles can be gathered from a satirical report in the *Freeman's Journal* in December 1786 listing 'the Rev. Pat Fay' as 'Archbishop of Botany (the *former*)' in the official Establishment intended for Botany Bay.[71] Two years later, the same newspaper also recounted an incident when he made an offer of his services as master of ceremonies at a children's concert to be performed at Dublin's Bethesda Chapel. When this were rejected, the *Freeman's Journal* remarked that 'all the water in the pool at the Bethesda could not wash him whiter than a raven'.[72]

During Fay's trial, it was claimed in the newspapers that after his training as a priest in France he had gone as a chaplain to China, serving for some time at Canton and later on the French island of Bourbon in the Indian Ocean. There he was supposed to have accumulated a sum of about seven hundred pounds which he brought back to Ireland and shrewdly invested in city and country properties, eventually owning eleven houses in Dublin and an estate in Co. Meath. He also married and fathered five children but was a widower by the time of his trial.[73]

Altogether, it seems that the authorities were much more concerned with preventing Fay's continued illegal activity as a marriage celebrant than they were with punishing him for the alleged forgeries, which may well have been trumped up. As he said at his trial, it seemed highly unlikely that a man of his substantial wealth would risk so much for so little gain. Further evidence that he was 'framed' was provided by a report in the usually well-informed *Dublin Chronicle* that he was being reprieved by the authorities every three months so that he could be considered 'dead by law, and therefore his marriages cannot ever be valid'. Keeping him in Ireland also meant that that he could not practise his vocation anywhere else,[74] although eventually the continuing publicity surrounding his case may have become too embarrassing. Altogether, his career possesses some remarkable similarities to that of another ingenious and enterprising Irishman, Laurence Hynes Halloran, whose exploits as a masquerading Anglican priest in South Africa and England and as a schoolmaster and publisher in New South Wales have been recounted elsewhere.[75]

A writer in the *Hibernian Journal* drew an unfavourable comparison between Lord Lieutenant Buckingham's rejection of Fay's petition for mercy and the clemency shown by him to a well-known brothel-keeper and bondage-mistress, Maria Lewellin, who had been pardoned on the morning of her planned execution. She had been capitally convicted for abetting the rape of a fourteen-year-old girl (herself the daughter of a prostitute) in the garden of her house in Blackmore-yard:

> the fate of the unfortunate Fay seems peculiarly hard, when contrasted with that of a certain harpy, whose crime, though infinitely more atrocious, has been compensated with life and liberty. Had the degraded Priest degraded even his bad character with acts of the *sporting* kind, he might have experienced the same lenity. In these times of vicious dissipation, what favour of the *crack of the whip*, by which so many, now living in splendour, have made their fortunes, must be considered as an ingredient highly meriting pity from the Cyrbernean votaries, who are numerous and powerful in every state. Had the exiled [illeg.] of departed priesthood mixed a drachm or two of p----n with his pound of forgery, he might have found friends capable of preventing a voyage to Halifax, Port Rosemary, or Maryland.[76]

After all his appeals had failed, Fay was finally put on board the *Duke of Leinster* in Dublin Bay on 13 June 1789, bound officially for Nova Scotia. Contrary to his wish that he be taken to the North Wall in the relative privacy of a coach, he was conveyed 'in an open machine, called the Kilmainham cart'[77] and, as we shall see, was injured when it overturned on the way to the docks. Unlike the usual practice for prisoners, however, he was accommodated in a comfortable cabin on the upper deck of the vessel and treated with uncommon courtesy. Before his departure, it was even reported in the newspapers that he was to be landed at St Vincent's in the Leeward Islands and that he would subsequently arrange for his children to join him there. By this time he had returned to the Roman Catholic faith, declaring that he would 'die in that doctrine, tho' for a time entertained some scruples [sic]'.[78]

When the *Duke of Leinster* was two days out from Dublin and Wicklow Head was still in sight, a sail was spied. It turned out to be a fishing vessel which came alongside and took off Fay with the full co-operation of Captain Harrison, who must have been paid to facilitate the rendezvous.[79] Within a day or two, Fay was landed at Whitehaven in England and, according to a subsequent newspaper report, 'from thence after a curious and interesting journey, through Great Britain, Germany and the Netherlands, visited Paris during the commotions which preceded the Gallic revolution, and is now established as an eminent cheesemonger in the city of Bordeaux ...'.[80]

According to another Dublin newspaper account, Fay took ship direct from Whitehaven to Bordeaux, but there was no dispute about the fact of his having established a business in the French port. His continuing problem, however, was that the two agents appointed by him before his departure could not collect rent on his Irish properties: his tenants obtained advice from eminent counsel that as he had not been transported according to law, he could not give a valid power of attorney to anyone to act on his behalf.[81] Although he did not subsequently establish a wealthy Hiberno-Gallic dynasty in the style of the celebrated Hennessy family, Patrick Fay must surely be regarded as one of the more colourful Irish entrepreneurs of his time.[82]

So well-known was Fay in Dublin that after his departure there were a number of satirical reports in the newspapers of his being sighted in different parts of the city. The *Morning Post*, for example, suggested in mid-July that he had been observed at a popular zoological garden outside the city and that the reason for his return was to officiate at the nuptials of the respited Lewellin and her pimp and lover, Robert

Edgeworth, who had recently been pilloried opposite the Tholsel for perjury:[83]

> Father Fay was seen last Saturday at the Green-house, Rathfarnham. The sight of the birds, beasts and reptiles, all that is curious and exotic, could not strike the beholders with more astonishment. It is said he is come over on the invitation of Lewellin, to marry, her legally to that pillar of the Tholsel, Bob Edgeworth.[84]

In his 1790 pamphlet, *Thoughts on Penitentiaries*, Sir Jeremiah Fitzpatrick referred to the freeing of Patrick Fay as an example of the common practice by ships' captains of 'breaking bulk' on the outward voyage. He also cited evidence of the involuntary return of transportees from America. During his travels around Ireland the previous year inspecting prisons, he had encountered no less than fifteen people who had been transported to America in 1788 but had been returned against their will:

> it is a well known fact, that the Americans re-ship every Convict they find, knowing him to be such, except he is a tradesman, with whom they generally dispense; so that we are not to be surprised at seeing them daily returning to their offended Country, apparently braving the laws.[85]

He estimated that, tradesmen apart, most of those transported during the previous ten years had returned within a year of their original embarkation and no less than four-fifths of those who had left during the previous three years.

6
The Revival of Irish Transportation

By the middle of October 1784, the Dublin newspapers had begun to express extreme impatience over the delays in arrangements to take away prisoners sentenced under the Hard Labour Act. The *Hibernian Journal* believed that

> It would be doing an act of the utmost utility to the citizens of Dublin, and the public in general, if Government would send off in the ship now getting ready for the convicts ... the several persons under the rule of hard labour, with whom our Gaols are at present crowded, and with whose maintenance the citizens of Dublin are, and have been, shamefully burdened.[1]

It was with some satisfaction, then, that the same newspaper reported on 25 October that the first shipment to leave Ireland for almost ten years was destined for the islands of Abaco in the Bahamas,

> where these unhappy wretches, if not wholly abandoned, may, in a rich and luxuriant soil, and the finest climate in the world, acquire habits of labour and industry, that comparatively will be a Heaven to the life of profligacy and misery they have hitherto led. By this excellent measure, the city of Dublin will save upwards of £500 per annum, which the maintenance of these wretches cost.[2]

It was by no means generally believed that the destination was the Bahamas. The *Freeman's Journal*, for example, thought that the ship was 'bound to the coast of Africa' where British prisoners had earlier been sent.[3] Nevertheless, few readers would have disagreed with its observation that

In the present very untenable state of the gaol [Newgate], it must be a great satisfaction to the public, as well as happiness to the gaoler, that such a number of dangerous prisoners are sent out of the kingdom.[4]

In a subsequent report which used the 1782 *Memoirs* of the eccentric Captain Peter Bruce as its authority,[5] the *Hibernian Journal* lyricised on the fertility of Abaco, claiming that 'there is not a spot within the tropics so desirable'. Vegetable seeds 'thrown loosely on the earth, will grow to a singular degree of luxuriance' and 'for poultry and fish, for the variety and value of its fine woods, and the salubrity of its air, it is unparalleled so near the equator'.[6] The only possible disadvantages of this earthly paradise were the presence of the 'musketo, the cokroche, and the trigger [sic]', but even these could be removed when the undergrowth was cleared away – as had been done on the neighbouring island of New Providence.[7] So enthusiastic was the newspaper about what promised to be 'a noble acquisition to England' that it believed its 'incitements ... should excite some clergymen to visit a people, who may be turned from vice to the purposes of becoming good men and useful subjects'.[8]

It is not clear why Abaco (or Albico, as it was also known at that time) was believed by the *Hibernian Journal* to be the destination. As we have seen, there had been an active Irish trade with the West Indies since the late seventeenth century, but the Bahamas were not a significant part of that pattern. Indeed, they were largely irrelevant to Irish commercial interests, which focused on Barbados, Jamaica and the Leewards. Furthermore, as we have also seen, the market for Irish indentured labour in the West Indies had virtually disappeared fifty years earlier. The most likely explanation is that September 1783 had seen the evacuation to Abaco of the first of about 8,000 American Loyalists and their slaves from New York and Florida. Some of those from East Florida subsequently began setting themselves up again as cotton-planters there.

An Irish connection with the Bahamas was established when Governor John Maxwell's appeal to London to help feed the influx of refugees resulted in the requisitioning and despatch of at least one shipload of salted provisions, clothing and tools from Cork in early 1784.[9] News of a shortage of field labour and the need for road-building brought back by Irish captains may also have suggested to the Dublin authorities that convict labour would be welcome there. Alternatively, Abaco may have been given out by the Lord Mayor both to distract the attention of the American authorities who were known to oppose the resumption of transportation and to reassure the convicts in Newgate who were growing extremely restive in the expectation of being sent to Africa.

News of their impending departure for what was as yet an uncertain destination caused the women prisoners under sentence of transportation at Newgate to make a concerted effort to escape on 31 August 1784:

> armed with their bolts, stones and glass bottles, they suddenly setting up a horrid yell, fell upon the hatch-keepers, and on Thornton the turnkey, whom they would in all probability have killed, had he not effected his escape by means of a cord from the execution window.[10]

The military guard tried to frighten the women with their bayonets, but when this did not have any effect they fired some shots, wounding two women and quelling the riot.

On 16 September the women made another attempt by making a hole in the wall opposite Green-street and two managed to get out before they were secured by the military guard.[11] On 8 November the women made yet another attempt, this time through the sewer which they penetrated for some distance towards King-street. One of them managed to escape into the street after stripping off all her clothes, but the others, 'terrified at their situation', gave the alarm and were re-captured.[12] Despite the posting of more guards in the surrounding streets, within a few days there was another attempt made by the men through the sewer, resulting in the escape of two prisoners. The *Freeman's Journal* was moved to comment:

> When we consider the untenable state of that prison, acknowledged by a committee appointed for that purpose, together with the vast numbers still confined therein under rule of transportation, who should have long since been sent to their destined places, it may not be wondered at, to hear of escapes from that prison almost every week, and the robber and the plunderer again let loose on the public.[13]

In the meantime, there had also been a serious outbreak of 'a dangerous fever' at Newgate due to overcrowding[14] and the *Dublin Journal* and *Hibernian Journal* were pleased to inform their readers in mid-

November that a chartered vessel to take the convicts 'to their defined places' was now in the harbour.[15] Indeed, it was probably relief at their imminent departure as well as their 'miserable appearance' which moved Sheriff Jenkin to prevail on the Dublin Grand Jury for enough money to provide warm clothes for their winter voyage across the Atlantic. In a fit of patriotic concern, the *Dublin Journal* remarked that 'the apparel they [previously] had on would be a disgrace to the country from whence they came'.[16] For their part, however, the ship's contractors were not so generous with the amount of food and water that was put on board.[17]

After the series of escapes from Newgate during previous months, it was not surprising that the one hundred or so convicts should have been accompanied from the prison to the North Wall by a strong party of horse and foot soldiers before embarkation on the *Nancy* on 17 November.[18] The *Freeman's Journal* must have expressed a common sentiment when it wrote:

> In the present very untenable state of the goal [*sic*], it must be a great satisfaction to the public, as well as happiness to the goaler, that such a number of dangerous prisoners are sent out of the kingdom.[19]

The *Nancy*

As it happened, this first expedition met with disaster when a party of thirty-six of the one hundred convicts on board the *Nancy*, including a dozen women and children, were put to the sword by the Spanish garrison at Fortaventura on the island of Ferra (Hierra) in the western Canaries. After landing them there on 14 December, Captain Michael Cunnin sailed on to St Kitt's in the Leewards where he sold most of the remainder as indentured servants. Basseterre, the capital of this prosperous sugar island, had its own 'Irishtown' quarter and a small number of Irish merchants[20] who may well have purchased the services of some of their countrymen.

Cunnin was disposing of the left-over rations to the merchants at Basseterre when a letter was received by the authorities there from the Spanish Captain-General of the Canaries in Teneriffe, de Braniforte, complaining about the illegal landing at Hierra. Hearing of this, Cunnin quickly sailed off to the nearby Dutch-owned island of St Eustatia but a sloop was sent after him with a letter for its governor explaining what had happened. Cunnin was duly held at Fort George,

12 Late eighteenth-century brig of the kind used by Irish contractors in the trans-Atlantic convict trade.

St Eustatia, for questioning but there is no record of any outcome and it can only be presumed that he was released.

In the meantime, some of the convicts who had been landed at St Kitt's were causing problems. In early 1785, Mary Farrel, James Sands and John Bennett were committed to gaol in Basseterre 'on suspicion of Felony' and in April the local legislature voted £30 to pay a ship's captain to remove them to one of the American ports.[21] One hundred years earlier, the Leewards had been the only West Indian colony prepared to take fifty British women convicts,[22] but in the meantime slaves had become the principal source of labour and the planters feared the destabilising influence of exported felons.

The first public report of the Hierra massacre appeared in April 1785 when the *Maryland Gazette* printed a letter from an English merchant of St Eustatia who held Cunnin responsible for the convicts being 'indiscriminately murdered by the natives on a supposition that they were infected with the plague'.[23] However, another report published in the same newspaper three weeks later portrayed Cunnin's actions in a more favourable light. According to this version of events, six of the convicts on board the *Nancy* had broken free from their shackles within a few hours' sail of Dublin and the crew and passengers were only able to keep control after a blunderbuss was fired amongst them. Four days later, there was a serious outbreak of the 'gaol distemper' from which four people died. Within a day of sighting the Canary Islands, the convicts once again indicated their intention of rising up against the captain and crew. Consequently, when they reached the island of Hierra and a number demanded to be put ashore, Cunnin, 'finding himself and his crew in danger from their violence and their distemper, was in his own defence, obliged to comply with their instant desires'.[24] No explanation was given as to why Cunnin had taken his ship so far off course as the Canaries, although it seems likely that the mutineers had insisted on this.

A more reliable summary of what happened at Hierra was given to Britain's Foreign Secretary, the Marquis of Carmarthen, by the British Consul in Madrid, Robert Liston, in an official dispatch of 31 January 1785. This was apparently based on a report sent to the Spanish capital by de Braniforte who had been in communication with the Spanish governor of Hierra:

> The circumstances, as related by the Governor himself are said to be:
> – that a vessel apeared upon the coast, and landed from a boat five or six people, who were almost naked, and seemed to be sinking under the weight of disease: – That the boat then returned and brought a similar number from the Ship; when the Governor attempted to prevent their disembarking, from an idea that they were infected with the plague: – but that the Captain pointed his Guns towards the land, and by force put on shore about thirty-six persons (of whom seven were women and five or six children); after which he stood out to Sea, without having hoisted any Colours, or had any communication with the inhabitants of the island. – The Governor put the whole of those that were landed to the sword, and had their bodies thrown into the Sea.
> What is very remarkable is that he does not appear to have thought of the possibility of providing for the Security of the island by confining the Strangers within a cordon, and obliging them to perform quarantine: and it is still more inconceivable that the Massacre is said to have been a deliberate act, done after a formal consultation upon the subject with the Clergy of the place.[25]

Liston told Carmarthen that orders had been sent from Madrid for 'a strict inquiry' into the incident and that the Governor of Hierra would doubtless suffer 'exemplary punishment'.[26] However, he made no reference to the outcome in subsequent despatches and it can only be concluded that the Spanish authorities did not pursue the matter. Liston's serious illness later that year may also have been a factor. As the nationality of the *Nancy* was uncertain, it was not an issue which the

British government could easily press. Strained relations between Britain and Spain over the fledgling British settlement in Honduras, to which British convicts were despatched as late as December 1785, may also have prevented Carmarthen from pursuing it. He was in no mood to risk another war with Spain. At any rate, it was not mentioned in his subsequent correspondence with Liston. Nor was the massacre referred to in correspondence between the Home Office and Dublin Castle and there is no indication that the Castle authorities took up the matter with the ship's agents or with Cunnin himself, if he ever returned to Dublin.

A Dublin newspaper in May 1785, citing a private letter from an Irish resident of St Kitt's, alerted the public to the convicts' fate.[27] The letter explained that the Spaniards at Hierra had mistaken the symptoms of typhus displayed by many of the convicts for bubonic plague, known to have been raging at Constantinople earlier that year.[28] Two of those killed were named as Thomas Stevens and William Rea, but the list of those originally embarked at Dublin has not survived.

The *Anne-Mary*

Within a month of the departure from Dublin of the *Nancy*, concern was being expressed by the newspapers that the recent shipment, together with the spate of recent public executions at Newgate and Kilmainham, was having no significant impact on crime or the swollen population of the gaols. Citing three recent robberies in the city, the *Dublin Journal* remarked:

> Notwithstanding the frequency of awful examples exhibited at our prison fronts, we are sorry to find that depredation is still prevalent through this city, and we fear our jails will in a short time be crowded as they were previous to the shipping of the convicts for Abaco.[29]

New regulations were proposed for Newgate by which convicted prisoners would be 'held in a situation consonant with their crimes' and 'the innocent treated as men and brethren',[30] but as usual nothing seems to have come of this well-intended initiative. In the meantime, the population of Newgate was increasing and by early May 1785 fears were being expressed in the newspapers that the approaching hot weather would bring a 'gaol distemper, which may prove a certain plague to the metropolis'.[31]

It was another four months before a transport could be arranged. On 20 September 1785, the two-masted snow or small brig *Anne-Mary*, owned by the Dublin merchant William Stockden and with Captain Duncan Nevin in command, embarked 126 prisoners at Dublin and subsequently a further fifty at Cork before sailing from there on 5 October. The newspapers of the day rarely provided detailed descriptions of convict embarkations, usually preferring to reflect on the benefit which they represented for the community. On this occasion, however, the writer for the *Freeman's Journal* was clearly moved by the drama he witnessed at Dublin's North Wall:

> To every spectator of feeling it must have been a distressing scene, to behold yesterday several infants and children taken from their unhappy mothers, who were among the number of convicts sent on board the transport ships [sic] for America. The cries, shrieks, and floods of tears at the moment of parting, never nore to behold, in all likelihood, their offspring, were exceedingly affecting to every humane observer, and clearly demonstrated, that however the mind might have been corrupted with vice, the pang of nature excruciated the mothers' poor hearts at having their little ones torn from them.[32]

The *Anne-Mary* was said to be bound for Nova Scotia, whose advantages were described by the *Hibernian Journal*:

> Considerable tracts of land ... were granted at the conclusion of the former war to several officers and privates in the British service, but were shortly deserted by them. At the late Peace numbers of refugees from the southern colonies settled there. The climate is cool and hospitable, and the lands, except in the neighbourhood of Halifax, uncultivated. The labour, therefore, of the transports may turn out [to be] of considerable service to the new settlers, if the convicts can be brought to reform their lives, and acquire the habits of industry, honesty and sobriety.[33]

The *Freeman's Journal* was more concerned with the waste involved in shipping off people whose industry was put to productive use 'in every other country of Europe except Great Britain and Ireland':

> What numbers of these unfortunate people sent off ... from our jails, that might have been rendered of general utility, by being compelled to work at some laborious and useful employment; ... it

is sincerely hoped, that the present injudicious mode may be shortly commuted for some other, that will be more conducive of national benefit.[34]

Rather than Nova Scotia, the convicts on board the *Anne-Mary* had been secretly consigned to the merchant house of Stewart and Plunket of Baltimore, Plunket himself being a Dubliner by origin.[35] However, when the ship reached the Virginia Capes in early December 1785, it was met by a pilot boat from Baltimore and taken up Chesapeake Bay and the Potomac River to George-Town, Maryland. On 23 December the convicts were advertised for sale as indentured servants by Nevin in conjunction with a local merchant, Col. William Deakins,[36] in the *Maryland Journal, and Baltimore Advertiser*:

JUST ARRIVED

At George-Town, on Potowmack, the Snow
ANNA MARIA, DUNCAN NEVIN, Master, from DUBLIN

With upwards of 100 MEN and WO-
MEN SERVANTS; among the former are several valuable
Tradesmen, viz. Carpenters, Blacksmiths, Stone-Cutters,
Shoemakers, &c &c. Their indentures will be disposed of on
reasonable terms, for ready Money, by the Subscriber, on board
his Vessel, or at the Store of Mr William Deakins, jun.

DUNCAN NEVIN
George-Town, December 15, 1785.

There was a demand for bonded labour at that time in nearby Virginia where the recently established Patowmack Canal Company was cutting channels for shipping at the Shenandoah and Seneca Falls and a canal to make a connection between the Potomac River and the tributaries of the Ohio River.[37] The most ambitious engineering venture in eighteenth-century America, it was largely the initiative of George Washington who became the Company's first chairman of directors. A major landowner in the Potomac valley, he saw the scheme as opening up the interior to navigation and making possible 'a rising empire'.[38]

By the middle of 1785, the Company was experiencing great difficulties with its workforce of more than one hundred free labourers. Fearful that the payroll would be robbed during the journey from

George-Town to the remote up-river work camps, it antagonised the workers (some of whom were Irish) by withholding their wages.[39] At the 9 September and 18 October meetings of the Company's board at Wise's Tavern in Alexandria, presided over by Washington, it was resolved that since the free labourers had proved to be 'irregular and disorderly in their Behaviour', sixty indentured servants should be purchased from Stewart and Plunket of Baltimore, or from John Maxwell Nesbitt of Philadelphia, as soon as the next shipment arrived.[40] Both firms had close Irish connections and had long been involved in the indentured servant trade.[41]

Subsequently, about ten of the convicts on the *Anne-Mary* were sold as servants by Deakins to one of the Company's directors, Col. John Fitzgerald, at ten guineas a head.[42] What happened to the other ninety is not recorded but they were almost certainly sold off as domestic servants. After taking on a cargo of wheat at George-Town, the ship sailed the following February for Cork and Liverpool with the intention of obtaining another load of convicts at Dublin in April.

Fitzgerald, an Irishman who had served as Washington's secretary and aide de camp during the war, was probably aware of the true identity of the passengers of the *Anne-Mary* but believed that as indentured workers they would be more easily controlled than free labourers had been. However, the fact that he purchased only ten of the sixty that had been authorised to acquire suggests that he had some doubts about them. Washington and his true fellow directors might have been politically embarrassed if their employees' identity became generally known, although he himself had been tutored by an English ex-convict and employed another as a painter at his 'Mount Vernon' estate. In June 1786 he employed an Irish tailor and an Irish shoemaker who had arrived as redemptioners on a later shipment from Cork which did not carry convicts.

At the Potomac works, the servants from the *Anne-Mary* were put to work from 7 a.m. to 5 p.m. each day, regardless of the weather, pulling out tree roots and stumps and shovelling spoil into wheelbarrows and ox-carts.[43] Required to dig a minimum of six cubic feet a day in order to qualify for three gills (about one pint) of rum, they received a daily ration of '1$\frac{1}{2}$lb. of fresh meat or 1$\frac{1}{4}$lb. of salt beef, or 1lb. of salt pork; 1$\frac{1}{2}$lb. of flour or bread ...' and one gill of salt and one of vinegar per week.[44] As indentured servants, they probably did not receive the £2 per month wage paid to free labourers. Accommodation was in crude huts which must have made winter a severe trial.

The greatest hazard of all was the crude black-powder blasting which caused many accidents. Drilling to lay the charges had to be done with hand-augers in solid rock; the holes were often too shallow and the charges of powder too large. In July 1786, Michael Bowman, an Irishman employed as a 'blower' or blaster at the Shenandoah Falls, was severely injured when the charge he had just laid exploded prematurely. According to the *Virginia Journal*, 'His Situation is hardly to be described, having had the Fore part of his Head blown to Pieces, one of his Eyes blown out, and his Breast and Limbs shockingly bruised and mangled'.[45] Miraculously, he survived.

Referring to this case, the original works foreman and manager appointed by Washington, James Rumsey, complained to the Company's treasurer, Hartsborne, about the theft of black powder by the workers:

> We have been much imposed upon the past Two weeks in the powder way. (We had our Blowers, one run off the other Blown up.) We therefore was obliged to to have two new hands put to blowing and there was much attention give to them lest Axedents should happen, yet they used the powder Rather Too Extravangant. But that was not all. They have certainly stolen a Considerable Quantity as we have not more by that will last until tomorrow noon. Our hole Troop is such Villains that we must fore the future give the powder into Charge of a person appointed for the purpose to measure it to them on the ground by a Charger.[46]

The hard and dangerous work, together with harsh treatment by the overseers under the supervision of Richardson Stuart, the new works manager succeeding Rumsey, caused a number of the Irish indentured workers to abscond. Within six weeks of their purchase by the Company, the *Virginia Journal and Alexandria Advertiser* reported that some runaway indentured servants from the *Anne-Mary* had been caught and subjected to a humiliating punishment:

> Alexandria, Jan. 26
> We hear that several Servants who had been purchased to work on the Potomack Navigation, lately ran away, but being soon after apprehended were sentenced to have their Heads and Eye-brows shaved, which Operation was immediately executed, and is to be continued every Week, during the Time of their Servitude, or until their Behaviour evinces that they are brought to a Sense of their Duty. This Notice, it is expected, will sufficiently apprize the Country should they again make a similar Attempt.[47]

13 'Potomac Company President, George Washington, overseeing the construction of the canal at Great Falls, Virginia'. Negro slaves were found to be more
reliable than Irish indentured workers.

The Company subsequently explained that due to the severity of the
weather, only the workers' eyebrows had been shaved and their hair
cut short. 'Should any come under the *shaving Laws* when the Season
becomes milder', it threatened, 'their *Heads* will also suffer'.[48]
Nevertheless, numerous newspaper advertisements by the Company
from May onwards for the return of further absconders[49] indicate that
these and other punishments including flogging had not achieved the
desired effect. According to the published description of runaway
Patrick Ready, 32, in August, 'his eye-brows lately shaved ... and had
on an iron collar when he ran away, and his back much cut for
running away some time ago'. The first of his two companions, Hugh
Maloan [sic], 28, had shaved eyebrows and 'a cross shaved on his head
at the same time ...'. The second, John Crowley, 30, had two damaged
fingers 'and sundry marks of gunpowder on his hands, and a blemish
on his left eye, having been hurt with a shot or blast'.[50] In July, two of
the Company's indentured Irish servants, Robert Meaghan and
Andrew Keating, broke out of gaol after being arrested for robbery and
riot.[51]

The recapture of Ready and a number of other absconders in August
cost the Company the hefty sum of £25,[52] but it chose to reject

allegations of ill-treatment of workers and other complaints made by Rumsey against Stuart that same month. The latter had allegedly been heard to declare that 'Old Convicts make the best of overseers as [they] themselves know what it is to be whipped'.[53]

'A load of serpents'

The revelation that the passengers from the *Anne-Mary* were convicts rather than indentured servants was first made locally by the *Virginia Journal* in mid-July 1786 when it reprinted without comment a report from a concerned correspondent to the *Dublin Volunteer Journal*. Believing that the illicit sending of convicts to America was damaging the 'harmony and trade' between the two countries, the Irish writer described in detail the deception that had been practised by the owner and captain of the *Anne-Mary*.[54] Later that month there was outspoken editorial comment by one of the New York newspapers after it had received the issue of the *Dublin Evening Post* for 22 April reporting the planned despatch of yet another shipload of Irish convicts in the *Charming Nancy*. The *Evening Post* had noted that as the *Anne-Mary* arrived back in Dublin on her return voyage from Baltimore too late to embark the spring cargo of convicts as originally planned, the Lord Mayor of Dublin had chartered another vessel which 'for prudence sake' and 'for fear of discovery' would not take them to the same destination.

Infuriated by this bare-faced deception, the New York newspaper described the system in some detail:

> the *genius* of the Irish nation have struck out a new mode [of transportation] viz. The Mayor of Dublin charters a ship, under the cover of sending out the convicts to Port-Roseway, Halifax, the Bahamas, or elsewhere, places within the limits of British America. The contracting merchant lets his ship for the government allowance of 5£ per head, and the cancelling of which, according to contract, is never looked after when the convicts are disposed of. Instead of going to British America, these desperadoes are run into the United States of America, under the cover of their being indented servants, after a sham form of indenture is made out in the Newgate of Dublin, or the other gaols of that kingdom.[55]

The newspaper asked citizens to watch out for the arrival of more convicts 'and on no account whatever admit them into the United

States'. It urged the different legislatures 'to pass such laws or regulations such as to prohibit such an import of the most wicked and abandoned wretches that can disgrace human nature'.[56] Every ship from Ireland and England carrying servants should be searched and the 'severest penalty, if not seizure of the ship' be laid on those found engaged in the convict trade. Finally, the newspaper expressed its indignation

> that this outrageous and abominable Insult given to an independent country (and which country has hitherto shewn every attention and affection to their Irish brethren) has only been practised from *Ireland!!!*[57]

The *Virginia Journal* of 10 August published a letter from 'A well wisher to good Settlers' also from New York which delivered a similar warning:

> A Gentleman arrived here from Dublin informs and assures us, that a Captain E ---- was about sailing from that place with a load of convicts out of the gaols there, but which the government, it is said, pay him for taking the vermin off. On his arrival in Philadelphia or Baltimore the passengers are to pass by the gentle name of redemptioners. You will have to dread robbers, murders. &c. if they are permitted to land.
>
> Query. Would not the Captain do an equal favor to the States by introducing a load of serpents?
>
> And, query. Ought not the citizens of the place where he so arrives, after inquiry made, and satisfaction obtained of the truth of such villainies, to favor the Captain with a coat of T. and F. &c. [and] send him with vessel and cargo to Nova-Scarcity [*sic*] or the Bahamas?

The New York report was duly reprinted in the *Maryland Gazette* and this, together with the letter, must have caused consternation for the Baltimore and George-Town agents anxious to profit from the renewed trade. Altogether, the newspaper reactions serve as a useful reminder of the conflict between the political pretensions and the economic needs of the young republic. Published in the busy port of Baltimore and serving the interests of its merchants, shipping contractors and captains, the *Maryland Journal* was unlikely to adopt a moralistic stance on what had been (and promised again to be) a profitable trade. The newspaper's owners were probably aware of the true nature of the indentured servants landed from the *Anne-Mary* but were not inclined to offend the merchants who provided most of their advertising revenue by reprinting the New York report. The *Maryland Gazette*, by contrast, was published in Annapolis, the seat of provincial government, and reflected the attitudes of the patriotic lawyers and land-owners who dominated the legislature.

News of the American reaction to Nevin's shipment no doubt reached Dublin by means of American newspapers and the reports of returning ship's captains. On 26 May 1786 the *Hibernian Journal* reminded its readers that the provincial assemblies of Virginia and North and South Carolina had made representations to London sixteen years earlier against the sending over of any more Irish convicts, claiming 'that the country was much better cultivated by negroes, who, in general, are more faithful and honest'.[58] It regretted that Ireland had no colonies of its own to which felons could be sent.

The *Dragon*

In the preceding months, the pressure of overcrowding at Newgate had become even more serious and there were no signs of preparations for another shipment. The *Hibernian Journal* warned that

> The prisons are now so crowded with felons, etc. and with the heat will probably in a few days become so intense, that fevers of the most malignant kind must inevitably ensue, if those who are sentenced to transportation are not immediately shipped off ... Let Government in pity to those wretches who are to remain, and those innocent persons who have occasion to visit them, thin their dreaded habitations, by executing the sentence of the law, as soon as possible, on those fated for banishment.[59]

Although the new Police Act had created a centralised system of transportation under the nominal control of the Lord Lieutenant who now paid the cost, the shipping arrangements were left as before to the Lord Mayor.

By the end of May, seventy convicts sentenced to transportation at different county assizes had been brought down under military escort to Newgate but there was still no news of a ship to take them away. In addition to these, eight of whom were dangerously ill from the epidemic of fever which had swept the prison during the previous week, there were fifty-seven others who had been sentenced to transportation in the Dublin courts. On the night of 30 May, both groups of prisoners were 'exceedingly riotous' and almost succeeded in making a mass escape after boring holes through the inner door of the prison.[60] No doubt it was this, together with the reports of fever, which caused the *Freeman's Journal* to complain that the delay was 'to the imminent danger, not only of their lives, but the lives of the citizens in general'.[61]

Arrangements had in fact been made by Lord Mayor George Alcock with a local shipping contractor for Captain Hamilton of the 150-ton brig *Dragon* of Dublin to take a shipment of 122 convicts to George-Town. Reporting this in mid-June, the *Hibernian Journal* remarked that the vessel was so small that 'it cannot possibly take any other cargo on board, than the victuals and water necessary to support so numerous a crew'.[62] Nevertheless, it seems unlikely that the contractors passed up the opportunity to turn an additional profit from the voyage.

When the 108 men and 14 women, 'all dressed in clean jackets',[63] were taken in separate groups from Newgate to North Wall on 17 June, they were accompanied by a 'regiment' of infantry and two troops of horse to guard against any attempt by the mob to free them. None of their names are recorded, but the Dublin newspapers noted that they included two bailiffs' wives convicted of shop-lifting who 'by grace especial' went by coach.[64] The *Dragon* called at Cork to take on 45 more prisoners before sailing for Alexandria, Virginia, where Hamilton hoped to dispose of his cargo as Captain Nevin had done the previous year.

Eight days out of Cork, there was a mutiny on board in which the second mate and the boatswain joined the convicts with the intention of throwing Hamilton, the supercargo and other officers overboard. However, this was quickly thwarted without loss of life and the mutinous crew members sent back to Bristol in irons on a passing ship. The *Dragon* reached Alexandria in August and, according to a subsequent report in a Dublin newspaper, Hamilton managed to dispose of all the convicts 'in one lump' to John Fitzgerald to work for the Patowmack Canal Company.[65] The Company's own records indicate that in fact it purchased only sixteen men and one woman as servants from the merchant firm of Hooe and Harrison of Alexandria on 23 November[66] and there is no indication of how Hamilton disposed of the others. As another charter member of the Patowmack Company and fellow magistrate for the city, Robert Townshend Hooe would have been closely acquainted with Fitzgerald and was no doubt aware of the Irish servants' convict origins.

These new acquisitions by the Company were no more satisfactory than the previous ones. Of the twenty-five runaways advertised for by the Company in the Maryland and Virginia newspapers between February 1786 and October 1787, no less than twenty were specifically identified as Irishmen and another four had Irish names.[67] There were

Stop the Villain !
RANAWAY, laſt night,
from the ſubſcriber, living near the eaſ-
tern Run, Baltimore County, 17 miles
from Baltimore Town, an *Iriſh Servant
Man*, named MICHAEL BURNS, a ba-
ker by trade, about 22 years of age, 5 feet
6 or 7 inches high, has remarkable black
hair, and is pitted with the ſmall pox ; had on when he went
away, a ſhort blue broadcloth coat, green jacket, blue ſtock-
ings, and new ſhoes, with ſtrings ; has two pair of breeches,
one of which are nankeen ; has lived ſome time in Baltimore-
Town, and was ſold for his priſon fees on the firſt day of March
laſt. He ſerved ſome time near Frederick, or Chambers-
Town, and probably has his old indentures and diſcharge, and
has a certain *Roger Ryan's* paſs, ſigned by *Jeremiah Johnſon*.
Whoever ſecures the ſaid Servant, ſo that I get him again,
ſhall have a Reward of *Thirty Shillings*, and *One Shilling* per
mile, if brought home, paid by
    April 3, 1788.   WILLIAM MATTHEWS.
    N. B. All maſters of veſſels and others, are forewarned
from harbouring, or carrying him off, at their peril.

Ten Pounds Reward.
RANAWAY, from the ſubſcriber, on
Sunday the 20th of the preſent month,
DENNIS HOLLAND, an *indented Iriſh
Servant Man*, about 28 years of age, about 5
feet 6 inches high, thick and ſquare made,
round viſage, ſwarthy complexion, black hair,
eyebrows and beard, bluiſh gray eyes ; he is a
tailor by trade, and has a number of ſcars on his left knee : He
had on and took with him, a white caot, breeches and ſtock-
ings, a ſnuff-coloured cloth coat, a waiſtcoat red and yellow
mixed, with black ſpots in it, a white ſhirt, oznaburg trouſers,
coarſe ſhoes with buckles, felt hat almoſt new, and an old black
ſilk neck handkerchief ; but it is probable he will change his
dreſs. Whoever will apprehend and bring home ſaid runaway,
ſhall, if taken 10 miles from home, receive *Forty-five Shillings* ;
if 20 miles, *Three Pounds Ten Shillings* ; if 40 miles, *Five
Pounds* ; and if out of the State, the above reward, paid by
        C H A R L E S   R I D G E L Y,
        Near the Northampton Furnace, Baltimore County.
    July 22, 1788.
    N. B. All maſters of veſſels, and others, are cautioned
againſt ſecreting or carrying off ſaid runaway.

14 Advertisements in the *Maryland Journal and Baltimore Advertiser* in February and April 1788 for runaway Irish servants.

at least as many advertisements for Irish servants absconding from private employers as there were for negro slaves, some of them accompanied by woodblock illustrations showing a young man fleeing with a stick and spotted handkerchief bundle over his shoulder.[68] Before long, the Company was replacing its indentured workers with slaves.

The *Dispatch*

Although it had been rumoured in Dublin in June 1786 that in future a vessel would be chartered every three months to take convicts away, there was no further shipment that year.[69] A likely reason for this, as we shall see below, is that the Irish authorities expected to be allocated space for some of their convicts in the First Fleet to Botany Bay. When this did not eventuate, two more transports were sent off from Dublin during 1787 through the instrumentality of Lord Mayor George Alcock.[70] On 2 and 3 May, 183 convicts from Newgate, including fifty women, were embarked on the *Dispatch*, Captain Napper, for what the newspapers thought was either America or Botany Bay. On the way to the North Wall, two of the male convicts untied their ropes and jumped out of the prison carts. Forcing their way through the guard 'like desperadoes', one of them managed to escape.[71]

Shortly after the ship's sailing, there was a report in the Dublin newspapers that a mutiny by the convicts a few days out of port was only put down by the decisive action of the captain who shot through the head 'one of the most audacious ringleaders'.[72] Even so, some of the convicts managed to escape to France. A more detailed account of the incident appeared in Cork's *Hibernian Chronicle* in May 1788:

> the convicts ... knocked off their fetters, and soon overpowered the crew; and having afterwards brought the vessel into a French port, went on shore. Three of them who have already returned to this city, and are, no doubt, following their old practice of marauding on the public.[73]

There was an earlier report from Dublin that one of these returnees, a 'noted robber' called Moran, was 'following the old trade' in Co. Kildare.[74]

According to a subsequent Irish newspaper report, when Captain Napper tried to dispose of the remainder of his convicts at the newly established Loyalist settlement of Port Roseway or Shelburne on the southern coast of Nova Scotia, the governor would not allow it and he was forced to land them instead on a remote and uninhabited part of the Bay of Machias where the British colony of New Brunswick bordered the American state of Maine. From there, the story continued, they 'begged' their way south to New England, representing themselves as indentured servants who had been put ashore after suffering from lack of water and provisions.[75] Although there is no record of any attempt to land convicts at Nova Scotia or the Bay of Machias in 1787,[76] Governor John Hancock of Massachusetts wrote to the Continental Congress in a letter of 11 August 1787 that

> a number of persons some probably convicts and all of them people whose maners and conduct will be detrimental to the state have been set on shore in the eastern part of the Commonwealth ... from a brig bound from Ireland to Baltimore.[77]

The brig referred to by Hancock was almost certainly the *Dispatch*.[78] Although Foreign Secretary John Jay appears to have taken no action over his report, the incident certainly alerted Congress to the possibility that there might be similar attempts in the future.

The popular belief in Dublin at the time was that both shipments were bound for America where the Irish were still thought to be welcome because of their sympathy for the Revolutionary cause. Shortly after the departure of the *Dispatch*, a writer in the *Freeman's Journal* suggested that its passengers ought to be well received in the United States:

> Both the ships, which lately received the male and female convicts, have sailed for their ports of destination – not to Botany Bay, as reported, nor to the coast of Africa, but to America, where indeed they ought to receive a welcome, from the infinite use which many of our former transported convicts were of to the American cause, in fighting its battles, and assisting in acquiring its present independency [sic]. It is not improbable, therefore, from the present state of the Western empire, but that the children of some of our late transported gentlemen and ladies will sit in Congress in less than half a century, as it is an indisputable fact, that some former convicts have already obtained that honour.[79]

The *Chance*

On 14 October 1787 the new double-decked brig *Chance* of Barmouth in Wales, commanded by an Irish captain, Patrick Stafford, sailed from Dublin, its officially-stated destinations being Baltimore and Charleston. On board were 92 male convicts, 26 women and about 13 free emigrants. The Dublin newspapers had first reported that they were bound for Africa and subseqently for Port Roseway, Nova Scotia, where they would be 'disposed of amongst the planters in that flourishing settlement'.[80]

Before the free emigrants were embarked on the *Chance* at Dun Laoghaire in Dublin Bay, they each paid the super-cargo, Connor, seven guineas to secure berths as cabin passengers and 'to be allowed Provisions during the Voyage at the Captain's Table'.[81] Connor was in charge of a consignment of linen, porter and coal from which the ship's contractors no doubt hoped to make a substantial profit. For the first month at sea on this longer than normal voyage the cabin passengers were well treated but henceforth they were rationed to a biscuit, half a pint of rum and a pint of water a day. What was given to the convicts is not recorded, but it cannot have been very much because no less than twenty-four of the men were reported to have died on the voyage. The predatory Connor and his crew also relieved the cabin passengers of all their possessions. In particular, Connor took the entire stock-in-trade of James Hamilton, a Dublin jeweller and goldsmith who had hoped to set himself up in business in Charleston or Baltimore after reading the handbills distributed in Dublin by the crafty super-cargo.

On 31 December after almost six weeks at sea, the *Chance* encountered another vessel and Stafford inquired whether the island which was now in sight had any watering place. As it transpired, this was Great Heneaga (Inagua), a desolate and uninhabited island in the Bahamas group. At seven o'clock that night, after the cabin passengers had been forced to remain below during the day with the convicts, Connor had them come on deck ten at a time, putting each group ashore in the ship's boat after telling them that they were at Trinidad. All that they were given by way of sustenance was a salted bullock's heart to be shared between two. Stafford told them that the island was well inhabited with three towns and that they would find plenty of fresh water and fruit. He also said that they would be able to make their way easily from there to any part of America.

When the first party of convicts who had been put ashore discovered that the island was uninhabited and one of the women was told by a sailor that 'they would want Provisions before Cloathing', they decided to make their way back to the ship. Attempting to get into the ship's boat, they were fired on by Connor and one of them, Patrick Cauldfield, was killed before Stafford could call on him to put down his gun. Three hours later, the *Chance* weighed anchor and sailed for Jamaica.

After four or five days without food and bedding and constant attack by 'musketos', the seventy-seven surviving castaways, including several young boys and twenty-four women, some in advanced stages of pregnancy, were rescued by two New England captains. Sailing from his home port of Bermuda, Captain Alboy had noticed the convicts when he ventured closer to shore than usual. Taking them on board, he subsequently landed twenty-three who were seriously ill at the nearby settlement of Long Island and the remainder at New Providence (Nassau) where Governor John Murray, the Earl of Dunmore, had to support them at his government's expense. Some found employment for a time, but 'returning to their old courses' they soon became 'a very great pest' to the inhabitants and a number were prosecuted for various thefts.[82] Amid fears that their continued presence posed a threat to life and property, Dunmore had twenty-four of them committed to gaol by the magistrates in July as 'persons of ill-fame, without any visible means of supporting themselves ...'.[83] Others were no doubt sent to work on Fort Charlotte, the massive fortification (or folly, as many saw it) which Dunmore had commenced in the previous year and where members of the 47th Regiment had been 'living in palmetto huts and dying like flies'.[84]

'A present to the Congress'

Two of the Irish convicts were amongst the fifty or more prisoners liberated from Nassau gaol by Dunmore to accompany William Augustus Bowles on a raiding expedition to Spanish Florida in September 1788. Bowles, a colourful and talented adventurer who had previously served as Director General of the Creek Nation, was apparently involved with some Nassau merchants to put a rival Florida trader out of business. Dunmore subsequently told Grenville that he had released the Irish prisoners to Bowles 'to save expences to the Country as well as to get quit of such abandoned wretches ...'.[85] According to Dunmore, Bowles had promised to land them 'on the Continent' and they had been willing to go. Dunmore also denied having supplied Bowles with arms, ammunition and provisions from the King's stores, although this seems to have been exactly what he in fact did. What happened to the Irishmen when most of Bowles' followers absconded during the expedition is a mystery, although they may have been the two thieves described by him as escaping to the Spanish garrison on the island of St. Augustine.[86]

On 2 June the General Assembly at Nassau had resolved 'that the introduction of Convicts into the Bahamas would be attended with consequences highly prejudicial to the Interests of the Inhabitants'.[87] Dunmore consequently arranged in late July with Captain William Thompson of Nassau to take about twenty of the remaining convicts, together with five local ex-prisoners and the child of one of the women, to Baltimore in the locally-owned schooner *Prince William Henry*. No doubt the governor hoped that they would all be accepted there as indentured servants.

When the schooner arrived at Fisher's Bay, Baltimore, in early August, Thompson managed to land about six of the convicts before the port authorities discovered that the schooner was not properly registered and would not allow it to berth. Thompson protested in vain that he needed a new jib and foresail before he could leave port and that he had no provisions. After his departure, the six convicts were apparently apprehended and sent by the Baltimore justices to Annapolis with a letter to Governor William Smallwood asking whether there was any legislation which would make it possible to eject them from the state.[88] In the words of the *Maryland Gazette*, Thompson and his super-cargo, John Kelso, were 'to take such orders as may be consistent with the safety of the citizens, and the dignity of government, which we think most grossly insulted by Lord Dunmore'.[89]

The Governor of Virginia before the Revolution, Dunmore was an easy target for the American newspapers who gleefully publicised his political problems.[90] The convicts incident was also seized upon by his domestic critics, notably the colony's former Attorney-General, William Wylly. Commenting on Dunmore's flouting of the principle of *habeas corpus* on this occasion, Wylly subsequently recounted in a published attack on his administration how the Irish convicts had been 'sent as a *present to the Congress*'.[91]

As his subsequent letter to them reveals, Governor Smallwood could give the Baltimore justices very little satisfaction:

Annapolis   In Council   August 7. 1788
Gentlemen,
    We have received your Letter of the 6th Aug. and can assure you it gives us infinite concern. We cannot find any Law prohibiting the importation of Convicts or vesting any Person in this Board respecting them so as to justify any Measure that might be devised by us for the Safety of the Inhabitants of the State.

15 The Earl of Dunmore, Governor of the Bahamas, 1786–97.

The last Act relative to Convicts was the Act of 1769 in which Act there is some Kind of Provision made by the Legislature for the security of the Citizens; the Purchaser of a Convict being obliged to recognise in the law of £20 for the good Behaviour of the Felon during the Time for which he was transported. As it does not appear to us that we have any [illeg.] Person to interfere or make any Order respecting these People we have declined doing anything and have ordered the Guard to return with them to Baltimore.

We are &c

W. Smallwood[92]

After spending some days in Annapolis, where they had to be fed and sheltered at government expense, the party of convicts were returned to Baltimore.[93] What subsequently became of them is a mystery, although it seems likely that they ended up as indentured servants.

In the meantime, Thompson had landed all but four of the remaining convicts at the Rapahanok River and gone on to New York and from there to Blandford, near New Haven, where he abandoned the schooner for another vessel about to return to the Bahamas. Left in charge of the *William Henry*, super-cargo Kelso decided to return to New York but fell overboard off Long Island when drunk and was drowned. When the schooner arrived in port in late August its mate, Leonard White Outerbridge, was at a loss what to do. Eventually, however, he was advised by Britain's Consul-General there, Sir John Temple,[94] to make a full deposition of events to the American Foreign Secretary, John Jay.[95]

By early February, the *Chance* had reached Baltimore from the Bahamas and Stafford was advertising in the *Maryland Journal* for a return cargo to Belfast.[96] However, it was altogether the wrong season and after a month of waiting, the ship slipped out of port without a loading. No doubt Stafford was beginning to fear that the news of what had happened in the Bahamas would catch up with him. The departure of the *Chance* was not recorded in the Baltimore newspapers and it subsequently ceased to trade between Ireland and Baltimore. As it happened, however, the first report of the Inagua affair did not appear in the American newspapers until early August.[97]

All that Governor Dunmore could do when Lord Sydney subsequently sought further information from him about the convicts of the *Chance* was to forward the deposition made by the unfortunate Hamilton to the Chief Justice of the Bahamas at Nassau the day after his arrival there. 'We have never been able to make any further Discovery in the matter than what is contained in Hamilton's Deposition' he told the Home Secretary in late February.[98] The cost of providing medicines and food for the castaway convicts had amounted to £160 and Dunmore urged Sydney to have inquiries made in Dublin so that he could 'be informed of the real state of the case ...'.[99] By this

16 Advertisement for the *Chance* in the *Maryland Journal and Baltimore Advertiser*, 1 February 1788.

time, Dunmore's governorship had reached crisis-point. He had suspended the colony's judges in May after a quarrel with them over the question of the Crown's interest and was under constant attack from Wylly.[100] The cost of the upkeep and disposal of the convicts no doubt provided further cause for criticism.

Some half-hearted efforts were made by the Home Office to trace Stafford, Sydney assuring Dunmore that 'the necessary steps will be pursued to bring him to punishment'.[101] However, as Sydney informed the Marquis of Buckingham in August 1788 when forwarding a copy of Hamilton's deposition, the Governor and the Chief Justice 'were totally ignorant of the description of Persons, of which the Passengers on board the *Chance* were composed, or of any other circumstances relating to the matter in question than is contained in the deposition ...'.[102] No inquiry was subsequently held by the Irish authorities into the twenty-four deaths on board the *Chance* before it reached the Bahamas and the fatal shooting of Patrick Cauldfield during the landing at

Inagua. By contrast the Home Office vigorously pursued with Dublin Castle the question of reimbursing the Bahamas government for the costs incurred on account of the convicts.[103] No action was subsequently taken against Stafford for what another captain properly called 'this inhuman piece of villainy'.[104]

When it was finally reported in the *Freeman's Journal* in October 1788, the Bahamas incident had taken on some macabre embellishments. According to six different letters which had been received in Dublin from Irish expatriates in the West Indies, forty-three of the convicts had died on the passage due to 'the allowance of provisions being so very small and disproportionable [sic] to their support'.[105] Half of the remaining fifty or so had 'perished for absolute want' on the island of Inagua where they were landed; and when they were picked up, 'the living were eating the carcasses of the dead ...'.[106]

'A gentle Remonstrance'

The important outcome of the bringing of the convicts to Baltimore in the *Prince William Henry* was a Congressional resolution advising the state assemblies to legislate against further shipments of convicts. When Outerbridge's affidavit was tabled before Congress by Jay on 3 September 1788, he advised members that

> A gentle Remonstrance on this Subject to the Court of London, would probably prevent such an improper Practice in future, as to the present Case, there is Reason to suppose that it arose from the unauthorised Interference of Lord Dunmore.[107]

Praising Temple for his assistance in the matter, Jay tabled before Congress on 16 September a letter he had drafted a few days earlier to Britain's Secretary of State for Foreign Affairs, the Marquess of Carmarthen. Accepting that the shipment had not been officially authorised by the British government, Jay was content to pass on the information. As he told Carmarthen:

> To insist on the impropriety of the practice which that Affidavit will explain, would seem to imply doubts of it's [sic] being considered in that point of light; I forebear therefore to enlarge on that topic, nor can it be necessary to hint that the same principles of honour and delicay should obtain between Nations, and between private Gentlemen. I am directed, My Lord, just to make known this

Business to You. Congress being well persuaded that His Majesty will, on receiving the information, give such orders on the occasion, as the nature of the case may require.[108]

Although Jay clearly intimated to Congress that the matter could be effectively pursued by this diplomatic means, it was nevertheless resolved on the motion of Abraham Baldwin (Georgia), seconded by Hugh Williamson (North Carolina)

That it be and it is hereby recommended to the several states to pass proper laws for preventing the transportation of convicted male-factors from foreign countries into the United States.[109]

As it happened, only the government of Virginia legislated accordingly on 13 November with 'An act to prevent the importation of convicts into this commonwealth ... whereby much injury hath been done to the morals, as well as the health, of our fellow-citizens'.[110] And it was George Mason of Virginia who was responsible for the section of the Constitution empowering the states to levy a tax of ten dollars on all persons imported into America – a clear disincentive to bringing in convicts.[111] Altogether, American opposition to transportation seems to have been more apparent than real. Nevertheless, Jay's letter was taken seriously by the British government, the King himself directing Grenville in July 1789 to tell Buckingham 'not to send any more of these Convicts to the Colonies, as far as depended on him'.[112]

7
Irish Anticipations of Botany Bay

Official Irish interest in alternatives to trans-Atlantic transportation was expressed as early as May 1785, by which time the American government had made clear its unwillingness to see the trans-Atlantic trade renewed. Thomas Orde, the new Chief Secretary brought to Ireland by the Duke of Rutland, wrote to Evan Nepean at the Home Office seeking information on the outcome of the Beauchamp Committee's inquiry into possible sites for a convict colony. 'We labour here under much Inconvenience for the want of effectual Provisions for the same Purpose', Orde told Nepean, 'and I should be most obliged ... that I may be furnished as soon as possible with any Proceeding upon this Subject, that similar Measures may be adopted here'.[1]

As we have seen, the first trans-Atlantic shipment of Irish convicts after the end of the American War had resulted in a massacre at Hierra in the Canaries in December 1784 and further problems in the Leewards. Orde would certainly have heard by May 1785 of Nepean's plan to send convicts to the island of Lemaine in the Gambia River and the blistering criticism of it by Edmund Burke and others in the British House of Commons in March which resulted in the appointment of the Beauchamp Committee.[2] Indeed, he was anxious to embrace any scheme that the Committee recommended. The ability to send off from Ireland at least one shipment of criminals a year underpinned the entire scheme of police and other public order reforms which he was to put through the Irish Parliament during the next three years.

The Police Bill

During the Irish Parliamentary session of 1785, Orde had to abandon legislation creating a commercial union between Ireland and Britain[3] and establishing an official militia as a counter to the Volunteers: an unofficial Protestant militia formed in 1778 in order to defend Ireland from anticipated French attack during the American war but by now the vehicle of radical nationalism. In November, however, he told Prime Minister William Pitt that he was determined to revive the Militia Bill at the next session and to introduce a Police Bill, 'chiefly for the regulation of the Capital'.[4]

The latter was no doubt intended to please Pitt, who had been told by Lord Lieutenant Rutland during the Dublin riots of August 1784 that the city was 'in great measure, under the domination and tyranny of the mob' and that 'the state of Dublin calls loudly for an immediate and vigorous interposition of Government'.[5] In order to reinforce this, His Majesty's ministers told Rutland in January 1786 that 'a police is much wanted in the Capital of Ireland, not much more than in that of Great Britain, and they hope that as the [Irish] Capital is much smaller, the Plan will in proportion be more easy to accomplish'.[6] Pitt's own Police Bill for London, which had been defeated the previous year, was to provide the model for the centralised system of urban policing planned by Orde and Under-Secretary Sackville Hamilton.

The provisions of Ireland's new Police Bill of March 1786 were to some extent a response to newspaper pressure for the reform of Dublin's notoriously corrupt and ineffectual system of parish watch-men.[7] However, they were largely motivated by the government's more pressing need to strengthen the mechanisms of public order in both city and country. The 1784 disturbances in Dublin, which saw the invasion of the Irish House of Commons on 5 April, had left Orde, Attorney-General John Fitzgibbon and other members of the government badly shaken.[8] The outbreak of Rightboy and Whiteboy violence against the collection of tithes in the province of Munster in the same year also demanded prompt action.[9] Subsequent legislation exclusively aimed at suppressing rural insurrection, the Riot Act and the Country Police Act of early 1787, were also premised on the ability of judges and magistrates to order transportation as an alternative to hanging.[10]

Orde and Sackville Hamilton were also determined to improve the organisation of transportation. They were anxious to broaden the range of authorised destinations so that the government would be well placed to take advantage of any new convict settlement on the west African coast or elsewhere that Pitt and his ministers decided on as an alternative to trans-Atlantic transportation. While Orde publicly dis-avowed any wish to have the Bill put through Parliament quickly, his obvious determination to do precisely this only helped to alienate its critics still further.

Part of the formal description of the Police Bill's purpose was 'for the more expeditious Transportation of Felons ...' and the immediately relevant sections were prefaced with a reference to Rightboy and Whiteboy violence:

> whereas great outrages are daily committed in many parts of this kingdom by desperate persons who assembled in great numbers, and strongly armed, forcibly and without any title, take and with-hold the possession of houses and lands, and oppose the execution of process of the law for giving or quieting such possession, in defiance of the civil power.[11]

The Bill authorised the transportation of anyone convicted of forcible possession and related agrarian crimes, and of anyone else found guilty of other offences punishable by transportation 'either to any of his Majesty's plantations or settlements in America, or to such other place or places not in Europe as such judges repectively shall order or direct ...'.[12] The broadened formula spelled out here meant that Irish convicts could be sent to whichever new destination the British government decided upon as an alternative to the American colonies, whether it was Africa, Nova Scotia, Botany Bay or anywhere else. To this extent, it followed the British enabling act of 1784 which re-established transportation without fixing any specific destination.[13]

In Section LXVII, the Bill also acknowledged the problems encountered by local authorities in arranging transportation, particularly since the outbreak of the American War:

> whereas the laws in being are not sufficient to provide for the speedy transportation of felons under sentence, rule, or order of transportation, and from the difficulty of procuring ships and vessels trading to his Majesty's plantations to convey such felons thereto, the several counties in which such felons have been convicted and confined, have been at considerable expence in the support and maintenance of such felons during their confinement, and in the transmission of such persons to the sea-ports from which they have been transported, and in contracting for their transportation.[14]

Accordingly, control of all arrangements for transportation were henceforth to be placed in the hands of the Lord Lieutenant, 'or chief governor or governors', with the optimistic stipulation that there would be a maximum of four shipments a year. In another important departure from past practice, the whole of the cost was henceforth to be borne by the Irish government rather than local authorities such as Dublin Corporation.

Nevertheless, when the Bill was given its first reading in the Irish House of Commons on 20 March by John Fitzgibbon, he did not make a single reference to the provisions relating to transportation. His main emphasis was on the reorganisation of the police in Dublin, with crimes such as forcible possession being mentioned only at the end of his speech. 'It creates no new offence', the *Freeman's Journal* commented approvingly on the Bill, 'nor does it enact any new punishment; it seems to be [designed] to enforce the existing laws, agreeable to the spirit of the constitution'.[15]

Most of the criticism of the Bill in Parliament by the Patriot opposition, which was virulent in the extreme, focused on what was seen to be its strengthening of the executive government at the expense of Dublin Corporation and other local authorities – and indeed the sovereignty of the Irish Parliament itself. In short, it was represented as being entirely contrary to the spirit of the new constitution of 1782. Henry Grattan, for example, attacked the Bill as 'the most obnoxious and alarming that ever, perhaps, arrested the attention of the Irish senate'.[16] Its provision for the direct appointment of police commissioners by the Castle was also represented as part of the executive government's practice of buying political support through places and pensions. In short, it was 'a bill of armed patronage'.[17]

On the other hand, there was nothing controversial in the transportation provisions and there were only two references to them during the entire debate. The first was a whimsical complaint by the member for Askeaton, Co. Limerick, Richard Griffith, that 'While the Bill was reading I thought myself transported back to Indostan [*sic*], and that I was listening to an edict of the Great Mogul to regulate the city of Delhi'.[18] The more serious reference was by Godfrey Greene, MP for Dungarvan, Co. Waterford, who observed that the clauses relating to transportation 'went to remedy an inconvenience very much felt in every county of Ireland, the difficulty of transporting felons'.[19] Although a number of amendments were made at the committee stage, none of the provisions relating to transportation was challenged.

The weak link in Orde's scheme was that the Irish authorities were still dependent on the agreement of the Home Office and British colonial governors in order to implement transportation. As the *Hibernian Journal* observed a month after the Police Bill received the Royal Assent in April:

> It is a peculiar defect in our criminal laws, that the sentence of transportation cannot be specified with respect to place, as we are possessed of no colonies, where such vagabonds might be useful.[20]

The other weak link was that the government was totally dependent on the Lord Mayor of Dublin to make the physical arrangements for transportation until a measure of responsibility was assumed by the Home Office in late 1790. Ireland had no naval establishment of its own which could assist in procuring suitable shipping from elsewhere. For the time being, Irish convicts continued to be sent to north American and Caribbean destinations for which Irish trading interests could make shipping available.

The Botany Bay announcement

The formal announcement in the King's Speech at Westminster on 23 January 1787 that the government was to establish a convict settlement at an unspecified location[21] had been anticipated for some time by the Dublin newspapers. They were aware by September 1786 from the London press reports that the site chosen was Botany Bay and quickly expressed the hope that the Irish authorities would avail themselves of this welcome opportunity to relieve the pressure on the city's gaols.

Nor did the first news suggest that the Botany Bay project would be very expensive. According to a London report of 20 September, reprinted in the *Freeman's Journal*, the British government had managed to take up 1,500 tons of shipping 'at the small price' of £7 per ton. This was said to be due to an arrangement with the East India Company which provided that after unloading their convicts the ships would carry home tea from China at £10 per ton. Indeed, it seemed to offer an ideal solution:

> This makes a very considerable saving to the Company, and by this mutual compact, the new colony will be annually recruited with our convicts, at a moderate expence [sic] to the nation.[22]

Towards the end of September, the *Hibernian Journal* published a glowing but almost certainly bogus account of Botany Bay by a man called Crewis, a Bristol merchant who claimed to have been there with Cook on the *Endeavour* in April 1770 and was now hoping to be sent out in charge of convicts.[23] In early October, the *Hibernian Journal* reported that 'Captain Philips [*sic*]' had been appointed commodore of the squadron which would take with it 700 male convicts and 150 women to Botany Bay.[24] A week later, the *Freeman's Journal* thought that 'It would save much trouble and expence [*sic*] if those sentenced to transportation throughout the kingdom were sent off in a vessel from this part to join the little fleet destined for Botany Bay. ...'[25]

Despite the universally condemnatory and dismissive descriptions by the Dublin press of the convicts despatched in earlier shipments to the Americas, the *Freeman's Journal* now believed for some unaccountable reason that most of those to be sent to Botany Bay would be 'young, healthy and active, filled by acuteness for industry and manufacture, and by age and constitution for the purposes of population'.[26]

The *Hibernian Journal* was enthusiastic about the reformatory potential of the scheme:

> Sending the convicts to Botany Bay is the most rational plan which has yet been found out, for disposing of the many hundreds who are annually committed to prison. For if there are any, and we hope there are, who have been driven by their distresses to thieving, and are not hardened in criminality, they will have an opportunity to regain, by industry and good behaviour, that character which it is impossible for them to attain in this country. As for the expence [sic] to Government, it is trifling, and were it not so, the urgency of the case is great. There are many thousands of poor wretches in the metropolis, who have no other means of subsistance [sic] but those which bring them to an untimely end.[27]

It also saw Botany Bay as the only effective punishment for petty offenders, and one which would act as a deterrent to others:

> The simple mode of punishment used in this country for petty offences will never deter the profligate and abandoned from their mal practices [sic], there being no medium between the halter and whipping, many escape through the lenity of the prosecution. The scheme of sending convicts to *Botany Bay*, we trust, will operate to the advantage of this country, as nothing but annihilation or transportation can prevent us being subject to the depredations of the hardened ruffian.[28]

The same newspaper reported in November that Irish convicts would indeed join the fleet of nine vessels already being prepared in England for the expedition to New South Wales. Seeds, agricultural implements and two years' provisions were being supplied, it revealed, 'but as the soil contains fifteen feet of black vegetable mould, it is thought, that in so luxurious a spot in the South latitude ... two harvests a year may be accomplished'.[29] It was also believed that Captain William Dampier's earlier description of New Holland as a 'naked land full of swamps, and the natives the most wretched of the human kind' must have been based on experience of another part of the continent. Captain Cook's account of the natives as 'scarce removed beyond the brutal condition' was not dissimilar to Dampier's, but he had given 'a luxuriant description of Botany Bay; says the land is fine, the woods free from bush or thorn, and the verdure abundant as the most temperate climate'.[30]

'Such acute beings'

Unlike the British press, which had published since September 1786 a number of letters from readers expressing serious misgivings about the Botany Bay scheme,[31] there was litle thought given by the Dublin newspapers and their readers to the destructive impact that convicted criminals might have upon the indigenous inhabitants of New South Wales. As we shall see, it was not until mid-1789 that the first public doubt was expressed in Ireland about the justice and wisdom of the entire proceeding.[32] Despite its deprecating attitude towards previous shipments of convicts, the *Hibernian Journal* asserted in November 1786 that their despatch to Botany Bay could only be for the best: 'though the inhabitants are in the most savage state, such acute beings as compose the body of convicts must make a greater progress of improvement among them in a year, than rude society could accomplish in centuries'.[33]

The *Freeman's Journal* saw the plan as being beneficial in a number of other ways to all the peoples of the Pacific islands, as well as to the needs of British shipping:

> The expedition to Botany Bay comprehends more than the mere banishment of our felons; it is an undertaking of humanity; for in all the islands of the South Seas there is not a four-footed animal to be found but the hog, the dog and the rat, nor any of the grain of the other quarters of the world, living merely on the bread-fruit tree and the cocoa nut ... by the number of cattle now sending over of

various sorts, a capital improvement will be made in the Southern part of the new world, and our ships which may hereafter sail
in that part of the globe, must receive refreshments in greater
plenty than from the exhausted soil of Europe, considering that all
New South Wales is formed of a virgin mould, undisturbed since
creation.[34]

Interest in the newly discovered Sandwich Islands (Hawaii), stimulated by a highly popular pantomime representation in Dublin's
Smock-alley theatre of Cook's death there in 1779, even encouraged
one writer in the *Freeman's Journal* to suggest that because of the
islands' wonderful fertility, it 'would be a fine spot to form a colony'.[35]
However, there was no suggestion this time that colonisation would
benefit the natives. Athough Hawaii boasted 6,000 fighting men, 'what
could such a number of savages, uninformed of the use of firearms, do
against 1000 convicts with European arms, if sent to that happy [sic]
island?'[36] A similar scheme was to be offered two years later to William
Pitt by an impoverished young law student called Theobald Wolfe
Tone then living in London.[37]

Apart from the mention of facilities for British shipping in the southern
hemisphere, there was no reference by the Dublin newspapers to the
economic advantages that a settlement in New South Wales might bring
to Ireland. The *Freeman's Journal* was aware of the benefits to Britain of
trade with India and China, but Dublin merchants were still oriented
towards continental Europe, North America and the Caribbean and there
was little if any commercial interest in the East Indies and beyond.

It was anticipated by the Dublin newspapers that by the spring of
1787, ships would have conveyed convicts from Dublin and Cork to
join the main British fleet bound for Botany Bay. The only problem the
Hibernian Journal could foresee was that because prisoners awaiting
transportation to Botany Bay would have to be detained for some time
in Dublin's Newgate prison until ships became available, the city's rate-
payers would bear most of the additional cost, amounting to three-
pence per day for each prisoner. It consequently suggested that in the
meantime they be found employment 'suitable to their different capa-
cities, and the avocations they had been originally intended for', half
their earnings to be given to them as an incentive.[38]

By early January 1787, however, hopes that Irish convicts would be
part of the first fleet to Botany Bay must have been dampened by the
publication of reports from London that it was likely to sail later that
month. While details were given of the civil and military establishment

which would accompany it, there was no reference to any Irish involvement.[39] In a final attempt to be optimistic, the *Freeman's Journal* suggested that the expedition would 'touch at Cork to take in the Irish felons'.[40]

'The Mixture and probable cross of Breeds'

Although Thomas Orde had expressed keen interest in the outcome of the Beauchamp Committee's deliberations on the siting of a convict settlement, it was from newspaper reports rather than from the Home Office that the Irish authorities learnt of the British government's Botany Bay decision. There is no record of Orde's reaction to the Committee's less than enthusiastic recommendation in July 1785 that Das Voltas Bay was the most suitable site in Africa, although he no doubt assumed that the scheme would go ahead. The widening of provisions for transportation in Ireland's new Police Act in March 1786 reflected his confidence that the Irish government would be allowed to participate in the new scheme when it was finally decided upon, whether it was to be located in Africa or somewhere else.

When the first news of the Botany Bay decision was revealed in the Dublin press in late September 1786, Lord Lieutenant Rutland immediately asked Sackville Hamilton, who was acting in Orde's absence, to write to Nepean for detailed information. Hamilton accordingly asked Nepean to be 'informed of the Nature of the Undertaking that if it be possible a similar Mode may be adopted here or some Advantage taken of that adopted in England so that the Transportation of Convicts from this Kingdom may be rendered more effectual'.[41]

In his reply to Hamilton of 24 October, Nepean merely copied the original Botany Bay proposal, now well known to Australian historians as 'Heads of a Plan', which had been sent to the Admiralty in July that year, but tactfully omitting the final paragraph referring to the possible cultivation of flax.[42] Nepean no doubt realised that if it were included, Irish linen manufacturers would be alarmed at the future prospect of antipodean linens competing with their own in the British market.

Nor did Nepean make any mention of the possibility that the Botany Bay scheme might also be made available for the despatch of Irish convicts, but this was something that Hamilton was quick to raise with him. In another letter to Nepean of 2 November acknowledging receipt of the 'Heads of a Plan', he wrote:

It would be of infinite Service to the Police of this Country if the Convicts under Rule of Transportation might be transmitted at

Portsmouth to take their Fate with the offenders from Great Britain under the like sentence; and I believe that his Grace [the Lord Lieutenant] intends to make Application upon this Subject to Lord Sydney.[43]

Orde, who was taking the waters at Bath after an exhausting Parliamentary session in Dublin, also raised this 'subject of much importance' just a week later in a private letter to Nepean. He inquired as to the date of departure of the 'Expedition' to Botany Bay and suggested, with a touch of wry but prophetic humour, that an Irish contingent might form a useful addition:

May we not be allowed to join it with a good number of *Adventurers* from the other side of the Water? Or, which wd. be best of all, could not the Commodore touch at Corke in his way out and take on board some of his Ships the Colonists, with whom we shall be able to furnish him? They shall be ready for him there, and the Establishment will certainly be improved by the Mixture and probable cross of Breeds.[44]

In all likelihood, Orde had a broader interest in the Botany Bay proposal than the two viceroys under whom he served and the senior officials who succeeded him. As Government Secretary sitting in Dublin Castle, law and order and the associated problems of police reform and transportation were his responsibility. However, it is important to remember that in 1781 in his previous role as a Westminster MP he had been elected to the secret committee on India. Further, as under-secretary and treasury secretary in Lord Shelburne's government he had developed an intimate knowledge of the India trade. There is no direct evidence that he saw Botany Bay in the context of Britain's commercial interests in the East, but it is unlikely that his enthusiasm for the project was derived solely from the need to rid Ireland of its convicts. True to his position as Government Secretary, his basic political loyalty was to London.

For its part, the Irish government was not interested in the India and East India trade and it is highly unlikely that Botany Bay fitted in with any of its economic plans. In February 1791, the Patriot opposition called for an end to the East India Company monopoly, claiming that 'by an East India trade, riches have flowed into Great Britain, and if we are to carry on a trade to the east, the consequence would be, that riches in a short period of time would flow into the kingdom'.[45] Government speakers argued that Ireland could not afford a trade with the prospect of such slow profits and the strong likelihood that her goods would not be acceptable anyway in that part of the world.[46] However, there was no real likelihood of Irish traders looking in that direction and the Patriots were more interested in political point-scoring than in fostering commerce.[47]

In his own despatch on the subject of transportation to Lord Sydney in mid-December 1786, Rutland made Orde's private suggestion to Nepean about Botany Bay a formal request, pointing out that with the implementation of the new Police Act, there were now no legal object-ions to the hundred or so Irish convicts currently under sentence of transportation in Dublin 'being sent to any Place out of Europe that Government may think proper'.[48] Indeed, he was prepared to send them to Plymouth – or any other British port – to join the fleet for Botany Bay, and to bear the cost of their transportation there:

> The effectual Execution of Public Justice respecting such Felons appears to me of such great Importance, as well for the Example as the Security of the Community, that whatever expence may prop-erty be induced for their Transportation, ought ... to be borne by this Kingdom, and I shall therefore be ready to take the necessary steps for reimbursing such Proportion of Charge as Ireland ought to be liable to in the sending her Criminals Abroad upon the same Footing as England does.[49]

By the end of 1786, Dublin's magistrates certainly seem to have believed that transportation to Botany Bay was a sentencing option which they could now exercise as an alternative to capital punishment and hard labour. On 7 December the *Freeman's Journal* reported that two robbers under sentence of death in Kilmainham who had been respited by the Lord Lieutenant 'have since been pardoned on con-dition of being transported to Botany Bay with the rest of the convicts'.[50] And on 11 December at the Dublin City quarter sessions held at the Tholsel, the Recorder or chief magistrate, Denis George,[51] sentenced no fewer than fourteen people 'convicted of various felonies' to be transported to Botany Bay.[52] The *Freeman's Journal* even reported satirically at the time that several of these convicts had petitioned the government that a murderous robber known as 'Scotch Andrew' who had recently been caught should not go with them. They thought their company 'much too good, and even Botany Bay itself much too favourable for such a monster of villainy and savage bloodshed'.[53]

One of the first to have his life saved by a reprieve of the death sentence 'on condition of transportation for life to Botany Bay' was Anthony Cunningham, who had originally been sentenced to be hanged at Newgate on 11 November 1786.[54] Cunningham was a member of an active and well-known criminal family in Dublin: his elder brother, Thomas, was a 'notorious' thief who had been hanged at St Stephen's Green eight years earlier to the very day of Anthony's conviction at the Commission of Oyer and Terminer on 27 October.[55] Described as 'a most desperate and daring robber' by the newspapers, Anthony had been found guilty by the jury of robbing James Magrath at Summerhill on 29 July of 'a pinchbeck watch and seals, value five pounds sterling.' Refusing his request for a 'long day' – an appeal to the Court of King's Bench for a stay of sentence – the Chief Justice, Lord Earlsfort, pronounced the death sentence 'in so solemn and awful a manner, as affected very forcibly every person present'.[56] Although the evidence against Cunningham had been unsatisfactory, he could not produce a character witness and the jury appears to have convicted him more on the basis of his assumed involvement in other crimes. He had also been indicted for having, in the company of a 'notorious robber' called Whelan (who was subsequently hanged in Co. Wicklow), 'snapped' a pistol early one morning at one of the police guard in Gardiner's Row, Dublin.[57]

The suspicions about Anthony Cunningham were shown to be entirely justified when he was granted a late reprieve of execution in return for his 'discoveries' concerning a gang of house-breakers and robbers with whom he had been involved. A few days before he was due to be hanged, one of his comrades handed over to Gaoler McKinley of Kilmainham no less than £5,000 worth of bonds, banknotes and securities which the expert gang had stolen from Prime Serjeant (*puisne* judge) Brown while he was asleep. This delicate and well-organised operation had involved entering his house in Sackville-street (now O'Connell Street) in the early hours of the morning. The postilion had let the gang into the courtyard where one of them was able to enter a window by means of a ladder, taking a key from clothes in the bedroom where the judge lay asleep and opening an *escritoire* in which he kept his valuables.[58]

It seems very likely that the respited Cunningham was transported instead to Cape Breton Island, Nova Scotia, in October 1788. He was probably also the brother of James Cunningham who was sent off on the *Duke of Leinster* to the Leeward Islands in November 1789[59] and of John Cunningham, a well-known Dublin criminal and returnee who was executed at Kilmainham together with George Robinson and another colleague in September 1792. Another returnee with whom Anthony Cunningham had been associated, Obadiah Davis, was convicted in December 1789 and transported for seven years to New South Wales on the *Queen* in April 1791.

James Cunningham may, like William Dalton, have returned from Antigua in the Leewards and been convicted once again: a James Cunningham, 40, and a John Cunningham, 24, were listed in the indent for the *Queen* transport in March 1791 as having been convicted in Dublin in June 1790 and sentenced to seven years' transportation.[60] This John Cunningham may well have been the son of the John Cunningham executed at Kilmainham a year later.

Satirical anticipations

In a light-hearted anticipation of the civil and military contingent soon to be sent to Botany Bay, the *Freeman's Journal* in December 1786 published a satirical report listing an *Irish* Establishment for the new colony under the command of Castle Under-Secretary, James Sackville Hamilton. Written in the same mock-heroic style as reports of the 'Kingdom of Dalkey' invented a few years earlier by the editor of Dublin's *Morning Post* in his 'Dalkey Gazette' column[61] and celebrated each year by a well-attended ceremonial coronation of the 'King of Dalkey', it amounted to a thinly-veiled roll-call of some of the better-known and even notorious Dublin personalities of the day. While senior Castle official Sackville Hamilton was cast in the role of 'Chief Governor', Patrick Fay was styled 'Archbishop of Botany (the *former*)'. The radical M.P. for Enniscorthy, Sir Edward Newenham, became 'Commander in Chief' and the eccentric Lord Mountmorres, 'Lord High Treasurer':

INTELLIGENCE EXTRAORDINARY

As the state of Botany Bay, and the formation of a new colony, seems at present to occupy the mind of the public, it must be pleasing to hear it is become a measure of the utmost attention, and is to be regulated by gentlemen of the most remarkable abilities, and which is the more necessary, as it is to be colonized by transports and party adventurers. It must be satisfactory to find, that preparations are accordingly making to establish this settlement, which, no doubt, will be productive of the most advantageous consequences.

This new colony, much more extensive than England, Ireland and Scotland, being possessed of the richest soil, and enjoying the greatest salubrity of air, and healthful situation, requires only the hand of man to make it the most fertilized spot in the universe. It is with satisfaction our correspondent mentions the following gentlemen are reported to fill such *ostensible* employments. Their well-known integrity and purity of conduct must do credit to the Government of Botany Bay.

Chief Governor – Sir J.S. H--lt--n,
Deputy Governor – Sir R. P--lm--n,
Field Marshal of the Colony – C-p-l M-ll-r,
Commander in Chief – Sir E. N-----,
Lord High Treasurer – Lord M--ntm-rr-s, (a place he could not obtain in England, Ireland or Scotland,)
Secretary of State – Captain T. B-gg-t,
Accountant General – Bob B-rch,
Primate and Metropolitan – the Rev. H.P.Q.,
Archbishop of Botany (the *former*) – the Rev. Pat. Fay,
Dean of Ditto – Rev. Dr. S-p--e,
Chancellor of the Exchequer – Coun. S-ha--n,
Attorney General – H. Ch----ne,
Solicitor General (in *half-crown* causes) – Francis Br. B-d--y,
Speaker of the House of Transport – Fr. Sp---ng,
President of the NEW Court of Conscience – Lord Viscount S--f--d,
Pawnbroker in Botany and Usurer General – Ed. G--g--n, Esq.,
Inspector-General of Buildings, Gravel-seller, and Comptroler of the Kitchen – J. H--t--b,
Master of Horse – Lord C--l--n,
Clerk of the Buttery – Lord C---l---n,
Poet Laureat – D. Gilburne,
Master of the Revels and Theatrical Manager – General Hughes, F.R.S.L.L.D.[62]

A further 'report' in January 1787 was in the form of an extract from the *Botany Bay Gazette Extraordinary*, said to have been recently received from New South Wales:

His Excellency Sir J--- S--- H--- had his levee, at which he was attended by Sir R--- P--- B---ch Esq. and the other state officers. We learn from Ireland, that James Sh--t-n, Esq; Counsellor at Law, has declined the office of Chancellor of the Exchequer in this state, having engaged himself to the completion of that learned, eloquent and laborious work, the *Companion of the Laws*.

The Solicitor in half-crown causes, F. B--- B--die, has returned to Ireland, having found leisure, from his employment here, to complete a work, for which, in his studies of that academy, he was perfectly calculated, namely, the complete Newgate Solicitor: He has also promised to publish the Accomplished Pawnbroker. He has, likewise, some love epistles (not after the manner of Abelard and Eloise) between Lothario and Calista. His Excellency, considering the great utility of these works to all of Europe, has given Mr. B---die leave of absence for six months.

On Thursday last, being the birth-day of his Excellency, an ode, set to music after the manner of the celebrated Volunteer's hornpipe, was presented at State House. It was written and composed by Dr. Gilb--n, except that verse which is to the air of 'Will you come to the circuit, my pretty miss?' which was written by Counsellor Sh---han, who was good enough to send it from Ireland to Dr. G----n. Such a happy intercourse between men of genius, learning and abilities, cannot be too much applauded and admired.[63]

The *Gazette Extraordinary* went on to list 'Promotions Extraordinary'. Amongst these, J. Napper Tandy, the flamboyant municipal politician and Dublin Volunteers commander of artillery, had been made 'Master of the blind ordnance', the journalist Jack Stevens 'Compiler of news and Gazette intelligencer' and Captain Marsh 'Gentleman Usher to the Female convicts'.[64]

Entering into the 'Kingdom of Dalkey' spirit, *Walker's Hibernian Magazine* for December 1786 and February 1787 also entertained its readers with two mock-serious reports from Botany Bay's 'House of Assembly', illustrated with a well-executed etching entitled 'The first Parliament of Botany Bay in high debate'.[65] First produced in London in 1784 to mark the fall of Lord North's government the previous December,[66] the anonymous etching in the style of Rowlandson depicts Lord North, Charles James Fox, Edmund Burke and other notables of the defeated coalition exiled in the political wilderness of Botany Bay. While North slumbers, Burke holds up a crucifix in parody of his liberal attitude to Catholic Emancipation and Fox's gaze seems fixed on a corpse hanging from a tree above him. Gathered beneath the tree where a leg-chained Speaker is installed in the fork, these worthies of the British Parliament are fringed by a crowd of armed ruffians

The first Parliament *of* Botany Bay *in High Debate.*

17 '*The first* Parliament *of* Botany Bay in *High Debate*'.

representing Fox's notorious Westminster electors. In the background a number of gallows are depicted, complete with dangling corpses.

Published at least two years before the Botany Bay decision was made, the cartoon was originally intended purely as a satire on contemporary British politics. Reprinted by *Walker's Hibernian Magazine* three months after the decision had been revealed in the press and at a time when Irish participation was assumed, it took on a new level of meaning. Relocated at Botany Bay, Lord North's government debated a subject of considerable relevance both to Ireland and the new colony – the role and purpose of an established or state church. This question had been raised by the Bishop of Cloyne, Richard Woodward, in December 1786 in his influential pamphlet *The Present State of the Church of Ireland* ... which helped spark off Dublin's 'Paper War' of the next three years.[67]

According to the mock-report of proceedings, the first resolution put to the *al fresco* Parliament at Botany Bay by the 'secretary to the executions', Mr Ketch, was reimbursement to the state of the cost of hangman's halters used in no less than thirteen executions for murder already carried out in the infant colony. Opposing this and suggesting instead the multiple use of the same halter, 'Father Luke' (most likely the protectionist MP for Co. Dublin, Luke Gardiner, later Lord Mountjoy) stressed the need for 'oeconomy' in view of the destruction of the colony's hemp plantations and the burning of the 'rope manufactury' by 'insurgents' in the previous year. This, together with the expected arrival of another fleet of transports from England, led him to predict that 'the demand for halters would encrease [sic] considerably'.[68]

In the guise of 'Mr Reynard', Fox advocated the institution of an established church in the colony, regardless of its denomination, in the belief that religion was a 'political law' necessary for the coercion of weak minds. 'Regularity and honour', he insisted, were as necessary among thieves as among honest men, for without principles to cement individuals to one common interest, a state would never subsist. He 'knew of no means so conducive to political union as religious influence'.

While he was supported by 'Mr Congreve' (most likely the military department under-secretary and brother of the dramatist, Charles Francis Sheridan[69]), Reynard's cynical views were strongly attacked by 'Lord Blaze', a thinly disguised George Gordon whose outspoken opposition to Catholic 'relief' had precipitated serious riots in London in June 1780.[70] Advocating the establishment of the Church of Scotland as the colony's state church, Lord Blaze's peroration caricatured conservative Scottish Presbyterian intolerance not only towards Catholics but the hapless indigenes of New South Wales if they refused to become good Presbyterians:

Who could doubt his religious principles? many of the colonists had benefited by their practice. He had associated with the faithful in their vindication. He had congregated and headed tag, rag, shag and bobtail, to vindicate them. From principles of freedom he had liberated debtors; from sentiments of honesty he had set thieves free; from motives of religion he had burned down chapels, and for the honour of God, and the good of their souls, he had persecuted the papists. He had not put his candle under a bushel – it had blazed out like the sun at noon day; it had brought down fire upon the modern Gomorrah – consuming her great buildings, and the habitations of her mighty men, which sent forth flames like so many volcanos, causing anguish, bitterness, and gnashing of teeth among her inhabitants. This was the *religion* which he thought most proper for the colonists of *Botany Bay*, living as they did in [sic] the neighbouring savages, ignorant of Christianity, and whom, if they refused to embrace the *pure faith*, as dictated by the kirk of *Scotland*, should be harrowed up, root and stem, and *extirpated* with *fire* and *sword* from the face of the earth.

Awakened by Lord Blaze's declamation, Lord North in the guise of 'Lord Boreas' revealed that he did not believe religion to have played any significant part during his time in government and that it would be a mistake to authorise an established church in the colony:

> to attempt the establishment of any particular system, would be only to lay the foundation of future dissension, and lead some future incendiary ... to attempt destroying the peace and harmony of the settlement.[71]

Altogether, the fictional debates of this first Botany Bay Parliament provided an ironically prophetic anticipation of subsequent events: the effective disestablishment of the Church of England in New South Wales by Burke's nephew, Governor Sir Richard Bourke, fifty years later and Australian historians' arguments about the significance of flax in the Botany Bay decision.

Pressure on the gaols

The prospect of Botany Bay must have become increasingly attractive to the Dublin authorities as overcrowding placed further pressure on the city's two main gaols during 1786 and 1787. In May 1786, even before country prisoners were brought down to the capital in the expectation that they would soon be removed by ship, a spell of hot weather had given rise to fears of 'fevers of the most malignant kind ...'.[72] The *Hibernian Journal* implored the authorities to do something quickly:

> Let Government in pity to those wretches who are to remain, and those innocent persons who have occasion to visit them, thin their dreadful habitations, by executing the sentence of the law, as soon as possible, on those fated for banishment.[73]

By early June, there were fifty-seven prisoners under sentence of transportation in Newgate from the city's quarter sessions and a further seventy who had been sent down from the county prisons, eight of whom were 'dangerously ill'. On the previous Monday, both the city and country convicts proved exceedingly riotous, and were nearly effecting their escape, having bored holes through the inner doors of the prison, and broke them in, but [for] the vigilance of the keepers, who are employed night and day in watching them.[74]

In January 1787, five prisoners attempted to escape from Kilmainham but were captured and sentenced to death for what had recently been made the capital offence of gaol-breaking.[75] Serjeant (judge) Toler 'expatiated with much energy on the atrociousness of the act, and intimated that it was necessary to make examples, in order to enforce a due obedience and submission, in prisoners, to the laws of the land'.[76] Nevertheless, their sentence seems to have been commuted to transportation.[77] In June there was another attempt, the prisoners managing to break down the wall of their cell with a crowbar and other tools which had been passed to them through the gratings. They were just about to break into Gaoler McKinley's own room when the alarm was given and they were secured.[78]

Conditions in Dublin's four marshalseas or debtors' prisons also prompted escape attempts. In early January 1787 when the police entered the City Marshalsea to arrest and convey to Newgate two sisters who had grievously assaulted a fellow prisoner, the other prisoners broke open the doors and almost tore down the walls for bricks to throw at them. As a consequence, one prisoner was killed and the gaol was left 'a scene of destruction which can be scarcely conceived or imagined'.[79]

The committal in May of fourteen more debtors to the City Marshalsea, 'where there was not a vacant corner before', led the *Hibernian Journal* to express concern about the likelihood of disease breaking out there with the advent of warmer weather:

thus many persons of reputation and advantage to the community, must fall sacrifice to contagion, whilst hundreds of felons of every description of infamy are daily transporting to a land of health and liberty. Pray whose [life] is most eligible, that of the felon or poor debtor?[80]

Later that month the Lord Chief Justice, Lord Earlsfort, who had just completed a tour of inspection of the city's gaols, told the Dublin Grand Jury that they demanded urgent attention, the horrors of some being 'shocking to humanity'. The City Marshalsea was an hovel dreadful to imagination, a number of persons huddled together without even a little straw to lie on, surrounded by noisome stenches ... yet even this was nothing when compared to the state of the Bridewell.[81]

Others described it as 'worse than the black hole of Calcutta'.

'Petticoat miners'

Another incident which focused public attention on Dublin's gaols during 1787 took place in September when a number of women prisoners at Newgate were detected completing a tunnel 'about the size of a coal vault hole' under the walls and nine feet towards the potato market immediately outside the prison. These 'petticoat miners', working with no tools except an old poker and 'the indefatigable execution of their hands', had carefully disposed of the spoil in the sewer and concealed the entrance to their tunnel with a large flagstone. Indeed, they were very close to success when one of their number 'peach'd' on them.[82] *Walker's Hibernian Magazine* observed that 'perhaps so astonishing an exertion was never made by a set of females in any gaol in Europe'; and the *Freeman's Journal* suggested that King George should lend 'this chosen band of Irish female miners' to his cousin, the *Staatholder*, to undermine the foundations of the city of Utrecht to which he was then laying siege.[83]

In May 1788 there was yet another incident at Kilmainham where prisoners broke holes in the wall of their cell with crowbars and almost managed to get away.[84] The lack of control within the gaols was also reflected in the shooting of two prisoners by the military guard at Kilmainham in response to taunting and bottle-throwing and in the near-fatal stabbing of a man at Newgate in August by another prisoner who had been sentenced to transportation for life.[85]

Overcrowding at Newgate led the *Hibernian Journal* to remark in May that 'riots and outrages almost every day occur' and to hope that there would be more opportunities to send convict transports to the western and southern hemispheres,

as their maintenance is not only an additional expence [sic] to the inhabitants of this city, but from their great numbers, there is great danger in the summer season of causing an infection.[86]

In Cork, too, where a new gaol was under construction, there was a daring attempt by prisoners on 5 October. Having set fire to a door of the gaol, they pelted the soldiers with brickbats and stones when they came to put it out and were only quelled after two of their number had been fatally shot. One prisoner, the notorious 'Jack-a-boy' who had escaped in 1783 only to be recaptured, continued to hold the leg of the commanding officer in a vice-like grip long after he had been chained to the floor.[87]

Nor was the movement of prisoners from county gaols to Newgate without its problems. In April 1787 when a party of green dragoons were escorting a group of seven prisoners from Co. Galway and King's Co. through the Curragh in Co. Kildare, some friends of the prisoners managed to persuade the local people that they were 'poor innocent oppressed people' and to lend assistance in rescuing them.[88] In the outcome,

> a numerous mob to[ok the side] of the culprits, who assailed the military with stones, and at length obliged them in their own defence, and for the security of their charge (when every remonstrance failed of effect), to fire among the rabble, three of whom … fell victims of their own temerity. The consequences would have been still more tragical, if several gentlemen from the Curragh, on hearing of the tumult, had not interposed and checked the misguided frenzy of the populace.[89]

Other incidents of this kind had already caused General Sir William Pitt, the commander of British military forces in Ireland, to press Orde the previous month for the appointment of a Peace Officer to each military detachment accompanying prisoners under escort. In the past, he complained,

> the Magistrate or Civil Officer absents himself as soon as he delivers the Prisoners to the Party who have often been insulted by the Mob, pelted with Stones, and their Prisoners attempted to be rescued, and being deprived of [illeg.] … are thereby prevented from [? serving the] use for which the Military [? are intended].[90]

In Dublin, the mob was no less sympathetic towards prisoners. In September 1787 a fourteen-year-old-boy, who had just been been sentenced to transportation at the Tholsel quarter sessions, scornfully told the Recorder, Denis George: 'Well, my Lord, that's the worst you can do'. On his way to the fortified cart which conveyed convicted prisoners to Newgate, popularly known as 'the *landau*', he escaped down

Nicholas-street but was promptly recaptured. During the journey to the prison he was 'extremely riotous', breaking off panels from the cart and necessitating the intervention of the military guard.

By the time they reached Essex-gate, a large mob had gathered and began to pelt the guard with stones. In the resulting melee, the teenage prisoner and his companion were cut by bayonets and one person was killed.[91] For reasons of this kind the *Dublin Journal* suggested in May 1788 that in order to avoid delays in transportation and the over-crowding and expense that resulted, it was desirable to charter ships more frequently and to send off half the convicts from Cork to relieve the pressure on Dublin's two gaols.[92]

'The most wretched footing'

We have seen that the Irish authorities and the Dublin press were not slow in suggesting that Irish convicts should form part of the first expedition to Botany Bay. Nevertheless, the Home Office was un-responsive to the idea: it does not appear to have even replied to Rutland's formal request of December 1786 and the informal inquiries made earlier by both Hamilton and Orde. Rutland's preoccupation with commercial questions during the first half of 1787 meant that the matter was not pursued and that consequently the First Fleet sailed from Portsmouth for Botany Bay in May 1787 without taking on any Irish-convicted prisoners. Rutland's sudden illness and death in October of that year and the time taken to replace him meant a further delay until his successor could renew the pressure on the Home Office. The retirement of Thomas Orde as Government Secretary late that year also saw the departure of the senior official who had taken the keenest interest in the Botany Bay proposal from the outset.

The question of transportation to Botany Bay was not raised again at official level until early 1788 when Rutland's successor, the Marquis of Buckingham, apparently approached the Home Office for assistance. At that time there were only thirty-nine prisoners at Newgate and ten at Kilmainham under sentence of transportation, but the next assizes would increase their numbers considerably.[93] Although there is no record of Buckingham's request in the official correspondence between Dublin and London, the *Hibernian Journal* reported in May that such an application had been made and that there was likely to be a favourable response.[94] Unable to wait any longer, however, Lord Mayor John Rose arranged a shipment to America which sailed later that month for New London, Connecticut.[95]

Another problem had arisen meanwhile at Newgate in the conflict between Dublin prisoners and those recently brought down from the county gaols to await transportation. Traditional antagonisms between Dublin *jackeens* and *culchies* from the countryside, exacerbated by over-crowding and hot weather, had spilled over into violence. According to the *Hibernian Journal* of 21 May,

> Yesterday a most dreadful affray happened in the New Prison between the country and city transports which raged [with] great fury for a considerable time – many of them were cut and severely bruised on both sides, and part of the door which communicates between the two yards on the men's side [was] broken.

There was another major disturbance at the prison a few days later, this time in the form of an attempted break-out. Taking place shortly before two hundred prisoners were due to be embarked on the waiting transport, it resulted in two of them being killed and several wounded by the military guard. Indeed, the break-out would probably have suc-ceeded had it not been for the assistance given to George Roe and the guards by a handful of co-operative country prisoners. Even after they had been secured in their cells, the rioters continued to throw bricks and stones at the soldiers between the bars, 'bidding them, in the same time, "fire away if they dare"'.[96] The *Hibernian Journal* was relieved to report that they were subsequently secured on board ship and that precautions had been taken to prevent a mutiny during the voyage.[97]

The incident caused the *Freeman's Journal* to question seriously the wisdom of bringing all prisoners sentenced to transportation to Newgate and keeping them there for long periods until a ship became available:

> Even the number confined within the walls of one prison might cause distempers, independent of the incitement to riot, dissipation, and mutiny, when so many desperadoes are together in one place.[98]

It suggested that two transports should be chartered and convicts embarked both at Cork and Dublin.

In October, when the quarterly assizes had once again filled the gaols around the country and there had still been no response from London, Buckingham wrote to Lord Sydney about the possibility of a Canadian alternative:

> I wish that you would be so good as to order Nepean to send over in a private letter the heads of a plan which we are told is arranged for sending some convicts to Canada[;] that whole subject is as you know on the most wretched footing here and something must be done upon it.[99]

Indeed, by this time, Lord Mayor John Rose had almost completed arrangements with Captain Debenham of the *Providence* for a shipment of convicts officially destined for Port Roseway in Nova Scotia.[100]

Although the Home Office had made no positive response on the question of making provision for the transportation of Irish convicts to Botany Bay, the Irish authorities still hoped that official assistance would be provided in sending them to North America instead. According to the *Annual Register*, Dublin Recorder Denis George had a long conference with Lord Sydney in London on 8 December on the prison situation in Dublin and the increased numbers of prisoners due to the Home Office's delay in arranging transportation:

> The season is over for sending them to Quebec and Nova Scotia; but assurances have been given that two ships, properly fitted up, shall be ready, by the latter end of March next, to carry convicts to America.[101]

It was also reported in the London newspapers that Irish convicts would be sent to Newfoundland in the annual fleet the following spring, although no such suggestion had been made by the Home Office to the Newfoundland authorities.[102]

Nothing came of Sydney's undertaking but the disastrous voyage of the *Providence* brought a strong reprimand in late July from Buckingham's brother, William Grenville, who had recently succeeded Sydney as Home Secretary.[103] Recuperating at Bath two weeks earlier after the strain of the Regency Crisis, Buckingham had told him that he had 'writ to Ireland about the convicts whom I am anxious to send to New South Wales ...'.[104] Noting that representations had been made by colonial governors in North America about 'the great inconvenience and distress' caused by transportation, he had assured the Irish Lords Justices that the cost of sending convicts to New South Wales was 'so little increase from our present system, that I am induced to hope that it may in future be adopted'.[105] Accordingly, he had directed them to examine whether Irish law allowed convicts to be sent there by way of commutation of capital sentence and to provide him with a list of all convicts transported since 1785, the cost incurred, and the numbers currently under sentence.[106] However, his resignation from the Lord Lieutenancy shortly after this left the matter in limbo and in the meantime the Dublin Castle authorities were obliged to allow Dublin Corporation to continue the trans-Atlantic trade.

By this time, the Dublin newspapers had abandoned the idea of Botany Bay. In addition to the apparent reluctance of the British government to provide shipping for Irish prisoners, there was the problem of the heavy cost that was still thought to be involved. According to the *Hibernian Journal* of 10 June 1789,

> The idea of sending our convicts to Botany Bay is entirely given up. The vast expence [*sic*] which would be incurred, as every man and woman would stand government in an hundred pounds, has been considered too great a charge. Nova Scotia, and the back settlements of Canada, and New Brunswick, want inhabitants, and if the traffic in human flesh [the African slave-trade] is set aside, our convicts can be sent to the West India [*sic*] islands.

8

The Voyages of 1788: New London and Cape Breton

During 1788, two further shipments of convicts were despatched from Ireland.[1] On 19 May, the brig *Charming Nancy* of New London, Connecticut, captained by Robert Winthrop, embarked 201 prisoners from Newgate after they had signed indenture papers there. As we have seen, many of them had been brought by gaol cart from Cork and Clonmel to Newgate during the previous weeks.[2] This time it was popularly believed that the ship would be taking convicts to a new destination and the Dublin and Cork newspapers suggested that this could be either Africa or Botany Bay.[3] Rejecting the latter possibility, the *Freeman's Journal* thought that because of the high cost involved, Irish convicts would probably never be sent to Botany Bay.[4] It subsequently offered an unflattering comparison of the likely destinations of English and Irish convicts:

> Such a voyage is too expensive for the resources of this kingdom. As Abbe Winkleman observed, when a statue of *Venus* was discovered some years ago at Rome, which surpassed that in the Medici gallery at Florence, 'it will fall into the hands of some Englishman, for who else can afford to purchase it?' We may say the same of the New Holland settlement, who could afford to send criminals [on] a nine months voyage, with all the materials for founding a new colony in thirty degrees of the other side of the Equator, but the opulence of Englishmen? The dregs of our society are bound for Nova Scotia, where many of them may, at a future day, become useful members of the British Empire.[5]

The *Freeman's Journal* had earlier suggested that the Bahamas were a preferable destination to Nova Scotia as the frequency of shipping contact with Halifax would lead to 'the affectionate return of our native rogues, to try over again their experiments of dexterity'.[6] Accordingly, it recommended that if the official contract could be altered, the convicts should be despatched to New Providence or one of the other many islands in the Bahamas group. There was 'no situation in the world better fitted for receiving and turning transports to an actual benefit for the British Empire'.[7] The climate and natural productions of the area were superior to anywhere else in the West Indies and all that was wanting was population. This 'could be well supplied by the *refuse* of this country, as we never will go to the expense of sending them to Botany-bay'.[8]

The other advantage of transporting convicts to the Caribbean was its likely effect as a deterrent to crime:

> If ... they were transported to the West India Islands, and made to share the same fate as the unhappy Afican, who is doomed for life to the hardest slavery, without a crime or having offended against the laws of any country, it would strike a much greater terror in others, and prevent many from the commission of offences against the community, as such a punishment would be very justly considered worse than death itself.[9]

Other newspapers were sceptical about just how welcome convicts would be in that part of the world where negro slave labour was in ready supply. The *Hibernian Journal*, for example, commented:

> may not a query arise, whether the planters of those islands can be obliged to receive them, even under a special act of our legislature for the purpose? Our liberty, in common with Great Britain, to trade with these islands, confer no privileges of furnishing them with our worst commodities against their will. Before we send out our abhorred cargo, it might be necessary to feel the pulse of our western fellow-subjects, otherwise we may be obliged to hawk about through all the regions of that quarter of the globe, as few or no purchasers would be found amongst islanders, confined to a small district, and already well stocked with negroes, over whom our goal [sic] people of Newgate, and the different goals, might in little time have no small influence.[10]

Responding to this, the *Freeman's Journal* thought that the Bahamas planters would not only admit them but pay very well for the transfer of their indentures.[11]

Nevertheless, for the time being the American ports seemed to offer a better chance of profit for enterprising captains. Encouraged by a payment of £5 per head and the prospect of selling the convicts as indentured servants, Winthrop had evidently decided to try for one of the American ports. The total cost of the shipment to Dublin rate-payers was actually £1,754.3s.1$^{1}/_{4}$d., or more than £8 per head, a good proportion of which must have been clear profit to the contractors and to Lord Mayor William Alexander.

It was even rumoured that the authorities had paid as much as £10 per head to have the convicts taken away, which would have been twice the normal cost. Remarking disapprovingly on this, Cork's *Hibernian Chronicle* also reported that no security was required for the performance of the contract, observing that it was 'very notorious of late that more cargoes than one were improperly disposed of'.[12]

'Quite transported'

Unlike the arrangements on previous voyages, men and women were supposed to be kept strictly apart, the former secured with shackles.[13] However, as the *Freeman's Journal* made clear, there were no such limit-ations placed on members of the crew:

> A petty officer on board, taking a liking to one of the female con-victs, honoured her with half of his hammock, and in his extacy [sic] exclaimed, 'Oh! I am *quite transported*' – then, my jewel, cried his *dulcinea*, I have no occasion to go, as you supply my place.[14]

It was also reported (mistakenly as it happened) that a thirty-gun frigate was to be provided as an escort in case of any break-out. The abnormally large number of prisoners on board – about twice that of other voyages – was thought to have made this a desirable pre-caution.[15] Furthermore, the mutiny on board the *Dragon* just a year earlier can hardly have been forgotten. Special measures had also been made necessary by the riot at Newgate on the night before the embarkation and sailing which left many of the convicts with 'their legs, thighs and hands tied up, where they had received wounds ...'.[16] Continued newspaper reports that the ship's intended destination was Botany Bay may well have helped to bring on this trouble.[17]

Indeed, Botany Bay was very much in the minds of the magistrates: at least one of the prisoners embarked on the *Charming Nancy* had his earlier sentence commuted to transportation there. Samuel Moore, former quarter-master and paymaster of the Prince of Wales' regiment of light dragoons, was originally condemned to death in 1787 for the rape of his daughter.[18] With three exceptions, nothing is known about the other prisoners on board. The first was William May, a school-master who had been employed as a children's tutor by some of the leading families in Dublin but had stolen a gold watch belonging to Dr Francis Flood's daughter and taken it to a pawnbroker.[19] Fortunately for May, the jury under-valued the watch at three pence less than five shillings in order to avoid a capital conviction.[20] The second was an unnamed but well-connected young man 'who in a fit of drunkenness, was the spectator of a robbery, where even the prosecutors swore he prevented murder'.[21] He had nevertheless been sentenced to fourteen years' transportation.

Finally, there was 'the noted [Charles] Dempsey', the Bishop of Dublin's postilion who had been charged with cutting the throats of two of his fellow servants when the Bishop's palace in Cavan-street was plundered and set on fire in December 1787.[22] Athough the circum-stantial evidence against Dempsey amounted to what *Walker's Hibernian Magazine* called 'the strongest proof of guilt', he was acquit-ted after Judge Kelly directed the jury to take account of the single character witness who came forward.[23] Through the idiosyncratic workings of the Irish judicial system, Dempsey was found guilty of the theft of 4s.9d. in the same court just a few days later and ordered to be transported.[24]

'A Suit of T-- and F-------'

Arriving at his home port of New London, Connecticut, on 15 July, Captain Winthrop managed to sell off some of the convicts as three-year indentured servants without needing to advertise in the news-papers. However, when the bulk of them were despatched further southwards in a smaller vessel he had hired, their true identity was dis-covered and he 'had much to appease the wrath of his fellow-citizens' over the deception he was seen to have practised on them.[25] The *Massachusetts Centinel* revealed Winthrop's scheme in a report from New London dated 27 June, and this was copied in at least two other New England newspapers:

> Last week arrived at Fisher's Head, the brig Nancy, belonging to this port, Captain Robert W-----, (a half pay British officer) master, and landed his cargo, consisting of 140 convicts, taken out of the British

gaols. Capt. W., it is said, received 5£ sterling a head from government for this job; and we hear he is distributing them about the
country. Stand to it house, stores, &c. these gentry are acquainted
with the business. Quere [sic], whether a suit of T-- and F-------
should not be provided for Capt. W. [as] a suitable compliment for
this piece of service done his country?[26]

Although Winthrop had been born in New London and was an
American citizen, he had served in the Royal Navy during the whole of
the Revolutionary War and was still on half-pay.[27] In response to this
unsought and dangerous publicity, he was obliged to take on board
again some of the convicts he had sold and land them at Sandy Hook,
New Jersey, from where many apparently found their way back to
Ireland.[28] A subsequent report in the *Freeman's Journal* had it that they
bribed Winthrop to let them off there and with 'the profits of their
plunder' managed to purchase their passage home, 'no doubt to the
very great *benefit* and *satisfaction* of the inhabitants of this – their
native city'.[29]

In view of the problems that Winthrop encountered in New England
and the publicity given to the returnees in Ireland, it is not surprising
that this proved to be the last Irish convict shipment to the United
States. Where was a captain now to be found who would run the risk
not only of a tarring and feathering but of failing to dispose of his
cargo at a profit?

There were already sufficient reports from North America and the
West Indies reaching Ireland by early 1788 to suggest that more
caution should be exercised in the despatch of convicts to that part of
the world. As we have seen, even before the *Charming Nancy*'s departure a Dublin newspaper had questioned the wisdom of continuing to
send off convicts with no guarantee of their being favourably received.

In September, when news of the less than successful voyage of the
Nancy had been received and a further one was rumoured, the
Hibernian Journal and the *Dublin Chronicle* published a brief but comprehensive history of the six shipments made since 1784, highlighting
the suffering endured by the convicts involved. By way of introduction, the *Hibernian Journal* remarked that

The fate of unfortunate convicts on former occasions, as mentioned
in the newspapers, is too great a reflection on the humanity of the
nation, and so disgraceful an infringement of the law of nations, as
to need no repetition.[30]

The *Dublin Chronicle* also referred to the 'very atrocious conduct' of the masters of vessels over the previous four years, reporting that the government had consequently instructed the city's magistrates to take large bonds of security from them in future for the proper performance of their contracts. Accordingly, it expressed the vain hope that

> from the attention paid hereafter to this melancholy business, an attention which both justice and humanity absolutely demand, that no such accounts as were some time since received of the unhappy fate of numbers of poor convicts, will again shock the ears of the public.[31]

There was also the question of the profit to be made from the voyage if the captain managed to sell the convicts as indentured servants. The one source of satisfaction for the *Hibernian Journal* was that 'after the tricks they have formerly played', this time the captain was 'bound under a severe penalty' to land all the convicts at the agreed destination.[32] The *Chronicle*, on the other hand, lamented that 'no place has as yet been assigned for the convicts sent off from this country but that they are obliged at times to be landed at desolate places, liable to perish in all the miseries of extreme distress'.[33] It suggested that land might be made available in Canada, in Labrador, for example, where convict settlers could make a 'competent livelihood' from cutting timber and trapping. Indeed, 'settlements or villages could be formed, tillage encouraged, and their descendants arrive to respectability, and of course become in time a flourishing colony'.[34]

The *Providence*

It was no doubt due to reports of Winthrop's troubles that this next shipment of convicts was specifically directed to the Canadian settlements. In October, Captain Debenham of the snow *Providence*, 200 tons, from north Yarmouth contracted to take 103 men and 23 women convicts from Dublin and Cork to Port Roseway, Nova Scotia, for £5.17s.6d. per head, with a guinea allowance each for clothing, under penalty of forfeiting final payment if he did not land them at the agreed destination. On 17 October when the fourteen cartloads of male and female prisoners were being taken from Newgate to the North Wall, guarded by a formation of horse and and two companies of foot-soldiers, some managed to untie themselves in Capel-street and almost escaped. One, who had dressed as a sailor in order to facilitate his escape, was also detected.

Anthony Molloy, a well-known counterfeiter and thief who had been sentenced to seven years' transportation 'for being strongly suspected of being concerned in taking out of the dwelling-house of Jeremiah Bacon, a large quantity of plate ...', had taken the easier course of bribing Debenham to put him off the ship after embarkation.[35]

As no ship's indent has survived for this or any of the other five earlier trans-Atlantic voyages, it is not possible to say very much about the convicts and the crimes they had committed. All that was specifically recorded in the newspapers of the time was that one man on the *Providence* had taken money illegally while masquerading as a hearth-tax collector, 'being furnished with printed receipts, &c.'[36] Another, Laurence Prendergast, had been sentenced at the Tholsel quarter sessions on 9 September to be executed two weeks later 'for robbing Murray Gorman on Ranelagh-road, and taking from him one double-cased silver watch, with a steel chain, seal and brass key, value 3£. sterling, and some other articles of value ...'.[37] His sentence was subsequently commuted to transportation for life.

An impressionable contributor to the *Freeman's Journal* was deeply affected by the plight of one of the convicts being taken to the North Wall on 17 October:

> a genteel young man, very decently dressed, and with a pair of new boots on, who sat on the bottom of one of the carts, with his hat slouched, so as entirely to hide his countenance. He seemed to be deeply affected with his unhappy situation, holding a white hand-kerchief to his face, that appeared wet with his tears. His contrition was in perfect contrast to the behaviour in general of the wretches his companions, who for the most part appeared callous to every reflection of shame. With this sensibility of heart, possibly the above young man possessed qualities that might have more than atoned to his country for the crime he committed; but which now, it is to be feared, will be entirely depraved by the miscreant crew with whom he is necessitated to mix.[38]

However, a few issues later it was revealed that through some fault in the evidence presented at his recent trial, this 'genteel young man' had only narrowly escaped capital conviction for the theft of £200 worth of goods from an auction room in Anglesea-street, Dublin. Furthermore, he was described as having 'committed more burglaries and robberies than has fallen to the portion of any other convict for thirty years past'.[39] He could well afford to appear 'genteel' as the trunk which he carried with him contained goods purchased with the £60 worth of plate which he had been been found guilty of stealing from a house in Stephen-street.[40]

A further incident was related by the embarrassed *Freeman's Journal* as a caution to the public against feeling too much pity for these involuntary exiles:

> Last Saturday, when the convicts were carrying from the New-prison to be embarked, an apple-woman piteously lamented the hard fate of the 'poor creatures who were going to be sent for nothing into slavery!' She accompanied her monody with imprecations against the cruel ones that disposed of her fellow creatures so barbarously. – One of the objects of her commisseration called her to the cart-side, and pretended to purchase some of her fruit, overset her sieve into the cart, and told her he would pay her at next meeting: Her tone was soon changed from pity to execration – but one had as much effect as the other – and the example was (before they reached the water-side) followed by others. The kingdom assuredly has an happy riddance of such incorrigible wretches![41]

Little regret was expressed by the newspapers at the departure of the shipment, the *Dublin Chronicle*, for one, remarking with satisfaction that

> Among the transports sent off Saturday last ... there were several of the most daring and desperate lawless villains, as well as of the most infamous and abandoned prostitutes with which the metropolis and its environs had been infested. The ridding the city of those dangerous pests must greatly contribute to the establishment of public peace and the personal security of its inhabitants.[42]

It seems likely that some of the women on the *Providence* were prostitutes who had been rounded up under the Vagabond Act. Before the embarkation, the *Dublin Chronicle* reported that there were in Newgate

> a considerable number of idle women, committed by the divisional Justices or police, as vagrants of infamous character, who nightly infested the streets of the metropolis at unseasonable hours, having no honest visible means of livelihood.[43]

Unaware of the arrangement made by Anthony Molloy with Debenham, the newspaper recalled previous instances of convicts who 'for a paltry bribe procured their liberty from the captain'.[44] Indeed, within ten days of the ship's sailing, there was a strong rumour amongst the 'lower orders' in Dublin that a number of those on board had come ashore on the southern coast of Ireland after extricating themselves from the heavy irons to which they been attached below deck.[45]

Main à Dieu Harbour

The voyage of the *Providence* was to provide further examples of 'very atrocious conduct'.[46] No less than forty-six of the convicts were subsequently reported to have died on board this ironically misnamed ship during its four weeks' voyage across the Atlantic. When the first landfall was made off the north-eastern coast of Cape Breton Island, it was the second week of December and there was already snow on the ground. The extreme lateness of the season made it impossible for the vessel to proceed up the St Lawrence River to Quebec, which may have been Captain Debenham's original plan. At any rate, he decided to land the remaining convicts on the wild and almost uninhabited north-eastern coast of Cape Breton Island where there would be no difficulties with the local authorities. Taking his ship through the Gut of Canso, Debenham anchored in the late afternoon of 11 December between Port Nova and Scatari in Main à Dieu Harbour. This was two or three miles to the east of a small fishing settlement near the site of the former French fortress of Louisbourg which had been destroyed by the British in 1763. The only sign of civilisation encountered by the *Providence* was a local fishing shallop which passed without responding to a hail.

Although there was already snow on the ground in what was to be an 'unusually severe' winter, the convicts' shackles were knocked off and they were forcibly landed from the ship's boat at different points on the coast without warm clothing, bedding or provisions. Some did not even have shoes and stockings.[47] Observing this surprising scene from the shore was Charles Martell, the local justice of the peace, who had been sawing up logs for his winter fire. From the account given a few days later by the government pilot at Main à Dieu, Francis Dixon, who no doubt had it from Martell, there is this description of the landing:

> the seamen, were armed with Pistols, cutlasses, and swords, and when the Boat reached the shore, they tumbled these people head-

long from the Boat into the surf among the Rocks and one man was killed by being thrown against a Rock.[48]

At about six o'clock that evening, when it was already dark, the *Providence* weighed anchor and stood out to the westward.

Seven of the convicts who had no shoes and were unable to walk in the snow remained where they had been landed. The rest walked westwards along the rocky coast in small groups, one of them encountering Martell. Taking them back to the settlement, he made sure that they were given food and warm clothing in the fishermen's huts. Then, together with Dixon, he organised the fishermen into different parties to search for the other convicts. The first group of convicts encountered by Dixon were the seven without shoes. Leaving them where he found them until a boat could be sent to pick them up, Dixon continued the search. That night he and Martell managed to collect 'between Thirty and Forty Persons straggling about, without knowing which way to go ...'. According to Dixon, most of them were 'little better than naked'. However, they were more fortunate than the seven he had left behind, six of whom had died of exposure in the woods by the time the boat reached them the next morning.

To celebrate their deliverance, two of the convicts, Joseph McDonald and Laurence Prendergast, produced a guinea piece to purchase rum, tea and other comforts for the whole of the party at the settlement store. A grim tale lay behind this apparent generosity, however. During the first night ashore, the pair had robbed and left for dead an old man, John Kirkpatrick, who had earlier entrusted his money to McDonald for safe-keeping during the voyage. When the old man refused to give it up to them after the landing in spite of their violent threats, McDonald knocked him to the ground with a piece of wood and Prendergast took the bag of money from his breeches. Unknown to them, the incident had been closely observed by another member of the party who had fallen behind the others out of exhaustion and was resting in the woods. He was to be the principal witness in the subsequent trial of the two men. When a young boy who had been friendly with Kirkpatrick during the voyage accused McDonald and Prendergast of murdering him, they promised that in return for his silence they would look after him and vouch for him when they went to the United States.[49]

A few days later, Luke Keegan, an Irish fisherman of Main à Dieu who had failed to respond to the hail from the *Providence*, took forty of the convicts, including the women and those crippled by frost-bite, to

Sydney. These were all that he could safely fit in his fishing shallop, the *Shilaly*, which would normally have carried a crew of three or four. The remaining thirty or so were probably taken by him to Sydney in a second trip.

Governor Macarmick

When he was informed by Dixon of the convicts' arrival at the military wharf at Sydney on 15 December and had read the explanatory letter which the pilot brought from Martell, Macarmick called a meeting of his executive council for that evening. In the meantime he ordered the town's principal merchant, Keith Stout, and the local justices of the peace to provide the convicts with food and clothing. The next day the Council met again and decided that in view of the shortage of provisions reported by the local merchants, as many of the convicts as possible should be sent in the Treasury brig *Relief* which was then making ready to sail for Halifax. Other vessels would be hired to carry the remainder there. However, Captain William Campbell of the *Relief* reported a few days later that due to the construction of the brig, the weather conditions and the description of the Persons', he could carry only ten or twelve of them and that even then they would have to 'lay upon the ballast'.[50]

Macarmick thus had little choice but to keep the convicts at Sydney in the house normally used as a gaol until they could be sent to Halifax in a larger vessel. When Provost-Marshall David Taitt pointed out to him the 'impropriety of confining such a number of people into that House, as the Gaoler was not obliged to take any person not legally sent', the governor had to hire a larger house at the north end of the town for their accommodation and to promise the gaoler a liberal reward for his trouble. A military guard was placed over the convicts until they could be sent to Halifax where Governor Parr could decide what to do with them. In the meantime, Macarmick was obliged to maintain them at the local government's expense. Writing to Lord Sydney on 18 December, he reflected:

> I hope the Law will overtake the unfeeling Author of such Barbarity. But to wherever their Destination was, or whatever their Crimes and Misfortunes may have been, they come to me in so miserable a State and by an Act so cruel, that were they not H.M.'s Subjects I could not resist the pressing Inducements to give them protection.[51]

No sooner had the convicts been safely housed, however, than there was a general scare that they were carrying the dreaded 'gaol fever'. Some members of the military guard had been taken ill and the surgeon and commanding officer of the 42nd Highland Regiment reported to Macarmick 'that some infectious disorder might have been brought in their rags'. Accordingly, the governor had all the convicts' clothing destroyed and arranged for them to be sent to a house on the coast about seven miles from the town as quarantine. He also issued a proclamation on 6 January warning of the danger of an epidemic and requiring that any convicts found straggling should be apprehended. Before the story of the epidemic was proven false, one woman died and a man carrying provisions from town to the house was frozen to death. During the next few months there were never less than sixteen or seventeen of the convicts in hospital recovering from the effects of severe frost-bite. Indeed, several had been rendered permanently lame by their ordeal in the snow during the night of the landing at Main à Dieu.

Although most of the convicts were once again accommodated at the secure house in Sydney and kept under guard, others were allowed to live elsewhere without restraint of movement. After a complaint on an evening in April that some of the convict women were 'rioting at a Public House of bad fame', Taitt sent a constable to take them to the secure house. However, they were released later that night by the Government Secretary, Abraham Cuyler, who had no knowledge of why they had been sent there. When Taitt subsequently told Macarmick that the 'Publican concerned kept a house of bad fame', the governor could only answer feebly that he 'understood so'.[52] Nor can supervision at the secure house have been very careful. After the convicts were released and the house had been vacant for some years, the new owner discovered 'several human skeletons in the cellar who were supposed to be the remains of convicts who had died or been murdered by their fellows during that winter [of 1788–9]'.[53]

Another complication was the trial of the two convicts, McDonald and Prendergast, who had been accused of murdering old John Kirkpatrick on the night of their arrival at Main à Dieu Harbour. Although the two men were found guilty by a Grand Jury on 12 March and sentenced to be executed two days later, Macarmick ordered a stay of execution. Not only had Kirkpatrick's body never been found and the cause of his death ascertained, but there were serious doubts about the evidence given by the convict witnesses. As the Attorney-General, David Mathews, pointed out to Macarmick, there was no means of ascertaining whether it was 'entirely purged of malice growing out of former animosities'.[54] The governor accordingly referred the case to Lord Sydney for advice, but while his reply was being awaited the two prisoners escaped with the connivance of the military guard.

If this caused Macarmick embarrassment, it was nothing to the other problems he had encountered from the time of the convicts' arrival. Chief Secretary Cuyler, together with other members of the Executive Council, used the convict issue to further their political and personal campaign against the Lieut.-Governor who had already dismissed Chief Justice Richard Gibbons in March 1788.[55] Although the Council had agreed unanimously with Macarmick's policy towards the convicts at the outset, Cuyler subsequently claimed that he had always argued strongly for their immediate removal on the grounds that the colony had insufficient supplies to support them.[56] As Macarmick told Sydney in April, he had been brought to the position of contemplating the suspension of his senior officials:

> I am sorry, My Lord, to add that a few of my Council (those who from Office are bound to give me aid), have taken this opportunity of the Convicts not having been sent from this Island, to shew a disposition to oppose every effort I make to restore and maintain unanimity in the Settlement, which thank God every where now prevail [sic], but in those few and they even go beyond the limits of common decency to establish a Principle that a Governor shall only be a Cypher and that the advice and elictation [sic] of a Council must be the sole Rule of his Conduct without leaving him a Will to plan or a Power to act. Notwithstanding I shall exercise my utmost patience and forbearance, and it will only be in the last extreme that I shall make use of the Authority which His Majesty has been graciously pleased to honor me with, to suspend their official powers of acting.[57]

It came as no surprise, then, when Macarmick suspended Cuyler from office three months later.

Macarmick had still received no orders from London about what do with the convicts, and as the cost of continuing to support them was prohibitive, he allowed them their freedom in the spring of 1789. Some apparently found employment on the island but others left, most likely for the United States. Although there were reports that a few were 'suspected of lurking about Halifax' in April,[58] Governor Parr wrote to Evan Nepean that month to say that the situation was now under control. At the same time, he implored him not to allow the same thing to happen again:

> I tremble at the Reports I see in the News Papers, that Convicts are to be sent here from England and Ireland, which will do more hurt to this Country, than you good People at home are aware of, for God's sake let this be prevented if possible.[59]

Writing from Sydney in early August 1789, one of the military officers on garrison duty there related the story of the Irish convicts to a friend or relative at home with more than a touch of black humour:

> I must not forget to tell you that the Master of a vessel from Dublin[,] not thinking there were rascals enough upon the Island, thought proper to land 60 male and 18 female convicts upon the coast and left them to pick out their road the best way they could[.] The consequence was that seven of them died immediately from the severity of the weather ... Two of them have since been hanged for murder, seven [are] in Prison to take their trials ..., and the remainder are travelling about the country at large to improve the morals of the people – one is comforted however from the reflection that the danger of their being corrupted is not too great.[60]

Accepting Macarmick's action in helping the convicts as 'a measure of unavoidable necessity', Home Secretary Grenville wrote in October to tell him that their 'reasonable Expences' (amounting to the not inconsiderable sum of £567.12s.5d.) would be met by the Treasury. However, as it seemed that those remaining on the island were now employed and 'no longer a Burthen on the public', no further support would be provided. Nor could he give Macarmick any advice about the legality of the conviction of the two convicts for murder until a full transcript of the evidence had been provided. Indeed, he added sharply,

> from your having omitted to do so in this present instance, the unfortunate People in question must from their long confinement in a severe Climate, suffer a Punishment to which, whatever their Crimes may have been, they ought not to have been exposed.[61]

However, he was able to reassure Governor Parr that while little could be done to punish Debenham, no more Irish convicts would be landed at either Cape Breton or Nova Scotia:

I should think it a fortunate circumstance for the sake of example if the Master of the vessel and any other persons who may have been concerned with him in this inhuman transaction, could be punished in an exemplary manner; but I fear, that consistently with the Law, as it now stands, nothing can be done than merely sue the penalties of the bonds which have been forfeited. Measures however will be taken to prevent the repetition of an Offence so detrimental to the end of public Justice, and at the same time time so injurious to the interest of His Majesty's subjects in North America.[62]

Grenville had already sent a strongly worded complaint to his brother, Lord Lieutenant Buckingham. On 27 July 1789 he wrote:

This transaction appears to have been attended with circumstances of so atrocious a nature, that it is highly proper that the most speedy and effectual Measures should be taken to recover from the Master of the Vessel the Penalties of the Bonds which he is required by Law to give.[63]

Grenville told Buckingham that as the transportation of convicts to North America was 'in so many respects objectionable', particularly on account of the 'extreme dislike' expressed by the former colonists to the 'introduction of persons of that Description amongst them', the British government's policy had been to avoid it and establish a convict settlement in New South Wales instead. As the same considerations applied to Irish convicts, Grenville signified that it was His Majesty's command that he should not use *26 Geo. III, c. 24* to authorise transportation to North America 'or to any part of His Majesty's Dominions than the coast of New South Wales, or the Islands adjacent thereto'. Grenville recommended that the relevant Irish legislation be amended if necessary by the Irish Parliament to allow transportation to New South Wales. He also suggested that there be some investigation of the means by which the Irish government could defray the expense of sending its own convicts there, indicating that this would be calculated on a proportional basis and that clothing and rations for perhaps three years would also have to be taken into account for the final cost.[64]

In the meantime, Buckingham had instituted his own inquiries into the Cape Breton affair after receiving separate advice from Macarmick of what had happened. When Captain Debenham revealed in his official return for the voyage in March 1789 that twenty-one convicts had died of 'a most inveterate Venereal Distemper', the Lord Lieutenant asked Lord Justice John Fitzgibbon to inquire whether legal action could be taken against the captain. Having obtained from the former Lord Mayor, William Alexander, a copy of the charter party 'signed by the Brute who had undertaken to transport them', Fitzgibbon had to tell Buckingham that the wording of the document made it practically impossible to proceed against Debenham. He had only been required to land the convicts 'at some port in N. America', and even this was subject to 'a Reservation for Stress of Weather'.[65] All that could be done, Fitzgibbon advised the Lord Lieutenant, was for Alexander to have Debenham declare on oath that he had in truth landed the convicts 'in any part of the British settlements in North America' – something that the captain could happily swear. At the same time, he promised to 'endeavour to prevent if possible a Repetition of this Sort of Barbarity by stating to the present Lord Mayor what has happened and desiring of him to guard against it'.[66]

Within a few months of this correspondence, Buckingham had resigned as Lord Lieutenant. Apart from the Home Office's request that the Cape Breton government be reimbursed by Dublin for the £786.19s.6$^{1}/_{2}$d. it had incurred on account of the convicts, the matter was subsequently allowed to rest.[67] However, the Dublin newspapers reported the high mortality suffered on the voyage and this can hardly have escaped the notice of those inmates of Newgate 'cast for transportation'.[68] The newspapers also remarked with mixed feelings of admiration and disapproval on the profitability of the voyage, which was believed to have secured the Dublin owners of the *Duke of Leinster*, George and Arthur Bryan, more than £500 profit.

9
The Newfoundland Voyage

The disastrous voyage of the *Providence* to Cape Breton Island in October 1788 had resulted in explicit instructions from the Home Office to Dublin not to send any more shipments of convicts to North America. Six weeks before these were received by the Marquis of Buckingham, however, the *Duke of Leinster*, captained by Richard Harrison, had sailed from Dublin on 14 June 1789 with 113 men and boys and 14 women convicts for a destination 'said to be Nova Scotia'.[1] Before the ship sailed there was a further report published in the newspapers that it was bound for Baltimore instead.[2] News of the fate of convicts despatched in the *Providence* would have reached Newgate by the time of embarkation.

On the morning of 13 June as Patrick Fay was being put into one of the fourteen carts mustered to convey the convicts from Newgate to the New Wall, there was a mild sensation amongst the onlookers when his children 'screeched' at the prospect of losing their father. As the *Freeman's Journal* writer described it: 'Many dropt a tear of pity at this circumstance, and for a moment forgot the crimes of the father at the wretched situation of his offspring'.[3] Accompanied by the sympathetic mob which always gathered on these occasions, the convicts 'behaved in a riotous and abandoned manner' as the procession of carts rattled through the streets of north Dublin with a squadron of mounted soldiers and four companies of foot as escort.[4] A number of prisoners were thrown out when one of the carts overturned at the junction of Little Britain-street and Capel-street. Amongst those injured by the spikes on the cart as they were tumbled into the street was Fay himself who was hurt in the mouth. For a moment there was some danger of a mass escape, but the vigilant guard quickly restored control.

While they were being taken in lighters down the river to join the ship in Dublin Bay, Anthony Molloy escaped by jumping into another boat which had evidently rendezvoused there for the purpose. Two brothers named Dwyer also escaped by jumping overboard and getting into a waiting boat.[5] Molloy was sensible enough to lie low for a time after getting away, but the Dwyers 'were so daring and fool hardy, that they soon appeared publicly, and were ... apprehended playing skittles in Thomas-street, and safely conveyed to their old quarters'.[6] Fortunately for them, the *Duke of Leinster* had already sailed with 'Father Fay' on board.

From contemporary newspaper accounts, it is clear that Dublin Corporation was maintaining the old system of deception by which convicts were given certificates of indenture signed by the Lord Mayor before their departure. It was reported in the press that Lord Mayor John Rose had gone on board the *Duke of Leinster* on 8 June for this purpose.[7] As the convicts had not yet been embarked, Rose's subsequent denial was honest enough: the indentures had been given out at Newgate instead.

Rose's reason for going on board the ship was to check the provisions and he had condemned some barrels of herring which were thrown overboard.[8] According to the *Dublin Chronicle*, the Castle authorities had recently issued an order 'that in future the provisions in every transport vessel shall be narrowly inspected, not only respecting their quality, but also their quality, and the regulations that compel these, like other vessels bound upon long voyages to make a sufficient provision of victuals, be duly enforced ...'.[9] No doubt this was in response to reports of insufficient or inferior rations on some of the earlier transports. Rose was also to arrange the shipping of another 89 convicts on the *Duke of Leinster* to the Leeward Islands in November of that year. As we shall see, it was these two voyages which were to bring to an end Ireland's revived trans-Atlantic convict trade.

Thanks to a sworn statement made by an English seaman, Richard Robinson, who deserted the ship shortly after its arrival at Newfoundland, and to court reports and official correspondence between St John's, London and Dublin, there is a relatively good record of what eventuated. This and the subsequent voyage of the *Duke of Leinster* are also the only ones from the period for which something like a ship's indent survives, providing the names and other details of more than half of the convicts originally embarked.[10] For the Dublin newspapers, the most notable feature of the June shipment was that it contained 'several very young boys'.[11]

In May 1789 when the 24-year-old Robinson signed on as able seaman at the St John's Quay counting house of Arthur and George

Bryan, the Dublin merchants who owned the *Duke of Leinster* and had contracted with Rose for the voyage, there was still no clear indication of the vessel's destination, 'some saying she was bound to Botany Bay, and others that she was bound to Nova Scotia'.[12] Captain Harrison told Robinson that they were going to America and would pick up a cargo of flaxseed and lumber there for Dublin in a round voyage that would last five or six months. Indeed, the amount of water and provisions taken on board suggested to him that the voyage might last from six to nine months rather than the normal two or three months for the trans-Atlantic return run.[13]

The convicts themselves had little idea of their destination, although they no doubt hoped to be landed at some American port. One of them had been alarmed to read in a newspaper in Newgate before embarkation that they were destined for Botany Bay, but there was no confirmation that the captain was ordered there. The Inspector-General of Prisons, Sir Jeremiah Fitzpatrick, had told another prisoner that 'such a voyage would cost the Irish Government One Hundred Pounds p. Man, and that no more convicts would be sent to Botany Bay'.[14] For reasons which are not entirely clear, Harrison asked the convicts to call the ship the *Charming Nancy*, after the vessel which had taken convicts to New London, Connecticut, in May 1788.

Talamh an Eisc

On 15 July, after a relatively swift voyage of thirty days, the *Duke of Leinster* made land at Cape Spear, the easternmost point of Newfoundland, and entered Bay Bulls[15] on the Avalon peninsula, nineteen miles south of the principal settlement of St John's. At about eleven o'clock that night, between eighty and ninety of the convicts were put ashore. Some provisions were given to them by Harrison but these were commandeered by the stronger men and some had to go without. It was during this operation that Robinson, because of his 'dislike to the trade' and his belief that the vessel was returning to Galway to await orders for a 'Northern Voyage', managed to slip away.[16] Walking fourteen miles north along the rocky coast, he reached St John's four days later and told the local magistrates his story. Early on the morning of 16 July, Harrison had landed the remainder of the convicts, including five women, at Petty Harbour, ten miles to the north of Bay Bulls, and sailed away. This group was not given any provisions, but it would have been easier for them to reach St John's.

Why Harrison chose south-eastern Newfoundland to dispose of the convicts is not clear. One explanation offered later was that the ship was short of provisions,[17] but this is highly unlikely in view of Robinson's account of what had been taken on board in Dublin. Harrison would have been aware that Bay Bulls was one of the traditional destinations of English and Irish 'bankers' (schooners) taking Irish workers and provisions to Newfoundland each spring for the fishing season.[18] Furthermore, Bay Bulls was a convenient and unobtrusive place for a ship to anchor safely after making land at what was North America's closest point to Europe.

The landing of small numbers of Irish convicts at Conception Bay and other isolated harbours by West Country banker captains had evidently become such common practice by 1731 that the then naval governor of Newfoundland, Captain Henry Osborn, sent a sharp complaint to the Board of Trade about the evil consequences of bringing over 'transported felons instead of Irish servants'.[19] A convict had been strongly suspected of the recent murder of a woman and four children at Muskitta, Conception Bay. Although there is no indication that the practice was kept up after Osborn's time, Harrison may have heard of it from other captains. He is much less likely to have been aware of the suggestion made in 1787 by an ill-informed critic of the Botany Bay scheme that convicts be used in Newfoundland to cut timber for the Royal Navy.[20] As we have seen, however, a meeting between Dublin's Recorder, Denis George, and Home Secretary Lord Sydney in London in December 1788 had led to rumours in the London press of Irish convicts being sent there in the fishing fleet the following spring.[21]

If Harrison had any previous experience of Newfoundland, he would have known that Bay Bulls, Ferryland Harbour and the other harbour settlements or 'outports' along what was called the 'Southern Shore' were inhabited predominantly by Irishmen of the servant class who could be expected to assist the new arrivals. The Newfoundland cod fishery had been employing seasonal Irish labour, mostly from Waterford but also from Kilkenny and Wexford, since the early seventeenth century. By the late 1760s, about 5,000 Irish male workers were making the crossing from Waterford to Newfoundland each spring, most of them returning in the late autumn at the end of the fishing season.[22] Waterford also provided most of the salted provisions, breadstuffs and cloth products for the Newfoundland market.[23]

The island known in Irish as *Talamh an Eisc* (Land of the Fish) had been familiar to many Munstermen since the late seventeenth century when Irish traders carried women servants there as well as goods.[24] The crop failures of the late 1720s and early 1740s badly affected Munster and further stimulated labour emigration to Newfoundland. The fishery was even the subject of a poem written by the celebrated bard, Donnchadh Ruadh MacConmara (Denis 'the Red' MacNamara), who made a voyage there from Waterford as a seasonal worker in about 1750.[25]

As one Newfoundland historian has pointed out, '[Newfoundland] had experienced a longer period of regular contact with Ireland than any other part of North America'[26] and was one of the principal points of entry for Irish migration to the American colonies. This may help to explain why, when they were subsequently interviewed by the magistrates at St John's, two of the convicts from the *Duke of Leinster* insisted that they had not been put ashore against their will. If Harrison deceived them as to their whereabouts, as Captain Stafford of the *Chance* had done in the Bahamas with another group of convicts two years earlier, they made no complaint. As one of them said subsequently, 'the Captain did not force them on the Shore, nor did they compel him to land them'.[27]

'Great disorders'

Left on the beach to fend as best they could, the convicts at Bay Bulls fought amongst themselves during the next few days for the limited provisions that Harrison had given them. According to a contemporary account, 'the strongest beat the weak, and over a cask of rank butter or beef, there was for a time as severe fighting as if a kingdom had been at stake'.[28] When the provisions were exhausted, they descended on the little fishing settlement of about five hundred people at Bay Bulls, burning a house and 'store' or shop owned by an English 'planter' or fishing master, Richard Hutchings.[29] 'I fear much we shall, before the fall is over, share the same fate in St John's', one of the town's leading residents wrote to a Dublin friend on 6 August when the convicts' presence there was known.[30]

Indeed, within a few days of the main body of convicts reaching St John's an attempt had been made to set fire to the town and it was only by prompt action that a disaster was averted. The settlement consisted at that time of two long 'streets' of about four hundred wooden row-houses and shops straggling along the wind-swept hillside which overlooked the narrow harbour. Towering over the houses were the fishing 'flakes' – the 30 feet high wooden racks or platforms for the drying of codfish which constituted the island's only industry. All

18 St John's, Newfoundland, 1780's. The ship is an English man-of-war of the kind that brought Vice-Admiral Milbanke to Newfoundland.

would certainly have been destroyed if the fire had taken hold.[31] Two men, probably convicts, were held on suspicion of setting the fire and a large reward was offered for information, but nothing could be proved.[32] The same correspondent told his Dublin friend that he hoped the master of the ship that brought the convicts would be punished on account of 'the colony [of criminals] he has planted in the most industrious part of his Majesty's dominions'.[33]

After Richard Robinson had revealed the origins of the voyage to the St John's magistrates on 20 July and made a deposition before the Vice-Admiralty Court the following day, the news that the arrivals were convicts quickly went around the town. No doubt their presence was also linked with a rash of petty thefts which had commenced a few days earlier and resulted in the arrest of a convict in the first week of August. 'Fearing if they are permitted to range at large it may endanger our Property and be the means of disturbing the Peace of the District', thirteen merchants and other leading citizens of St John's (including the Irish merchant, John Gleeson) met and petitioned the town's magistrates on 22 July to 'cause their immediate Confinement under a proper Guard' until the arrival from England of the newly appointed governor. Vice-Admiral Sir Mark Milbanke was due to take up his first tour of duty of two months in early September.[34] Although he had performed a useful service to the community, the unlucky Robinson was arrested as a deserter and thrown into gaol until Milbanke could decide what to do with him.

Sixty-three male convicts were subsequently rounded up by the magistrates and further details of their origins and the voyage were obtained from an interrogation of two of them. James McGuire was a 25-year-old labourer from Enniskillen, Co. Fermanagh, who had been transported for seven years for 'keeping forcible Possession of a House and Land'. Matthew Dempsey was a 21-year-old ribbon-weaver, born in either Queen's or King's County ('does not know which', the magistrates recorded) but long settled in Dublin's Liberties. He had been sentenced to death at Co. Dublin's Kilmainham assizes for 'forging a note to obtain a pair of Silver Buckles from a Pawn Broker'[35] but this was respited to transportation.

The Winter house

Faced with the novel problem of dealing with immigrant criminals, many of whom were ill, the magistrates of St John's decided to confine them in the merchant and planter James Winter's large summer house on his 'plantation' or estate. This building, which had been previously used as a hospital, was located on 'the Barrens', the wind-swept hills a mile or so inland from St John's. Anxious about the security of their property, which was so vulnerable to arson, the petitioners subscribed money to help meet the cost of feeding the convicts until Milbanke arrived. At the same time, they managed to have a military guard posted at the house to prevent any attempt at escape.

Although no account of this time was recorded by any of the convicts themselves, there is a contemporary description of their incarceration at the Winter house which suggests how they might have been by the respectable townspeople:

> here the Irish howl was nightly sung in full chorus and the sentinels were frequently affrighted with the noise while on their posts. A bottle or two every half hour kept them festive all day, and when the provisions supplied to them were lessening, they broke away and laid hold of everything that was eatable, without inquiry whether it had an owner.[36]

When the funds were used up after ten days, the merchants petitioned the garrison commander and Lieut.-Governor, Major James Elford, on 31 July to supply the prisoners with rations from the garrison stores, promising to reimburse government for the cost.[37] This action was also brought on by a threatened 'mutiny' by the convicts who had already caused considerable damage to the house. Thanks to the condemnation of some of the garrison's stores six weeks earlier, Elford was able to authorise their transfer to the gaoler for the convicts' consumption.[38]

As by no means all of the convicts had been rounded up, there was need for vigilance against those who were still 'walking about' in the town. The solution resorted to by the property-holders of St John's was to appoint six-man patrols led by a constable and a householder who stayed out from ten o'clock at night checking the two 'paths' or streets until the cannon at Fort Townshend on the hill overlooking the town signalled the dawn.[39] According to a letter from a resident of St John's in late August to Benjamin Lester, a prominent Poole merchant and Westminster MP with extensive fishing interests in Newfoundland, even this precaution was insufficient to deal with the twelve women convicts, 'more abandoned than you can conceive of ... ', who had been 'suffer'd to remain at Large'.[40] Newfoundland was a predominantly male society and unattached women would have been in keen demand.

'The Goal Disorder'

One of the further problems posed by the Irish convicts was what one resident of St John's called 'the Goal Disorder', most probably typhus, which they had brought with them from Newgate. Indeed, their 'much diseased' appearance had been one of the reasons for their rapid confinement by the magistrates, Lester's correspondent describing the illness as 'a kind of Spotted putrid Fever'.[41] Despite the precautions, it was soon contracted by the military guards and many of the residents of St John's, causing at least two hundred deaths within the town's population of about 3,000 and probably many more at Bay Bulls and other outports.[42] One of the first victims at St John's was the gaoler himself.

According to Fr James O Donel, the epidemic was the last straw in what had been a difficult time for the settlement. Writing to his friend John Troy, Archbishop of Dublin, on Christmas Eve 1789, he lamented:

> This is the worse [sic] year ever remembered in this country; the low price of fish, together with the great reductions of the servants [sic] wages brought the inhabitants to extreme poverty & to increase this misery we've had a most malignant jail fever imported to us by some unhappy convicts landed here from your city, of which no

less than 200 people already died in this Harbour which is as yet an intire [sic] Hospital. I've the Lord be blessed escaped it tho' of a most infectious & dangerous nature.[43]

Another indication of the high mortality was that the Anglican chaplain at St John's had officiated at the burials of no less than 102 people by mid-November, including that of his own son.[44] As carriers of the disease, the convicts seem to have been relatively immune to it and only one death was recorded from their number, the Protestant John Keeley on 13 August.[45]

'The most outrageous Set of People that ever lived'

In addition to the immediate threat they posed to property, another reason for the hostile response to the convicts from the *Duke of Leinster* was the danger they were seen to offer to general peace and good order. Indeed, Irish immigrant workers in Newfoundland had been regarded as a problem by the local authorities long before the arrival of the *Duke of Leinster*. As early as 1705 when England was at war with France, the resident English naval officer at St John's warned 'of the Irish resideing in this Country for they by our daily [sic] Experience have proved detrimental to the Governmt. here ffor when the Enemy makes any Incursion upon us they doe take up armes and informe our Enemy. And prove very treacherous and our greatest Enemy'.[46] When St John's was taken by the French in 1714, the loss was attributed to Catholic Irish deserters.[47] At the same time, however, there was a steady increase in the resident Irish merchant community.

During the 1740s there were frequent complaints from officials about the loyalty of the Irish Catholics, particularly in the 'outports' (harbour settlements) along the Southern Shore where the Irish were in a clear majority. In 1749, for example, Governor Rodney reported to London that the Irish Catholics were 'most notoriously disaffected to the Government'.[48] And in one of the first comprehensive accounts of Newfoundland, published in 1765, Capt. Griffith Williams, a Welsh military officer who had been posted at St John's, wrote of the period after the Treaty of Aix la Chapelle:

At this Time great numbers of *Irish Roman Catholics* were in the Island as Servants; but no sooner had the [British] Troops been sent away, than they became the most outrageous Set of People that ever lived: Robberies were committed almost every Day in one Place or other, the Magistrates insulted in the Execution of their Office, and the Chief Justice murdered; many hundreds of the West of *England* People were afraid of going over, many of the *Newfoundland* men left the Island, and the Roman Catholics transported themselves by Hundreds from *Ireland*: So that at the Time the *French* took the Country, the *Irish* were above six Times the Number of West Country and *Newfoundlanders*: In short, they were in Possession of above three Quarters of the Fish Rooms and Harbours of the Island, who consequently welcomed the French with open Arms. And during the time the French were in Possession of the Island, the Merchants and Inhabitants suffered more cruelties from the *Irish Roman Catholics*, than they did from the declared Enemy.[49]

About 700 Irishmen were reported by Sir Joseph Banks to have served with the French during their brief seizure of Newfoundland in 1762[50] and Williams held them largely responsible for the French success. The murder of the Chief Justice to which Williams referred was probably the robbery and killing of William Keen, one of St John's leading English Protestant merchants, by Catholic Irish in 1753. Williams advised accordingly that 'none but the Inhabitants of Great Britain, *Newfoundland*, with Jersey and Guernsey (being Protestants) should have the Privilege of being possessed of any Fish Rooms, or Plantations in the Island of *Newfoundland*'. 'The *Irish Roman Catholics*', he warned, 'are useful as Servants, but very dangerous in that Part of the World, when in Power'.[51]

Political loyalty was a vital issue during these decades when the British and the French were battling for control of North America and the West Indies. This explains the new set of regulations issued on 31 October 1764, after the British re-occupation of Newfoundland under Governor Palliser, for 'the better ... preserving the peace, preventing robberies, tumulteous [*sic*] assemblies and other disorders of wicked and idle people roaming in the country during the winter'.[52] The restrictions were clearly aimed at stemming the flow of Irish immigrant workers and preventing them from spending the winter on the island.

A repressive policy towards Catholic Irish had already been practised under governors Bonfoy and Dorrill, largely in the guise of restricting permanent settlement on the island. In 1755, Dorrill even authorised the unsuccessful search for an Irish Augustinian priest in the Conception Bay area, which resulted in the burning of a building where Mass had been said and the fining of Catholics who had attended.[53] However, the Poole and Dartmouth merchants who financed and controlled most of the Newfoundland cod industry told the Board of Trade in London in 1764 that the behaviour of the Catholics had 'given no cause to apprehend any Danger to the well affected to His Majesty's Person & Government residing there'.[54] They knew very well that the industry was dependent on seasonal Irish labourers who were preferred to the English because of their steadiness and capacity for hard work.[55]

Although they had supported the French, the Newfoundland Irish did not side openly with the American colonies during the Revolutionary War. This may well have been in response to the policy of free exercise of religion adopted by the British governors of the island following official instructions in 1779 which in turn reflected the lifting of some of the penal laws in England and Ireland.[56] Religious toleration was confirmed in 1783 during the governorship of Vice-Admiral John Campbell. Permission was obtained to build a chapel and the first Roman Catholic priest, Fr James Louis O Donel of the Franciscan Order, arrived at St John's in July 1784. A well-educated and cosmopolitan man appointed by the Vatican as Prefect Apostolic of what was to become the separate ecclesiastical territory of Newfoundland, O'Donel also had a good knowledge of the Irish language. This was essential as the great majority of his parishioners were Waterford men who could speak little else. Court hearings in Newfoundland in the 1780s and 1790s frequently necessitated the employment of an interpreter.[57]

Prince William Henry

In the outport communities where the Irish outnumbered the English, the maintenance of official authority was sometimes a problem. Writing from Bonavista to Governor Elliot in September 1786, magistrate Langdon begged for assistance in maintaining good order in his community of more than 3,000, 'mostly a low Class of People and so difficult to be governed that I am often in danger of violence from them'.[58] He had recently put a man in the stocks for petty theft, only for him to be released by forty or fifty others who sent word to Langdon that it was fortunate he had not fallen in their way. The uncertain basis of the whole judicial system in Newfoundland also meant that crimes could be committed with impunity.[59]

In August 1786 there was an incident at Placentia Harbour, Newfoundland's second largest settlement, which illustrated the potentially turbulent behaviour not only of the Irish workers but of the youngest scion of the Royal House of Hanover.[60] During his visit there

19 HMS *Pegasus* at the entrance to St John's harbour, 1786.

as commander of the 28-gun frigate HMS *Pegasus* from July until September 1786, the 20-year-old Prince William Henry, Duke of Clarence and England's future King William IV, took his turn as 'surrogate' or deputy judge of the Court of Vice-Admiralty as was customary for naval officers posted to the Newfoundland Station.[61]

A staunch upholder of the Anglican ascendancy, Clarence was deeply concerned about the influence being exercised by the newly established Catholic mission in Newfoundland. With Governor Campbell's permission, O Donel had recently completed the first Catholic chapel at St John's and was ranged in an unlikely alliance with the Congregational minister, the Revd John Jones, against the Anglican chaplain, the Revd Walter Price, who bitterly resented their presence. Nor was the Catholic mission's influence limited to St John's. O'Donel had installed a Dominican priest, Fr Edmund Burke, at Placentia who was building another chapel there while celebrating Mass in the local court house.

Angered by what he saw as unnecessary concessions to Papists, Clarence took immediate steps to shore up the weak position of the Church of England at Placentia and to harass Burke. Banning the further use of the court house for Mass, Clarence publicly accused the priest of treason for making converts and prohibited him from marrying Protestants to Catholics and burying them in the same cemetery, as had long been the custom. He also dismissed a constable and an Ordnance blacksmith who were Catholics.

When a disturbance broke out in the town on 6 August, probably as a result of these initiatives, the firm-handed Clarence took prompt action. In a letter to his father, King George III, he gave what was probably a tactfully edited account of his forceful response:

> as it was a Sunday, the Irish servants came in from fishing, & after having got drunk they assembled to the number of 300 before the Fort where the magistrate lives and abused him grossly, upon his going out to disperse them. They attempted to break the constables' staves & threw large pieces of rock & stones at the civil officers. The magistrate immediately came on board to acquaint me of the riot. I then went on shore with the boat manned & armed & the marines: upon our landing they dispersed & I pursued them over the beach till the ringleader was apprehended: I then called a Court, & sentenced him to receive a hundred lashes, which punishment was immediately inflicted with the utmost severity.[62]

This, together with his examination of another man from an outlying harbour settlement the next day for 'a multiplicity of crimes [too] shocking to mention', moved Clarence to assemble all the male inhabitants over the age of twelve at the court house and have them swear an oath of allegiance to the British Crown.[63]

In a subsequent letter to Governor Elliot, Clarence issued a strong warning about Burke:

> I found that the priest from his very great ascendancy over the weak minds of weak People had made in the course of these last twelve months, a number of Proselytes & I have observed Since I have been in this Port that more Respect and Regard is shown him, by the lower Class of Inhabitants, than the Surrogate himself or any of the Justices of the Peace & as there are none of his Majesty's troops here, I have every reason to believe, that at my departure, most fatal Consequences will arrive, without the Growing Power of the Roman Priest in the outer harbours be now restrained in its Present State of Infancy.[64]

When he discovered on his return to St John's that O Donel had written to Elliot asking him to intercede over the measures he had taken at Placentia, Clarence flew into a rage. O Donel gave a graphic account to Archbishop Troy of Clarence's threat to his life and his preservation by the Irish merchant, Gleeson:

> This [letter], together with the squawks of our good and virtuous ladies, so embittered His Highness against me that he insulted me

with obscene language and with great violence threw a heavy iron file at me from a window which, however, did not seriously injure me but only caused a slight wound on my shoulders. But he had really determined to take my life in the following way. He was supposed to have had two sailors as onlookers who would have sworn I had insulted him and that he, without taking time to think about it, had run me through with his sword, and at the same time determined to set fire to our chapel. All [of] which was discovered through Divine Providence the day before it was to have been carried out. Whereupon Mr. Gleeson ... brought me hastily to his house, and hid me in an attic where I remained for twelve days, without a spark of fire, and deprived of any other comfort, even without the servants in the same house knowing I was there. But all the while handily looked after by Mr. Gleeson who carried to his house under cover of night all the things of value belonging to the chapel, and he spread the rumour that I had fled by land to Portugal Cove.[65]

The headstrong Clarence certainly seems to have over-reacted to the situation he found in Newfoundland, but his fears that the Catholic Irish posed a threat to the security of the island were not entirely unfounded. Fourteen years later, in April 1800, St John's was to see the repercussions of the 1798 Irish Rebellion when the predominantly Irish members of the Newfoundland Fencibles Regiment garrisoned at Fort Townshend conspired to seize control of the town and hold it to ransom until the British government made concessions in Ireland to the Society of United Irishmen.[66] Even so, it was O Donel who played a crucial part in persuading the Catholic Irish population not to support the rebels and was subsequently rewarded with a government pension at the instigation of grateful merchants and military officers.[67]

The Ferryland 'riots'

During the winters of 1788 and 1789, unemployed young Irish workers, many of them 'masterless men' who had been laid off by their employers before the end of the normal eighteen months engagement period, converged on St John's and Ferryland Harbour further south to find employment as 'dieters', an arrangement by which they worked for the fishing masters without wages for their board and lodging. Those unable to find even this basic form of support had to beg for their existence. It was probably for this reason that in June 1788 the

St John's magistrates had ordered the repatriation to Waterford of William Condron and Elinor Connery in the brig *Ann and Francis*. According to Thomas D'Ewes Coke, the controller of customs and principal magistrate of the town, Condron was 'an incorrigible Rogue and Vagrant'. For her part, Elinor Connery had been convicted of being 'a lewd disorderly Woman and a Common Prostitute having had a Child and left it exposed to the open Air upon a Common Wharf ...'.[68]

The problem with repatriation, however, was that the Irish executive government was not disposed to accept the legality of actions taken by Newfoundland magistrates or – perhaps more importantly – to meet the costs involved. Complaining to Grenville's predecessor, Lord Sydney, that the magistrates had signed warrants of banishment to Ireland for Condron and Connery, the Marquis of Buckingham in July 1788 requested him to 'take such Measures as may appear ... best calculated to Put a Stop to a Practice of this Nature, the illegality and inexpedience [*sic*] of which are sufficiently obvious'.[69]

During the autumn of 1788, fighting between rival groups of Leinstermen and Munstermen had broken out in the predominantly Irish Catholic outport of Ferryland Harbour. Violent factional disputes of sometimes ancient lineage were a feature of life in late eighteenth century Leinster and Munster.[70] Brought to Newfoundland, together with the vigorous game of hurling, they provided an explosive combination at what seems to have been an annual end-of-season gathering of the fishery workers. The Surrogate Court at Ferryland had fined more than one hundred of those involved in the September 'riots', repatriating six and banishing another twelve who had escaped prosecution.[71] Governor Elliot subsequently agreed to build a gaol and a court house there to help the local magistrates maintain order.

The conflict at Ferryland Harbour between the Leinster and Munster 'boys' had been sparked off by a bitter dispute between the officially-appointed O Donel and a maverick Irish priest at Ferryland, Fr Patrick Power, over the ecclesiastical jurisdiction of the Southern Shore.[72] While O Donel was a Tipperary man, Power was from Kilkenny and as a result of the latter's provocative speeches, 'the old quarrels were renewed & brought to such a pitch that no man was safe in appearing either by day or by night unless attended by numbers of wel armed men'.[73] Believing their personal dispute to be the cause of the riots, Governor Elliot took O Donel to task while the Ferryland magistrates admonished Power. Writing in late October 1788 about the two priests, Elliot reassured the Ferryland magistrates that 'their diabolical proceedings will be not suffered to pass unnoticed or with impunity ...'.[74] This was a milder response than had come from the Surrogate Judge, Captain Edward Pellew, RN, who 'denounced Pope, Popery, Priests & Priestcraft' from the bench and called on the governor to banish them both.[75]

Strenuously rejecting the accusation that he had been responsible for the disturbances, O Donel told Elliot:

> As for the riots in Ferryland they cou'd by no means proceed from the disagreement between this clergyman & me, as there have been riots there & in every quarter of the Island those [sic] 40 years past & often brought to an higher pitch than they have been this winter, for there is a deep-rooted malice in the hearts of the lower class of Irishmen to each other from the great abuse & horrid mangling they have receivd from time to time in those Provincial Quarrels.
>
> These quarrels partly originated from drinking & idleness but chiefly for the want of [religious] instruction, of which they were then debarr'd by the laws, which were so rigorously executed in this Island as to burn the very House in which a few clergymen lurked or even said their prayers.[76]

Indeed, O Donel claimed that he had done everything possible to discourage members of his flock from pursuing old factional antagonisms and from attending the hurling matches at Ferryland that year 'which were generally productive of the riots'.[77] Insisting that the presence of priests had actually dampened down the conflict, he claimed that the 'Seneschals of sedition, if there be any, could be rather found among the envious merchants of Ferryland than among the Popish priests as the voice of prejudice now runs'.[78] It was certainly true that until the establishment of the Catholic mission, the West Country captains, together with the merchants and planters who controlled the magistracy, exercised an almost unbridled authority over their Irish servants.[79]

A dramatic example of how this was abused was the axe-murder of Captain Henry Brooks of Teignmouth by three Irish servants on board his banker at Newfoundland in 1790, which was believed to have been the result of 'some gross maltreatment'. According to a Waterford source cited by the *Hibernian Journal*,

> Last year he took a number of fishermen passengers from Newfoundland for Waterford. On the passage he used them very severely, and put them, unnecessarily, on short allowance; on

making the land he obliged them to go ashore in the county Cork, from whence the poor men had to walk to this city. This not being thought sufficient to fill up the measure of their disappointments and misfortunes, he sailed to England with their chests, etc although at landing his passengers he had solemnly promised he would come round and deliver their chests here, according to his original agreement.[80]

'Such a Banditti'

When Vice-Admiral Milbanke arrived at St John's on board HMS *Salisbury* on 4 September 1789, he was informed about the convicts and promptly wrote to the town's magistrates expressing warm support for their action:

> I am to acquaint you that altho' there does not appear to be any charge made against them, so as to authorize their being committed to Prison, yet, as the safety of the Place was at stake I think you acted very prudently in complying with the desire of the Inhabitants and thereby prevented many irregularities in the Fishery, which would have been the consequence of suffering such a Banditti to go at large about the Island. It now remains to be considered where they are to be sent to and what more is necessary to be adopted for defraying the Expence [sic] of conveying them from hence.[81]

Milbanke proposed to the magistrates that they call a public meeting to decide the best means of raising a levy to pay for the repatriation of the convicts, the basic principle being that St John's should meet half the cost and that the remainder be shared 'by the rest of the Island'.[82] Following the meeting's recommendations, he issued an order that the owners of every merchant ship and banker should pay 10s., every four-man shallop 4s., every skiff 2s. and every inhabitant 3s..[83] Unaware of the problems that might arise from enforcing the collection of tax in a community which as yet possessed no form of constitutional representation, Milbanke blithely told the hapless magistrates that they could 'distress' or confiscate goods or property to the appropriate value from any person who refused to pay. This, he assured them, could be done under the authority of a British Act (*17 George II, c. 5, sec. 2*) which obliged local communities to bear the cost of removing vagrants.[84] Not surprisingly, this unprecedented and almost certainly illegal form of

voluntary taxation was highly unpopular and Milbanke was to experience great trouble enforcing it. Although it did not result in a 'no taxation without representation' agitation, the issue no doubt contributed
to the subsequent clarification of the island's constitutional and
judicial status.[85]

'The best Shoplifter in Ireland'

On Milbanke's direction, a list was made on 7 September of the 64
male convicts then being held at the Winter house, including their age
and place of origin and in some instances the nature of their crime
and sentence.[86] Ten or eleven more subsequently brought in from Bay
Bulls were not included. Of those listed, 22 were from Dublin, one was
from Belfast and one from Cork, while the others represented almost
all the other counties of Ireland. Most were in their early twenties.

Although their offences and sentences were not recorded in every
instance, it is clear that the majority were petty thieves or robbers who
had been sentenced to seven years' transportation. John O Neal, 20, of
Dublin, who headed the list, was described (no doubt from his own
proud boast) as 'the best Shoplifter in Ireland', and had been transported for seven years for 'Stealing Waistcoats'. He had escaped from
custody two weeks earlier. More seriously, James Myler, 20, of
Donaghadee, Co. Down and Dennis Newenham, 19, of Dublin had
been sentenced to death at the Dublin City quarter sessions in October
1788 for 'having assaulted Henry Jolly, at Stephen's Green, and taking
from him a silver watch, value 3£'.[87] John Keough, 22, also of Dublin,
was described as 'A famous Porter Stealer but does not know for what
he was Tried'. Patrick Leonard (or Lennon), 40, of Kinnagad, Co.
Westmeath, had been sentenced to death in Dublin in January 1789
for knocking down and robbing a man in Dublin's Smock-alley and
trying to sell his hat, shoes and other belongings to a pawnbroker.[88]
Three men had been convicted of coining, two of swindling, three of
burglary and one of highway robbery. Only two had committed the
distinctively rural offence of animal-stealing. Francis Lacey, 41, of
Castle Dermot, Co. Kildare, had been convicted of stealing a sheep and
John Byrne, 22, of Co. Dublin had stolen a cow. Thomas McDermot,
20, of Edgerstown, Co. Longford, had stolen a pound of tobacco.

The most serious offender was Cornelius Brosnahan, 23, of Tralee,
Co. Kerry, who had been found guilty of murder and sentenced to
death, 'but from some Error in the Trial changed to Transportation'. At
the other end of the scale were John Coyle, 21, of Dublin, Samuel Ellis,

18, of Co. Carlow and Daniel McAleese, 20, of Belfast who had apparently been transported under the Vagabonds Act as vagrants. William Gibbeons, 22, of Dublin had been accused of attempting to break into a house but was ordered to be flogged and transported 'for want of Bail'. Amongst the others were two 13-year-old boys and two 14-year-olds. Of these, the only one whose offence was recorded was John Farrell of Dublin who had been convicted 'For Theft'. As the twelve women had been allowed to remain at large in the town, their names and offences were not recorded in this document. However, six of them were listed together with the 74 or more men and boys who were returned to England in late October.

One of the twelve or more of the Newfoundland convicts who, after many vicissitudes, were subsequently transported to New South Wales was Michael Delaney, 30, 'a most notorious offender' originally convicted and sentenced to seven years' transportation at the Commission of Oyer and Terminer in October 1788 for obtaining a silver watch under false pretences from Frederick May, watchmaker, of Capel-street, Dublin.[89]

In the meantime, security at the improvised prison on the Barrens proved difficult to maintain. The first to escape on 22 August were John O Neal and young John Farrell. O Neal was apparently recaptured but Farrell, who may have found a place for himself with a sympathetic fishing master, disappeared henceforth from the official record.

'Cruising' in Newfoundland

Before Milbanke's arrival, the magistrates of St John's had instituted a system whereby sick convicts could obtain a written pass permitting them to stay in the town. However, the experiment went badly wrong when one of the first beneficiaries resumed his old habits. James Reily, 28, linen bleacher of Cootehill, Co. Cavan, had been sentenced to death for highway robbery, subsequently commuted to transportation. On 18 July he stole a leather case of medical instruments from the shop of surgeon John MacCurdy of St John's in the mistaken belief that it contained money and valuables. Then on 4 August he stole a shirt left drying on a garden fence by an Irish washerwoman and used it to pay for his night's lodging at a boarding-house kept by a certain Margaret Welsh. Unfortunately for him, the shirt's owner was the Clerk of the Peace at St John's, William Easton. The same night Reily smashed a window of the house of the Revd Walter Price and stole a table cloth and an unfinished linen shirt. The Prices had helped him when he was ill and had even given him dinner some nights earlier. He also broke into the house of William Humphrey, the government store-keeper, and stole his hat and great-coat.

Suspecting that Reily was responsible for the burglaries, news of which must have spread quickly in the small community, his landlady searched his room the next morning and found the table cloth in his bed. According to the evidence she later gave in court,

> He fell down upon his knees, and told her that a woman had given it to him, but that he would not tell her name ... That in that posture he lifted up his Hands and said 'my dear Mrs Welsh, my dear Christianable woman, my Life is in your Hands, my dear Mrs for God's! sake spare my life'.

A further search of the room by Welsh and her husband brought to light the other items which had been stolen, including MacCurdy's razor.

Brought before the magistrates at a specially summoned assizes on 30 September, Reily was tried on two charges of Grand Larceny. His defence was that two other convicts, Daniel McAleese and Patrick Leonard, had come to his room at the lodging house and threatened to 'blow his brains out' if he did not conceal the stolen articles for them. Another convict, John O Neal, who was sharing a room with McAleese and Leonard at the Winter house, testified that he heard the two men saying on the night of 4 August that they knew how to escape the notice of the guard and were determined to 'go to the Town on a Cruise'. However, they had returned later, saying they 'had done no Good, meaning that the Cruise had been unsuccessfull [sic]'.[90] Found guilty on both charges, Reily was sentenced to be 'Burnt in the Hand with a hot iron having upon it the Figure of the letter T ...' and to be 'dismissed'. The normal penalty for larceny of this kind was death but as most of the offences had taken place over a twenty-four hour period, the magistrates decided to be merciful.[91]

'Every means in my power'

When Milbanke learnt on 13 September that one of the convicts held at the Winter house had been allowed to 'go into the Town upon leave', he immediately issued an order that 'none of the convicts for the future, be upon any pretence whatsoever permitted to go out of the Charge of the Centinels [sic] appointed to take care of them'.[92] In spite of this precaution, six more escaped a month later and not all were recovered.[93] Milbanke subsequently directed that the officer responsible for the guard at the time be court-martialled for negligence.[94]

Writing to the newly-appointed Home Secretary, William Grenville, on 20 September to report on the convicts, Milbanke subsequently enclosed a report of Reily's trial and a number of other documents relating to the unwelcome arrivals whom he described as disturbing what had been a flourishing and peaceful settlement:

> Till those wretches came into the Country, open and professed Villainy, it seems, was little known amongst the lower order of people engaged in the Fishery, but since their arrival, very frequent punishments have taken place for petty crimes (not very common heretofore) and I am afraid, unless the greatest precautions are taken to prevent it, the Spirit of thieving will soon find too good root in the Island to be eradicated (if at all possible) without much difficulty. This [,] joined to the consequences to be dreaded from a fever, which was rife amongst them when they first came to St John's (but is now subsided) has determined me to use every means in my power to get them sent away.[95]

Anticipating that it might well meet with disapproval in London, he nevertheless announced his intention of carrying out the principal merchants' plan of sending the convicts back to Spithead 'to wait the Commands of His Majesty's Ministers'.[96]

In his despatch to Grenville, Milbanke painted a somewhat rosy picture of Newfoundland's rough-and-ready frontier society, about which he would learn a good deal more during the following month. After some years of rapid growth in the fishing industry after the end of the American war, 1788 had seen a dramatic increase in the catch of cod but a decline in the price that it could bring.[97] By early 1789 the island's highly vulnerable economy was sliding into the doldrums. In the meantime, the availability of winter work had boosted the 'wintering' or resident population of the island to almost 20,000.[98] A prominent planter at Conception Harbour noted 'a great number of unshipped men' staying on in the autumn of 1789 and 'a vast number' in the following year.[99]

As the winter of 1789 approached, the numbers of would-be dieters in St John's increased to such an extent that they were becoming a serious nuisance. On 17 September, Milbanke wrote to Capt. Walter Rose of the military garrison at Fort Townshend:

In addition to the Irish Convicts, there are so many Idle persons now about this Town, that it is becoming absolutely necessary for the safety of the Fishery, to take some steps for their removal ... and that those that have been brought hither, by Persons engaged in the Fishery, and left without Masters during the Summer, should be carried back again to the country from which they came (or at any rate taken off from the Island) by the same persons.[100]

Four days earlier, the governor had issued a proclamation warning seamen or fishermen intending to come to St John's for the winter, that they would be 'punished as Vagrants and sent back to the places whence they came by the earliest opportunity that offers'.[101] And after his departure for England on 31 October, the town's magistrates duly ordered the repatriation of a number of Irish, the cost of their passages presumably to be met once again by the Irish government.

While Captain Edward Pellew who prosecuted the Ferryland rioters had been influenced against O'Donel, Governor Elliot seems to have accepted the priest's defence. However, Governor Milbanke shared the minority Protestant Establishment's anxiety about the loyalty of the Irish at Ferryland and the other harbour settlements and his attitude to O'Donel was less sympathetic than that of his predecessor. For example, he not only refused O'Donel permission to build a Catholic chapel at Ferryland but indicated that he would place the two existing chapels at St John's and Placentia 'under particular restrictions'.[102] He also asked the Revd Richard Harris, who had just been posted to Placentia by the Society for the Propagation of the Gospel, to make a confidential report to him 'on the exact situation of the Romish Church at that Place, withholding nothing'.[103]

The *Elizabeth and Clare*

Determined to 'get the Convicts away in the best manner I can, for at all events such a Banditti cannot be suffer'd to remain here during the Winter',[104] Milbanke advertised on 17 September for a ship to take 'between sixty and eighty' convicts back to England. He stipulated that each was to be supplied with $3\frac{1}{2}$ pounds of bread, 2 pounds of flour, 3 pounds of pork, 3 pints of pease, half a pound of butter and 7 gallons of water per week.[105] It is unlikely that many captains would have been enthusiastic about the prospect of taking on such a troublesome cargo and it must have been a relief for Milbanke when for a total cost of £400 he managed to charter the 114-ton Teignmouth-registered brigantine, *Elizabeth and Clare*, commanded by an experienced West Country captain, Robert Coyshe. At £5 per head with rations provided, this was the normal rate for a trans-Atlantic passage.

Anxious about the security of the convicts on board the vessel, Milbanke commissioned a local blacksmith to make sets of shackles for them. However, he was also concerned about their well-being on the voyage, ordering the barracks master at Fort Townshend to supply them with forty beds, bolsters, blankets and coverlets previously used by the garrison.[106] In addition, 'as the Convicts were in a wretched state and daily falling sick for want of Cloathing, which some of them were almost destitute of at the time of their landing', he directed Captain Domett of HMS *Salisbury* to issue each of them with 'navy slops', consisting of a shirt, frock (jacket), trousers, shoes and stockings.[107] These were promptly bartered for rum and by the end of the voyage most of the convicts were reported as being half-naked with only biscuit-bags for clothing.[108]

In his letter of instructions to Coyshe, Milbanke told him to make the best of his way to Spithead where he was to inform Grenville of the ship's arrival and await further instructions. He was to be 'particularly careful of the ... Convicts during the time they shall remain on board the Brig and to let nothing be wanting on your part to carry them safe to the Port of Destination'.[109] By stipulating Spithead, Milbanke obviously had in mind that Grenville would arrange their transportation from there to New South Wales. Portsmouth had been the gathering place in May 1787 for the First Fleet of convict transports bound for Botany Bay and Milbanke may have been aware of plans for the Second Fleet to assemble there in early 1790.[110]

In the meantime, Milbanke was experiencing great difficulty in collecting subscriptions from the harbour-based fishing communities towards the cost of removing the convicts. By 7 October no payments had been made to the Treasurer, Aaron Graham, although the magistrates at Ferryland and Harbour Grace had written seeking permission to raise the money in a way more agreeable to themselves. In his response to the Harbour Grace magistrates, Milbanke expressed some of the frustration he felt about an affair which had occupied most of his time and energy since his arrival:

> I beg you will assure the Gentlemen of [your] District that as I have nothing more at heart than the public good, I cannot but be pleased with this instance of their readiness to assist, in a Matter, which altho' not so much mine, as it is the business of almost

every other person in the Island, yet has given me infinite trouble, and uneasiness.[111]

When the merchants of the only predominantly Protestant outport of Harbour Grace subsequently sent him the £90 which they had raised, Milbanke was quick to thank them, adding appreciatively that 'while I have the Honor to Govern this Island, I cannot possibly forget there is such a place in it as Harbour Grace'.[112]

To Milbanke's disappointment and embarrassment, however, the money finally raised from the levy on the other harbour communities amounted to no more £184, less than a quarter of the £775.1s.7d. which had been spent on the convicts. The total annual vote by the House of Commons for the governance of Newfoundland was only £1,182.10s.0d., all of which was committed to nornal expenditure. Milbanke had also been obliged to find money to pay for the new courthouse and gaol at Ferryland authorised by his predecessor. Accordingly, after his return to London in late November that year he wrote to Grenville that he had 'been obliged myself to advance most of the money for chartering the said vessel [*Elizabeth and Clare*], making the Irons and paying for the House ... and a Doctor for his medicines and attendance'.[113] William Easton, the Clerk of the Peace at St John's whose shirt had been stolen by James Reily, subsequently claimed that he, too, had spent a good deal of his own money on the convicts.[114]

When the convicts were finally embarked on the *Elizabeth and Clare* at St John's on 24 October 1789, Captain Robert Coyshe was provided with a list of the names of 74 men and boys, including Matthew Dempsey and James McGuire who had first provided information to the magistrates, together with six women who had been allowed to remain free in the town.[115] During the period since 7 September when the original list of 64 convicts had been compiled by the magistrates, at least seven had escaped from the Winter house and a dozen or so others may have been released to find employment in the fishing industry.

There were at least eighteen names on the 7 September list which did not appear on Coyshe's list. At the same time, there were at least 24 names (excluding the women) on Coyshe's list which were not on the 7 September list. It is also clear that Coyshe's list did not include all those who were embarked. For example, James Myler (Millar) was included but not his former partner in crime, Denis Newenham, although both were later recorded as transported to New South Wales on the *Queen* in April 1791.[116] Apart from the women, a significant number of the convicts who had not been rounded up by the magistrates in August must have been subsequently apprehended or had given themselves up to the authorities, including Newenham and ten late arrivals from Bay Bulls. James Reily, who had been branded on the hand for thieving at St John's, was not on board, although he was one of the most likely people to have been sent back.

Richard Robinson, who had first alerted the authorities to the convicts' arrival, was included in Coyshe's list and was taken on board the *Elizabeth and Clare* in irons with the convicts. Happily for him, however, the mistake was discovered and he was put on board HMS *Salisbury* instead.[117] Another passenger when the ship sailed for Portsmouth on 31 October was the chief magistrate of St John's, Thomas D'Ewes Coke, whom Milbanke had wisely decided to take along for support in case his actions were questioned by the Home Office or the Admiralty on his return.

Three days after Milbanke's departure, the remaining magistrates of St John's ordered the whipping of four men and the deportation of one of the women convicts who had been allowed to stay behind. No names or other details were recorded, but it seems that she had been involved in prostitution and that the men punished were her clients. As the cost of her passage was only £2, she was probably taken to one of the New England ports rather than across the Atlantic.[118] What happened to the nineteen or more male convicts and the five other women who remained behind in Newfoundland is impossible to determine. It seems likely, however, that the women quickly found themselves partners in the predominantly male society and that the men originating from Waterford and Cork found employment with their compatriots in the fishing industry. Some of their surnames appear in the island's 1794 census, but these were already common because of earlier Irish immigration and it is difficult to establish any definite correspondence.[119] On the other hand, the total absence from the census of the more identifiably English family names of the Protestant convicts suggests that they made their way south to New England as those landed at the Bay of Machias in late 1786 had done.

10
The Newfoundland Convict Crisis

It was the return of the Irish convicts from Newfoundland which set the final seal on Irish transportation to North America. In the correspondence between London officials and Dublin Castle which ensued from Governor Milbanke's action, we can trace the extraordinary course of events which brought about the final abandonment of the trans-Atlantic convict trade.

On 17 November 1789, the badly-leaking *Elizabeth and Clare* made Spithead with seventy-nine convicts on board. As it was already very late in the season, the voyage had no doubt been a rough one and many of the convicts were in a lamentable condition on arrival. Nor was there to be relief for very long in the thought that they were now close to home: some unexpected legal and political problems meant that it was another two months before they were to see Dublin again.

Carrying out Milbanke's instructions, Captain Coyshe informed Grenville of the ship's arrival, sending on to him a packet containing the Admiral's official dispatch with its various enclosures relating to the convicts. However, Milbanke himself had arrived at Portsmouth two days earlier and a set of the documents were already with the Home Secretary. When Grenville passed these on to Lord Chancellor Edward Thurlow for his opinion on 17 November,[1] the latter advised him the same day that the convicts should be returned to Ireland forthwith. In his view, they ought to be dealt with there 'according to their law, as their sentence seems not to have been executed'.[2] He enclosed a draft warrant which he suggested could be sent with them.

Not entirely satisfied with this advice, Grenville returned the warrant to Thurlow with some suggested alterations to the wording. He told him that there was no point in referring to the convicts as having to be tried in Ireland when it was clear from their own testimony that they had already been convicted and sentenced there. Emphasising the 'novelty and peculiarity of this case', he thought that an order of the Privy Council would be more appropriate than a warrant in his name and he sought a meeting to discuss the matter.[3]

'As to the Council', Thurlow replied dismissively, 'I don't think it a subject to discuss'. If Grenville still wanted a meeting, however, he thought that it should be a small one with only half a dozen Councillors, mostly the lawyers, present. Anything more 'would elevate the thing too much to make it the subject of *eclat*'.[4] Indeed, after cross-examining Milbanke, d'Ewes Coke and Robinson on 24 November, Prime Minister William Pitt and the other Councillors decided that the convicts should simply be sent back to Ireland with a warrant from the Home Secretary.[5]

In a letter which was probably written just before the meeting, Thurlow told Grenville that the 'short method' they had first discussed – of ordering Coyshe to proceed to Ireland – 'might have been sufficient'. However, the leaking condition of the *Elizabeth and Clare* posed a problem and there was also the question of American sensitivities: 'if the sending [of] transports to the American States be a point upon which that country takes an obstinate turn, it may be proper, on that account also, to observe more form'. He concluded:

> Something must be hazarded at last; because it is of course impossible to manifest their true condition by the best evidence, the record of their conviction, and proof of personal identity. But considering that examinations have been taken in the island from some of them, who have confessed their situation, and that other grounds to establish the belief may be deposed by Admiral Milbank [*sic*] ... there will be ground enough for the usual warrant, founded on suspicion, to send them over.[6]

As the Lords Justices of Ireland constituted the executive in Dublin until the new Lord Lieutenant, the Earl of Westmorland, was installed at Dublin Castle in January of the following year, it was to them that Grenville wrote on 25 November after the Privy Council meeting saying that he had signed a warrant for the convicts' return to Dublin. A transport lying at Portsmouth, the *Deptford*, had been commissioned to convey them with an accompanying sloop of war, the *Drake*.[7] This precaution suggests that Grenville was still concerned that their return to Ireland might not be a straightforward affair. Indeed, in his private letter of the same day to the new Irish Secretary, Major Robert Hobart, informing him of his action, the Home Secretary wrote:

> Although our lawyers here are all agreed that the proceeding thus far is perfectly legal and regular, there seems to be more doubt with respect to that which is to take place in Ireland on the arrival of these convicts in Dublin.[8]

While acknowledging that the Irish decision rested with the Court of King's Bench and not with the executive government, Grenville thought that 'any delay or difference of opinion may lead to some awkwardness'. He suggested to Hobart that it would be 'highly expedient' for him to talk to Lord Chancellor Fitzgibbon and perhaps to the Lord Chief Justice, Lord Clonmel. The solution he hoped for was that the Court of King's Bench would remand the convicts to the prisons of the courts where they had been tried until the Irish Parliament could amend its legislation to authorise their transportation to New South Wales. To this end, Grenville advised Hobart that if the King authorised the reception of Irish prisoners at the new settlement, the cost of their passage would be £17 per head, together with provisions for their passage and for a year after their arrival. The Irish government would also have to make a contribution towards the garrison which would be needed to guard them – perhaps in the form of an Irish company to be added to the recently-formed New South Wales Corps in the same way that Irish troops had been helping to protect the West Indian colonies. This was the most positive response that the Irish government had yet received to its continued requests for participation in the Botany Bay scheme, although it was still hedged with the formality of the King's permission – a device which allowed Grenville to stop short of committing himself completely.

At the same time, the Home Secretary had some sharp things to say about the Irish authorities' continued recourse to transportation to North America and the West Indies:

> The awkwardness, inconvenience, and expence [*sic*] of the whole business is so very great, that I must earnestly request of you to consider again with the Lord Chancellor as to the means of preventing any repetition of it. The landing [of] convicts in the territories of the United States (even if the masters of the ships perform their contracts in so doing) is an act highly offensive to a country now foreign and independent; and as such, very improper for the

Government to authorize. And it is besides an act of great cruelty to the convicts, who, being turned on shore without the necessities of life, are either left to starve, or (as sometimes has been the case) are massacred by the inhabitants. And as to transporting to the King's American colonies, you may depend on it, that after the example set them by Admiral Millbanke [*sic*], none of our Governors will suffer any of these people to be landed in their governments; and that, if landed by stealth, they will send them back at very heavy expense [sic] which must fall upon the Irish government.[9]

'Scurvy and the Flux'

In the second week of December, the Newfoundland convicts were transferred from the *Elizabeth and Clare* to the *Deptford* which then sailed for Dublin accompanied by the *Drake*. However, stormy weather forced the two vessels to shelter at Cowes and it was there that the deplorable physical condition of the convicts was brought to the attention of the naval authorities and ultimately the Admiralty and the Home Office. From Cowes, Captain Countess of the *Deptford* told Captain Onslow of HMS *Magnificent* at Portsmouth that they were 'seiz'd with a Fever, that many of them are very bad with the Scurvy and the Flux, with great black blotches breaking out on them, tending to putrefaction'.[10] Instructions were promptly given by Onslow for them to be examined by the surgeons from the *Magnificent* and the *Edgar* who reported on 21 December that while there were no signs of fever for the time being, an outbreak of serious infection was highly likely:

> The Convicts are now from want of Clothing, Bedding and every necessary in a small vessel in an inclement Season [and] are obliged to sleep on the bare Deck, which with the want of proper Provisions (their Diet consisting altogether of salted Meat) has produced the Scurvy among some of the number to the most inveterate degree. As this is the case there is reason to apprehend from what they have suffered since the first embarkation that the Disease in a few days if not counteracted may become general and fatal.[11]

Accordingly, they were declared unfit to proceed to Ireland until they had been 'cleansed and clothed' and the *Deptford* was ordered to take shelter in Stoke's Bay for that purpose. A sergeant's party of marines also had to be put on board to guard against their escape.[12]

The Home Office paid for the services of the two naval surgeons and authorised the issue of 'the requisite necessaries and Remedies', including fresh provisions, while the good citizens of Portsmouth raised enough money through a public subscription to provide the convicts with some badly-needed warm clothing. According to the Portsmouth correspondent of the *Hampshire Chronicle*, 'nine out of ten had arrived with no other covering than a biscuit bag. They sold their jackets and trowsers [sic] at Newfoundland'.[13] By 6 January they had been reported by the surgeons to be fit to travel and the Treasury officer sent down from London to supervise arrangements had received instructions that they were to sail immediately from Cowes. The *Hampshire Chronicle* remarked that the behaviour of the men was 'very orderly' but that the five women 'are said to give more trouble than 40 men'.[14] One of the women embarked at St John's had evidently died on the voyage to Spithead.

'A national indignity'

In the meantime, Lords Justices Fitzgibbon and Foster had been informed of the intended repatriation of the convicts by Nepean's despatch to them of 23 November.[15] While they were preparing their response, Fitzgibbon, who had become Lord Chancellor in June, wrote privately to Grenville on 28 November complaining of his action and warning of the problems that it had created:

> we have now, for time immemorial, been in the habit of sending our convicts to the British colonies in America without objection on the part of the colonies, till very lately. And if an objection had been stated whilst our Parliament was sitting, certainly we would have been bound to make some provision for the disposal of our convicts, which could not be deemed injurious to Great Britain or her colonies.[16]

He pointed out that if transported convicts were found at large in Ireland, they could be indicted and capitally punished under Irish law. However, if they were sent back under order of the British government there was no law which would allow Irish magistrates to detain them. Entreating Grenville to postpone their repatriation until some means had been found of dealing with them, he was nevertheless pessimistic that this was possible. 'I am free to acknowledge', he concluded, 'that, at the moment, it does not occur to me that we can in any way get out of the difficulty, if they are returned to us by an act of Government'.[17]

20 John Fitzgibbon, Earl of Clare.

In their official reply of 1 December, Fitzgibbon and Foster informed Grenville of Lord Clonmel's view that under Irish law he could not commit the convicts to custody under their former sentences. Nor, under the circumstances, did he think that it would be just to commit them under the Irish statute of 1722 for returning from transportation. However, they emphasised that the same law could be applied to the Home Office messenger and the captain of the ship responsible for their return. Indeed, 'any Magistrate of the City of Dublin would be satisfied in committing both the Messenger and the Captain for a Capital Felony'. Accordingly, they had taken the precaution of ordering out a revenue cruiser to intercept the transport carrying the convicts ship and warn the captain not to enter Dublin port but to take shelter at one of the neighbouring English ports 'till a Determination can be made in what Manner these Convicts can be disposed of'.[18]

Fitzgibbon and Foster remarked finally on the need to repeal the Police Act of 1786 and to make provision for 'disposing of ... [felons] in such Manner as may suit the Interest of Great Britain and Her Colonies ...'. It was their view that the Act explicitly authorised transportation only to His Majesty's plantations in America. In fact, as Fitzgibbon must have known very well since he had introduced the legislation in the Irish Parliament, it also provided for transportation *'to such other place out of Europe as shall be expressed in such sentence rule, or order. ...'* To admit this, however, would have weakened his political argument that the Irish authorities had no choice but to send their convicts to North America.

The Regency crisis

There was an important political dimension to the whole affair. As Hobart advised Grenville in a private letter from Dublin of 1 December, any attempt by the British government to support Milbanke's expulsion of the Newfoundland convicts would be bitterly resisted by the hypersensitive Irish Parliament as 'a national indignity'. Although he had not seen the official response prepared by Fitzgibbon and Foster after their consultations with Lord Carleton and the Attorney-General as well as with Lord Clonmel, he felt obliged to warn Grenville that

> unless the greatest caution is used in the further progress of this business, one of the most angry and unpleasant questions is likely to arise in Parliament here that has been agitated for many years.[19]

At the same time, he revealed that the revenue cruiser had been despatched to 'bribe the Captain of the ship to delay until he received directions from England'.[20]

The principal reason for this heightened sensitivity was that the Irish Parliament had taken serious umbrage at not being properly consulted during the 'Regency Crisis'.[21] When the continued illness of King George III led to the proposal of a limited regency in late 1788, the Protestant nationalist members of the Irish Parliament (known as the 'Patriots') were filled with the expectation that the known Whig sympathies of the Prince of Wales would make him more accommodating to their call for further parliamentary reforms than his father had been. Accordingly, it was agreed on 11 February to send an address to the Prince urging him to assume unrestricted royal powers. When Lord Lieutenant Buckingham refused to forward the document, a deputation of six members from both houses was despatched to London to wait on the Prince, only to learn on their arrival at Holyhead that the King had fully recovered his health. In the outcome, the disappointed Patriots complained that the dignity of the Irish Parliament had been affronted by lack of consultation. Indeed, there were bitter reactions in both houses and in the sympathetic sections of the Dublin press.

The tide of Irish Protestant nationalism had been running high since the establishment of a substantial measure of Irish legislative autonomy through the constitutional changes of May 1782 and the launching of what became known as 'Grattan's Parliament'. It was further encouraged when the British Parliament passed the 'Renunciation Act' in 1783, explicitly renouncing any claim to control Ireland's internal affairs. Designed by Grenville himself during his time as Irish Secretary under the earlier Lord Lieutenancy of his brother, the Marquis of Buckingham, this marked a high point in the Patriots' campaign for complete Irish autonomy.[22] Although they had provided only a lack-lustre opposition between 1786 and 1788, the Regency Crisis inspired them with a new vigour.[23]

Furthermore, there was one key member of the acting Irish executive who had been sympathetic to the Patriot cause at one point. 'Copperfaced Jack', as the obdurate Lord Clonmel was popularly known, had himself been dismissed from his position as Attorney-General by Lord Lieutenant Northington in 1782 when he denied that England had any right to bind Ireland by its Acts of Parliament.[24] Consequently Fitzgibbon, as leader of the Parliamentary faction loyal to the Castle, would have been anxious to avoid any issue which might antagonise

Clonmel and hand the Patriots the initiative in the forthcoming session of Parliament.

While the official purpose of sending out the revenue cruiser was to prevent the landing of the convicts at Dublin until their exact legal status could be established, the political overtones of the Lords Justices' extraordinary action could hardly be missed. 'As the matter now stands', Hobart told Grenville in his letter to him of 1 December, 'Admiral Millbanke [*sic*] has superseded an Irish Act of Parliament, and you may well imagine what a ferment that will create in the Irish House of Commons'. Pointing out that the Lord Lieutenant had acted entirely in conformity with the Police Act of 1786 in authorising the despatch of the convicts, he added sarcastically that 'it is presumed [this Act] was considered by His Majesty's Ministers in England previous to the Great Seal being put to it ...'.[25] Nor did there appear to be any ready means of dealing with the convicts if they were sent back to Ireland. Lord Clonmel had advised that he could not commit them for wilfully returning from transportation, which meant that they would have to be identified by the gaolers of the various prisons from which they had been drawn. 'I would submit to you', Hobart concluded hopefully, 'whether it may not be right for the British government to send them back to some part of America, or to some place out of Europe'.[26]

Fitzgibbon wrote privately to Grenville the next day, also emphasising that the convicts had been shipped off in strict conformity with the Act of 1786. The added complication, however, was that the Act made it 'utterly impossible' to commit the returnees to custody in the counties of Ireland where they had been convicted. 'I entreat it of you', he pleaded, 'if it is possible to devise any means of disposing of these wretched creatures, except by sending them here by act of the British Government, that it may be done'.[27] Anticipating that Grenville was unlikely to co-operate, however, he found it expedient to shift the blame from His Majesty's ministers to the hapless Milbanke:

If he had even shipped them off directly for Ireland, and had them landed on our coast, we could easily have managed matters so as to prevent any difficulties with the Irish Government; but proceeding as he has done to send them to England with a regular invoice to the British Government, to be re-exported from that Government to us, I cannot but feel that he has done an act highly indiscreet at best. And I am very well satisfied that if he had acted in such a manner by any description of the King's English subjects, that he would hear of it very unpleasantly at Westminster Hall. And if we are driven to the necessity of defending their return upon us under all these circumstances, I freely own to you that it appears to me as difficult a task as could be assigned to the friends of Government in this country.[28]

Altogether, the Admiral provided an ideal scapegoat:

Let the act of returning them to us, if they must be sent here, be the act of Governor Milbank [sic]. Probably he never will come to Ireland, and I do not suppose that he will very much feel any comments that our worthy Whigs may make upon him.[29]

'This ill-advised step'

When Grenville received Fitzgibbon's private letter of 28 November, he explained in measured tones the government's decision and the legal advice on which it was based. Apparently unaware that the three shipments of convicts made by Moore at the instigation of North and Sydney between 1783 and 1785 had been officially destined for Nova Scotia, he added:

No convicts have been transported from this country to any of the British colonies in America since the last peace, and all the colonies have uniformly expressed a decided resolution not to receive them.[30]

When he received the official despatch from Fitzgibbon and Foster, together with Hobart's letter, on 5 December he could scarcely control his fury over the sending out of the revenue cruiser. 'I cannot enough lament the precipitation of this ill-advised step', he wrote immediately to Westmorland who was at that time preparing to depart for Dublin. He told him that he had sought a special meeting with Prime Minister Pitt to discuss the consequences.[31] Conveying the same message to Hobart in a private letter to Dublin that day, he also took the opportunity to point out apropos the 1786 Police Act that the King's assent to an Irish Act of Parliament 'neither gives it, nor was ever supposed to give it, the smallest force in any of the King's colonies'. Indeed, it was 'no more ... than the King's assent to an Act of the States of Jersey would do'.[32] Consequently, the legality of Milbanke's action had to be decided solely on the basis of his instructions and English laws.

Admitting that while the point was 'so unquestionable' it was desirable to avoid making it the subject of discussion in the Irish

Parliament, Grenville nevertheless believed that this was a risk that had to be accepted:

> But when the case has arisen we have no other mode of acting; as the proposal of our sending them to any place out of England, except Ireland, would, if acceded to, put us in the situation of doing an illegal act because the judges in Ireland feel an unwillingness to do what all our lawyers consider as a legal act.[33]

When it came to the political fall-out, the Home Secretary was not too concerned about the storm that might be aroused in the Irish Parliament by the return of the convicts.[34] His own experience with the administration of Ireland in 1783 disposed him to call the Patriots' bluff.

'Neither colony nor plantation'

The technical weakness of the Irish Lords Justices' position was that the island of Newfoundland was, strictly speaking, neither a colony nor a plantation under His Majesty's dominion as required by the amended Police Act of 1786, which now provided the sole legal basis of Irish transportation. Legally, Newfoundland was a 'fishery' with no formally established civil government and only an ad hoc Vice-Admiralty Court where, as we have seen, British naval captains posted to the Newfoundland Station acted as surrogate judges. Governor Milbanke had thus been entitled in law not to accept the convicts who had been dumped on the Newfoundland coast, although he may have gone too far in detaining them until they could be repatriated.

As Grenville had told Fitzgibbon in his reply of 2 December to the latter's letter of 28 November, 'Newfoundland is in no respect a British colony, and is never so considered in our laws'.[35] As a fishery, it had been official British policy since the seventeenth century to curtial its permanent settlement even by British subjects, although this had never been seriously enforced and the resident population had been allowed to increase to almost 20,000 by 1789. Nevertheless, the legal formula that it was neither colony nor plantation was to serve a useful purpose on this occasion, enabling Grenville to conclude that the convicts 'must be considered as standing in the same situation as if their sentences had never been attempted to be carried into execution'.[36]

Responding to the stern tone of Grenville's letter, Fitzgibbon immediately gave orders for the recall of the revenue cruiser. Together with

Lord Clonmel, he was disposed to accept that Newfoundland was not a British colony and that the best course of action was to commit the convicts on arrival 'upon the ground of their sentences never having been carried out'. Always anxious to curry favour with the ministers and high officials in London whose control of patronage in Ireland ensured the dominance of the Ascendancy interest that he headed, he now (somewhat disingenuously, it has to be said) represented himself as performing a valuable service in facilitating the return of the convicts. At the same time, he could not resist a little sarcasm at Grenville's expense:

> I trust it is unneccessary for me to assure you that I am truly anxious to relieve the British Government from embarrassment in this business. The Speaker and I, acting under very particular instructions from Lord Westmorland, thought it our indispensable duty to state to him and you the difficulties which are likely to occur in this country, upon the return of these convicts to us in custody by your warrant; and to give the opportunity to the King's Ministers to weigh the difficulties on all sides before the measure of retaining them was put into final execution. But if they do come back, you may be assured, whenever the matter may become the subject of public discussion, I shall be very anxious to prove their return to us to be a mark of high respect on your part to the people of Ireland.[37]

Once he was satisfied that Milbanke was within his rights in sending the convicts back to England, he would then take the offensive by calling on Lord Mayor Alexander of Dublin 'to account for his breach of contract'.[38]

In the meantime, Grenville had written again to Fitzgibbon in response to his letter of 2 December to defend Milbanke and emphasise that the British government did not have the authority to override his actions. Furthermore, as the convicts had committed no crime and incurred no sentence in Britain, the British government had no jurisdiction of any kind over them:

> It is equally impossible to detain them in custody in any prison in England, or on board any transport or prison ship. Because, if they were once within the body of any county in England, they might claim their *Habeas Corpus*.[39]

Consequently, all that could be done was to send them to Ireland.

Repeating the earlier point that the convicts' transportation to Newfoundland could not be seen as constituting an execution of their sentence, Grenville also had some sharp things to say about the actual mode of their treatment:

> Another doubt may be started; whether setting the wretches on shore without provisions, tools, or clothing in a place where they must have perished but for the humanity of the inhabitants, is a mode of transporting them that falls within the the purview of the laws for transportation, or within the contract which the master of the vessel makes with the Irish Government.[40]

As for the possible prosecution of the Home Office messenger and the ship's captain for returning the convicts from transportation, Grenville confessed that he had no knowledge of the relevant statute but properly dismissed the whole idea as ridiculous:

> if any magistrate in Dublin was so absurd as to commit them for this offence, the Government could have no difficulty in offering, nor the King's Bench in receiving bail; and the King's pardon must of course be granted, if it should be thought necessary ... I have great difficulty in believing that any words [in the statute] could make it criminal in the messenger or captain to land these men under circumstances in which the men themselves who are landed will clearly incur no guilt.[41]

Hobart responded more stiffly to Grenville's criticism and to his determination to press ahead with the convicts' repatriation:

> If, notwithstanding the representations made from hence, you persevere in your intention of sending the convicts, they will of course be received; and we must get out of the scrape as well as we can.[42]

He had discussed the matter once more with Fitzgibbon and Lord Clonmel and it now appeared that the latter would remand the convicts 'to their several prisons' on the grounds that their sentences had not been executed. Still dubious about this, however, Hobart was anxious to defend the shipment to Newfoundland on the basis of principle:

> Permit me to say that I have never conceived that the King's assent to an Irish Act of Parliament could give it force in the King's

colonies; but that His Majesty having given his assent, and thereby authorised his Lord Lieutenant of Ireland to transport convicts to the colonies, it was a justifiable presumption that the English law enabled the Governors of the British colonies to receive them, and that his Majesty's instructions ordered them to do so.[43]

Grenville was relieved to learn of this breakthrough which he hoped would avoid any difficulties with the Irish Parliament. However, he had just learned of the despatch of another shipment of convicts from Dublin to Nova Scotia and hoped that 'however unwelcome guests they may be' the Lieutenant-Governor would not send them back.[44]

'A loop hole'

The solution to the thorny problem of what do with the Newfoundland returnees in Ireland had been found by Lords Thurlow and Kenyon. They had pointed out to Grenville that as the convicts had not actually been transported according to Irish law to one of His Majesty's colonies or plantations, they were thus in the situation of not having had their sentences executed. The Irish government was consequently empowered to execute their sentences by transporting them to another destination.

'I am in great hopes, that you have given us a loop hole, which will get us out of the scrape …', a greatly relieved Hobart wrote at last to Grenville on 22 January 1790.[45] The convicts had been landed from the *Deptford* the previous evening at Poolbeg Fort in Dublin Bay where they were identified and committed to the custody of the city sheriffs. Nine days later they were once again committed to Newgate under an order issued by Lord Chief Justice Clonmel.[46] There had been no outcry in the radical press and the affair had not been raised by the Patriots in the Irish Parliament at the opening of the new session on 21 January as Hobart and Fitzgibbon had feared it would.

The tense and sometimes sharply-worded exchanges between Dublin and London over the Newfoundland convicts had little to do with the convicts themselves but everything to do with the respective jurisdictions of the two governments and the problematic new relationship between them created by the constitutional changes of 1782. As Fitzgibbon's political biographer, Ann Kavanaugh, has pointed out, Grenville and Thurlow had 'acted out of broad imperial interests', but in the process 'rode roughshod over the fears and sensibilities of their Irish servants'. While she goes too far in concluding that 'the business of the convict transports prefigured the far larger conflict over Catholic emancipation', it can certainly be said that it highlighted the basic reality of the political relationship between London and Dublin which was to be formalised in the Act of Union of 1800.[47]

The first report in the Dublin newspapers in mid-November of what had transpired in Newfoundland was copied from the London press, whose sympathies were entirely with Milbanke and the St John's magistrates. According to this account, 'the appearance of these gigantic ruffians threw the inhabitants of St John's into unspeakable consternation – for they neither could infer whence they came, or how they got there'.[48] It was believed that the master of the vessel who had put them ashore would be 'severely proceeded against' for breaking his contract to take them to the United States.[49] As the report stood, it implied that 'this desperate phalanx' of eighty convicts now on their way to England were all who had survived the original shipment.

A few weeks later when more was known about the circumstances of the convicts' disposal at Newfoundland, the *Freeman's Journal* took a far more sympathetic line:

> As the unfortunate wretches were put on shore, on that island, without their consent, and experienced considerable hardships before relieved by the inhabitants, it may not, perhaps, be an abuse of the clemency of Government, if on their remittance to this country, some mode of employing them on public works, at home, was tried, as probably the sufferings they have undergone on their passage to the place of their intended destination, may have taught them such a lesson, as to lay a strong foundation for their future good behaviour, and reformation of their lives.[50]

The newspaper was also critical of Captain Harrison's treatment of the convicts and of his 'open and notorious abuse of justice' in liberating Patrick Fay.[51]

Just how the Newfoundland veterans were to be dealt with was very much a matter of conjecture once it was known that they had been returned to Ireland. Dublin's *Morning Post* of 30 January 1790, for example, reported a popular belief that they would be sent to 'recruit' (reinforce) Britain's military garrisons in Senegamba and Guinea, which it charitably thought would be 'a much better provision for those who survive the change of climate, than from their vicious and abandoned profligacy they had reason to expect'. Apart from the *Freeman's Journal*, little sympathy was expressed for them in their extraordinary misadventure. Indeed, there was much more interest in the vicissitudes of Patrick Fay from the time he parted company with the *Duke of Leinster* off Wicklow Head.[52]

News of the Newfoundland convicts' return had nevertheless spread throughout Dublin's under-classes and there was a crowd of curious onlookers when they were landed from Poolbeg Fort at North Wall on 1 February and put into six prison carts to be conveyed to Newgate. Handcuffed in pairs, they were wearing the new blue jackets and worsted nightcaps given to them by the good citizens of Portsmouth. Indeed, the *Dublin Chronicle* remarked that they 'looked in general, far better than when they left this kingdom'.[53] However, the *Morning Post* hoped that 'much more care will be taken in future to prevent such unfortunate wretches from being left a prey to famine and misery, than has been of late years the case'.[54]

Indeed, it had been reported by the Dublin newspapers a month before the convicts' return that at the forthcoming session of the Irish Parliament, legislation would be introduced to make it a felony for any master of a convict transport not to fulfil the terms of his engagement.[55] Nothing of the kind eventuated. Nor was the return of the Newfoundland convicts to Ireland represented by Patriot politicians and their sympathetic newspapers as an affront to the

21 Poolbeg Fort, Dublin Bay, where the Newfoundland convicts were landed in January 1791.

authority of the Irish Parliament in the way that Hobart and Fitzgibbon obviously feared would happen. As we shall see, however, it was not long before the convicts themselves made clear their feelings about their treatment.

11
The Barbuda Affair

In what was to be the final trans-Atlantic shipment from Ireland, eighty-eight convicts[1] were embarked at Dublin on 7 November 1789 on the *Duke of Leinster*, commanded this time by Captain William Christian. The 'charter party' or shipping contract was signed on 18 September by Christian and the Lord Mayor of Dublin, John Rose.[2] The ship's owners, Arthur and George Bryan,[3] also provided Rose the following day with a bond of £1,000 'for the true and Faithful Performance of the said Charter Party ...'.[4] As we have seen, the Bryans had been involved in the previous shipment of convicts to Newfoundland in the *Duke of Leinster*, which must have brought them a handsome profit.

At that point, the Dublin Castle authorities were unaware of the embarrassing outcome of the Newfoundland voyage but had evidently encouraged Rose to instruct Christian that the convicts be landed at Nova Scotia. Despite Governor Parr's protestations over the Cape Breton shipment the previous year, Grenville had encouraged Hobart to believe that they would be landed at Nova Scotia with 'no difficulty'.[5] However, on 22 December when he had been informed by him of the details of the Newfoundland fiasco, Hobart wrote to the Home Secretary that there was at least a possibility of the most recent shipment being landed at Newfoundland as well and of being 'dealt with in the same manner as those who have lately been the object of much discussion'.[6]

'A great gainer or loser'

The contract bound Christian to provide rations, clothing, bedding, proper accommodation and irons for the convicts and to land them 'at some Port or Ports in North America' in return for a payment of five guineas per head. However, Christian was carefully instructed in a private letter from Arthur Bryan a few days before their embarkation to make for the island of Antigua in the Leewards, giving the nearby island of Barbuda a wide berth on account of its surrounding reefs. He was told to land small groups of the convicts at Antigua and at Anguilla or other islands, *'but not a great many at one place, for fear of a commotion'.*[7] Bryan also instructed Christian to

> tell them on leaving you, the advantage it will be to them, that they conceal what they are and that should their future behaviour be good, that they may get to be caretakers, and in situations of trust in the Plantations.

Although the official contract stipulated 'some Port or Ports in North America', Bryan was doubtless aware of the problems encountered by Captain Robert Winthrop of the *Charming Nancy* in July of the previous year and was disinclined to take the risk of trying Baltimore or George-Town.

To his credit, Bryan gave Christian detailed instructions on the care that was to be taken of the convicts:

> You cannot be too attentive to these poor people put under your care; – so that they be treated with humanity, at same time that you hold them under steady authority – that their meals be regularly dealt to them, & that above every thing else, you see that they are kept clean, not only in their persons, but their Births [sic], & that their beds be brought up every day to air, and on each day, that your tween Decks get a thorough cleaning of all wet or other filth – as to keep the Ship healthy is of the utmost moment, and nothing will contribute so much to health as cleanliness, and even to amuse them, when it can be done with safety – would be a means of giving health to yr Ship.

All this was admirable, but it was in reference to rations that Bryan showed his hand. He told Christian that the merchant firm of Condy and Bryan in Charleston, South Carolina, had been apprised that 'there would be such a Surplus of Provisions, as would yield there something handsome ...'. Expecting that 'at least one half' of the provisions on board would be available for sale on the *Duke of Leinster*'s arrival at Charleston, he gave Christian careful instructions that the first to be used for the convicts were the eight or nine barrels of beef out of his own cellar, 'the first that was put on board last Summer. ...' It seems likely that some of this meat apparently left over from the voyage to Newfoundland in July was none the better for its travels. Bryan also urged Christian that care should be taken to issue the exact quantity of rations and that there should be proper weighing equipment on board for that purpose.

Barbuda

The convicts were escorted to Dublin's North Wall on the appointed day by a troop of horse and a company of foot in order to prevent any more escapes. The *Hibernian Journal* was disappointed to observe that 'so far from having been decently affected by their ignominious situation, the hardened wretches, to an individual, carried the strongest marks of shameless indifference'.[8] Indeed, the very sight of the convicts prompted the newspaper to reflect on the inutility of imprisonment and to conclude that some other form of punishment should be devised for the public good:

> So dangerous and so dreadful to society is the usual imprisonment of malefactors, already grown familiar with the horrors of vice; – but deriving such energy of wickedness and infamy from the immoralities, blasphemies, and other similar contagions, peculiar to such habitations, that a few weeks, spent among the dregs of human nature therein, impress such a habit of delinquency as never can be erased by any subsequent cultivation.[9]

It also expressed the hope that sufficient security had been obtained from Christian by the authorities to ensure that he fulfilled his contract.

In fact, Christian sailed without telling even his first mate where they were bound and on 1 January 1790 the ship made the tiny, coral-fringed island of Barbuda. The private leasehold property of the Codrington family since 1685, infertile Barbuda was useless for sugar cultivation but it supplied livestock to the larger sugar island of Antigua a few miles away. With a population of about 500 negro slaves, it had also benefited from the numerous shipwrecks that had occurred on the surrounding reefs.[10] Although he had been warned of these, Christian must have initially mistaken the island for Antigua.

After landing forty-eight of the men and five of the women convicts at Barbuda 'destitute of every necessary and without waiting to know if there was any subsistence for them' (as Sir William Codrington's Antigua agent, Langford Lovell, later reported to him), Christian sailed on to Anguilla.[11] Three days later, the Barbuda castaways were taken to St John, the capital of Antigua, in a ship belonging to Codrington, a wealthy and influential London merchant whose family had extensive interests in the Leewards.

According to the report subsequently made to Home Secretary Grenville by General Sir Thomas Shirley, Captain-General or Governor of the Leeward Islands, on their arrival at St John in Antigua they 'gave out they were indented Servants and other Emigrants from Ireland going to Philadelphia' who had been forced to make for the West Indies after being at sea for three months.[12] Accepting this in good faith, and moved by the 'naked, miserable condition of these people', six of whom seem to have already died, the compassionate citizens of St John provided them with food, clothing and a house.

'A great uneasiness and alarm'

On 18 January, news came from Anguilla in a ship bearing the mate of the *Duke of Leinster*, Sylvester Dowling, that the deputy governor there, apprised of the true identity of the arrivals, had not allowed the remainder to be landed from the ship. According to the account given to Shirley by Edward Bryan and Thomas Freeman on 22 January on behalf of the two houses of the Antigua legislature which had just met to discuss the matter, the deputy governor had also impounded the ship until he could be advised by Shirley what to do. Once the convicts' real character was revealed in Antigua, Bryan and Freeman told Shirley, 'a great uneasiness and alarm took place in the minds of the Inhabitants on having such a Set of desperate wretches at large in the Town of St John's [sic], and at liberty to go to any part of the Country they choose'.[13] Consequently the magistrates had them imprisoned until some way of disposing of them could be found. Already, four of the convicts had robbed the Anglican parish church at St John of its communion plate and had broken into a watchmaker's shop, stealing fourteen watches.[14]

Believing it to be 'an Evil pregnant with the most dangerous consequences that Convicts should be brought hither', and 'apprehensive also that unless further measures are taken to prevent it, we may be again loaded with another Importation of them', the two houses requested Shirley to send them back on the same vessel to Ireland.[15] Indeed, they were prepared to meet the cost if necessary. They also wished Shirley to ask the Lord Lieutenant in Dublin for an assurance that no more convicts would be sent. As William Hutchinson, the Antigua government's London agent and Shirley's nephew, told Evan Nepean, it was not willing to become 'a Botany Bay to Ireland on any future occasion'.[16]

Ironically, the Presbyterian merchant Edward Bryan who was so closely involved in the legislature's efforts to remove the convicts was himself related to Arthur Bryan of Dublin who had contracted to ship them to the Leewards. Arthur's elder brother, George, had spent some years at nearby St Kitt's before establishing himself in Philadelphia. There also seems likely to have been a connection between the Dublin Bryans and the firm of Condy and Bryan in Charleston who were supposed to purchase half of the provisions put on board the *Duke of Leinster*.

Apart from the spate of robberies and fears of more, the main reason why the convicts of the *Duke of Leinster* were not welcomed by the sugar planters of the Leewards was their historical reputation for disloyalty. As we have seen earlier, they had been in political alliance with the French during the late 1660s and were in rebellion in 1689 after news of the Williamite Revolution. In 1706 they had once again assisted the French.

By the late 1780s, the Irish proportion of the white population of the West Indies had been greatly reduced, mostly by further migration to the United States. The Irish had always accounted for a smaller proportion of the European population of Antigua than of St Kitt's and Montserrat and the Irish merchant community which had developed at St John since the late seventeenth century was predominantly Presbyterian.[17] However, the capital still had its separate Catholic settlement known as 'Irishtown'.[18]

Responding to the Antigua legislature's appeal, Shirley wrote to the deputy governor of Anguilla, only to find that the *Duke of Leinster*, after landing the remainder of the convicts on the western part of the island, had left for the Dutch settlement on the nearby island of St Martin. Responding to Shirley's request that the ship be impounded there, Governor Johannes Gibbes told him that it had already been seized for the non-payment of wages due to Dowling. However, Christian had been taken seriously ill in the meantime and was not expected to live. Furthermore, his ship was in such a poor and leaky condition that it could not put to sea again without extensive repairs.[19] Finding a copy of the charter party and Arthur Bryan's private letter of instructions to Christian on board, Gibbes had these copied by the government secretary and sent to Shirley who subsequently forwarded them to Nepean at the Home Office.

Any possibility that the convicts might be sent back to Ireland in the *Duke of Leinster* now seemed remote. Faced with this 'unusual and embarrassing circumstance', the Antigua legislature subsequently asked Shirley to request Commodore William Parker of HMS *Jupiter*, commanding officer of the Newfoundland Station which was then anchored in Antigua's English Harbour at the south-eastern tip of the island, to send the convicts back to England in one of the frigates under his command. In justification of this, they referred to Vice-Admiral Milbanke's removal of the convicts from Newfoundland the previous October when he was commanding officer there. Although Parker was sympathetic to the plight of the colonists, he could not account for Milbanke's action and was unwilling to oblige them by imitating it. As he told Shirley:

> That these people are a nuisance, I am perfectly sensible, and as an individual no one wishes their removal more than I do, but the part I am required to take in doing it I should apprehend cannot have been well considered.

22 'View near St John's Antigua'. Government House is on the left and in the centre is the parish church robbed by the Irish convicts.

What orders could I give a Captain upon such an occasion; to turn them on shore at the first place he arrives would be a cruel, as well as an unjustifiable proceeding.

To refer him to the Admiralty, as it would bring embarrassment there, 'twould bring censure upon me (people being little inclined to feel things other than as it affects them) for what is the authority in England to take these people into custody? If none, they must be turned on Shore: then the cruelty of their being sent thither to commit depredations and possibly murder upon innocent people will fall upon me; and even if there is a power of doing it, they become an additional encumbrance and evil to the too great a one already. Beside, as I have no authority to incur any expence upon such an occasion, I should be called to account upon that, and be open to every censure public and private and most likely obliged to make good every expence, the Crown might be put to upon the occasion.[20]

Parker suggested instead that the convicts be sent back to Ireland and, because of the 'little delicacy' of the Irish government over the Newfoundland affair, that they be put on shore at the first convenient place with an explanatory letter from Shirley addressed to the chief magistrate. This, Parker thought, 'might not be improper, and [might be] the means of preventing such practices in future'.[21] Faced with this unhelpful response, the Antigua legislature asked him to reconsider their request, 'as we look upon it to be an essential part of the duty for which he was sent out to these Islands, to afford them every sort of protection in his power'.[22]

Even a guarantee to indemnify him for any expense incurred did not sway Parker from his sensible decision. Accordingly, the Executive Council proposed on 18 February that in order to deal with the 'Calamity so unjustifiably and illegally thrown upon it ...', there should be a joint committee established with the authority to contract for the convicts' removal 'either to Ireland or some place to Leeward of Saint Martin's and Tortola'.[23]

A partial solution was eventually found when thirty-nine of the convicts landed at Antigua entered into articles of agreement as indentured servants with a certain Captain Burk who, in consideration of £566 advanced from the colony's treasury, undertook on security not to release them on any of the neighbouring islands and to ship them 'to some part of America'. This he did on 2 March, although two days later a resident of St John wrote to a friend in Dublin: 'it is probable you may hear of this precious cargo being carried back to Dublin by

23 'Cutting The Sugar Cane'. The sugar planters of the Leewards used negro slaves in the 1780s and had no interest in white workers.

the time this letter reaches you'.[24] The remaining sixteen who 'refused peremptorily to Indent' stayed in the gaol at St John and by the end of April their upkeep had cost the colony's government £1,200.[25]

In the meantime, three of the four convicts found guilty of theft and sacrilege and sentenced to death, William Dalton, Francis Tyrrell and Peter Kean, had been reprieved by the St John magistrates and only Michael Mooney had been executed. 'No one knows why', Langford Lovell complained to Codrington in March, 'for such bad people cannot easily be met with'.[26] However, the magistrates had made it clear to Shirley that mercy had been extended to the three on the clear understanding that they would soon be removed from the island.[27] One of them, Dalton, subsequently managed to make his way back to Dublin where he resumed his old lifestyle.

Reporting all this to Grenville, Shirley implored him to prevent any repetition of the event, warning that the Antigua legislature now had it in mind to bring in a bill 'making it felony to bring Convicts hither'.[28] Replying in May, Grenville suggested that the sixteen remaining convicts at St John be employed in public works 'so as to prevent their being reduced to the necessity of committing further depredations on the Community for their Support'.[29] While reassuring him that there would be no further shipments of Irish felons, he did not want the legislature of Antigua or any other West Indian colony to pass a law which would make transportation there impossible in the future:

> It is not his Majesty's intention to authorize the sending [of] Convicts to his West India possessions and effectual measures have been taken to prevent the sending [of] any more persons of the description from Ireland, but I cannot think it would be by any means proper that any Act should be allowed to pass in any of the Colonies for inflicting Penalties on persons who might under the King's authority convey thither persons of that description and you will therefore on no account give your Assent to any Act of that nature, which may be brought forward.[30]

'Such an amazing expence'

This unsympathetic response from the Home Secretary seems to have been the last straw for poor Shirley, who was already exhausted when he received Grenville's dispatch. Since the beginning of his second tour of duty as governor of the Leewards in 1787, he had been defending himself against charges of corruption by an influential faction of the colonists. Furthermore, he had from the outset been in the unhappy position of attempting to govern what was not much a colony as an unwieldy federation of tiny colonies, each with its own bicameral legislature, judicial system and militia.[31] Wearied of all this, he wrote in November to his nephew, William Hutchinson, in London asking him to intercede with Lord Ailesbury on his behalf:

> having been so very unwell these last two or three months ... I have been almost incapable of Business. My present Complaint is an inward decay with loss of Appetite, sleep and total debilitation, that I am extremely doubtful, if I shall last long enough for the proper time of leaving this Country. I wish you would speak to his Lordship upon this subject and state to him my situation, devices and present circumstances. I am at present so ill, that I cannot do myself the honor of writing to his Lordship but beg his ... good Offices in obtaining some small provision for me during my life upon the Resignation of my Government.
>
> I dread dying in this country[,] they put you to such an amazing expence [sic] in laying you in the Ground.[32]

There was also the problem of the substantial cost incurred by the colony's governmment in dealing with what the Antigua legislature stiffly called 'the late unwarrantable importation of Irish convicts ...'. Imprisonment, food, clothing, a special sitting of the Court of Oyer and Terminer and the cost of shipping them from the island had amounted to no less than £1,541.8s.8d. and Shirley was called on to request the British government to reimburse the colony for this amount.[33] When the ailing Shirley eventually returned to London in January 1792, he sent the relevant documents to the new Home Secretary, Henry Dundas, in the hope that this would be done.[34]

In addition to the reports sent to Grenville by Shirley, the Home Office had also received a strong formal complaint from Codrington who enclosed Langford Lovell's description of events. Codrington made it clear to Grenville that no planter in the Leewards would employ the remaining convicts. Nor would the public bear the continued cost of maintaining them in gaol or the risk of releasing them. As well as 'their Habits of thieving and house-breaking', they might 'corrupt the Negroes to a very mischievous and lasting Degree'. He wrily suggested that as Commodore Parker was soon returning to England, he might at least bring with him 'the worthy Commander of [the] Brig *Duke of Leinster* ...'.[35] Parker did not take Christian back with him to England and indeed it is not clear what became of the unfortunate captain who, as Codrington later pointed out to Nepean, had followed his orders so faithfully. It is likely, however, that he died at St Martin.[36] As for the *Duke of Leinster*, it was probably sold at auction to meet the wages of Dowling and the crew. Altogether, Arthur Bryan was to be 'a great Loser' from this ill-fated final shipment of Irish convicts to the Americas.

'This horrible abuse in Ireland'

Writing to Nepean in early October about Bryan's secret letter to Christian, a copy of which he had left at his office earlier, Codrington expressed concern that although 'the alarm, the mischief and the expence [sic] and trouble occasion'd by these Wretches is almost inconceivable', the 'atrocious behaviour of the Irish Contractor' had not yet been censured or punished.[37] Consequently, as there was no awareness on the part of those involved in the business that they 'shall be obliged to do better than their predecessors', there was no reason to think that their conduct would be any different. And as a large number of convicts were then known to be awaiting transportation from

Dublin, there might well be a repetition of the same problem and Codrington was anxious that Grenville should do something to prevent it:

> It may be necessary to keep the Corporation of Dublin in good humour, and the Lord Mayor of Dublin has the *perquisite* of this Contract, but there is no person in or out of office, whose mind would not be irritated against such shocking Villainy as A. Bryan's. I am sure 'tis but to state it, to have it redress'd and ought not a Contractor to bring some Voucher of having perform'd the Service, he is amply paid for performing – but Mr Bryan under authority of Government makes War of the worst kind upon his fellow Subjects. I entreat you [illeg.] to remind Mr. Grenville of this horrible abuse in Ireland.[38]

Enclosing copies of Lovell's and Codrington's letters, Nepean penned a sharp complaint to Government Secretary Hobart on 18 March 1790 that the embarkation of convicts on board the *Duke of Leinster* at Dublin for the Leewards must have taken place some time after the return of the convicts from Newfoundland,

> when it was hoped and expected that the difficulties which were then stated with respect to the disposal of Convicts in the Colonies, would have induced the Government of Ireland to have refrained from carrying the Transportation Laws into effect, until some plan had been considered for the disposal of Persons of that description.[39]

Hobart could honestly reply, however, that the *Duke of Leinster* had left Dublin on 7 November 1789, eighteen days before Grenville had written to him about Milbanke's return of the Newfoundland convicts.[40] At the same time, he was able to inform Nepean that the Irish Parliament's recently enacted legislation authorising transportation to New South Wales was now awaiting the Royal Assent. He also passed on Westmorland's request to Grenville that Irish prisoners sentenced to transportation 'be taken up and disposed of as shall be thought fit until they can be carried out with British Convicts to Botany Bay, or such other Place as shall be resolved upon; and the expence [sic] thereof shall be borne by the Government here'.[41]

'We are not yet quite rid of the troublesome subject of Irish convicts', a weary Grenville had told Westmorland a week before Nepean's despatch to Hobart, referring to the Barbuda affair and the previous problem of the Newfoundland shipment. 'This untoward accident must, I fear', he continued in reference to the latter, 'bring forward the question which we have before so much discussed, and it will now come in the case of an island that *is* a British colony'.[42]

It had been suggested by Codrington that the sixteen convicts remaining at Antigua who had refused to sign indenture papers might be employed on the construction of military fortifications there under Lieut.-General Mathew, but there was still some uncertainty as to whether the colonial authorities possessed the power to do this. The question was duly referred to Dublin Castle by Nepean and on 11 June, after consultation with Attorney-General Arthur Wolfe, Sackville Hamilton wrote to Nepean that as their sentence had been executed, the Lord Lieutenant had no power over them and that they were now subject to the laws of the colony. If they declined to enter into indentures to work under Mathew, they could be sent back to Ireland,

> from whence the Government may then legally direct them to be transported to Botany Bay or send them under Indentures as proposed to serve in the West Indies; and that if they shall choose under these Circumstances to indent with General Mathews [sic], such Indentures will be legal and valid.[43]

Forty-eight of the convicts, probably including those who had been taken on to Anguilla, were said to have been set to work in May on the extensive military fortifications being constructed at Shirley Heights, overlooking English Harbour. However, according to V.L. Oliver's *History of the Island of Antigua*, 'they were not liked' and were probably employed instead in deepening the harbour. There is no record of what happened to them subsequently.[44]

By this time, Hamilton had called for an account of the number of convicts in Ireland under sentence of transportation and promised to send it to Nepean as soon as it was ready. Accordingly, he passed on Westmorland's request to be informed 'as early as possible of the Time when the Transportation to Botany Bay is intended to take place, and what port of Ireland the Vessels will be directed to touch, in order to take the Irish Convicts on Board'.[45]

It was this pressure, together with the prospect of further problems from continued Irish transportation to North America and the West Indies unless some alternative was found, which by the end of 1790 had at last forced Grenville and Nepean to find space for Irish convicts on what was to be the Third Fleet to New South Wales.

12
Crisis in the Gaols

By early June 1790, when it had been known for some months that Irish convicts were to be sent to New South Wales, there were already some popular doubts that the desirability of the new system. The *Freeman's Journal* pointed out that the long delays bound to elapse between shipments of convicts to Botany Bay

> will always be attended with inconvenience, on account of the very riotous and almost ungovernable state of the felons disembogued, we may say, from all the jails in the kingdom to the general receptacle in Green-street, by which the [illeg.] for only bread, straw and medicines for the sick, must become very heavy on the inhabitants of Dublin.[1]

Referring to the Newfoundland convicts whose return had swelled Newgate's numbers to more than 250, it hoped that they could be put to hard labour, as in England, and required to 'earn their support'.[2]

The cost of the convicts' upkeep and of sending them halfway across the world to New South Wales was certainly disadvantageous, but the *Morning Post* believed that it would be 'amply compensated' for by the certainty that 'few, if any, will ever return' and the deterrent effect that this would have on other criminals. Referring to the continuing problem of returnees, it reported that more than one hundred had returned from America during the last twelve months. Some of these had subsequently been convicted of various felonies, 'while others belong as formerly to the most desperate gangs which infest this metropolis and its environs'.[3]

The *Morning Post* nevertheless believed that the best means of employing 'able-bodied felons' was in Britain's armed forces. Indeed, it invoked a noble set of precedents:

Who composed the original inhabitants of Rome? robbers. Whence came the regency of Algiers? Transported prisoners from Constantinople. Who, of the old or new world formed the bravest people? The Romans and the unconquered Algerines [sic]. Historical facts, and modern experience prove, that domestic desperadoes, will make the best fighting people. Let our criminals therefore be tried in a service of danger. He that escapes the gallows, will glory in a more honourable fall. The onset of his life sets death at defiance. Therefore, in every hour of danger, he will not be found a coward.[4]

Repeating this argument in a later issue, the newspaper suggested that a large number of the young men held in Newgate should be drafted into the Navy, thereby saving a considerable cost to the city.[5]

Despite the official indication in February 1790 that Ireland was to participate in the Botany Bay scheme, there was no subsequent evidence that this would materialise. By early July it was being claimed in the Dublin newspapers that there were plans afoot to send convicts to the Bahamas instead, possibly to the island of New Providence. This destination, which had been enthusiastically canvassed by the *Freeman's Journal* in 1788, now found a new advocate in the *Morning Post*:

> Here they must be deemed useful, as of the eleven principal islands, there are only three thinly inhabited, and as there are eighty others, with proper necessaries, they might be made truly useful, within reach of assistance, which is not the case at Botany Bay. These islands being situated in the Gulph of florida, should there be a Spanish war, in the privateering line, such desperadoes like the Algerines [sic], or Buccaneers, will make an uncommon degree of resolution and battle.[6]

There was an even more imaginative suggestion that Ireland's potential trade with Nootka Sound on the north-west coast of America made it a suitable destination for transportation. Not surprisingly, however, the still greater cost and delays involved were seen as making it more impracticable than Botany Bay.[7]

What made a shipment to the Americas more problematic than before was not just the clear disapproval of the Home Office (which had also expressed concern about the fate suffered by convicts on some of the previous voyages), but the financial losses incurred by Arthur and George Bryan from the *Duke of Leinster* and its cargo in the

Leewards and the difficulty of finding another Irish contractor who would run the same risks. What made the need for another shipment absolutely pressing, however, was the dramatically worsening situation in Dublin's two gaols.

The Newgate riot

The development which persuaded the Dublin authorities that they would have to maintain trans-Atlantic transportation, despite stern and repeated warnings from the Home Office that this was now highly undesirable, was an unprecedented riot and attempted break-out at Newgate on 6 July 1790. Newspaper reports of this extraordinary event reflect the critical situation which had developed in the prison following the return of the Newfoundland prisoners in late January and further delays in securing Home Office permission to send Irish convicts to Botany Bay. They also make it clear that the seventy Newfoundland returnees played a central part in the organisation of the riot.[8] Six months after their return to Newgate, there was still no indication of when and where they were to be sent. Furthermore, according to the letter of the law they had still not served any part of their original sentences. Other prisoners at Newgate had been waiting as long as three years for transportation and it was probably this gnawing grievance that was the root cause of the riot.[9]

A warning of potential trouble came in April when the *Morning Post* observed that Newgate was now so crowded with prisoners that the keepers were 'barely competent to keep them fully in subjection'.[10] Unless something was done to clear Newgate, the newspaper believed that another prison would be needed. Many of the prisoners had unsuccessfully petitioned the government to be drafted into the Royal Navy in the expectation of war with Spain. When that prospect seemed less likely at the end of June, the *Freeman's Journal* suggested that putting them to work building the proposed new docks near the Customs-house 'would be turning their labour to much better purpose, than either imprisonment or transportation'.[11]

There was a further indication of the lack of proper regulation at Newgate in April when John Redmond, *alias* Raymond, *alias* E. Ponsonby Esq., *alias* Captain Uniake, *alias* Stepny, a young American protégé of Barrington and his gang of pickpockets managed to make his escape. As we have already seen, he had been sentenced to seven years' transportation at the Tholsel quarter sessions on 8 March for the theft of a pair of stockings. It later transpired that Matthew

Nulty, the man who assisted him, was 'a kind of messenger' – one of a favoured group who made a good business out of running errands for the wealthier prisoners. As we have already seen, Nulty himself was subsequently convicted and sentenced to transportation for helping Redmond to escape, although one newspaper wondered how this could be when he had no official status in the gaol.[12]

It was not long before there was an even more serious attempt at a mass break-out, occasioned as was so often the case with disturbances at Newgate and Kilmainham by a planned execution. John Read and Anthony McDermot, two journeymen sawyers from Dublin who had been found guilty at the Commission of Oyer and Terminer on 5 July under the amended Chalking Act of 1778 of 'cutting and wounding' fellow workers in a yard at Queen-street were due to he hanged in front of Newgate on the morning of 7 July. Under the terms of the Act, they had to be executed within forty-eight hours of their sentence and their bodies sent to the College of Surgeons for dissection.[13]

On the night of Monday 5 July, the prisoners broke all the windows that they could reach. The following morning a number of them knocked over the under-turnkeys and seized their keys, forcing them out and barricading all the doors so that they 'became absolute masters of the interior of the prison'. Liberating the other prisoners and helping to remove their shackles, they then proceeded to strip the building of all its fittings and to demolish the roof. By the time Lord Mayor John Exshaw and the sheriffs arrived, it was late afternoon and the occupants of neighbouring houses were apprehensive of what might happen that night. Indeed, the entire city was described as being in 'a continued state of alarm'. Soldiers comprising the entire 22nd Regiment and most of the 39th had been posted in a connected line around the prison and all the streets leading to it 'were lined with horse and foot'.[14] When the prison chaplain, the Revd Gamble, bravely offered himself as a hostage to the prisoners, he was refused.[15]

There was no option but to order the light infantry of the 22nd to knock down the inner door with sledge hammers and attempt to regain control of the main courtyard. When this had been done, 'a regular attack and defence took place', with the military keeping up a constant fire with their muskets in the passages of the prison until the rioters retreated to their apartments and were locked up again just before midnight.[16] The next morning, Read and McDermott were hanged at the front of the prison as originally planned. So large was the crowd gathered at Little-green that the military had to form a 'circumvallation' or cordon to prevent people from being smothered in the summer heat.[17]

The 6 July riot focused public attention on conditions at Newgate. According to the *Hibernian Journal*,

> There are near 300 felons confined in the New Prison, most of them desperadoes of the most abandoned, profligate, and daring description. Seventy of them are convicts returned from transportation, who have now remained there above six months; a tax on the citizens of Dublin, though long since promised to have been removed by the Government, either by transportation or embarked on ships of war. To keep this miscreant horde in subjection, the goaler [sic] is allowed only one turnkey; and out of his salary he is obliged to pay his deputy, who with himself, is occasionally called, not only to attend prisoners to the Quarter Sessions, Commission of Oyer and Terminer, – but continually to attend out-door duty, at the different Law Offices and City Committees, and other occasions about town. With this assistance he is possessed of but thirty pairs of bolts – but one main door, all the wooden doors, erected for temporary convenience being nearly demolished from time to time by connivance or the wickedness of the prisoners. The wall which divides the men's yard, from the women's, being wholly unsecured at [the] top by anything like a *Chevaux de Fraze* [sic]. Though such a security has been repeatedly applied for – and owing to this defect, joined to that of bolts, the wall has been repeatedly scaled and surmounted by the male prisoners, who have thus obtained a communication with the females, and to which no other barrier remained within the power of the goaler [sic] but the sanguinary use of the musketry of the guards, who defend the outside of the prison.[18]

The *Dublin Chronicle* also warned:

> There are now near three hundred men in this prison, many of them under rule of transportation; as they are in general muscular, active and desperate young fellows, very serious consequences are to be apprehended from their machinations to escape.[19]

On about 10 July a hole was discovered in the main wall 'which required nothing but the removal of a single stone to admit the escape of the whole gaol ...'.[20] Newgate was in the news again ten days later when no less than forty prisoners crawled through the prison 'necessary' into the main sewer, escaping where it disgorged into the river Liffey.[21] On the following day a further fourteen travelled the same route, six of them escaping and five dying of suffocation.[22] The whole of the first party were observed in groups of five and six in the Phoenix Park, heading for the Lucan road. Dermot Byrne, who had already been transported on no less than two previous occasions, was retaken at Smithfield when he was unable to give a constable a satisfactory explanation for his 'horrid appearance'. Sentenced once more to transportation in the Recorder's court, he may well have had Africa in mind as his most likely destination. Anticipating the traditional request made by Dubliners of departing seafarers, he playfully promised the Recorder that he would 'bring him home, on his return, a baboon, in reward for his indulgence'.[23]

On 20 July the prisoners at Newgate redoubled their efforts to escape. According to the *Dublin Chronicle*,

> The gaol at noon-day today has bore [sic] more the resemblance of a town besieged, than the prison of the second city in the British Empire – within, a constant yell of blasphemy and execration – showers of stones and brickbats – all the inner doors broken and the windows demolished; – without, an army in the street, and on the leads [roofs] of the opposite houses, keeping up a regular fire; the felons on the roof of the prison defending themselves and annoying the regulars by flinging among them huge fragments of stone and large flags![24]

Reporting the second escape through the sewers, the *Hibernian Journal* observed that 'nothing can more strongly mark the desperation of the prisoners in that jail, nor the insecurity of the means designed for their imprisonment, than this attempt'.[25] The *Morning Post* was prompted to suggest that there should be another prison in Dublin for all country convicts sent down to await transportation:

> The inhabitants of Dublin would, by this means, be eased of the great cost of maintaining and transporting rogues convicted, and transmitted from the country; but this additional gaol ought to be built at the expense of Parliament, and levied on the inland counties. Thus all parts would be impartially burthened, in the support of its outlaws.[26]

Moved to action at last by these alarming events, the commons of Dublin Corporation appointed a committee to supervise the management of Newgate. Finding in its report of 13 October that there had been 'great supineness and neglect' and that 'great irregularities' had been permitted by Gaoler Richard Cox and his assistants, the committee insisted that regulations be set out for their control. It also recommended that a sub-committee of the commons attend the gaol once a week to listen to the complaints of the prisoners and 'to form such internal police, as will in future prevent the attempts lately made to break gaol'.[27]

Kilmainham

Security at Kilmainham also continued to be a major problem. In what was to be the first of several such incidents that year, in February 1790 eleven prisoners picked a hole through the walls of their cell and managed to escape.[28] In the first week of September, there were two further efforts by prisoners to make a mass escape. In the more serious of these,

> some resolute villains among them having disengaged themselves from their irons, cut a hole through the door of one of the cells and were creeping out – the design was to rush up to the hall in a body, and if possible, to get the keys and force their passage through the military with bolts in their hands; the jailer brought in the guard, and after a struggle each time they were all happily secured.[29]

Reporting this, the *Hibernian Journal* remarked:

> The length of time since the convicts have been sent off, has occasioned such numbers to remain in the different prisons of this kingdom, but especially in the city and county of Dublin, as render it extremely difficult to keep then in any order and obviate their different designs and efforts for again getting loose on the public.[30]

County gaols were also experiencing serious problems during 1790. In early September, about eight prisoners, most of them under sentence of transportation, escaped from Maryborough (Portlaoise) gaol in Queen's Co. by 'breaking and removing some huge stones and flags out of the back wall of the prison ...'[31] and there was an attempt at Carlow.[32] During the previous three years there had been similar problems at Galway, Limerick, and Mullingar, Co. Meath.[33] On other occasions, convicts being brought under escort to Dublin for transportation had managed to escape from the sometimes make-shift gaol accommodation provided.[34]

Nor was the problem of security limited to the gaols. In March 1789, eight prisoners being held for trial at the Tholsel for the next Dublin quarter sessions managed to break out of the holding cell. Built in 1683 and formerly the Guildhall of the Dublin Corporation, the Tholsel in Skinner's-row was used for the city's assizes until the completion of a new court at Little-green near Newgate in 1794.[35] While its spacious hall lent some dignity to the process of justice, the rapidly decaying state of the building meant that the facilities for holding prisoners were highly insecure. The leader of the escapees, Michael Delany, 'a most notorious offender', was already under sentence of transportation and had just been acquitted together with Patrick Hughes on a charge of robbery committed within Newgate itself. A few days after the escape, he was caught having his hair cut at a barber's shop in Francis-street and was returned to Newgate. Subsequently found guilty of yet another robbery in the prison, this time on a police corporal visiting a prisoner, he was hanged, together with the teenage returnee John O' Neal, in front of Newgate on 24 October.[36]

In response to the continuing crisis at Newgate, the Dublin Sessions Grand Jury in late September 1790 produced an ambitious plan for the improvement and greater security of the prison. There was to be a new entrance, new quarters for the staff, a proper guard room for the military, a new infirmary and a proper division of the male and female prisoners by means of two parallel walls surmounted by a *chevaux de frize* of broken glass. Finally, a new sewer would make that traditional avenue of escape impossible and a perimeter wall would prevent escape from the roof. A sum of £1,000 was voted towards work estimated to cost £3,000.[37]

Even as these plans were being prepared for public display at the Royal Exchange, however, the prisoners at Newgate were busily engaged in yet another daring escape attempt. In the last days of September, they dug a tunnel under the foundations of the prison with the intention of coming up into Gaoler Cox's own apartment, killing him and making their way to the front of the gaol. Unfortunately for them, the noise of their nocturnal excavations alerted one of the turnkeys and they were quickly secured.[38] Cox was subsequently fined £50 at the Commission of Oyer and Terminer for 'neglect' resulting in the escape of one of the prisoners.[39] However, the situation at Newgate was now clearly beyond his control.

By this time, the Dublin newspapers were reflecting the alarm which must have been widespread amongst the city's respectable classes since early July. Reporting this latest escape attempt at Newgate, the *Morning Post* remarked:

> The numerous attempts made by 300 wretches huddled together in the above prison should incline government to take some effectual steps for disposing of the convicts in a proper manner, and not leave the public in the hourly dread of being again a prey to their depredations; a shame not less to the executive power than it is to the want of laws to put them into execution.[40]

Penitentiary houses

Although new transportation legislation was passed by the Irish Parliament in February 1790, the government was also considering the establishment of a system of penitentiary houses throughout the country. As we shall see, this had been publicly advocated by the Inspector-General of Prisons, Sir Jeremiah Fitzpatrick, in his *Thoughts on Penitentiaries* published earlier that year. It was also strongly supported by his friend Peter Holmes, who chaired the parliamentary committee on the state of the prisons for some years and had drawn up the new prison regulations of 1788. Chancellor of the Exchequer, Sir John Parnell, indicated his support for the principle when introducing the transportation bill and shortly after its enactment, judges and county authorities were asked by Government Secretary Hobart for their responses to such a system. The county authorities were generally favourable to the idea, although they wanted more details and were apprehensive of the additional cost that it might involve. The Cavan grand jury, for example, be-lieved that a local tax for the purpose could not be borne 'to any extent'.[41]

The idea of a penitentiary was also being taken up by the Dublin newspapers and their readers. A correspondent to the *Morning Post* in March 1790 offered the example of Holland where every principal town possessed an institution called a *Rasphuis*. Prisoners were put to practical tasks there for the duration of their sentence and those found to be 'incorrigible' were transported to Surinam in South America or Batavia in the East Indies.[42] Indeed, the penitentiary system was enthusiastically embraced by most of the newspapers, the *Freeman's Journal* testifying to the 'astonishing effects' of the scheme in those British counties where it had already been tried.[43] Its only concern was that the work of setting up the institution should be put in the hands of some 'respectable and honourable characters',

For it has too long been the *curse* of this country, at least of this metropolis, that some *needy ignorant* adventurers have found means to get into the direction of our public buildings and work, where scenes of the most shameful *jobbing* and peculation have been and still are carried out. Our public prisons are a reproach to our civilization – the Four-courts Marshalsea, the New-jail, and some lately erected Hospitals, stand as undesirable proofs of this assertion; and for the yearly repairs and additional amendments of such, the public are highly taxed.[44]

It was against this background that Dublin Corporation decided in June that the old city Bridewell in St James-street would be 'appropriated' as a penitentiary 'for the confinement of convicts to labour', the cost to be borne by the government.[45] At the same time, a newspaper report that a bill for the reform of the criminal laws would be introduced at the next sitting of Parliament stimulated some more thoughtful discussion of the penitentiary as an alternative to transportation. Accepting that 'vindictive justice' was not possible, the *Freeman's Journal* believed that '*public utility*' must supply the measure of human punishment 'which would ever be proportionate to human example'.[46] By this criterion, transportation was totally inadequate:

But where a set of desperadoes, as well as the giddy and unthinking, are seen exulting and carousing at the idea of being banished from this country, to be removed to a foreign quarter, equally happy, healthy, and in their opinions more wealthy than that which they have offended; and where, it is well known to them, slavery is abolished, it will seem to many rather as a temptation to offend, than a cause of dread or terror; some other mode of punishment should be adopted, salutary to the morals and useful to the interests of the country.[47]

The July riot prompted further newspaper debate on what might be done to reduce the pressure on Newgate, including the possibility of building penitentiaries. One writer to the *Morning Post* later that month referred to the system practised in France, Spain and Italy where prisoners put to the galleys in summer were transferred in winter to secure houses and employed in various skilled and unskilled tasks. He concluded:

Such an institution, well conducted, would surely answer all the ends of transportation with less than a quarter of the expense, as the malefactors would more than maintain themselves, and instead of quitting, become highly beneficial to themselves and their country.[48]

A few months later, the first official steps were taken by the government to pursue the idea proposed by Fitzpatrick of establishing penitentiaries 'for the reception of felons heretofore sentenced to transportation'.[49] On 21 October, forty or fifty male convicts under sentence of transportation were removed from Newgate to the St James-street Bridewell which had been converted for the purpose. Although the *Dublin Chronicle* report did not make this clear, it seems likely that amongst these first inmates of the new institution were three young boys – an eleven-year-old, a twelve-year-old and a thirteen-year-old.[50]

Within a short time, there were signs that the experiment would not be without its problems. The *Freeman's Journal* reported in mid-January 1791 that four of the young prisoners employed in hemp-dressing had broken through the ceiling and slate roof of the building and let themselves down to the street using ropes made from hemp and their own shirts.[51] On 23 April it noted that 'a few nights ago, the penitentiary *cage* in James-street, was forced open at the top, from which some of the *impenitent birds* flew away'.[52] However, by January 1792 the Dublin police commissioners found that some progress was being made in instructing the thirty-nine inmates in shoe-making, ribbon-weaving, silk-winding and beating hemp.[53] Recognising that the main limitation of the new scheme was the size and nature of the building, Fitzpatrick consulted his mentor Jeremy Bentham in early 1791 on the planning and management of a more suitable one which the Inspector-General no doubt intended as a prototype for the whole country.[54] Bentham's subsequent plan found approval but, as similar proposals made by him to the British goverment, it was rejected by Chancellor Parnell on the grounds of excessive cost. Nevertheless, the government remained committed to the penitentiary principle and legislation was enacted in late 1792 (*32 Geo. III, c. 27*) to establish it as an alternative to transportation for offenders, especially younger ones, considered capable of reformation.[55]

13
Irish Transportation to New South Wales

The resignation of the Marquis of Buckingham as Lord Lieutenant of Ireland in October 1789 after the furore of the Regency Crisis, and his replacement the following January by the Earl of Westmorland, meant that the Irish government's long-requested participation in the Botany Bay scheme was once more delayed. It was only in early January 1790 that Government Secretary Robert Hobart again raised the matter with Evan Nepean after the latter had told Westmorland that there might be a cheaper system than had originally been anticipated. As it was, Hobart emphasised, 'the great expence [sic] now attending the transportation of convicts to Botany Bay, will create much difficulty here'.[1]

In the meantime, Hobart was responsible for ensuring that new legislation was passed by the Irish Parliament which would authorise transportation to Botany Bay. Apparently unaware of the terms of the 1786 Police Act whose broad definition of where convicts might be transported would certainly have covered New South Wales, both Nepean and Grenville had made it clear to Dublin Castle from as early as July 1789 that a new Act, was required before they would assist in the despatch of Irish convicts.[2]

When the Irish Parliament met on 21 January 1790, the strain in relations between the executive government and Whitehall brought about by the Newfoundland and Barbuda affairs was not generally known. However, on 15 February in the House of Commons the Chancellor of the Exchequer, Sir John Parnell, referred to the convicts who had 'been lately compelled to return' from Newfoundland and the likelihood that no further shipments could be sent to North America. Consequently, he said, consideration would have to be given to two possible alternatives – transportation to Botany Bay, or the establishment of a penitentiary system along the lines of what was then being initiated in Britain. This latter alternative had been discussed at some length in Sir Jeremiah Fitzpatrick's *Thoughts on Penitentiaries*. Dedicated to Fitzgibbon and strongly reflecting the ideas of the pioneer Italian reformer, Cesare Beccaria, whose work had been published in English in Dublin in 1767, the pamphlet was also influenced by the writings of William Eden, John Howard and Jeremy Bentham. In all likelihood, it was put out hurriedly by the Inspector-General of Prisons with the intention of influencing the Parliamentary debate.

'Vindictive justice not being possible', Fitzpatrick had written as a true Benthamite, 'public utility must be the measure of human punishment, and that will ever be proportionate to the efficacy of example ...'.[3] Transportation to the Americas had been ineffective as a deterrent, he went on. Indeed, it had been eagerly embraced by many convicts in Newgate who were not under sentence of transportation but were confined for their inability to pay fees or find security for their release. He had seen as many as ten of these young men in one day volunteer for transportation in the belief that they would be 'bettered by the change'. Transportation had by this means lost its intended effect,

> but were the most dangerous miscreants ... to have to dread the horrors of being sent to Tunis, Algiers, or other Barbarian ports, for the redemption of unfortunate Christian slaves; or be sent to the coast of Africa, or to Botany Bay, (which perhaps might be done through the medium of Great-Britain) we should hear no more of volunteering, for then transportation, in the vulgar opinion, would become punishment: whilst the less artful and hardened, whose youth or other circumstances might presume the possibility of reform, and the heinousness of whose offences, would not render it absolutely political or necessary to extirpate from the land, might be confined and employed in penitentiaries, for such time as the courts should award.[4]

Although the expense of transporting convicts to Botany Bay might seem 'enormous', Fitzpatrick believed that the 'most atrocious offenders, *doomed never to return*' would scarcely number forty each year, the rest being capable of reformation by servitude in penitentiaries.[5]

The transportation debate

Clearly reflecting Fitzpatrick's approach, Parnell told Parliament it was his belief that persons convicted of lesser crimes should be employed in hard labour, or in some manner beneficial to the country, and that those guilty of greater should be transported for life; for certain he was, that wherever they might be placed, they would be bad subjects.[6]

The costs involved in transportation to Botany Bay, Parnell emphasised, were 'enormous': about £18 per head for the actual cost of conveyance, £28 or £29 for clothing and other necessaries on the voyage, and further outlays including eighteen months' provisions which would amount to a total of between £70 and £80 per convict. 'However', he added, 'expensive as it was ... the greater crimes ought to be so punished – though, for the lesser, hard labour and penitentiary houses would be better, *but in any case money would be wanting* [emphasis added], and therefore supply must be opened'. Parnell's idea was that most prisoners should be set to labour in Ireland, but that the cost of maintaining them should be borne by the county authorities, as had been the custom before the Police Act of 1786 had centralised control of transportation under the Lord Lieutenant. At this point, the draft bill authorising transportation to Botany Bay was already completed and Parnell was simply taking the precaution of appealing to members for their suggestions. While he favoured transportation to New South Wales for more serious criminals, he knew that the problem of its high cost could only be overcome by persuading leading members of Parliament that it would be effective.

Dominating the ensuing discussion was Peter Holmes, MP for Banagher, King's Co., and Comptroller of Stamps. A close associate of Fitzpatrick's and the leader of a group including Richard Griffith and Parnell himself which had been campaigning for prison reform and the introduction of a penitentiary system, Holmes had chaired the gaols and prisons committee of the House of Commons for some years. Intimately acquainted with prison conditions, he and Griffith were the architects of the Prisons Act of 1784.[7] Echoing the Inspector-General's economic arguments against transportation, the man whom Fitzpatrick had called 'Ireland's Howard' told the House that it was a reproach to Ireland's laws 'to see the number of wretches daily lost to this country, most of whom, by judicious management, might be reclaimed and made useful members of society'. He cited the example of one such institution at Wymondham in Norfolk, described in detail in Fitzpatrick's pamphlet, where the costs of upkeep were met by the 'labour and industry' of the convicts. Under that system, prisoners recommended by the gaoler on account of their useful services could be released with warm clothes on their backs and sufficient money to take them wherever they then wished to be employed.

Holmes was also critical of what he saw as the inhumane nature of transportation, pointing out that amongst the Newfoundland returnees, '*some of the convicts were under the age of twelve, and that six were under the age of fourteen!*'. This, he felt, was a strong argument for penitentiary houses, 'for there was something shocking in thus abandoning early youth to infamy without the hope of reclaiming their pliant minds'. 'Could there be any doubt', he went on, 'but that solitary confinement, with hard labour and spare diet, might retrieve from destruction, such young and unhardened minds?'. In his view, 'it was time to amend the sanguinary code of criminal laws'.

The only other speaker was John Forbes, the influential member for Drogheda, Co. Louth, and friend of Henry Grattan who was aligned with the Patriot opposition. He was concerned not only with the cost of a penitentiary system but (as with the Police Bill of 1786) the number of 'place-men' he believed it would create. Forbes promised that he 'would oppose every scheme of establishing penitentiary houses, it would only be to create new offices for members of parliament, or lay the foundation for pensions'. Instead,

> he thought it better to get rid of bad members of the community by exporting them to Botany Bay, were the expence [*sic*] 50 or 60 pounds each, than to keep them within the precincts of our own society, where they might possibly have an opportunity of corrupting the honest and the industrious.

Parnell was thus handed the opportunity to suggest that Forbes and other 'country gentlemen' might alter the government's bill 'to their own likeing [sic]' in order to avoid the problem of adding to the already lengthy pension list. This was a not-so-subtle reference to the possible revival of the old system of local responsibility for the support and disposal of convicts, something which the Chancellor and other members of the government knew was most unlikely to be acceptable. Having offered this bluff, Parnell promised to bring down the Bill in four or five days.

The new Act

On 1 March 1790 the legislation foreshadowed by Parnell was given its first reading in the House of Commons by the Attorney-General,

Arthur Wolfe, and quickly went through the committee stage and third reading in both houses with no amendments and negligible discussion. Although the committee stage was usually reported in detail in the *Parliamentary Record* and the *Freeman's Journal*, not a word was recorded about the Bill's reception and there may not even have been any debate at all.[8] The issue was not a controversial one and the cost of transportation to Botany Bay, which had certainly been seen by the Castle authorities as a difficult political obstacle to overcome, did not loom large. Honourable members were perhaps too preoccupied with a sensational legal case involving Lord Chief Justice Clonmel and the proprietor of the *Dublin Evening Post* to be interested in the cost of sending away each year a few hundred irreclaimable villains to the ends of the earth.

The new 'Act for rendering the Transportation of Felons and Vagabonds more easy' (*30 Geo. III, c. 32*), which received final confirmation in the House of Lords on 5 April when the Earl of Westmorland conveyed the Royal Assent, contained nothing very new or controversial. It simply enlarged the geographical scope of transportation to include 'such part or parts beyond the seas, and in such manner as the lord lieutenant ... shall think proper ...' and made the Irish Treasury responsible for all the costs involved.[9] With a definition as broad as this, there was no need to stipulate New South Wales as one of the places where Irish convicts sentenced to transportation could be sent. The formula adopted may indicate, however, that the Irish authorities were still by no means confident that they would be able to participate in the Botany Bay scheme or that it would be a success.

Thus it was that members of the Irish Parliament, Patriots and Castle supporters alike, enacted a piece of legislation which made possible the despatch to New South Wales of a largely Roman Catholic body of Irish petty criminals whose presence in the new settlement would help prevent the erection of any new Protestant ascendancy in the antipodes.[10] The satirist in *Walker's Hibernian Magazine* a few years earlier would prove to be remarkably clairvoyant in his description of Botany Bay society.

'I was in hopes'

Forwarding the Bill to Nepean on 25 March after its third reading, Hobart told him that once it received the Royal Assent, the new legislation would empower the government to send 'all Felons and Vagabonds under sentence of transportation to such Part or Parts beyond the Seas, and in such manner, as Government shall think proper'.[11] However, this would not be possible without the co-operation of the British government:

> The Obstructions given of late to the landing Persons of this Description in any of the United States of America, and the Prohibition in the British Colonies and Plantations against their being received there, makes it impossible for the Government of this Kingdom to transport Convicts out of this Country, unless they can be assisted by Great Britain in the sending them with the Convicts from thence.

Hobart told Nepean that letters had gone out to judges seeking their opinions on the advantages of confining lesser criminals in 'Penitentiary Houses' and that special measures were being taken in Dublin itself to give this scheme a trial. 'If such a Plan should be found practicable', he added,

> it will not however alter the Wishes of Government to transport beyond the Seas, felons whose Crimes are atrocious, or whose desperate inclinations afford little promise of their being better'd by milder Punishment.

Under the new arrangement, the Lord Lieutenant hoped to be able to send prisoners sentenced to transportation at both the Lent and Summer assizes to Portsmouth. There they would be placed in the hands of the authorities responsible for the transportation of British convicts:

> The Irish Convicts to be put upon the Footing and Transported at the same time, in the same manner and to the same place as the British Convicts. Government here would then either repay to Great Britain the actual Expense of the Transportation in proportion to the Number of Persons sent from hence, or pay at once a certain Sum for each Man to be stipulated upon a reasonable Estimate of every Charge attending his Transportation.

While there was now no doubt about the Lord Lieutenant's authority under the new Act, there was still the question of whether any further legal powers were required by the British government 'for the receiving and detaining Irish convicts or transporting them from thence'. However, Hobart was confident that these would be 'readily furnished' by the British Parliament if need be.

24 John Fane, Earl of Westmorland. It was during Westmorland's Lord Lieutenancy that the transportation of Irish convicts to New South Wales was finally agreed upon by the Home Office.

Westmorland himself had written to Grenville two weeks earlier assuring him that the new Bill would cover the retransportation of the convicts at Barbuda and Anguilla (of whom the Home Secretary was to learn at about the same time as he received this despatch) as well as those returned from Newfoundland. Suggesting that it might be better to allow the former to sail direct from the West Indies to Botany Bay, he confessed: 'The less we hear of them in Europe and particularly in Ireland the better'.[12] He hoped that convicts would be sent from Ireland at the same cost as those from England, as provided for by Chancellor Parnell, but evidently expected that this might not be possible. 'If you are resolved to drive a very hard Bargain with poor Ireland' he added in a cynical postcript, 'lay the cost upon each individual Convict and then nobody will take notice'.

The other issue raised by Westmorland with the Home Secretary was Grenville's earlier suggestion that Ireland should supplememt at its own cost the military establishment at Botany Bay. 'There would be great awkwardness in the accounts', he wrote, 'the proposal wd. be much objected to in and out of Parliament and the Irish will say, you might at least afford a company from your Treasury'. He emphasised that various schemes were under way to dispose of felons either through public works or solitary confinement. 'I am in hopes', he told Grenville, 'that after we have cleared our gaols of present incumbents, we shall not trouble Botany Bay with such numbers as can make an increase of Force necessary'.

In mid-June, when there had been no response from the Home Office to Hobart's inquiry of early January about costs, Sackville Hamilton told Nepean that at Hobart's instigation he had called for an account of all those under sentence of transportation which he would pass on as soon as he received it. Westmorland had also asked him to request information 'as early as possible' about when the next fleet to Botany Bay was to assemble and at which Irish port the transports would touch to pick up Irish prisoners. Such was the need to relieve the pressure on Dublin's gaols that Westmorland expressed his willingness to send the Irish convicts to Portsmouth to join the fleet of transports there if need be.[13] A month later, Hobart informed Nepean that from the returns that had come in from Ireland's county gaols it appeared that there were about 200 prisoners under sentence of transportation – 175 men and 25 women.[14]

On 28 July when these repeated inquiries had still produced no response from London and the situation at Newgate was at crisis point, Hobart wrote impatiently to Nepean: 'I am very much afraid that our

Convicts have in the hurry of business been forgotten – as I was in hopes long ago to have heard from you on that subject'.[15] Two weeks later he asked him for 'notice of the time the Botany Bay ships are to sail' so that he could commence the process of collecting the convicts.[16] When there was still no response by late September, he wrote again in desperation to Nepean, emphasising both the material problems and the political embarrassment that any further delay would bring for the government:

> I was in hopes long before this to have heard from you upon the subject of Convicts, which I can assure you is now become very serious in this country – our Prisons are so crowded that the worst consequences are to be apprehended, both from Pestilential disorders, and the escape of Prisoners[;] in either case much clamour would deservedly be rais'd against the Government. You will recall that we have no hulks, and that the Convicts of two years are now upon our heads. I have therefore to request you would inform me what prospect there is of our being able to send those now under sentence of transportation, as it is absolutely necessary that something should immediately be done.[17]

Hobart's increasingly strident appeals for assistance were finally answered, Grenville himself writing to Westmorland on 31 October to say that the delay had been due to the need to reduce costs but that the Navy Board had recently advertised for transports.[18] At the same time, the Home Secretary suggested that the Irish government might follow the British practice of pardoning convicts 'whose crimes have not been of an atrocious nature' on condition of their entry into the armed forces. This had been resorted to extensively in Ireland during the American War, but in peacetime British regiments preferred not to recruit Irishmen, particulary convicted felons. At any rate, Grenville thought it undesirable 'that any part of such Convicts whatever should be selected by Government, and forced into either Service'.[19]

In early November, Hobart received a letter from the First Fleet shipping contractor, William Richards Jr., tendering his services for the conveying of convicts to New South Wales. Although he promised 'reasonable terms', Richards did not reveal what these would be, only saying that as 'no Shipping proper for the purpose' could be found in Dublin, it would have to be hired per ton per month.[20] It seems from this that the Home Office favoured for a time the idea of the Irish authorities should make their own arrangements for transportation to

New South Wales, especially in view of the delays. However, Nepean subsequently informed Hobart in a despatch of 5 January 1791 that the *Queen*, one of the ships recently contracted by the Navy Board, would shortly be despatched to Cork to embark 175 male and 25 female convicts.[21]

A week later, the Dublin newspapers carried reports of these long-awaited arrangements to send Irish convicts to New South Wales. According to the *Morning Post* of 15 January, 'it is at length determined by Government to empty the New Prison of its foul contents: a vessel will be immediately chartered for Port Jackson, Botany Bay, to carry thither its abandoned crew'. Two weeks later it reported that proper clothing and accommodation for the long voyage were being prepared. 'The project will certainly be expensive', it observed, 'but it is at the same [time] expected, that it will be effectual, in the intent of punishment, as there can be no kind of probability of a return from transportation'.[22] Readers were reminded that legislation had already been enacted which would authorise transportation to this conveniently distant location.

Although the Dublin Castle authorities were greatly relieved to have Nepean's advice of the imminent arrival of the *Queen*, there was as yet no indication of how much the shipment would cost the Irish government. Hobart made a number of inquiries seeking information on this question from the Home Office in January and February,[23] but it was not until the end of March that he received a copy of the 'charter party' or contract signed in London on 18 November 1789 by the Revenue Commissioners with Messrs Camden, Calvert and King. This well-known slave-shipping firm had taken British convict conscripts to the garrison at Cape Coast Castle (Ghana) in January 1784 and had also offered to transport them to the island of Lemain in Gambia in February 1785.[24] They had successfully tendered for the Second Fleet in 1790. Although their record in caring for convicts in the latter shipment would be subsequently revealed as nothing less than disastrous 25 , the charge of £22,370 for transporting 1,250 convicts was substantially less than the £54,518.16s.1d. received by Richards for transporting only 775 convicts in the First Fleet.[25] William Grenville, who had replaced Lord Sydney as Secretary of State in June 1789, was evidently determined to cut costs and to expedite arrangements for the next shipment to New South Wales.[26]

Under the terms of the contract for what was to be the Third Fleet, Camden, Calvert and King agreed to transport 2,000 convicts (including 200 Irish) to New South Wales at a cost of £45,000, or £19.10s per head.[27] Consequently, the Botany Bay scheme was not nearly as expensive as the Irish government had originally feared. When its contribution to the cost of supplies, clothing and the military guard was calculated, the total bill for this first shipment on the *Queen* was £6,800, or £34 for each of the 200 convicts allowed in its quota. This was about half the cost that Parnell had originally anticipated, but the convicts were to pay a high price for the savings.[28]

'Of an incorrigible description'

In accordance with Nepean's indication that a transport would shortly be sent to Cork to embark convicts, county sheriffs were directed by Hobart to prepare lists of all prisoners currently being held under sentence of transportation in the gaols under their control. Following this, Hobart sent out warrants authorising their despatch under military escort to Cork to await embarkation.[29] The sheriffs of Limerick, for example, received their warrant from Hobart in mid-January[30] and a week later the city gaoler set off for Cork with a party of ten convicts in his charge.[31]

At Newgate itself, the chaplain and gaol inspectors were called in to decide on those prisoners who might be reclaimed through hard labour and those, according to the *Morning Post*, '*of an incorrigible description (which are very numerous) ... allotted to Botany Bay ...*'.[32] Regardless of what had been said by the *Freeman's Journal* a few years earlier (and the opinions of historians in more recent times) about the worthy character of these first Irish settlers of New South Wales, there can be no doubt that many despatched on the *Queen* were considered by the prison authorities as hardened and irredeemable offenders. At least twelve of them were from the group of Newfoundland returnees believed to have instigated the attempted break-out at Newgate in July 1790.[33] Indeed, their selection for Botany Bay could be interpreted as confirming this. In addition, there were at least two returnees from the earlier trans-Atlantic shipments who had been reconvicted after committing further offences.[34]

There is no indication that the selection of the convicts at Newgate had any connection with useful skills that they might have possessed. As we shall see, the 'indent' or list of convicts transported on the *Queen* provided no information on their occupations or level of literacy which might have been of assistance to the authorities in New South Wales.[35] Nor were the basic details of their sentences received by the Sydney authorities until 1799. What can be said on the positive side is that as most of them were young men between the ages of twenty and thirty, they were probably chosen with a view to their ability to survive the long and arduous voyage and to perform some kind of physical labour on their arrival in the new colony. The women were also young and the willingness of the authorities to allow four of them to take their young children on the ship suggests that they were not regarded as being totally abandoned.

The convicts of the *Queen*[36]

While two-thirds of the 155 convicts embarked on the *Queen* were between the ages of twenty and thirty, boys of 11 to 19 years accounted for a significant 14 per cent. David Fay and James Blake from Dublin were 11 and 12 respectively and John Heally from Limerick City was 12. Another 15 per cent were between 31 and 40. The oldest person on board was Patrick Fitzgerald, 'yeoman' of Ballinline, Co. Limerick, who was sixty-four years of age. The average age of the twenty-two women was 27, the youngest being Sarah Brazil of Waterford and Mary Whelan of Dublin who were both eighteen. The oldest was Margaret Stephenson of Co. Armagh, who was 50.

Although there were no physical descriptions of the convicts in the indent, there is one vignette which provides some idea of their appearance. In their assizes records for Queen's County, it was reported that William Riely (or O' Reilly) and Ann Clark *'alias* Murphy' *alias* Cleary had been held 'under rule of transportation' in Maryborough (Portlaoise) gaol since 6 August 1790. Aged 'about twenty six years' and five feet ten inches in height, he had black hairy eyebrows, wore a dark wig and had greyish hair. He was from Naas, Co. Kildare, and had been convicted a second time for escaping from gaol where he was originally sent to await transportation for life for counterfeiting. She was 'about thirty years of age' with a smooth face, brown hair, grey eyes and with a small cut between her eyes.[37] Sentenced to seven years' transportation, her crime is unrecorded.

About 60 per cent or the great majority of the convicts despatched on the *Queen* had been sentenced to seven years' transportation. Another category of about 40 per cent who were classified by the law as more serious offenders had either been sentenced to transportation for life or had their capital sentences commuted to life. Eighty-two of the convicts had been convicted at the Dublin City or Co. Dublin assizes and there were another twenty or so urban offenders from Cork,

Limerick and Belfast to make up more than half of the total. The remainder represented the counties of Antrim, Cavan, Down, Fermanagh, Galway, Kildare, Kilkenny, King's Co. (Offaly), Leitrim, Longford, Louth, Meath, Monaghan, Queen's Co. (Laois), Tipperary, Waterford, Westmeath and Wexford.

There is a major problem in analysing the offences committed by the 155 convicts. With fifteen exceptions, all the assizes records for them have been destroyed. While the Dublin, Cork and Belfast newspapers recorded the proceedings of their own quarterly assizes and those of nearby counties, assizes of more remote counties often went unreported. Nevertheless, it seems reasonable to conclude from the evidence that can be found that the most common offences were of an urban nature – stealing from a shop or a house or the robbery of theft of money and belongings.

Although their legitimate occupations were rarely recorded in the newspapers, it seems likely that some of the urban offenders were servants found guilty of stealing money or belonging from their employers. Sarah Brazil and James Cahir of Waterford were jointly convicted at the Waterford city assizes on 19 July 1790 'for certain Felony to the value of four shillings nine pence'.[38] On 12 July 1790 at Dublin's Commission of Oyer and Terminer, Andrew Berrall, 22, was convicted of robbing his master, John Hatch Esq. of Harcourt–street and ordered to be transported for seven years.[39]

Others were clearly members of organised shop-gangs of the kind so frequently described in the Dublin newspapers. On 13 January 1791 at the Dublin City quarter sessions, Charles Marshall, 'a boy about thirteen years of age', was convicted of stealing diamond, gold and other rings to a very considerable amount 'from Richard Williams, jeweller, of Grafton-street'. He was sentenced to seven years' transportation but his accomplice, Catherine Connome or Connolle, who had received several of the rings knowing them to be stolen, got off with two pilloryings at Coal Quay and one year's imprisonment.[40] Terence McDaniel, 24, and John Cunningham, 24, were members of a gang of burglars acquitted of burglary after many hours of evidence from witnesses but found guilty of felony to the value of five shillings.[41]

Two juvenile criminals who worked together were James Blake and Christopher McMahon, both of them 12 years old. They were found guilty at the Dublin City quarter sessions in October 1790 of stealing a pair of silver buckles, the property of John Ash. Both were sentenced to seven years' transportation but only Blake's name appeared on the *Queen* indent.[42]

Two young Dublin women, Mary Ennis, 30, and Mary Whelan, 18, were transported as 'idle vagabonds', most likely prostitutes, when they failed to produce the necessary security to the same court.[43]

Bridget Nowlan, *alias* Rossiter, 35, was convicted at the Dublin City quarter sessions on 16 July 1789 of stealing from the Linen Hall. She had been caught by Constable Smith on the morning of 26 March carrying away on her back six pieces of white linen in a bag which she told him contained greens from the market. It was revealed during the trial that she was an accomplice of Patrick McDaniel who had probably passed the cloth to her from linen factor (dealer) John Chambers' room without being noticed by him.[44] Under the mandatory terms of the statute designed to deter thefts of this kind, she was sentenced to be executed. Being recommended as 'an object of mercy', however, she was given 'a long day 'or stay of execution until 7 December, by which time the penalty was commuted to seven years' transportation.[45] McDaniel had been arrested in a 'night–house' (brothel) in Thomas-street shortly after the crime but the other woman working with him, Catherine McEnnallan, was not apprehended.[46]

Perhaps the most daring criminal of all was Patrick Leonard, 45, of Dublin who had conspired with a solider and other prisoners while committed to Newgate for another offence to rob the Treasury in the Lower Castle-yard. The plan was that when the solider returned to duty in the yard he would give them the opportunity that they needed. Instead, however, he 'discovered' the plot of this 'national robbery' to the authorities and Leonard was apprehended.[47]

A significant number of the male convicts had committed street or highway robbery. Hugh Lynch, 25, was convicted at Dublin's City quarter sessions in early August 1788 for 'stopping Mr Denis Murphy in Grafton – street and clapping a pistol to his breast with intent to rob him'.[48] James Grant, 26, seems to have been one of the many footpads preying on pedestrians on the fringes of the city. On 9 December 1788 he was found guilty at the Commission of Oyer and Terminer of stopping Charles Lindsay late one night on New – street and taking from his person four shillings in silver, a pen – knife, a steel toothpick case and a watch chain. He also took a caroline hat from Lindsay's son, these being very much in fashion.[49] Garret (George) Kitwan, 29, sentenced to be hanged at Kilmainham on 31 July 1790 for highway robbery was 'shaved and prepared for death' when the letter bearing his respite to transportation arrived.[50]

Nor was highway robbery an entirely male preserve. On 14 October 1789 in the Dublin City quarter sessions, Catherine Devereux, 30, was found guilty together with Richard Andrews of stopping John Burke on the highway and taking his hat, purse and £4.13s.3d. in cash. Sentenced to be hanged on 31 October, she was subsequently reprieved to transportation for life when she revealed to the court that she was pregnant. Andrews had been reprieved earlier when it was pleaded on his behalf that he had prevented his other associates from ill-treating Burke.[51]

Only two convicts can be described as having committed offences of a recognisably agrarian or political kind. Francis McClernan, 20, was one of five men sentenced to death at the Co. Armagh assizes on 4 April 1790. Believed to be members of a gang of Defenders or Break o' Day Boys, secret vigilante groups formed in the 1780s to intimidate landlords and officials seen to be oppressing Catholic tenants, they had been found guilty of the murder of John Weir. Possibly due to his youth, McClernan gained a reprieve of transportation for life. His four companions were duly hanged on 13 April.[52]

Eyre Jackson, 21, had been convicted with his brother Charles for 'forcible possession' of land at the Co. Galway assizes in April 1790 and sentenced to seven years' transportation. Eyre was the only convict on board the *Queen* who apparently petitioned the Lord Lieutenant for the commutation of his sentence. This document does not survive but there is a letter from the foreman of the jury who convicted them, Christopher St George of Tyrone, Co. Galway, asking the Lord Lieutenant to 'Extend such Mitigation as to His Excellency's Wisdom shall seem fit'[53] The appeal was at least partly effective as Charles Jackson was not transported with his brother.

It is true that a higher proportion of those convicts sentenced to transportation for life came from rural areas, reflecting the relatively harsh penalties for offences such as animal-stealing. However, there is no basis for T.J. Kiernan's claim that 'about one-fifth of the men convicts (twenty-four out of 133) were transported for agrarian offences'.[54] The case of Eyre Jackson seems to have been an unusual one.

Typical of the rural offences recorded was Patrick Fitzgerald's crime. He had been convicted at the August 1790 Co. Limerick assizes for stealing clothing from a house to the value of 4s. 6d. and after pleading benefit of clergy as a first offender was sentenced to seven years' transportation 'to plantations in America or elsewhere out of Europe'.[55] More seriously, Edmund Kennedy and Thomas Dwyer had assaulted Charles McDonald on the highway in Co. Clare, 'feloniously and violently taking from his person Forty Three Dozen of Yarn value £1.3.3.$\frac{1}{2}$ one bagg value 10d one gal of whiskey value 3d one snuff

25 Petition to Lord Lieutenant Westmorland on behalf of Eyre Jackson of Co. Galway, 13 April 1790.

box value 2d one pocket handkerchief value 6d one pair of shoes and buckles value Two Pounds five shillings ...'. At the Co. Clare assizes on 22 July 1790 they had been sentenced to death, commuted to transportation for seven years.[56]

Animal stealing, especially of horses and sheep, was a common rural offence represented amongst the convicts of the *Queen*. James McKelvey alias McGrath, 24, had been sentenced to death at the Co. Monaghan assizes on 16 August 1790 for stealing a bay mare valued at £9.3s.0d from Terence McVeagh. Like most offences of this kind where the harsh penalty was supposed to act as a deterrent, his sentence was commuted to transportation for life.[57] At least six other men on board and probably a good many more from rural areas had been convicted of horse or sheep-stealing. However, these can hardly be considered to have been crime of protest.

Crime against the person seem to have been uncommon, although violence was frequently used in the course of highway and other robberies. One notable exception was the case of Thomas Mullen, 32, who was convicted at the Co. Antrim assizes at Carrickfergus on 5 August 1790 for assaulting and 'feloniously ravishing and carnally knowing against her Will and Consent' Mary Clark on 22 April. Sentenced to be 'hanged by the neck until dead', he was respited by the judge to transportation for life after 'some favourable circumstances' were represented to the court.[58]

Another case involved a Dublin constable, Thomas Regan, 34 who was convicted by a jury at the Commission of Oyer and Terminer in Dublin on 9 December 1788 of assulting Patrick Sheil in Hammond-lane a year earlier and giving him a 'desperate cut with a hanger [sword]'. Regan had gone there to assist in the arrest of Catherine Connolly and had become involved in an altercation with Thomas Connolly, who was no doubt her brother. When Sheil called out that he was killing Connolly, Regan slashed at the former with his sword. The mob which had gathered by this time then pursued Regan to Pill–lane where he must have found sanctuary. Sentenced to be executed at Kilmainham on 27 December, Regan was respited to seven years' transportation.[59]

William Rieley the Naas counterfeiter would have found a kindred spirit on board ship in Felix Owen from Co. Meath who had been sentenced at the Trim assizes on 7 April 1790 to be hanged and quartered for being found with instruments in his possession and for making counterfeit coin.[60] However, cases of fraud seem to have uncommon. The one case of what might be called 'white collar' crime was that of George Carr or Kerr, 39, of Tallagh, Co. Cork. A 'dealer in a very extensive way', he had been found guilty of forging and uttering a bill of exchange directing a firm of London merchants to pay £ 348.1s.8d. to the account of Sir Riggs Faulkner, Sir James Laurence Cotter, Charles

Little and Sir Richard Killet. Condemned to death at the Court of King's Bench in Dublin in February 1791, his sentence was promptly mitigated to transportation for life. At the time of the offence, he owned unencumbered (debt-free) property to the value of about £1,000. He had attempted to take ship for America while awaiting trial but an unlucky impulse caused him to return to shore at the Cove of Cork for some goods left behind and was immediately seized.[61]

'A sailing party'

By early 1791 the prospect of Botany Bay had undergone what might be called a 'sea change'. A good deal more was known about New South Wales than had been the case when the possibility of sending Irish convicts there was first mooted publicly five years before. The earliest reports of the arrival of the first fleet had been published in the Dublin press in March 1789, indicating that very few of the convicts had died on the voyage out and that the new settlement 'was going forward with alacrity and success'.[62] In May, a letter brought back to Cork by Captain Sharp of the *Golden Grove* store ship which had accompanied the first fleet revealed the surprising news that male convicts were receiving exactly the same rations as the soldiers guarding them.[63] More comprehensive accounts of the settlement were available by early 1791. *The Voyage of Governor Phillip to Botany Bay* had been published in London in 1789 and a Dublin edition of Capt. Watkin Tench's *Narrative of the Expedition to Botany Bay* ... appeared in the same year. Substantial extracts from Tench's book and John White's *Journal of a Voyage to New South Wales* ... of 1790 were also printed in *Walker's Hibernian Magazine*.[64]

Indeed, such a rosy picture was painted of the new convict colony at this early stage that a Dublin wit referred to it in his fanciful list of the 'natural curiosities' recently said to have been added to Cox's Museum in Dublin:

> A Priest – double bolted!
> A Bawd – without business!
> Coiners – without money!
> Felons – invited by the Crown – to [a] sailing party, even as far as Botany Bay!
> And Highwaymen – in Hovels![65]

There was also a highly romantic evocation of the natives of the South Seas in *The Death of Captain Cook*, a dramatic presentation performed at Dublin's Peter-street theatre in December 1789 with a popular actor known as Young Astley playing the part of Koah, the Hawaiian prince. In a 'rave' notice, the *Hibernian Journal*'s reviewer wrote:

> The pantomime entertainment ... may be pronounced the grandest spectacle ever exhibited in this metropolis; the music is most pathetic and expressive – the scenery, decoration and dresses truly picturesque, and the characters well supported; but inimitable, indeed, is the action of young Astley in the character of Koah; nor is it more than justice to say, that we never witnessed such theatrical excellence before – every beholder was lost in admiration, and we cannot cease to wonder how he could obtain such just notions of the people who inhabited the remote regions in the South Seas, as it must be a very difficult task by lecture alone, to form such true ideas, and above all, to represent so strikingly the customs and manners of savages who have so little intercourse with Europe.[66]

'A desert corner of the earth'

Private reports received in London earlier in 1789 and duly reprinted in the Dublin newspapers nevertheless suggested that not everything was proceeding favourably in the new colony. No less than forty-two convicts had died since the departure of the expedition from Portsmouth in May 1787, although this had been balanced by a similar number of births. The cattle and sheep were not faring well and some cows had strayed away from the settlement. More disturbingly, the natives were 'dissatisfied' at the presence of the Europeans and had made this clear this by killing and devouring two of them. In April the *Hibernian Journal* reported that

> Three of the convicts were induced to try their fortunes among the natives, where they hoped to have a favourable reception. Two of these were in this expedition killed and eaten, and the third, after subsisting for some time in the woods, almost perished through hunger. This operated to deter further adventures of a like nature.[67]

A more detailed report on the state of the colony brought back to the Admiralty in London by Lieut. Maxwell in March 1789 and subsequently reprinted in the Dublin press revealed that the 'poor convicts were in a wretched state for want of bedding: a very shameful improvidence at home!'[68] Furthermore, as if exile at Botany Bay were not bad enough, a mode of secondary punishment was already being practised:

> A rock at some distance from the shore is fixed upon as a sort of Bastile [sic]; here some offenders are sent, exposed to the weather, and with no other food than bread.[69]

Later reports told of discord in the settlement caused by the shortage of provisions. The supply ship *Sirius* had been sent from Sydney to the Cape of Good Hope to remedy this, but 'should she fail in her voyage, upwards of twelve hundred souls will be exposed to want, in a place which offers little sustenance'.[70] Shortly afterwards came a story of the execution of a convict for the theft of food from the government stores within a month of the original disembarkation at Sydney Cove.[71]

Governor Arthur Phillip's optimistic despatch to Grenville of 12 February 1790 was reprinted in the Dublin and Cork newspapers in March 1791.[72] However, the inmates of Newgate would probably have taken more notice of a graphic account by a surgeon's mate of severe privations suffered by the settlement following the disastrous loss of the *Sirius*. This letter was reprinted from the London newspapers in the *Hibernian Journal* in January 1791, just a month before the Dublin convicts 'cast for transportation' were due to be sent by tender from Newgate to Cork for embarkation on the *Queen*:

> It is now so long since we have heard from home that our clothes are worn threadbare. We begin to think the mother country has entirely forgotten us ... in this deplorable situation famine is staring us in the face ... and happy is the man that can kill rat or crow, to make him a dainty meal ... I dined most heartily the other day on a fine dog, and hope I shall soon again have another invitation to a similar repast. The animals that were meant to flock the country are almost butchered ... Hunger will be appeased while any eatables remain. Several of the convicts have perished by the hands of the natives, by rambling too far into the woods.[73]

The *Morning Post* was moved to comment that the shortage of meat in New South Wales would make it particularly hard for the Irish peasant condemned to live there.[74]

Indeed, the future of Botany Bay now seemed so bleak and unpromising that the Dublin newspapers had reason other than the expense involved to dismiss the new penal settlement as a practical solution to the problem of disposing of prisoners sentenced to transportation. North America and the West Indies were now represented as far more attractive alternatives, not least because of their relative wealth of natural resources and potential for trade, which compared very favourably with remote and unpromising New South Wales. As the *Hibernian Journal* put it in June 1789,

> The settlement in [New] South Wales must be considered from a different point of view: Liberty is not the object; timber there appears not fit for building; very little animal food can be procured. The whole Globe must be circumnavigated by ships in their sailing there and return, and great difficulty will arise in obtaining sappers before tillage can be properly exercised for that purpose. In process of time, indeed, a trade to China, Japan as contraband on the Dutch Spice Islands, the Phillipines [sic], and even the western coasts of South America, may be carried on, provided that [illeg.] material for industry can be reared or discovered. If the country be found unproductive in such articles the project must be, after much expence, entirely laid aside.[75]

For the first time, too, some thought was being given to the ethical aspects of establishing the new settlement, notably its impact on the indigenous peoples of New South Wales. Clearly affected by the newspaper's earlier report of conflict with the natives, a correspondent to the *Hibernian Journal* wrote that

> the policy [of] Great Britain has adopted a mode of punishing reprieved criminals, more cruel than the death they have escaped. A desert corner of the earth, in the almost unknown terra Australis, far removed from converse, except with each other; surrounded by desperate cannibals, that devour men's flesh, whose territories, however savage, we have no right to invade, are considerations that should have struck the Minister with horror, at the cruelty and injustice of the proceeding. Suppose a failure of the crops our fellow subjects have or may sow in lands to which they have not even the shadow of title, must not a multitude of miserable exiles perish, by the slow, but dreadful disease of famine, which ends in rage, madness and death? Suppose again, that the savage islanders should never be reconciled, but manifest a constant warfare, and take all opportunities of murdering the unhappy settlers, and destroying their plantations? What is to be done? Will not Government be reduced to the necessity of removing the convicts, or of exterminating their enemies

by superior force? Should the latter be chosen as the most politic remedy, with what face could we reproach Pizarro, Almagro, and Cortes, with the cruelties practised on the natives of Mexico and Peru, whom those chiefs alleged they had destroyed only in their own defence?[76]

In all the Irish discussions about the proposed new settlement, there was very little to suggest that New South Wales was seen by the authorities and the public as anything other than a suitable repository for felons. However, in May 1789 the pro-government *Dublin Chronicle* suggested supportively that while the British authorities had conceived a much broader economic and strategic purpose for the settlement from the outset, this could not be sustained in the light of further considerations:

The settlement of ... [New South Wales] has hitherto been thought by the public to be intended solely as a [illeg.] for criminals.

Our Government, however, was induced to it by political motives, no less advantageous to a great and commercial nation than the punishment and employment of delinquents. The New Zealand hemp was said by the projector to be superior to the European; and the timber of Norfolk island equal in goodness to the English in regard to ship building. With these important articles it was intended to supply the East Indies in time of war, when our convoys would be intercepted or delayed.

The situation is also peculiarly fitted to annoy the commerce of Spain, during a war with that power, and during peace, is well calculated for an intercourse with China and Japan.

However good the intentions of our Ministry might have been, their hopes are now entirely frustrated in regard to all their expectations.

The timber, which is excellent on Norfolk island alone, cannot be brought off on account of the violence of the surf; the settlement itself will undoubtedly be attacked by Spain in case of a upture; and the trade with China and Japan will excite the jealousy of the East India Company, whose charter it will also infringe.[77]

'Clear the way till I mount my *landau*'

Although the prisoners at Newgate and Kilmainham under sentence of transportation had become increasingly restive since early 1790 over the delays in their removal, they were by no means relieved at the prospect of being exiled to Botany Bay. On the morning of 17 February 1791 as the sixty men and fifteen women, manacled in pairs, were being taken in the gaol carts under military guard from Newgate to North Wall for transfer to the two hired tenders, *Dolphin* and *Hazard*, due to take them to Cork, they made a desperate attempt to escape. According to the *Dublin Chronicle*'s report,

> Last Thursday as Sheriffs Dickinson and Williams conducted through Thomas-street, between sixty and forty convicts, under rule of transportation, the Magistrates were resisted by a riotous mob, who in the first sallies of their fury liberated the prisoners, broke their hand-cuffs, and unyoked the horses from the carriages which conveyed them.[78]

Two of the prisoners managed to escape into a house entry but were quickly reported by the owner and secured.[79] The *Hibernian Journal* took up the story:

> These desperate fellows, assisted by the unthinking mob, with the aid of stones, kept the soldiers at bay for some time, as the humanity of the Sheriffs would not suffer them to fire … but at the commencement of the affray the Sheriffs having judiciously sent for a reinforcement of horse, the two convicts were retaken, the whole reduced to order, and sent under a proper escort to their place of destination.[80]

The convicts were actually lodged in Kilmainham for a few days until they could be accompanied to North Wall by a stronger escort of one hundred mounted troops. Not all were unreconciled to their fate, the *Hibernian Journal* observing that 'most of the women seemed to have less feeling for their situation than the men'.[81] Indeed, there were some, like Bridget Nowlan, *alias* Rossiter, who made light of it all in a way that that might have been expected from a witty and resourceful 'Dub'. She entertained the crowd gathered outside Kilmainham to watch the manacled convicts climb up on the carts by calling on the military guard to 'clear the way till she mounted her *landau*'.[82] In the meantime, a sweep of the gaol had failed to bring to light the man convicted in April 1790 of robbing Lord Charlemont in broad daylight at his Slane Castle estate in Co. Meath.[83] Through the special exertion of Gaoler McKinley, he was eventually found and personally conveyed on board ship to join what the *Evening Post* wrily called the 'hopeful fraternity'.[84]

In the meantime, there had been some delays in readying the *Queen* for the voyage to New South Wales and the ship did not sail from London for Portsmouth and Cork until the beginning of March. By then, the Dublin convicts due to be embarked had been brought down by ship and those from the various county gaols overland to Cork where they were all were being held at the Provost or guard-house within the New Barracks.[85] The city's old gaol could not accommodate the numbers and the new gaol planned by Fitzpatrick was still under construction.[86] Conditions at the barracks must have become impossibly overcrowded with the new arrivals because on 17 February Cork's Lord Mayor, Richard Harris, advertised in the *Hibernian Chronicle* for 'a large ship sufficient to contain 170 convicts, to be well victualled and manned, and properly fitted up for their reception immediately and to be continued until the arrival of the Queen transport'.[87] As it happened, the *Queen* arrived at the Cove of Cork on 5 March before the contract could be filled and the sixty men and fifteen women brought by sea from Dublin, together with a further eighty brought by road, were put on board a week later.[88] However, more problems were to arise and it would be another month before the *Queen* finally set sail for New South Wales.

Despite long anticipation of the event, the embarkation at the Cove of Cork of these first Irish convicts for New South Wales went unnoticed by most newspapers. In Dublin, only the *Hibernian Journal* and *Magee's Weekly Packet* recorded the event in a brief paragraph.[89] Perhaps the newspapers' lack of interest reflected the fact that much of their earlier enthusiasm for Botany Bay had evaporated during the long delay since late 1786. By March 1791 the most likely response (at least on the part of the propertied classes who provided their readership) was relief that the highly dangerous condition of Dublin's gaols had been eased for the time being.

'An epitome of Botany Bay'

Although there had been few Irish critics of transportation to New South Wales since the plan was first made known, they found encouragement in the increasingly negative reports from the colony to pursue once again an alternative suggestion which we have seen was raised as early as 1787. In early March, the *Evening Post* anticipated that a scheme for 'a general Penitentiary house' for 1,000 prisoners at Dalkey Island would be settled on during the current Parliamentary session. Although the capital cost would be 'considerable', it would save £7,000 a year by doing away with transportation. Furthermore,

In point of humanity its advantages will be still greater – for we need but read the accounts of Botany Bay, and of the state of affairs there, to be convinced of the accumulated sufferings [to] which the wretched beings sent there are exposed when a speedy death rescues them not from them.[90]

Just two weeks after the *Queen* had sailed, a correspondent to the *Freeman's Journal* furnished more details:

The general outlines of the plan are – that a Castle should be built surrounded with moats – that the male convicts, ordered for labour, should be employed in quarrying – building walls – and working on such parts of the harbour as may require it.[91]

Unable to say who was the author of what it clearly regarded as a quixotic plan, the newspaper quipped that 'it would seem as if he wished to be *Governor of the Castle*, and form an establishment that might be not unaptly termed *an epitome of Botany Bay*'.[92] Few of its readers, least of all the officials at Dublin Castle, would have taken very seriously this stern new role for the 'King of Dalkey'. Nor was the suggestion of penal servitude on the tiny island in harmony with what the young poet Tom Moore represented as its benign traditions, although some of these were to be unexpectedly echoed in far-off New South Wales:

> Hail, happy Dalkey, Queen of Isles,
> Where justice reigns and freedom smiles.
> In Dalkey Justice holds her state,
> Unaided by the prison gate;
> No subjects of King Stephen lie
> In loathsome cells, they know not why;
> Health, peace, and good humour, in music's soft strains,
> Invite and unite us in Dalkey's wide plains.[93]

14

The *Queen* Transport

After some delays in readying for the long voyage to New South Wales, which included the preparation of secure quarters for the convicts to be taken on board, the *Queen* sailed on 5 March 1791 from the Port of London for Portsmouth and Cork. Built in Beaufort, Carolina, in 1773, she was first listed by Lloyd's as the *Queen Charlotte*, a 'French' London-registered privateer of seventeen guns making voyage to Trinidad in 1779. By 1781 she had been acquired by Fraser & Co., making a voyage that year to Jamaica and during the following two years serving as a transport to the West Indies.

During the last days of the Revolutionary War in early 1783 the *Queen Charlotte* was probably captured by the Americans before being seized as a 'prize' by a British naval force under Admiral Hood and 'condemned' (confiscated) by a Court of Vice-Admiralty at St Jago de la Nega on 28 February 1784. Acquired by the partnership formed by the merchant Daniel Shea of Ely Place, Holborn, with his brother Richard and a Jamaica merchant, Alexander Etches, she was registered in London on 19 December 1786 as the *Queen*. During the next few years she made at least one voyage to Jamaica but was without registration for a time. In early 1790 she was purchased by the partnership of William Camden, Anthony Calvert, Thomas King and Timothy Curtis who sent her to Jamaica again that year with Richard Owen as master.[1]

Displacing only 387 tons and with four officers, a surgeon, two carpenters, a boatswain, a cooper, a cook and fifteen crewmen on broad, together with space below decks to accommodate two hundred prisoners at close quarters, the *Queen* was one of the smallest ships ever to take convicts to New South Wales. Although there is no surviving pictorial record, she was a three-masted, ship-rigged (square-sailed) West Indiaman with a strong American oak frame designed for the bulk

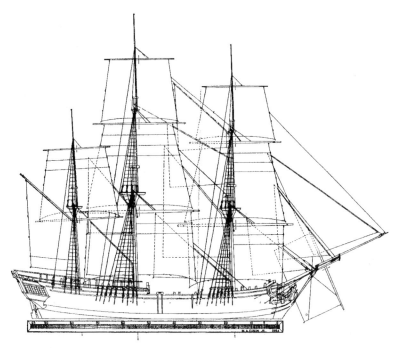

26 No image of the *Queen* survives, but this drawing of a c. 1770 New York-built merchantman, the *London*, provides some idea of what she would have looked like.

trade. While she was originally built with a flush deck, a quarter deck was added later and she was pierced for four guns. She was 112 feet in length and 30 feet in width and the height between her three decks was just five feet three inches. In appearance she probably resembled two similar-sized transports of the First Fleet, the *Alexander* and the *Scarborough*.[2]

According to the maritime historian, Charles Bateson, the poor standards of shipping prevailing in the Third Fleet resulted from the reluctance of shipowners to tender their ships 'in the face of the storm clouds gathering over Europe...'.[3] Although she had been condemned in February 1784, there is no real evidence that the *Queen* was a bad ship. Less than twenty years old and registered as El in Lloyd's list of voyages for 1791, she was then considered to be a second-class merchant vessel in good repair, with no defects and capable of carrying dry cargo in safety.

Nevertheless, Camden, Calvert and King needed to cut costs to the minimum in order to make any profit from what was a very low tender and they may have skimped on the preparation of the ship to take convicts. A similar point could be made about the skimping on rations by Captain Richard Owen and some of his officers who signed on for the voyage in London in the third week of January 1791. No such explanation can be offered, however, for the agent appointed to the *Queen* by the Naval Board, the altogether unreliable Lieut. Samuel Blow, who joined the ship at Portsmouth. Also taken on board there were Ensign William Cummings, a drummer and twenty-five soldiers of the New South Wales Corps who had been ordered to take up garrison duty in Sydney. They were also expected to guard the ship against possible mutiny by the convicts and seizure by the French with whom Britain was soon expected to be at war.

In their letter of instructions of 25 January 1791 to Lieut. Blow, the Navy Board required him 'to take particular care' that the terms of the contract relating to clothing and rations were 'punctually complied with'. They were even more concerned, however, that the ship should sail immediately after the convicts were embarked at Cork so that no demurrage or harbour charges were incurred.[4] In the contract that had been signed with Camden, Calvert and King on 19 November 1790 for what was to be the Third Fleet, the Revenue Commissioners on behalf of the Navy Board had undertaken that embarkation would be completed within fifteen days of the ship's arrival in port, accepting liability for the costs incurred by any delay. Blow was supplied with a copy of the document.

Camden, Calvert and King

According to the terms of the contract,[5] Camden, Calvert and King had undertaken to provide sufficient rations to support the soldiers and an anticipated two hundred convicts on board the *Queen* for a voyage of eight months. These were to be computed on the basis that the weekly requirement for each mess of eight male convicts was 16 lbs of bread, 12 lbs of flour, 14 lbs of beef, 8 lbs of pork, 12 pints of pease, $1^1/_2$ lbs of butter and 2 lbs of rice. The weekly allocation for each mess of six women provided them with only half the men's meat ration, but with more bread and the additional luxuries of tea and sugar. Each mess was also to be allowed 2lb. of soap each month.

The weekly ration for each soldier was to be rather more generous:

Seven pounds of Bread
Seven gallons of Beer
Three pints and one half of Rum
Seven Pints of Wine
Four pounds of beef
Two pounds of Pork
Two pints of Pease
Three pints of Oatmeal
Six ounces of Butter
Twelve Ounces of Cheese

In addition, the ship was to be supplied with 120 gallons of water for each convict. A qualified surgeon was to be on board with medicines and the following 'Necessarys' were also to be provided for the convicts:

Five hundred pounds of Barley
Three Hd Oatmeal
Two cwt Sugar
Two cwt essence of Malt
One hundred gallons Oil of Tar
Two Hund. do Vinegar
One hogshd Wine

Male convicts were to be supplied with clothing, 'agreeable to the pattern seal'd and kept at the Navy Office', consisting of:

One outside jacket	Two pair stockings
One Waistcoat	Two pr. Trousers
One Hat	Two pr. Shoes
One worsted Cap	Two pr. Drawers
Two Shirts	A Bag to contain each Kit

And the women:

One striped jacket	Two pair Stockings
One striped petticoat	Two pr. Shoes
One Hat	Two Caps
Two flannel Petticoats	A Bag to contain each Kit
Two Shifts	

Beds and bedding were also to be supplied to the convicts 'as may be approved of by the Naval Agent'.

'The most dreadfull instance of Cruelty'

Embarkation of most of the 133 male and 22 female convicts, four of them with young children, who were to sail on the *Queen* was apparently completed on 12 March,[6] well within the stipulated fifteen days of the ship's arrival at the Cove of Cork on 5 March. However, Lord Mayor Richard Harris's official receipt for their safe reception on board ship was not signed by Lieut. Blow until 11 April, a month after embarkation.[7] Owen had been ready to sail on 7 April but it was to be another five days after the completion of the essential documentation before the *Queen* departed from the Cove of Cork for New South Wales.

The official receipt for the convicts took the form of an 'indent' or list compiled by Blow of all those embarked, specifying their ages, places and approximate dates of trial, and terms of sentence. No information was provided on the nature of their crimes, their marital status, religious affiliation, literacy, or occupational background. The original document was presumably given to Lord Mayor Harris for his record, but the copy which should have gone with Blow on the ship for the information of the authorities in New South Wales seems to have gone astray.

Consequently, the convicts of the *Queen* were to arrive in Sydney in late September 1791 with no details of any kind accompanying them. Indeed, it was not until early 1799 that a copy of Blow's original indent, together with warrants for transportation and court papers for fifteen of those listed, was finally received by Governor Philip Gidley King.[8] During the intervening seven years there was no means by which the convicts who survived the voyage could document the terms of their sentences.

Why the Irish authorities did not fill their quota of 175 male convicts for this first shipment to New South Wales is something of a puzzle. It would not have been at all difficult to collect that number in Dublin's Newgate and Kilmainham alone without having to draw on the county gaols, although there was an obligation to answer the needs of the latter. Perhaps it was simply a matter of clerical ineptitude on Hobart's part. If the *Queen* had been supplied according to the terms of the contract, it would have been carrying rations for forty more convicts than were actually embarked – a comfortable surplus for the voyage. However, Camden, Calvert and King appear to have given

Ship Queen April 5th 1791

Honourd Sir

the deplorable State of the Convicts on bor
the Queen of London now in this Harbour is
perhaps the most dreadfull instance of Cruelty
you Ever hard of Each poor Creature is to the
allowence of ½ pound of beef & 6 politoes in the
twenty four hours neither Bread or Lig? of Any Kim
Except bad water the third of them will not Survive
the Pasage there Letters are opend by the Cruel Capts
& Agent who are in favour of Each other & of Corse
the poor Wretches dare not Complain Adress them
Worthy Sir as it is your Character to be good & Chara all
& heaven May for Ever reward afou is the Prayer of
An unhappy Convict

27 Letter from an anonymous convict to Captain Alexander Hood of HMS
Hebe, Cove of Cork, 5 April 1791.

Owen the responsibility of provisioning the ship and he seems to have
done most of this at Cork where he could make a substantial saving.
Not only is he likely to have been paid for forty more convicts than he
had to provide for, but some of the supplies he purchased from the
Cork merchants were clearly of very inferior quality. Blow, whose

responsibility it was to ensure that the *Queen* was provisioned according to the terms of the contract, seems to have been totally derelict in
his duty. Without actually condemning him by name, an inquiry in
Sydney in October 1791 concluded that the stipulated rations had not
been supplied to the convicts during the voyage:

> it does not appear that the proper steps were taken by those who
> had the means to see the full ration of provisions was served to
> them on complaints being made of deficiencies.[9]

One of the reasons for the *Queen's* long delay before sailing was the
extreme dissatisfaction expressed by the convicts and the soldiers on
board about both the quality and quantity of provisions distributed
from the time of embarkation by the Second Mate, Robert Stott, at the
behest of Captain Owen. Needless to say, it was a difficult and risky
business for the convicts to make their complaints known, particularly
since there was no readily accessible authority to whom they could
appeal. However, on 5 April one of them penned an anonymous letter
and managed to get it into the hands of Ensign Cummings. Addressed
to Captain Alexander Hood of HMS *Hebe*, which was expected in port
at any time, the letter pleaded for his intercession on their behalf:

> Ship Queen April 5th 1791
> Honourd Sir
>   the deplorable State of the Convicts on bord the Queen
> of London now in this Harbour is perhaps the most dreadfull
> instance of Cruelty you ever heard of Each poor Creature is to the
> Allowance of $^1/_2$ pound of beef & 6 potatoes in the twenty four
> hours nether Bread or Liqrs of Any Kind except bad water the third
> of them will not survive the Passage there Letters are opend by the
> Cruel Captn & Agent who are in favour of Each other & of corse the
> poor Wretches dare not Complain Adress them Worthy Sir as it is
> your Character to be good & Charatable & heaven may for Ever
> reward you is the prayer of An unhappy Convict.[10]

There was very little that Cummings would have been able to do until
9 April when the *Hebe* came into the Cove of Cork to 'press' seamen for
the Royal Navy in preparation for the anticipated conflict with France.
In the course of his duty, Captain Hood visited the *Queen* and met
Cummings who complained to him about the rations and accommodation on board. The sensible Hood asked Cummings to put it all in

writing and Cummings' letter to him of the same day enclosed 'a few of the many complaints my party has made to me', together with those of the anonymous convict and some of his own:

> As for myself the Language & Treatment I have met with is so illiberal that I cannot by any means express it to you. My Cabbin is too confined for myself much more so for my Wife & Child I have no place to put my things by in safety my Trunks & other things nocking about at the Mercy of every one even the small Cabbin I have the Master has threatened to pull down.[11]

In his letter to Cummings on behalf of the rest of the soldiers, Corporal Thomas Tyler produced a 'Statement of facts which we are Confident that Impudence itself dare not contradict in any Particulars'.[12] Although the bread was satisfactory, their requests for butter and cheese to which they were entitled had been met with 'absolute denial' from Owen and 'evasive answers' from Blow. The beef supplied to them was

> of a quality (generally speaking) altogether unfit for use and purchased by Mr Owen at an inferior price for the Convicts[,] the [captain] having declared that such was sufficiently good for soldiers whom he considered little better than Convicts.

Although their official allowance entitled them to 66 lbs of oatmeal and 43 gallons of pease worth £3.10s., the soldiers had received 'at the Largest Computation' 8s. worth of greens a day and sometimes none at all. As if all this were not bad enough, the beer grudgingly supplied by Owen after 'much trouble and repeated Solicitation' had often been given to them 'in a state of Fermintation' and 'unfit for Cabbin use'. This was all the more galling when there was known to be good beer on board of the quality normally supplied on His Majesty's ships.

Adding insult to injury was the captain's demeanour towards them:

> whenever we have represented these our grievances to Cap. Owen or his mate they have agravated [*sic*] injustice by insult and we have received abuse instead of reasons. Our Centinels have been abused in the Execution of the Duty pointed out to them by Lieut. Blow and Mr. Cummings in general and we have been treated with the most abusive language and scurilous invictives [*sic*] that a low mind instigated by malice could devise.

Lieut. Blow

The main reason for delay, however, was the mysterious disappearance
ashore of Lieut. Blow. Some days before Hood's arrival in port, Blow
had gone to Cork city with Owen to see Lord Mayor Harris and Sheriffs
Charles Ferguson and Sir Henry Brown Hayes[13] on business but had
not returned. As well as turning a blind eye to the quantity and quality
of the provisions purchased by Owen, Blow may well have been
involved with him and the Cork merchants in shipping goods on the
Queen with a view to making a profit.[14] The vessel was subsequently
discovered in Sydney to be carrying substantial private consignments
of cordage, copper, lead and iron intended for sale in India on the
return voyage.[15]

Before Owen set off from Cork to return to the ship, Blow had given
him the keys to the iron gratings over the hatches which were all that
prevented the convicts from escaping. When Cummings, no doubt
angered by his dispute with Owen over rations, seized the keys from
him, the convicts below decks 'Hussar'd and Cheered' him whenever
he passed by the gratings. Apprehensive of their 'making an Insiration
[*sic*]' with the encouragement of the soldiers, Owen asked Hood on
9 April to have another officer appointed to the ship in Blow's place.
Accordingly, Nicholson, 1st Lieutenant of the *Hebe*, was sent over to
the *Queen* the same day. Reporting his action to the Navy Board on
14 April, Hood added that 'from the disagreements that had arisen on
board her' he did not think it was safe for the ship to go to sea. He had
asked Nicholson to make a written report on the dispute.[16] In the
meantime, Cummings had also brought his dispute with Owen to the
knowledge of the officer in charge of the military garrison at nearby
Fort Camden.

When all his efforts to locate Blow in Cork had been fruitless, Owen
took the wise precaution of going ashore again on 6 April and having
a Cork notary prepare a sworn 'protest' against the delayed sailing of
the ship on the grounds of Blow's absence so that the Revenue
Commissioners would be responsible for 'all Delays Losses Damages
costs Charges and Expenses suffer'd or to be suffer'd sustain'd or
incurr'd'.[17] This was standard procedure for any sea captain who would
otherwise be held personally liable for costs resulting from a delay
beyond the stipulated time in port.

On 14 April, Hood wrote to the Navy Board confessing that he found
himself 'rather unpleasantly situated not knowing in what respect to
act with respect to Lieut. Blow in the Queen transport who I am sorry

to say in my opinion is very unfit for his situation'.[18] Hood sent a second message to the *Queen* that morning requesting Blow to present himself on board the *Hebe* and when the delinquent lieutenant finally appeared later in the day, 'gave him a severe lecture upon his past conduct...'. The chastened Blow accordingly 'promised never to be guilty of the like again'.[19] In the meantime, the Navy Board had belatedly taken note of Hood's complaint about Blow and on 21 April despatched a Lieut. Nairne to Cork with instructions to take his place.[20] However, by the time Hood had received a letter from his uncle, Admiral Thomas Hood, informing him of this decision,[21] the *Queen* was already ten days out for New South Wales with Blow on board.

Before sailing, Blow had also given Hood a letter signed by Cummings, Owen and himself testifying that they were all 'perfectly satisfied' with the settlement of the dispute on board and thanking him and the military commander in Cork for the assistance they had given. 'We ... flatter ourselves', the letter concluded hopefully, 'that unanimity and a good understanding will prevail among us, on board this Ship (from the arrangements that have been made) during the rest of the Voyage'.[22]

An important part of the settlement was an undertaking by Owen to provide 'a Decent Table, and C' for Blow, Cummings and the other soldiers.[23] However, Cummings had not been so solicitous on behalf of the convicts who had cheered him two weeks earlier when he challenged Owen's authority. And with Blow unwilling to assert himself on their behalf, no doubt because he was a party to the fraudulent scheme, there was little to prevent the continued systematic bilking of convict rations by the rapacious Owen and his second mate during the voyage to Sydney. The inevitable result was the one-third mortality predicted by the anonymous convict complainant, although this only became apparent some time after the completion of the voyage.

As far as can be ascertained, it was not the intention of the authorities to restrain the convicts on board ship. However, after the threat of insurrection over rations, Blow had taken the precaution before leaving Cork of acquiring twenty-seven pairs of bar irons, four pairs of chain irons and two pairs of handcuffs which, as he said at the time, 'I found Necessary to Keep on Board the Queen Transport'.[24]

'Sailed, *Queen*'

The date of the *Queen*'s final sailing from the Cove of Cork, 16 April 1791, was only recorded in the shipping movements column of Cork's

Hibernian Chronicle of 21 April and went unnoticed by all the Dublin newspapers. Nor, significantly enough, has it been accurately ascertained by the historians of convict transportation to Australia until now.[25] The despatch of the first direct shipment of Irish convicts to New South Wales, an event which was to be of considerable significance for Irish and Australian history, received only this economical acknowledgement:

> Cove 16. Wind W.S.E.
> Sailed, Queen, London, Owen, Botany Bay, convicts;
> Thomas, Lancaster, Powson, St Kitts, beef, butter
> etc.; Mary, Glascow [*sic*] ditto, ditto, ditto;
> Olive, Whitehaven, Butler, Maderia [sic], St Kitts,
> beef, butter; Triumph, Maryland, Dillon, ballast.[26]

15
Irish Transportation 1792–1795

Athough the British authorities had finally agreed to Irish participation in the Botany Bay scheme, arrangements by the Home Office for transportation of convicts from Ireland subsequent to the sailing of the *Queen* were, if anything, more unsatisfactory than they had been before 1790. At the same time, so profitable had the shipping of convicts to North America been for Dublin's Lord Mayors and contractors that they were reluctant to see the business pass into the hands of the Home Office and London contractors. Undeterred by the anti-transportation sentiments of Congress and the legislation enacted by the Assembly of Virginia in November 1788, the Dublin contractors were willing to try the American ports again, and even Africa or South America if need be, but not Botany Bay. New South Wales was irrelevant to Irish commercial interests, which were focused firmly on the Continent, North America and the Caribbean. Nor did it offer the opportunity to sell convicts as indentured servants, as the North American ports had done.

Learning in June 1791 that more transports were preparing for New South Wales, Hobart wrote to Nepean asking whether one of the ships could be sent to Cork to take on board Irish convicts there on the same terms as before.[1] Expressing some surprise at this request, Nepean told him it was his understanding that the *Queen* had taken away all the convicts in Ireland under sentence of transportation and that 'so little time having elapsed since her departure, the number since convicted must be inconsiderable'.[2] However, another transport was due to depart from Portsmouth in September and he promised to find space on it if necessary. Scrope Bernard eventually informed Sackville Hamilton in the second week of December that a transport had been taken up for the conveyance of female prisoners.[3] Seventeen women convicts were subsequently despatched from Dublin to Portsmouth in late December on the *Four Brothers* for transportation to New South Wales on the *Kitty* in March 1792.[4]

In the same month, Hobart wrote to Scrope Bernard to tell him that with the completion of the quarterly assizes on 16 April, there would probably be as many as 250 men and 60 women convicts under sentence of transportation in Ireland. Emphasising that 'it will be of the most material Importance to have them ship'd as soon as possible', Hobart passed on Westmorland's request for information on when a vessel might be expected to receive them.[5] Six months later, however, there was still no news from the Home Office of any transport being arranged. Whitehall officials were far more interested in pressing the Dublin authorities to reimburse the local governments of Cape Breton, Newfoundland and Antigua for the costs incurred by the convicts sent to those places some years earlier.[6]

Westmorland himself wrote to the new Home Secretary, Henry Dundas, in early August saying that because of delays in shipping, 'the Prisoners have become so mumerous as to create considerable Danger of Infection, their Turbulence renders it difficult to guard them from Escape, and they are a heavy Burthen on the respective Counties, of all which strong Representations have been made to me ...'.[7] Writing again to Dundas at the end of the month, Westmorland emphasised that the delays had brought representations from the Lord Mayor and sheriffs of Dublin, together wth county magistrates, 'of the very great Danger of the Gaols being broke by the Number of Prisoners confined therein, and the Apprehension of Disorders from their crowded states ...'.[8]

Henry-Gore Sankey

A few days later, Hobart forwarded to Nepean a proposal from Dublin's Lord Mayor Henry-Gore Sankey for a seven-year contract to transport two shipments of convicts annually from Ireland to Sierra Leone, Savannah (Georgia), Baltimore or Alexandria. The first proposed shipment would be of three hundred convicts at ten guineas per head.[9] Remembering that Virginia had passed legislation in November 1788 forbidding the landing of convicts, Sankey subsequently substituted Cartagena in Colombia for Alexandria. 'As to the Law of the United States respecting Servants or Convicts', he assured Hobart, 'it does not extent [sic] to either Maryland, Georgia, North or South Carolina. It is only a popular Clamour that deters the Merchants there from being concerned'.[10] His proposal was clearly premised on the ability to sell the convicts as indentured servants at Sierra Leone or the American ports.[11]

After the previous embarrassments, it is somewhat surprising that Westmorland and Hobart should have seriously entertained Sankey's proposal. They may have been using it as a means of placing pressure on an as yet unresponsive Home Office. However, Hobart took the trouble of asking Nepean if there would be any objection to convicts being sent to the alternative destination of Cartagena, which was under Spanish control.[12] In an increasingly desperate situation, the Irish authorities may well have tempted by Sankey's proposal.

When there was still no reply by late September, Hobart wrote again to Nepean repeating the request. Saying that he was now receiving daily visits from the Lord Mayor, the sheriffs and magistrates wanting to know how the convicts were to be disposed of, he referred to an attempted escape at Newgate the previous Sunday when the military guard had been attacked and forced to fire. As on earlier occasions, the prisoners were aggrieved that the time they had spent at Newgate 'was not deducted from the time they were to be transported for'.[13] Hobart concluded with a terse summary of the dilemma which the Irish authorities now faced:

> We have not any means of employing our Convicts at Home so as to expect a Reformation in their Conduct. To turn them loose in Society would be the most objectionable of all Measures. They cannot now be sent to any of the British colonies, we must therefore depend on the assistance of Great Britain for transporting them to New South Wales.[14]

In early October, John Hamilton, Marquess of Abercorn, wrote to Dundas about the crowded state of the gaols in the northern counties, which he attributed to the unwillingness of judges to order executions and to delays in transportation. A friend of Pitt and an aspirant to the Lord Lieutenancy, his views would have carried considerable weight:

> The County Goals [*sic*] (I believe throughout Ireland but I will particularise only my own Counties) of Tyrone and Donegal are Crowded with Felons sentenced to Transportation. Among them through the culpable capriciousness and incapacity of some of the Irish Judges are some most desperate Housebreakers and murderers. Of these several have been sentenced more than a year, and the whole subsequent time has been passed by them in endeavouring to

break Prison in rioting with the money they had stolen and what is worst of all in forming amd forwarding plans of Burglary with a gang of villains at large who are the terror of the Country. The bad effect of this to the peace, the Police and the good Government of these Counties is inconcievable [*sic*]. For our Prisons instead of being places of Punishment are in fact schools of education and headquarters for Villains. No longer ago than yesterday a Housebreaker who was taken confined himself under the orders of Captn Murray in Omagh Gaol, who I in vain endeavoured to persuade Lord Westmorland to hang last year for the most atrocious and numerous Villainies, of which he was convicted on the first count, a dozen others remaining untried.

When I apply ever so strongly to Government here the answer is that it is the fault of the English Government in not sending the Convicts to Botany Bay and that they cannot help it.[15]

Three weeks later, Hobart told Nepean that there was very little hope of obtaining an Irish contractor to convey convicts to Botany Bay and that the situation in the prisons was becoming more critical each day. 'We must therefore entirely rely on you', he concluded.[16]

In the meantime, after the embarrassing mortality in the Second and Third Fleets, Dundas had been investigating the alternative of sending out convicts more cheaply and safely to New South Wales on East India Company ships. Nepean consequently asked Hobart in a letter of 13 October if it was possible to secure those under sentence of transportation until such an arrangement could be made. If the state of the gaols meant that there could be no further delay, he had no objection to the use of Irish shipping to remove convicts to New South Wales. If this proved to be too difficult, he undertook to 'make the best bargain' in London on the Irish government's behalf. He would not enter into any definite arrangement with a contractor because of the problem of security. 'I find people in general adverse to the taking out of Irish convicts, without a military Guard', he concluded, 'and we have no such Guard to furnish'.[17] Just a week later, however, Nepean was able to send Hobart a proposal from William Richards Jr. who promised to despatch a ship to Dublin within three weeks of an agreement being reached. There was also the good news that some members of the New South Wales Corps 'could be spared as a Guard ...'.[18]

Much relieved by all this, Sackville Hamilton told Nepean that there were 230 men and 40 women waiting to be transported and suggested that two ships be sent by the contractor, one to Dublin and one to

Cork.[19] When there was no further news during the following month, Hobart wrote again to Nepean on 27 November asking that Richards be pressed to despatch the transports as soon as possible in the light of the political situation. 'It is of much importance to us to get them away as soon as possible', he told him, 'the scenes before us in Europe and the questions presented to the public may possibly agitate the multitudes'.[20]

Hobart was finally informed by Nepean on 28 November that two transports, the *Boddington's* and the *Sugar Cane*, would be ready to sail from the Cove of Cork by the middle of December.[21] However, the *Boddington's* was delayed in reaching Cork, where the convicts brought from Dublin had to remain cooped up on board the *Hibernia* tender for seven weeks, and was badly overcrowded when she finally sailed for New South Wales on 15 February 1793; the *Sugar Cane* did not sail from Dublin until 12 April. Although the *Sugar Cane* suffered an attempted mutiny, better supervision of convict health by the doctors on board both vessels meant that there was only one death during the entire voyage.[22] At the same time, William Richards' bill for shipping 301 convicts to New South Wales in 1792 came to £20,000, or more than three times the amount paid to Camden, Calvert and King for shipping half that number on the *Queen* in April 1791.

The penitentiary option

No doubt it was the delay in arranging this shipment and its high cost that stirred the authorities to examine other options. As we have seen, the St James-street penitentiary had been initiated in late 1790 under Sir Jeremiah Fitzpatrick's supervision to deal with younger offenders considered capable of reformation. And in late 1792 the Irish government enacted legislation designed to establish a penitentiary system as an alternative to and possible replacement for transportation.[23]

Visiting St James-street in early July 1793, members of the gaols and prisons committee of the House of Commons led by Peter Holmes were pleased to find 'several young Creatures, some not more than nine years old, at different Trades, Shoemaking, Ribband-weaving, etc., under proper Masters ...'.[24] Of the thirteen inmates who had been pardoned, four had returned to their counties of origin 'where they behave themselves properly' and nine were 'employed at their usual Occupations, as Tradesmen, Dealers & Servants in this city, [where they] conduct themselves with Honesty and Propriety'. The committee advocated a stricter system of discipline, the enlargement of the building and the purchase of more materials which would ensure constant employment and allow the institution to meet its costs. Indeed, they believed that a system of penitentiaries throughout the country, supported by local grand juries, could replace transportation altogether:

> a considerable Saving of Public Expense would be made by substituting this Mode of Confinement and Correction in the room of Transportation, as now practised, there having been transported in this Year [1792] three hundred and one Persons, at a very great Expence [*sic*].

Accordingly, the committee recommended that sentencing certain types of offenders to 'close Confinement and hard Labour, under Certain Regulations and Controul' would be to the security and advantage of the public, 'and that such Punishment would better answer the ends of Justice than the present practice of Transportation ...'.

Nevertheless, only seventy-nine prisoners had been drawn from Newgate to St James-street during the first two years of operation – hardly enough to reduce pressure on the prison. Furthermore, no less than nineteen of these had been returned as 'incorrigible'. Even before Fitzpatrick's departure in late 1793 for England, where he was to supervise conditions on board army transports during the war with France, the dishonesty of the overseers and Dublin Corporation's lack of interest in the institution meant that the scheme was in disarray. Fitzpatrick's extended tours of inspection of country gaols and his ambitious building programme had also meant that there was no one immediately responsible for its supervision. Most of the male convicts had been allowed to enlist in the army after the outbreak of war with France and the keepers had absconded with the income produced by the inmates during the previous two years. By 1796, the eighteen 'penitents' remaining at St James-street were described as being unemployed, 'almost naked' and living on bread and water.[25] The institution continued to function and was given a new lease of life with the appointment of Fitzpatrick's successor and the provision of material assistance by the Howard Society. However, it was not until 1801 that Ireland's first purpose-built penitentiary for young offenders was established at Smithfield.[26]

Acknowledging the penitentiary experiment's dependence on the departed Inspector-General, Sackville Hamilton told Nepean in May 1794 that it could not be sustained in his absence:

While Sir Jerome [*sic*] inspected and directed the Institution it throve extremely well, but he knows that even when he turned his back tho' but for a short time, it went to ruin. Nothing certainly can be more true, with respect to personally executive offices, than Sir Jerome's observation that 'it is impossible to discharge duties on this side and the other side of the water at the same time and by the same person.[27]

As in Britain, the criminal justice system would continue to rely on transportation as a sentencing option.

In March of that year, Hobart's replacement as Government Secretary, Sylvester Douglas, had written to Nepean seeking assistance in emptying the gaols of 250 prisoners under sentence of transportation, including a number of Whiteboys in Co. Cork.[28] The request was repeated in May and again in June but, as before, there was no response from the Home Office.[29] In October, Westmorland himself had to take up the matter directly with the new Secretary of State, the Duke of Portland.[30] In the meantime, there were further problems in the gaols arising from the long delay. One of the two prisoners who managed to escape from Newgate in April 1795 had been awaiting transportation for no less than five years.[31]

When the *Marquis Cornwallis* transport eventually arrived at the Cove of Cork in June 1795, serious difficulties developed with the detachment of the New South Wales Corps on board and the ship did not sail until 9 August. This time, mutinous convicts formed an alliance with the soldiers and it was only the determined action of Captain Michael Hogan that prevented them from seizing the ship.[32] It was not until the onset of the Irish Rebellion in early 1798 had created an urgent need to exile convicted members of the Society of United Irishmen that the Home Office was finally willing to make transportation from Ireland a high priority and to ensure a proper supervision of shipboard conditions. By then, the Irish had established themselves as part of the founding population of New South Wales.

Appendix I
Expenditure on Irish Convict Transportation, 1787–89

'An ACCOUNT of the Sums paid in the Treasury Office for the Transportation of Convicts within the four last Years' [*JIHC*, vol. XIII (1790), p. ccli]

		L.	s.	d.
1787, May 24	Paid George Alcock, Lord Mayor of Dublin, for the Cloathing, Victualling and Passage of one hundred and eighty-three Convicts, and for providing a Vessel for their Transportation, and all other Charges incident thereto	1888	4	4
1788, Feb. 8	Paid more, on account of the Cloathing, Victualling and Passage of one hundred and eighteen Convicts shipped by him in October 1787	944	–	–
June 2	Paid William Alexander, Lord Mayor of Dublin, for the Cloathing, Victualling and Passage of two hundred Convicts shipped on board the Brig Nancy for America	1754	3	$11^1/_4$
October 29	Paid more, the like for one hundred and twenty-six Convicts shipped on board the Snow Providence for America	1105	14	$10^1/_2$
1789 July 15	Paid John Rose, Lord Mayor of Dublin, the like for one hundred and fifteen Convicts shipped on board the Duke of Leinster for America	1009	7	$0^3/_4$
November 8	Paid more, the like for eighty-nine Convicts shipped on board the Duke of Leinster the 7th November 1789	781	10	4
		7483	–	6

H.T. Clements, Deputy Receiver-General

Appendix II
The Newfoundland Shipment, 1789

(i) 'Return of the convicts &C St John's Newfoundland the 7th day of September 1789' [CO 194/38, ff. 94–6].

Names	Age	Born	County	Crime	Sentence	Remarks
John O Neal	20	Dublin	Dublin	Stealing waist-coats	7 years	The best Shoplifter in Ireland Escaped 22d Aug.
Matthew Dempsey	21	Clonslee	Kings Co.	Picking a lock and taking out a Pawnbroker's Duplicate	Death & afterwards trans.	
James Myler	20	Donaghadee	Down	Robbing a man in Stephen's Green of a Watch	Death	
Denis Newenham	19	Dublin	Dublin	Do.	Do.	
John Coyle	21	Dublin	Dublin	Vagrant		Accomplice

Names	Age	Born	County	Crime	Sentence	Remarks
Martin Kelly	20	Old Court	Wicklow	Stealing wool	Trans.	
Samuel Ellis	12	Tullow	Carlow	Vagrant		
Daniel McEleese	20	Belfast	Antrim	Do.		
James Halfpenny	23	Drogheda	Drogheda	Stealing lead	Trans.	
William Gibbeons	22	Dublin	Dublin	Attempting to break into a House	Flogged & transported for want of bail	
John Keogh	22	Dublin	Dublin	A famous Porter Stealer but does not know for what he was Tried		
William Franklin	23	Dublin				
John Farrell	14	Dublin	Dublin	For theft		Escaped 22d August
John Walsh	25	Carrick on Suir	Waterford	Supposed for combination to rob a House		
Robert Fisher	25	Dublin	Dublin			

Names	Age	Born	County	Crime	Sentence	Remarks
William Butler	27	Limrick	Limrick	For a Robbery		
Conelius Brosnahan	23	Tralee	Kerry	Murder	Death & from some error in the trial changed to trans.	
Charles O Brien	26	Rathfriland	Down			
Michael Pendergast	13	Dublin	Dublin			
Patrick Hart	14	Dublin	Dublin			
John Foley	19	Dublin	Dublin	Stealing a Table Cloth		
Patrick Nugent	40	Omagh	Tyrone			
James Finn	19	Odennahaugh	Armagh			
James Grant	19	Dublin	Dublin			
Patrick Neal	27	Kilkenny	Kilkenny	Swindling	Death	
Patrick Leonard	40	Kinnagad	Westmeath	Do.	Do.	

Names	Age	Born	County	Crime	Sentence	Remarks
James Sheridan	40	Cornegall	Cavan	Stolen Goods found in his House	Trans.	
John Burleigh	19	Garahstown	Meath	Theft	Do.	
John Gainford	8	Dublin	Dublin			
Michael Flynn	21	Cork	Cork	Theft	Trans.	
Francis Lacey	41	Castle Dormoth	Kildare	Sheep stealing	Do.	
Martin Ryan	25	Humewood	Wicklow	Burglary	Death	
Daniel Stewart	19	Baltinglass	Wicklow			
James McGuire	25	Tanhousewater	Fermanagh			
Patrick Lee	24	Drogheda	Drogheda	Forcible Entry		
William Walpole	23	Cashell	Tipperary			
Nicholas Carpenter	25	Cramlin	Dublin			
James Cashell	23	Limrick	Limrick			

Names	Age	Born	County	Crime	Sentence	Remarks
John Mahony	44	Mitchelstown	Cork	Theft		
Patrick Mealy	19	Dublin	Dublin			
John Hurley	22	Parteen	Clare			
David Hogg	16	Edenacligh	Fermanagh			
Lausht Vance	40	Skeagh	Fermanagh			
Abraham Palleh	20	Cramlin	Monaghan			
Peter Parker	20	Carlow	Carlow	Coining		
James Rieley	20	Coot Hill	Cavan	Highway Robbery	Death	Died 13th August
Timothy Byrne	30	Mountrath	Queens			
John Byrne	22	Sagart	Dublin	Stealing a cow	Trans.	
Charles McCarthy	55	Ballymurphy	Cork			
Darby Carey	54	Calban	Kilkenny	Swindling	Trans.	
John Murphy	13	Dublin	Dublin			
Thomas Walsh	30	Mayvoir	Westmeath			

Names	Age	Born	County	Crime	Sentence	Remarks
James Murray	23	Drumclan	Monaghan			
Patrick Malone	19	Dublin	Dublin	Theft	Trans.	
Thomas Kelly	20	Rathcoole	Dublin	Stealing two saddles	Trans.	
Michael Delaney	22	Ballymore Eustace	Wicklow	Theft		
John Kelly	30	Athlone	Roscommon			
John Reiley	28	Cavan	Cavan	Coining		
Bartholomew Mooney	29	Dublin	Dublin			
Timothy Connors	16	Dublin	Dublin			
Michael Sullivan	18	Bruff	Limrick	Picking pockets	Trans.	
John Lawler	16	Dublin	Dublin			
Thomas Duncan	13	Kilcock	Meath			
Thomas McDermot	20	Edgerstown	Longford	Stealing a pound of tobacco		
*Peter Parker	20	Carlow	Carlow	Coining	Trans.	In Town at sick quarters

* Listed twice

(ii) 'List of 74 Men and 6 Women Convicts embarked on Board the Brigantine Elizabeth & Clare Robert Coyshe Master' [CO 194/38, f. 112]

Men

John Welsh
William Ibbson
Patrick Neal
John Taylor
James Millar
Thomas Nugent
James Moor
James Mory
John Neal
Matthew Dimsey
John Coyle
Samuel Ellis
James Baily
Patrick Malloney
William Butler
Patrick Nugent
John Croak
Thomas Kelly
Michael Delany
John Mansfield
John Burk
James Halfpenny
Patrick Hart
Patrick Fling
Martin Ryan
Nicholas Sullivan
Thomas Ragan
Cornelius Brirenham
John McDormet
Martin Kelly

William Franklin
William Warpole
John Soler
James Murphy
Michael Pendergrass
Francis Linsay
John Tally
John Gainford
Francis Laky
John Smith
Charles Bryant
James Quin
John Folly
John Folly
Robert Fisher
John Burn
Bartholomew Money
Patrick Danun
Peter Sullivam
Timothy Burn
Darby Carew
John Harley
Timothy Connor
Arthur Young
James Kahell
Patrick Mealy
Patrick Leanord
James Grant
Patrick Leigh
James Maguire
Daniel McClees
Thomas Shannon

Richard Robinson
Michael Murphy
Michael Fling
Thomas Duncan
Daniel Sturit
Nicholas Carpenter
Abram Pallate
John Macketty
Walter Linehan
John Mahany
Charles Carty
David Hague

Women

Mary Maloney
Judith Kelly
Eleanor Watson
Mary Connell
Mary Nan
Nancy Farrol

recd. 24th Oct 1789 at St John's [sd.] Robert Coysh   Milbanke

Appendix III
Virginian Legislation Prohibiting the Landing of Convicts, 1788

An act to prevent the importation of convicts into this commonwealth
(Passed the 13th of November, 1788)

I. WHEREAS it has been represented to this general assembly by the United States in congress, that a practice has prevailed, for some time past, of importing felons convicts into this state, under various pretences, which said felons convicts so imported have been sold and dispersed among the people of this state, whereby much injury hath been done the morals, as well as the health, of our fellow-citizens: For remedy whereof, *Be it enacted*, that from and after the first day of January next, no captain or master of any vessel, or any other person, coming into this commonwealth, by land or by water, shall import, or bring with him, any person who shall have been a felon convict, or under sentence of death, or any other legal disability incurred by a criminal prosecution, or who shall be delivered to him from any prison or place of confinement, in any place out of the United States.

II. *And be it further enacted*, That every captain or master of a vessel, or any other person, who shall presume to import, or bring into this commonwealth, by land or by water, or shall sell or offer for sale, any such person as above described, shall suffer three months imprisonment, without bail or mainprize, and forfeit and pay for such person so brought and imported, or sold or offered for sale, the penalty of fifty pounds current money of Virginia, one half to the commonwealth, and the other half to the person who shall give information thereof; which said penalty shall be recovered by action of debt or information, in any court of record, in which the defendant shall be ruled to give special bail.

[W.W. Hening, ed., *The Statutes at Large; Being a Collection of all the Laws of Virginia, from the First Session of the Legislature, in the Year 1619*, vol. XII, Richmond: George Cochran, 1823, pp. 668–9.]

Appendix IV
Documents Relating to the
Barbuda Voyage, 1789

(i) 'A List of Convicts sent off [to Barbuda] on 7th November 1789' [*HO* 100/29, f.98]

Hugh Griffin	Wm. Brady	Timothy Donovan	Thomas Holmes
Willm. Turner	John Hughes	Chas. Ryan	
Willm. McCane	Michael McCane	Js. Dunn	Elizth. Barlow
Francs. McMahon	Pat Thompson	Michl. Rafferty	Anne Clarke
Pat Moran	Michael Mooney	Barney Egan	Mary Orr
Jas. McNeal	Wm. Davis	James Brady	Alice Balf
Hugh Lyndsay	Danl. Moloney	Michl. Corrigan	Cathn. Keating
Neal Michin	Robert Gaynor	Jas. McNamara	Jane Gibson
Andw. Jones	Michl. Murphy	John Sheehan	Cathn. McNally
Robt. Hazlet	Michl. Carter	James Riordan	Cathn. Keogh
Thoms. Hughes	Danl. Farrell	James Hennessey	Margt. Madigan
Roger Skevington	Patt Kelly	John White	Cathn. Grady
Alio Beamish	Thomas Coyle	Thos. Fitzmaurice	Mary See
James Dillon	John McDonald	John Burke	Anne Denny
George Morley	Patrick Town	Darby Moriarty	
James Moran	Michl. Keogh	Thos. Molony	
James Cox	Henry McGee	John Ryan	
Thos. Finnigan	Henry McGuire	Danl. Read	
Geo. Cambridge	Pat McDonald	John Bluett	
Patt O'Brien	Wm. Dalton	Wm. Fulton	
John Halloran	John Boyle	Archibd. Newing	
Michl. Morgan	Peter Kane	John Rahaney	
Timothy Dwyer	Peter Bushe	David Smithson	
Frans. Read	James Keogh	Neal Nugent	
Thomas Manner	Patt Browne	James Cunningham	
John Byrne			

(ii) Legal contracts relating to the voyage of the *Duke of Leinster*, September–
November 1789 [*HO* 100/29, ff. 194–6]

This Charter Party of Affreightment indented witnesseth that William Christian
Master or Captain of the Brigantine or Vessel called the Duke of Leinster Burden
Three Hundred Tons or thereabouts Doth hereby covenant and agree to and
with the Righ Honourable John Rose Lord Mayor of the City of Dublin for a
Voyage to be performed by her as follows, that is to say the said Master or
Captain doth hereby covenant and agree to and with the said Affreightor that
he will on or before the first day of October next ensuing the Date hereof have
his said Vessel well securely and properly fitted for Sea, with all and every the
usual and necessary Accommodation for receiving and carrying Convicts or
Servants to America, and shall then forthwith receive and take on Board the
said Vessel from the said Affreightor or his Order as many Male and Female
Convicts as he shall then have in readiness or think proper to Ship, and after so
receiving the same he shall and will as speedily as possible with the first fair
Wind proceed to Sea with the said Convicts to some Port or Ports in North
America and shall there safely land and deliver the aforesaid Convicts or
Passengers, Mortality or the Danger of the Seas excepted, and shall not permit
any of said Convicts or Passengers to remain back in said Ship. And the said
Master doth hereby further covenant that he will find furnish and provide all
Manner of Provisions, Bedding, Cloaths, Medicines and Irons to secure them,
and all other necessaries fitting and proper for said Convicts during their said
Voyage, in Consideration whereof the said Affreightor doth hereby covenant
and agree to and with the said Master or Captain, that he will well and truly pay
or cause to be paid to the said Master or his Assigns the Sum of five Pounds five
shillings per Head for each and every Convict or Passenger which the said
Affreightor shall so ship or put on Board his said Vessel as and for a compensation for the said Master in providing Provisions, Irons and Accommodation as
aforesaid for said Convicts or Passengers during their said Voyage upon his the
said Master entering into and perfecting the usual and accustomed Security to
the said Affreightor which the Law in such cases prescribes such Payment to be
made by the said Affreightor by good Bills or Notes at three months Light or
Date the same to be paid in one Calendar Month after the said Vessel shall have
so set Sail from Dublin with the said Convicts provided the said vessel shall
have got clear to Sea and no Account of her having put back or put into any
Port or Place in Great Britain or Ireland or in Europe and in Case certain
Intelligence shall be received that the said Vessel hath by contrary winds or
Stress of Weather been put into any Port or Ports or Places in Great Britain or
Ireland or in Europe before the Expiration of the said Calendar Month then the
said Freight to be paid in one Calendar Month after the said vessel's sailing and
proceeding from such Port or Place where she may have so put in and getting
clear to Sea. And lastly for the true and faithful Performance of all and singular
the Covenants herein before contained the said William Christian doth hereby
bind himself his Executors, Administrators, and Goods, and the said Ship her
Rigging, Tackle and Appurtenances and the said Freight unto the said
Affreightor his Executors, Administrators and Assigns in the penal Sum of One
Thousand Pounds Sterling. And in like Manner for the true and faithful
Performance hereof on his Part the said Affreightor doth hereby bind himself

his Executors, Administrators and Assigns in the like penal Sum of One Thousand Sterling each to the other mutually and firmly by these Presents. In Witness whereof the Parties aforesaid have hereunto put their hands and seals this eighteenth day of September 1789.

Signed Sealed and Delivered   William Christian
in Presence of   John Rose
Moleswth. Greene
Thos Greene

Know all Men by these Presents that We Arthur Bryan and George Bryan both of St John's Quay in the City of Dublin Merchants, are firmly bound unto the Right Honourable John Rose Lord Mayor of the City of Dublin in the Sum of One Thousand Pounds Sterling of good and lawful Money of Great Britain to be paid to the said Right Honourable John Rose or his certain Attorney, Executors, Administrators, or Assigns for which Payment well and truly to be made We bind ourselves and each of us by himself for the whole our and each of our Heirs Executors and Administrators jointly and severally firmly by these Presents.

Sealed with our Seals and dated this nineteenth Day of September 1789.

Whereas it was agreed at and before the ensealing and Delivery of the foregoing or annexed Deed or Charter Party of Affreightment and the same wsa accepted of by the above named Right Honourable John Rose on the Express Condition that the above bound Arthur Bryan and George Bryan should become Security and Guarantees for William Christian in the said annexed Charter Party named for the true and faithful Performance of the said Charter Party so far as relates to the said Master's fitting up his said vessell, and taking on Board the said Convicts and proceeding from Dublin therewith, and all other Matters on the said Master's Part to be done and performed. Now the Condition of the above Obligation is such that if the said William Christian doth in all Things well and truly perform, fulfill and keep the said Covenants, Clauses and Agreements in the said Charter Party of Affreightment contained on his the said William Christian's Part to be done and performed agreeable to the true Intent and Meaning of the said Charter Party of Affreightment, or if the said William Christian should make Default and not duly perform and fulfill the said Covenants and Agreements If then the said Arthur and George Bryan or one of them, their or either of their Heirs, Executors, Administrators or Assigns do and shall at all Times hereafter well and sufficiently save keep harmless and indemnified the said John Rose his Heirs, Executors, Administrators and Assigns of and from all Losses Costs Expenses or Damages which he shall or may suffer or be put to thereby, that then the foregoing Obligation to be void and of none Effect or else to stand and remain in full Force and Virtue in law.

Signed sealed and delivered   Arthur Bryan
in presence of   Geo. Bryan
Moleswth. Greene
Thos. Greene

(iii) Private instructions relating to the voyage of the *Duke of Leinster*, September–October 1789 [*HO* 152/70]

Capt. Wm. Christian   Dublin 4th November 1789

Sir!

You are to proceed with the Brigantine Duke of Leinster under your Command, to the Island of Antigua in the West Indies & when you have made the Island, you are to stand off towards the Island of Barbuda, giving it a good Birth [sic] on account of the reefs of Shoals, that surround it – & when you have discovered a good Situation desire you may disembark a Boat Load of yr. Convicts unded the care of the most steady and trustworthy of your people, perhaps your second Mate may answer for this Purpose for othewise you may lose your Boat & people & perhaps your vessel be stopped – ; & from this you are to proceed to another side of the Island & at a convenient place, make a further disembarkation, or go to Anguilla or other of these Islands, & divide the whole among them, but not a great many at any one place, for fear of a commotion – : & tell them on leaving you, the advantages it will be to them, that they conceal what they are – & that should their future behaviour be good, that they get to be caretaker, & in Situations of trust in the Plantations. The moment you are clear of these people, I wish you to proceed with the brig to Charleston, & there address yourself to the house of Messrs Condy & Bryan, & deliver these Gentlemen the inclosed letters. I have desired these Gentlemen to procure for yr. Brig the best fret. [freight] in their power – the nearer to home so much the better, however that wch is most advantegeous I wd. give a preference to, & doubt not your Seconding these Gentlemen procuring a good one & with dispatch.

You cannot be too attentive to these poor people put under your care; – so that they may be treated with humanity, at same time that you hold them, under a steady authority, that their meals be regularly dealt to them, & that above everything else, you see that they are kept clean, not only in their persons, but their Births [sic] & that their Beds be brought up every day to air, & on each day, that your tween Decks get a thorough cleaning of all wet or other filth, as to keep the Ship healthy is of the utmost moment, & nothing will contribute so much to health as cleanliness, & even to amuse them, when it can be done with safety, would be a means of giving health to yr. Ship. You have herewith a regulation for the dealing out the provisions, the Qtys & kinds of each, at each meal, & for every day in the week, also the Qty of Water.

I have told the Gentlemen at Charleston, that I expected would be such a Surplus of provisions, as would yield there something handsome – in this I do not include the Forty Barrels of new Beef; the Qty of Salt provisions exclusive is thirty six Barrels, including Beef, pork, herrings & Hearts & Skirts – that I would appreciate on your arrival at Charleston, you would have at least one half of this Qty to dispose of that is to say the house there, to sell for my acct. There is five Teirces of Prime Beef, which were shipped for the uses of the Crew – ; but there are some in Barrels nearly as good, but what I wish you to use first, is nine or ten barrels that are pretty low down in yr Vessel – Walsh knows the beef I mean – ; it came out of my Cellar and was the first that was put on board last Summer –; whoever you put yr. care of provisions, that is yr. dealing of it out duly and regularly, you had best promise such a person a gratuity, if he is attentive and exact in its distribution, & if you have everything on board necessary for exactness.

You have a Cask of Vinegar on board, which will be a means of preventing infection. The water casks [I] wish to have disposed at Charleston, also Arms. The Irons & Bolts to be brot. back in yr Vessel, also bedding after being well cleaned and put into casks. Much depends on you at present and your Steadiness will be required in its utmost exertion. I have a very great property under yr. Care, & according as it is attended to I shall be a Great Gainer or Loser – : yr. Vessel is well fitted, & her materials are well attended to, & that you have a good offset I think little will be required to send her to sea on her return.

I am wishing you health & a good Voyage.

> Sir!
> your hble
> A. Bryan

Appendix V
Reports from the Botany Bay Parliament

Botany Bay – House of Assembly
A hasty sketch of yesterday's Debate.
(Illustrated by a humorous print)

Halters
The speaker having taken the *tree*, Mr *Ketch*, secretary to the executions, produced several papers – which had been called for on the preceding day of meeting; from which it appears that thirteen colonists had been hanged for murder.

He then moved the assembly, that the sum of six shillings and eight-pence be voted to reimburse the state for the expence of *halters*.

Father Luke objected upon principles of oeconomy, and entered into a long and learned argument to show that, notwithstanding the stretching quality of ropes, one halter, if used with caution, might serve for several executions, and it was the more necessary to be oeconomic in this article, as the insurgents of the last year had destroyed the *hempen* plantations and burned down the *rope manufacturey*; and also because it was probable that when the next fleet of transports arrived from England, the demand for halters would encrease considerably – he therefore moved that the question be postponed for the consideration of the *civil list establishment*.

On the question being put, it was ordered accordingly.

State of the Colony
Mr Reynard now arose to bring forward his promised motion, for taking the state of the colony into consideration. He prefaced it by a candid retrospect of the life and actions of his father and himself, and observed that from the biographical anecdotes he had laid down, he trusted, it must be allowed that he had strong, unequivocal claims, both hereditary and personal, to the confidence of the Assembly of *Botany Bay* – he believed no man would accuse him of *hypocrisy*, his actions had been *notorious*, and that therefore when he brought forward opinions upon the state of the colony, however contrary they might appear to his *former principles*[,] however diametrically opposite to antecedent declarations, he must hope for a patient hearing. Circumstances and events changed opinions. Measures prudent on one day might be imprudent on another; and this was no new doctrine with him, for he had brought it into practice when, in his native country, he coalesced with his noble friend asleep on the ground, though once the bitter enemy.

He observed, there were as many species of *religion* in the colony as there were species of *thieves* – a circumstance which caused sourness, bickering and quarrels; and that though he considered religion a mere *political law*, in which opinion he believed he was supported by most of the assembly, yet taking it in that light, it was necessary there should be a form of belief by law for the purpose of coercing weak minds, and rendering them amenable to order. *Regularity* and *honour* were as necessary among thieves as among honest men, for without principles to cement individuals to one common interest, a state should never subsist, and he knew of no means so conducive to political union as religious influence.

The species of religion was a matter entirely indifferent to him. He had no objection to *Jewism*, for he had found many good friends among the *Jews*, and owed several of them very heavy obligations. To Mahometanism he had but one objection, that was only to the ceremony of circumcision, which was also practised by the Jews; and if Christianity could be adopted, it was equal to him whether the establishment was to be popish, protestant, presbyterian, new Light, old Light, methodist or Armenian. He then moved as follows: Resolved that it is essential to the good order of the state that *religion* be established by *laws*.

Mr Congreve coincided with his honourable friend. Religion, he observed, was the main spring of every state, and in many cases served as an excellent mask to cover entrenched and political views, which he illustrated by the conduct of the Dutch in treading upon the cross in the island of Japan. He was equally indifferent, with his honourable friend, as to the form to be established; for though he had the highest veneration for Christianity, yet the sectaries were so vindictive against each other, they carried [on] a continual warfare, and repudiated from their bosoms the principle of meekness and brotherly love. In his private opinion, a *good conscience* was the best religion, and he could safely say *his conscience* was never yet *injured*; but as that was not the case with every man, he considered an established religion of *some kind* or *other*, necessary to the good order of the state, and therefore seconded the motion of his honourable friend.

Lord Blaze rose with great warmth and indignation, to reprobate the indifference with which the preceding speakers had opened the debate, and particulary the impiety of the mover of the resolution, who called religion a political law, whereas politics in his opinion had not the least connection with either *religion*, *morality*, or *common honesty*. That religion was necessary to the protection of the person, he allowed, but the honourable gentleman did not seem to have any idea of its use to the *soul*. He was for establishing the protestant religion according to the forms of the kirk of Scotland. No man could doubt his *zeal* or his sincerity; he had had difficulty escaping *hanging* for the former, and his perseverance in opposing the process of the ecclesiastical court, was the undoubted proof of the latter. He had fought the good *fight* of *faith*, and if happily he had not been supported by a Scotch advocate, before a Scotch judge, probably he would have died a martyr to the cause. Who could doubt his religious principles? many of the colonists had benefited by their practice. He had associated with the *faithful* in their vindication. He had congregated and headed, rag, tag, shag and bobtail, to vindicate them. From principles of freedom he had liberated debtors; from sentiments of honesty he had set thieves free; from motives of *religion* he burned down chapels, and for the *honour of God*, and the good of their *souls*, he had persecuted the papists. He had not put his *candle* under a bushel – he had *blazed out* like the sun at noon day; it had brought down fire upon the modern Gomorrah – consuming her great buildings, and her mighty men, which sent forth flames like so many volcanos, causing anguish, bitterness, and gnashing of teeth among her inhabitants. This was the *religion* which he thought most proper for the colonists of *Botany Bay*, living as they did in [sic] the neighbouring savages, ignorant of christianity, and whom, if they refused to embrace the *pure faith*, as dictated by the kirk of *Scotland*, should be harrowed up, root and stem, and *extirpated* with *fire* and *sword* from the face of the earth.

Botany Bay – House of Assembly.
A hasty sketch of yesterday's Debate.

Debate on the State of the Colony
The noise which Lord *Blaze* made in the conclusion of his speech, had disturbed Lord *Boreas* from the state of insensibility in which seems constantly to be immerged [sic] during a debate, and raising his unwieldy carcase from the green sward, he begged leave to deliver his sentiments.

His Lordship said, that during twelve years, in which he had guided, (we are not sure whether his Lordship said *mis*-guided) the helm of government in Great Britain, he had never considered religion to be of any great moment in a kingdom; that the higher classes of life were too enlightened to pay any regard to it, and the bulk of the people were best left alone to enjoy their own whimsies, and follow the worship of their forefathers: that it was evident from what Lord *Blaze* had said, and indeed what he had already done, that to attempt the establishment of any particular system, would be only to lay the foundation of future dissension, and lead some future incendiary (here Lord *Blaze* looked very angry) to attempt destroying the peace and harmony of this settlement. That the different members of this new colony, his Lordship supposed, had more reliance upon their own *good works*, than upon any degree of *saving faith*, as all the *faith* of the island, he believed, would not procure them a dinner; – that he had constantly observed,

> – where religion over-grown prevails,
> Pure reason sinks, and moral virtue fails.

His Lordship had no idea of appearing a saint to heaven, while he acted the part of a scoundrel to his fellow vagabonds: he was indeed of opinion with his worthy and right hon. friend, that *regularity* and *honour* were highly necessary, even among *thieves*, and he thought that mutual *interest* was a much stronger tie than any speculative systems, or any confessions of religious belief. And why should any,

> Missed by faith, from scripture learnt by rote,
> Hold up a dagger to his brother's throat?

which would undoubtedly be the consequence of attending to the last speaker's (Lord Blaze's) inflammatory project.

That should it, however, be judged necessary to establish a regular system of faith and exterior ceremony, he had, for his part, no objection whatever to the Mahometanism creed, with the alteration of one article only – he meant the ceremony of circumcision, which at his time of life would be rather a disagreeable operation: – and in this opinion he flattered himself his right hon. friend would certainly coalesce with him. And as Lord Blaze had now foregone every hope of his favourite dulcinea, the Jewess in Duke's Place, probably his lordship would not find so many charms in the Jewish persuasion, as he had formerly conceived.

[*Walker's Hiberbian Magazine*, December 1786, pp. 685–7 and February 1787, p. 90]

Appendix VI
Documents Relating to the Voyage
of the *Queen*, April 1791

(i) Shipping contract between Messrs. Camden, Calvert & King and the Navy
Commissioners for the Third fleet [GMM MKH/9 (part of the papers of Capt.
Alexander Hood, 1758–1798)]

It is covenanted Concluded and agreed upon this the 18th day of November in
year of our Lord 1790, and in the 31st year of the Reign of our Sovereign Lord
George the Third of Great Britain France and Ireland King Defender of the Faith
and so forth by and between Messrs Camden Calvert and King of London
Merchants of the one part and the principal Officers and Commissioners of His
Majesty's Navy for and on behalf of His Majesty on the other in manner and
form following that is to say the said Messrs Camden Calvert and King have
agreed and by these presents do agree to provide a sufficient Number of Ships
and such as shall be approved by the Naval Agent at Deptford for Transporting
2,000 Convicts Male and Female with such Officers Soldiers Provisions and
Stores as shall be ordered to be put on Board to such Ports in New South Wales
as shall be required and the said Messrs Camden Calvert and King do Covenent
promise and agree that the said Ships shall be strong firm tight stanch and substantial both above Water and beneath and of Sufficient Capacity to allow of
Two Tons for each person to be embarkd on Board them and shall and will sail
forthwith to such ports in Great Britain or Ireland as shall be required Wind and
Weather permitting, equipt fitted and furnished with Masts Sails Yards Anchors
Ropes Cords Tackle Apparel also with proper Iron Bars and Gratings to their
Watchways Necessary for such a Voyage and for the Security of the Convicts
and such Bulkheads and Cabbins as shall be directed by the Naval Agent and
may be proper for the accomodation [sic] of the Soldiers and Convicts and such
Irons and Handcuffs as may be Necessary for the securing of the Latter to be
embarked in them also with Furniture and all other Materials and things neces-
sary proper convenient and fit for such Ships for their intended Voyage and
Service and two proper Boats and not less than three large Cables of 120
Fathoms and one stream Cable all in good condition for each Ship and and all
proper Sails and not less than two Mainsails Two Main Top Sails and two Fore
Sails Two Fore Top Sails Two WindSails and one Osbridges Machine to sweeten
Water for each Ship which is to be Man'd in the proportion of Six Men and a
Boy to every 100 Tons and capable to manage and sail her and the said Ships

shall in like manner be furnished and provided with Coals fire Hearths Coppers or Furnaces for the Boiling and Dressing the Provisions for such Number of Soldiers and Convicts as shall be orderd and Directed to be put on Board them and also with Cans and pumps for serving the said Soldiers and Convicts with Beer and Water on their Voyage as well as with platters spoons Candles and Lanthorns and also all Necessarys that may be wanted or required for their accomodation also the Masters of the said Ships shall receive and take on Board the said Ships from time to time such number of Soldiers Convicts Provisions and any kind or sort of Victuallling [sic] or other Stores and whatever else there shall be occasion for the service of His Majesty as shall be directed and required and as they can reasonably store and carry the whole Tonnage of the Shipping to be for the use of Government as far as their destined port except such part as may be necessary for the ships' stores and provisions for the Ship's Company and shall and will therewith proceed and sail to such place or places in New South Wales as the said Commissioners or Naval Agent whose command they shall be under shall order and direct landing and Delivering the same Accordingly and that during the Voyage the Masters of the said Ships shall obey all orders and Directions of the said Naval Agents and so from time to time during their continuance in the said Service in performance of which the said Masters and their men with their Boats shall aiding and assisting to the utmost of their power also the said Masters shall and are hereby obligd to give and sign Receipts Bills of Lading and other Indents for what they shall receive on Board Men and Women Except, and be accountable for the same and the said Masters are hereby obligd to to keep true Journals of the Wind and Weather and other Remarkable Observations and at the End and determination of the said Service to deliver the same into the Navy Office upon Oath if required together with all Orders and Instructions that they shall have received and in case any of the said Ships should depart from the Company of the Naval Agent under whose Command they shall be the Master of the Ship which has departed from the Company of the Naval Agent shall upon his arrival in any port or place whatsoever by the first Opportunity send immediate notice thereof to the said Commissioners and if the ships which have departed from the Company of the Naval Agent under whose Command they were at first shall afterwards fall in with any other of the Naval Agents who are appointed to this service the Masters of the said Ships shall obey his orders and Directions in the same manner as they were to obey those of the Naval Agent under whose Command they were at first and it is hereby declar'd and agreed that Each of the Naval Agents shall have the choice of the Ship in which he is to sail and that he shall be accomodated [sic] with a Birth [sic] in the great Cabin or else where as he shall judge most proper and fitted in such manner as shall be most Convenient for his Employment and that each of the Commissioned Officers commanding the Soldiers shall have proper Births in the Great Cabin of the Ship in which they are to Embark in which proper accommodation are to be Reservd for the use of the Master and that the Gunroom fore Castle and Steerage or such part thereof as shall be necessary shall be reservd for Lodging the Seamen and Soldiers And it is also hereby further agreed that the said Messrs Camden Calvert and King shall put on Board the said Ships a sufficient Quantity of Provisions to victual the Soldiers and Convicts for Eight Months at the following Rashions [sic] and shall victual them accordingly.

Rashion of Provisions for each Mess of Six Male Convicts for Seven Days successively

Bread	Flour	Beef	Pork	Pease	Butter	Rice
lb	lb	lb	lb	pints	lb	lb
16	12	14	8	12	$1^1/_2$	2

Each Mess to be allowed Two Pounds of Soap pr Month

Rashion of Provisions for each Mess of Six Female Convicts for Seven Days successively

Bread	Flour	Beef	Pork	Pease	Butter	Rice	Tea	Sugar
lb	lb	lb	lb	Pints	lb	lb	lb	lb
20	12	7	6	12	$1^1/_2$	2	$^1/_4$	3lb

Each Mess to be allowed two pounds of Soap pr Month

Rashion of Provisions for each Soldier for Seven Days successively

Seven pounds of Bread
Seven gallons of Beer
Three pints and one half of Rum
Seven pints of Wine
Four pounds of Beef
Two pounds of Pork
Two pints of pease
Three pints of Oatmeal
Six ounces of Butter
Twelve Ounces of Cheese

And the said Messrs Camden Calvert and King do hereby oblige themselves to provide and put on Board the said Ships 120 Gallns of Water for each Convict also a Qualifyd Surgeon on Board each Ship to attend the said Convicts and to provide Medisines [sic] and the following proportion of Necessarys for every 200 Convicts

Five Hundred of barley
Three Hd Oatmeal
Two cwt Sugar
Two cwt Essence of Malt
One hundred gallons Oil of Tar
Two Hund. do Vinegar
One Hogshd Wine

Spices and such other Articles as may be Necessary and in such proportions as the Surgeon may think proper

And the said Messrs Camden Calvert and King have also agreed to Furnish each of the said Convicts with the following articles of Cloathing agreaable to a pattern seal'd and kept at the Navy Office

Clothing for the Male Convicts

One Outside Jacket	Two pair stockings
One Waistcoat	Two pr. Trousers
One Hat	Two pr. Shoes
One worsted Cap	Two pr Drawers
Two Shirts	A Bag to contain each kit

Clothing for the Female Convicts

One striped Jacket	Two pair Stockings
One striped petticoat	Two pr. Shoes
One pair Stays	Two Handkerchiefs
One Hat	Two Caps
Two Flannel Petticoats	A Bag to contain each Kit
Two Shifts	

And also such Bed and Bedding for each of the said Convicts as may be approved of by the Naval Agent. It is also further agreed that the said Messrs Camden Calvert and King shall furnish each of the said Soldiers and Convicts with Fresh Provisions Two Days in the Week of value eaqual [sic] to one shilling Sterling for each Soldier and Nine pence for each Convict during their Continuance in any foreign Port and that these sums shall be allowd without any Deduction for Salt provisions upon a Certificate being produced from the Naval Agents that they were so supplyd

In Consideration whereof the said principal Officers and Commissioners of His Majesty's Navy on His Majesty's behalf do hereby oblige themselves to allow and pay unto the said Messrs Camden Calvert and King the sum of Nineteen Pounds Ten Shillings for each Convict embarked on Board the said Ships and one Shilling a Day for each Soldier Embark'd as a Guard to the said Convicts Exclusive of the allowance for supplying the said Convicts and Soldiers with fresh Provisions as before Mention'd the whole to be paid for in Navy Bills with this Discout aded [sic] thereto in the Manner following that is to say five pounds for each Convict when all the Ships have their Cabbins and Bulkheads fitted upon a Certificate thereof being produced from the Naval Agent five Pounds – for each Convict when all the provisions Clothing and Necessarys are on Board and all the said Ships are ready to Receive the Convicts upon a Certificate thereof being also produced from the Naval Agent and the Remainder on the final settlement of the Freight on a Certificate being produced from the Commissary of New South Wales of all the Stores and provisions sent out on account of His Majesty being safely Landed and delivered when agreeable to the Bills of Lading it is also agreed between the said Messrs Camden Calvert and King and the said Commissioners that fifteen Days shall be allowed for Embarking the Convicts at whatever Port they are to embark After all the Ships at their port of Embarkation are ready to receive them and Twenty one Days to Disembark the Convicts and land the Stores and provisions afer their arrival at their destined port in New South Wales but in case it should Happen that any of the Said Ships shall be Detaind longer than the Number of Days above limited either by Orders from the Government or from the Convicts not being ready to be Embark'd or Disembark'd then the said Messrs Camden Calvert and King are to be allowed after the rate of Twenty Pounds per Day for every One Thousand Tons of Shipping so detain'd and in that proportion for a greater or lesser number of Tons and likewise six pence a Day for each of the Said Convicts in case of Detention in manner above Mention'd in witness to that part of the above mentiond Covenants Conditions and Agreements to be kept done and perform'd on the part of of the said Messrs Camden Calvert and King and they the said Messrs Camden Calvert and King have set their Hand and Seal and to the other part thereof on His Majest's part to be paid done and performd the said principal Officers and Commissioners of His Majesty's Navy for and on His Majesty's behalf have causd the common Seal of the Navy Office to be affix'd the Day and Year first above Written

Attested
sigd   George Marsh

(ii) 'List of Prisoners under Sentence or Order of Transportation as received from the different Parts of the country and transported from Cork in the Queen Transport April 1791'
[The following alphabetical list is based on the original prepared and signed by Lieut. William Blow at the Cove of Cork on 11 April 1791, with variations and additions, signified in square brackets, derived from two other versions which can be found at AONSW SZ115 and 4/4003, together with a partial listing located in Musters and Papers 2/8274, pp. 257–9, and Irish newspaper reports of trials.]

Name	Age	Where convicted	When convicted	Term
Edward Allen [Alleyn]	40	Limerick	[22 March 1790]	Life
John Armstrong	24	Monaghan		7 years
John Bennett	30	Aramagh		Life
Mathew Berral	22	Dublin	1791	7 years
James Blake	12	Dublin	Octr 1790	7 years
John Boulton als Dogherty	18	Dublin	1790	7 years
Sarah Brazile [Brasil]	18	Waterford	[19 July] 1790	7 years
Dominick Brennan	26	Dublin	May 1790	7 years
Patrick Brennan	40	Dublin	Sept 1790	7 years
Sarah Brennan als Howe	20	Dublin	1790	7 years

Name	Age	Where convicted	When convicted	Term
William Burnes [Burns]	42	Down	1790	7 years
James Byrne	25	Dublin	June 1790	7 years
John Byrn	56	Dublin		7 years
James Cahil [Cahill]	34	Waterford	[19 July] 1790	7 years
George Carr als Kerr	39	Dublin	Feby 1791	Life
*Michael Carpenter [Nicholas]	50	Dublin	Jany 1790 [Jan 1789]	7 years
Thomas Carthy	20	Dublin	1790	7 years
James Clark	49	Dublin	1790	7 years
Anne Clerk als Murphy als Cleary	27	Queen's Co.	1790	7 years
Michl Collins	20	Cork City	1790	7 years
Edward Connolly [Conolly]	32	Armagh	1790	7 years
Danl Connor	30	Cork City	1790	7 years
James Connor [John Conners]	30	Limerick	[15 August 1789]	Life
Mary Connor	35	Dublin	1790	7 years
Edward Conroy	20	Dublin	March 1790	7 years
Catherine Corrigan	25	Dublin	1790	7 years
James Cunningham	40	Dublin		7 years
John Cunningham	24	Dublin	[October] 1790	7 years
Mary Davidson	23	Armagh	1790	7 years
#Obediah Davis	35	Dublin	Decr 1789	7 years
*Michael Delaney	30	Dublin	October 1788	7 years
*Matthew Dempsey	28	Dublin	1790	Life
Catherine Devereux	30	Dublin	October 1789	Life
Edward Dogherty	26	Cavan	[17 March 1790]	Life
Hugh Dogherty	20	Dublin	April 1790	7 years

Name	Age	Where convicted	When convicted	Term
John Doran als Dolan	17	Dublin	July 1790	Life
John Doyle	45	Kilkenny	1790	7 years
Timothy Driscoll	26	Cork City	1790	7 years
James Dwyer [Thomas]	22	Tipperary	[22 July 1790]	7 years
Catherine Edwards	28	Dublin	1790	7 years
Joseph Ellis	28	Dublin	June 1790	7 years
Mary Ennis	30	Dublin	[October] 1790	7 years
#Roger Fane	28	Limerick	[1790]	Life
John Farmer	20	Dublin	April 1790	7 years
David Fay	11	Dublin	Octr 1790	7 years
Michael Fennigan	45	Dublin	1790	Life
Michael Finn	25	Limerick	[31 July 1790]	Life
Patrick Fitzgerald	64	Limerick	[31 July] 1790	7 years
*Michael Flyn	28	Dublin	1790	7 years
Thomas Flynn	50	Down		Life
Hugh Foley	18	Dublin	April 1790	Life
*John Foley	19	Dublin	July 1790	7 years
William Frazer	18	Dublin	1789	7 years
*James Grant	26	Dublin	July 1790	7 years
Cornelius Halpin	22	Limerick	[31 July] 1790	7 years
William Harrison	26	Armagh		Life
*Patrick Hart	17	Dublin	January 1789	7 years
John Heally	12	Limerick	[31 July] 1790	7 years
Mary Heally als Gill	35	Limerick	[31 July] 1790	7 years
Mary Heron	25	Dublin		7 years
James Higgins	30	Westmeath	[25 July 1789]	Life
Eyre Jackson	21	Galway		7 years
Alexr Johnings	22	Westmeath	[19 July 1790]	7 years

Name	Age	Where convicted	When convicted	Term
*James Jordan als Sheridan	25	Dublin	March 1789	7 years
Matthew Keane als Kearney	28	Dublin	February 1790	Life
Daniel Keeffe	23	King's Co.	1790	7 years
Edward Kelly	29	Meath	[Summer] 1790	7 years
Edward Kennedy [Edmund]	22	Tipperary	[22 July 1790]	7 years
Thomas Kenny or Kelly	16	Dublin	1789	7 years
Peter King	28	Wexford	[19 July 1790]	Life
George Kirwan [Garrant]	29	Dublin	July 1790	Life
David Lane	26	Cork City		Life
Michael Lamb	18	Dublin	Octr 1790	7 years
Frances Lawless	19	Galway	1790	7 years
+John Lawlor	20	Dublin	1790	7 years
John Lawson	29	Louth	1789	7 years
James Leary	27	Cork City	1790	7 years
Patrick Lee	25	Dublin	1790	7 years
*Patrick Leonard	45	Dublin	Jany 1789	7 years
Francis Little	30	Down		Life
Christopher Loughlin [Laughlin]	36	Tipperary		7 years
William Lydale	24	Dublin	Decr 1790	Life
Charles Lynch	37	Cavan	[17 March] 1790	7 years
Hugh Lynch	25	Dublin	Septr 1790 [Aug. 1788]	7 years
John Lynch	25	Dublin	Sept 1790	7 years
Daniel McCann	38	Antrim	1790	7 years
Patrick McCann	22	Armagh	1790	7 years
Francis McClernon	20	Armagh	Life	

Name	Age	Where convicted	When convicted	Term
Daniel McDaniel	20	Dublin	Octr 1790	7 years
Terence McDaniel	24	Dublin	Octr 1790	7 years
Willm McDaniel	26	Dublin	1789	7 years
Elinor McDonald Bridget McDonnell	23	Armagh	1790	Life
Pat McEvoy [Patrick]	38	Louth	1790	7 years
Patrick McGawran	26	Leitrim		Life
Patrick McInerney	20	Limerick	[31 July] 1790	Life [7 years]
James McKelvey als Magrath	24	Monaghan	[16 August 1790]	Life
Patrick McKernan	28	Leitrim	[23 July 1789]	Life
Peter McShane	30	Louth		Life
Hugh Magennis	20	Dublin	May 1789	7 years
Mary Mandeville	35	Kilkenny	1790	7 years
*John Mansfield	18	Dublin	Decr 1788	7 years
Monica Marlow	35	Dublin	1790	7 years
Charles Marshall	14	Dublin	1791	7 years
James Marshall	40	Down	1790	7 years
Lawrence May	18	Dublin	Sept 1790	7 years
James Marshall	40	Down	1790	7 years
John Martin	33	Dublin	Feby 1790	7 years
Owen Martin	18	Fermanagh	1790	7 years
Denis Mohair als Murtagh	20	Dublin	1790	7 years
Patrick Mooney	22	Dublin	Octr 1790	7 years
William Montgomery	25	Westmeath	[19 July] 1790	7 years
Thomas Mullen	32	Antrim	[5 August 1790]	Life
Mulloy als Hines	36	King's Co.	1790	7 years
Jeremiah Murphy	21	Cork City	1790	7 years
Michael Murphy	18	Waterford	1790	7 years

Name	Age	Where convicted	When convicted	Term
Michael Murphy	21	Dublin	October 1790	Life
Patrick Murphy	30	Limerick		Life
*James Myler	20	Dublin	October 1788	7 years
*Dennis Newenham	21	Dublin	October 1788	7 years
Bridget Nowlas als Rossiter	35	Dublin	1789	7 years
Matthew Nulty	35	Dublin	May 1790	7 years
+Charles O Bryan	29	Dublin	Septr 1790	7 years
William O Reilly	25	Kildare	[18 March 1790]	Life
Felix Owens	27	Meath	[Spring 1790]	Life
+John als Peter Parker	22	Kilkenny [Carlow?]	1790 [?]	7 years
Mary Plunkett	23	Dublin	1790	7 years
James Randles	25	Down	[August]1790	7 years
*Thomas Regan	34	Dublin	April 1789 [Dec. 1788]	7 years
James Reilly	30	Dublin	June 1790	7 years
Patrick Reilly	40	Longford	1790	7 years
William Reilly	26	Queen's Co.	1790	Life
Patrick Shane	23	Meath	[Summer] 1790	7 years
Anne Slater	30	Dublin	1788	7 years
Mary Smyth	30	Dublin	1790	7 years
Terence Smyth	18	Dublin	Jany 1791	7 years
Michael Stafford	26	Dublin	Feby 1790	Life
Margt. Stephenson	50	Armagh	1790	7 years
*Daniel Stewart	25	Dublin	1789	7 years
Andrew Toolen	25	Longford	1790	7 years
Francis Tyrrell	45	Dublin	Sept 1790	7 years
John Vardy	35	Fermanagh	[22 March] 1790	7 years
James Vaughan	20	Dublin		Life

Richard Vowell	19	Dublin	July 1790	Life
James Walsh	30	Dublin	Augt 1788	7 years
Thomas Watson	24	Dublin	Octr 1790	7 years
Anthony West	26	Armagh	1790	7 years
John Whelan	25	Dublin	July 1790	7 years
John Whelan	38	Dublin	July 1790	Life
John Whelan	38	King's Co.		Life
Mary Whelan	18	Dublin	[October] 1790	7 years
Francis Wild	24	Dublin	April 1790	7 years
Thomas Williamson	19	Down	[July] 1790	7 years
*Arthur Young	20	Dublin	1789	7 years

Received from the Right Worshipful Richard Harris Esqr Mayor of the City of Cork Charles Ferguson Esqr and Sir Henry Brown Hayes Knt. Sheriffs of the said city the Bodies of One Hundred and Thirty Male and Twenty Two Female Convicts (whose Names are in the foregoing and annotated Sheets) on Board the Queen Transport, in order to be Transported to New South Wales agreeable to their Several Sentences. Say Received the Whole in Good Health and I have Signed a Duplicate of this Receipt on Board the Queen in the Cove of Cork this 11th day of April 1791

Saml Blow. Naval Agent.

List of three Children Gone With Their Mothers (Convicts) on the Queen Transport to New South Wales

Childrens Names	Mothers Names	Ages
John Edwards	Catherine Stewart	2 Years
Betty McDonald	Mary McDonald	1 do
Judy Connor	Mary Connor	9 Months
Margaret Brennan	Sarah Brennan	2 Weeks

Recd. with the foregoing Convicts from the City of Cork Twenty-Seven pair of Bar Irons, four pair of Chain Irons, and two Pair of Hand Cuffs, which I found necessary to keep aboard the Queen Transport, and for which there is a Duplicate Receipt, dated on Board the Queen at the Cove of Cork this 11th Day of April 1791.

Saml Blow Naval Agent

Male Convicts	133
Female	22
Children	4
Total	159

* Returned from transportation to Newfoundland, January 1790.
+ Possibly returned from transportation to Newfoundland, January 1790.
# Returned from transportation to another destination than Newfoundland.

Notes

Introduction

1 For the fullest account of this voyage to date, see K. Johnson and M. Flynn, 'Convicts of the *Queen*', in Bob Reece, ed., *Exiles from Erin: Convict Lives in Ireland and Australia*, London: Macmillan, 1991, pp. 10–26. The First Fleet which reached New South Wales in January 1788 also contained about 80 convicts charged with 'return from transportation', mostly mutineers who had escaped from the *Swift* and the *Mercury* shipments to North America in 1784 and 1785. John Cobley, comp., *The Crimes of the First Fleet Convicts*, Sydney: Angus & Robertson, 1971, pp. xi–xiii. The *Swift* and *Mercury* shipments are dealt with below in Chapter 4.

2 For the most recent contributions to the debate, see A. Atkinson, 'The First Plans for Governing New South Wales, 1786–87', *Australian Historical Studies*, no. 94 (April 1990), pp. 22–40; M. Gillen, 'His Majesty's Mercy: The Circumstances of the First Fleet', *The Push*, no. 29 (1991), pp. 47–109; A. Frost, 'Historians, Handling Documents, Transgressions and Transportable Offences', *Australian Historical Studies*, no. 99 (October 1992), pp. 192–213; D. Mackay, '"Banished to Botany Bay": The Fate of the Relentless Historian', *Australian Historical Studies*, no. 99 (October 1992), pp. 214–16; A. Atkinson, 'Beating the Bounds with Lord Sydney, Evan Nepean and Others', *Australian Historical Studies*, no. 99 (October 1992), pp. 217–9. See also, A. Frost, *Convicts and Empire: A Naval Question, 1776–1811*, Melbourne: Oxford University Press, 1980; M. Gillen, 'The Botany Bay decision, 1786: convicts, not empire', *English Historical Review*, (October 1982), pp. 740–66; A. Frost, 'Botany Bay: an imperial venture of the 1780's', *English Historical Review*, 100 (April 1985), pp. 309–27; D. Mackay, *A Place of Exile: The European Settlement of New South Wales*, Melbourne: Oxford University Press, 1985.

3 D. Mackay, '"Banished to Botany Bay"'.

4 Frost, *Botany Bay Mirages: Illusions of Australia's Convict Beginnings*, Melbourne University Press, 1994.

5 E. O'Brien, *The Foundation of Australia (1786–1800): A Study in English Criminal Practice and Penal Colonisation in the Eighteenth Century*, London: Sheed & Ward, 1937.

6 A.G.L. Shaw, *Convicts and the Colonies: A Study of Penal Transportation from Great Britain and Ireland to Australia and Other Parts of the British Empire*, London: Faber, 1966.

7 W. Oldham, *Britain's Convicts to the Colonies*, Sydney: Library of Australian History, 1990, pp. 202–4.

8 *Ibid.*, pp. 83–94.

9 A.R. Ekirch, 'Great Britain's Secret Convict Trade to America, 1783–1784', *American Historical Review*, vol. LXXXIX, no. 5 (1984), pp. 1285–91.

10 Gillen, 'His Majesty's Mercy'.

11 O'Brien, *The Foundation of Australia*, pp. 188–91.

12 Oldham, *Britain's Convicts*, p. 167.

13 J. Martin, 'Convict Transportation to Newfoundland in 1789', *Acadiensis*, vol. 5 (1975), pp. 84–99.

14 For a more detailed account of the Newfoundland and its consequences, see Bob Reece, '"Such a Banditti": Irish Convicts in Newfoundland 1798'. Part I, *Newfoundland Studies*, vol. 13, no. 1 (1997), pp. 1–29; Part II, vol. 13, no. 2 (1997), pp. 127–41.

15 Fr Aubrey Gwynn, 'Cromwell's Policy of Transportation', Part I, *Studies*, vol. xix, no. 76 (December 1930), pp. 607–23; Part II, *Studies*, vol. xx, no. 78 (June 1931), pp. 291–305.

16 Joseph J. Williams, *Whence the 'Black Irish' of Jamaica?*, New York: Dial Press, 1932.

17 J.W. Blake, 'Transportation from Ireland to America, 1653–60', *Irish Historical Studies*, vol. iii, no. 10 (September 1942), pp. 267–81.

18 A. Lockhart, *Some Aspects of Emigration from Ireland to the North American Colonies Between 1660 and 1775*, New York: Arno Press, 1976, pp. 80–97.

19 A.E. Smith, *Colonists in Bondage: White Servitude and Convict Labor in America 1607–1776*, Chapel Hill: University of North Carolina Press, 1947.

20 A.R. Ekirch, *Bound for America: The Transportation of British Convicts to the Colonies, 1718–1775*, Oxford: Clarendon Press, 1987.

21 R.B. McDowell, *Ireland in the Age of Imperialism and Revolution 1760–1801*, Oxford: Clarendon Press, 1979, p. 71.

22 A. Kavanaugh, 'John Fitzgibbon, Earl of Clare: A Study in Politics and Personality', Ph.D. thesis, 2 vols., Trinity College, Dublin, 1992.

23 Oliver MacDonagh, *The Inspector General: Sir Jeremiah Fitzpatrick and the Politics of Social Reform, 1783–1802*, London: Croom Helm, 1981.

24 B. Henry, *Dublin Hanged: Crime, Law Enforcement and Punishment in Late Eighteenth-Century Dublin*, Dublin: Irish Academic Press, 1994, pp. 157–67. See also his 'Which Transportation: Irish or English, 1784–1791', *Alumnus* (1992), pp. 1–12.

25 Shaw, *Convicts and the Colonies*, p. 56.

26 For general works addressing this theme, see Lawrence McCaffrey, *The Irish Diaspora in America*, Bloomington: Indiana University Press, 1976, and D.A. Akenson, *The Irish Diaspora: A Primer*, Toronto: P.S. Meany Co. Inc., 1993. For a more specific discussion of the eighteenth century, see L.M. Cullen, 'The Irish Diaspora in the Seventeenth and Eighteenth Centuries', in Nicholas Canny, ed., *Europeans on the Move: Studies on European Migration, 1500–1800*, Oxford: Clarendon Press, 1994.

Chapter 1

1 'An Advise for Ireland. 19 Decemb. 1607', Lansdowne MSS., vol. 156, Caesar Papers, Ireland, British Museum, reproduced by Fr Aubrey Gwynn, 'Documents Relating to the Irish in the West Indies', *Analecta Hibernica*, no. 4 (October 1932), pp. 157–8.

2 *Ibid.*, p. 158.

3 Letter from the Lord Deputy, 8 December 1620, State Papers (Ireland) 235 (36) 1620, reproduced by Gwynn, 'Documents', p. 159.

4 For an account of Virginia's early Irish connection, see Brian McGinn, 'Virginia's Lost Irish Colonists', *Irish Roots*, 1993, no. 4, pp. 21–4.

5 J.C. Ballagh, *White Servitude in the Colony of Virginia: A Study of the System of Indentured Labor in the American Colonies*, New York: Burt Franklin, 1969, p. 35.

6 Smith, *Colonists in Bondage*, p. 65. See also pp. 14–15. This tenuous arrangement lasted until 1713 when the British finally took over the entire island.

7 Carl and Roberta Bridenbaugh, *No Peace Beyond the Line: The English in the Caribbean 1624–1690*, New York: Oxford University Press, 1972, p. 145.

8 *Ibid.*, pp. 144–5.

9 *Ibid.*, p. 15.

10 *Ibid.*, p. 17.

11 See Gwynn, 'Cromwell's Policy of Transportation', Part II, p. 301. In this article, Fr Gwynn documents the four known cases of Catholic priests exiled to Barbados from January 1655.

12 John W. Blake, 'Transportation from Ireland to America, 1653–60', *Irish Historical Studies*, vol. III, no. 10 (September 1942), pp. 267–281.

13 G.P. Prendergast, *The Cromwellian Settlement of Ireland ...*, London; Longman, Green, Reader & Dyer, 1865, p. 92, estimates that there were 'about 6,400' shipped to the West Indies by the Bristol 'slave dealers'.

14 Bridenbaugh, *No Peace Beyond the Line*, p. 196. The Bridenbaughs provide no further information about the petition.

15 Gwynn, 'Cromwell's Policy of Transportation', Part I, pp. 610–11. The Bridenbaughs, *No Peace Beyond the Line*, p. 17, state misleadingly that after Drogheda, 'a few hundred Irish common Irish soldiers were exiled to Barbados ...'.

16 Gwynn, 'Documents', pp. 614–5.

17 Thomas Carlyle, *Oliver Cromwell's Letters and Speeches: With Elucidations*, 2nd edn., 3 vols., London, 1844, II, p. 47, cited by Hilary McD. Beckles, 'A "riotous and unruly lot": Irish Indentured Servants and Freemen in the English West Indies, 1644–1713', *William and Mary Quarterly*, 3rd Series, vol. XLVII (October 1990), p. 506.

18 'The Political Anatomy of Ireland' in Charles Henry Hull, ed., *The Economic Writings of Sir William Petty*, 2 vols., New York: Augustus M. Kelley, 1963, I, p. 151.

19 Prendergast, *The Cromwellian Settlement*, pp. xxiii. Fr J.J. Williams, *Whence the 'Black Irish' of Jamaica?*, New York: Dial Press, 1932, p. 31, followed Prendergast in this misinterpretation.

20 Williams, *Whence the 'Black Irish'*, p. 17.

21 Gwynn, 'Cromwell's Policy of Transportation', Part I, 22. 616–7.

22 *Ibid.*, p. 621.

23 *Ibid.*

24 Smith, *Colonists in Bondage*, p. 104.

25 Ballagh, *White Servitude*, pp. 294–5.

26 *Calendar of State Papers, Colonial Series, America and West Indies 27 October, 1697, 31 December 1698*, London: H.M.S.O., 1905, p. 1.

27 Prendergast, *The Cromwellian Settlement*, p. 90. See also, Revd A.E. D'Alton, *History of Ireland from the Earliest Times to the Present Day*, 2 vols., London:

1911, and Elliott O'Donnell, *The Irish Abroad: A Record of the Achievements of Wanderers from Ireland*, London: Isaac Pitman & Sons Ltd., 1915.

28   Gwynn, 'Cromwell's Policy of Transportation', Part I, p. 623.

29   *Ibid.*

30   Ballagh, *White Servitude*, pp. 38–9.

31   Williams, *Whence the 'Black Irish'*, pp. 14–15. See also, Gwynn, 'Cromwell's Policy of Transportation', Part II, p. 305.

32   Cited by Prendergast, *The Cromwellian Settlement*, p. 92.

33   'Letter of John Grace' (5 July 1669), Gwynn, 'Documents', p. 257. See also, Patrick J. Corish, 'The Cromwellian Conquest of Ireland', in T.W. Moody, F.X. Martin and F.J. Byrne, eds., *A New History of Ireland*, vol. III, Oxford: Clarendon Press, 1978, p. 364. For the enduring influence of the Irish in the Leewards, see Brian McGinn, 'How Irish is Montserrat?', *Irish Roots*, 1994, no. 1, pp. 20–23; no. 3, pp. 16–17; no. 4, pp. 20–21.

34   T.M. Truxes, *Irish-American Trade, 1660–1783*, Cambridge University Press, 1988, pp. 94–102.

35   R.C. Nash, 'Irish Atlantic Trade in the Seventeenth and Eighteenth Centuries', *William and Mary Quarterly*, vol. XLII (July 1985), p. 352.

36   Cited by Williams, *Whence the 'Black Irish'*, pp. 19–20.

37   *Ibid.*, p. 19.

38   Richard Ligon, *A True and Exact History of the Island of Barbados*, London, 1673, p. 43, cited, *ibid.*, pp. 20–21. For further evidence of the status and treatment of Irish servants in Barbados, see 'Some Observations on the Island of Barbados', in Gwynn, 'Documents', p. 250.

39   John Scott, 'Some Observations on the Island of Barbados', *CO* 1/21, no. 170, cited by Beckles, 'A "riotous and unruly lot"', p. 511.

40   'Extracts from the Minutes of the Council of Barbados', in Gwynn, 'Documents', pp. 233–9.

41   'Order of Governor and Council', 22 September 1657, in Gwynn, 'Documents', p. 238.

42   Beckles, 'A "riotous and unruly lot"', p. 507.

43   *Ibid.*, p. 506.

44   *Ibid.*, p. 508.

45   Atkins to Lord of Trade, 15/25 August 1676, *Co* 1/37, no. 48, cited without reference by Bridenbaugh, *No Peace Beyond the Line*, p. 300.

46   Francis Sampson to John Sampson, 6 June 1666, Gwynn, 'Documents', p. 244.

47   Gwynn, 'Documents', p. 243. Bridenbaugh, *No Peace Beyond the Line*, p. 174, gets the date wrong.

48   Netheway to King and Queen, 27 June 1689, *CSP (CS)*, 1689–1692, no. 212., cited by Gwynn, 'Documents', p. 279.

49   Beckles, 'A "riotous and unruly lot"', p. 519.

50   Carpenter and Belchamber to Commissioners of Customs, 19 August 1689, *CSP (CS)*, 1689–1692, no. 361, cited by Gwynn, 'Documents', p. 279.

51   Codrington to Lords of Trade and Plantations, 31 July 1689, *CSP (CS)*, 1689–1692, no. 312, cited *ibid.*, p. 279.

52   Gwynn, 'Documents', pp. 266–7.

53   Beckles, 'A "riotous and unruly lot"', p. 521.

54   *Ibid.*

55 *Ibid.*
56 Cited by Warren B. Smith, *White Servitude in Colonial South Carolina*, University of South Carolina Press, 1961, p. 39.
57 Colonel Hart to the Board of Trade, 20 January 1723, *CO* 152/14, no. 195–6, cited by Gwynn, 'Documents', p. 281.
58 Hunter to the Board of Trade, 13 November 1731, *CO* 137/19, nos. 108–13, cited, *ibid.*, p. 282.
59 Truxes, *Irish-American Trade*, p. 144.
60 Historical Manuscripts Commission, *Tenth Report, Appendix. Part V. The Manuscripts of the Marquis of Ormonde, the Earl of Fingall, the Corporations of Waterford, Galway, &c.*, London: H.M.S.O., 1885, pp. 94–5.
61 *Ibid.*, pp. 71–2.
62 *Ibid.*, pp. 91–2.
63 *Ibid.*, p. 35.
64 *Ibid.*, p. 26.
65 *Ibid.*, pp. 46–7.
66 *Ibid.*, pp. 84–5.
67 *Ibid.*, p. 85.
68 For the English practice, see F.H. Schmidt, 'Sold and Driven: Assignment of Convicts in Eighteenth-Century Virginia', *The Push from the Bush*, no. 23 (October 1986), p. 5.
69 *Irish Statutes*, vol. IV (1703–19), pp. 44–8.
70 *Ibid.*, pp. 86–7.
71 *Ibid.*, vol. IV, pp. 537–41.
72 *Ibid.*, vol. V (1721–31), p. 46.
73 *Ibid.*, vol. V (1721–31), p. 176.
74 *Ibid.*, vol. V (1721–31), pp. 363–6.
75 *Ibid.*, vol. VI (1733–47), pp. 192–8.
76 Lockhart, *Some Aspects of Emigration*, p. 81.
77 *Irish Statutes*, vol. XIII (1785–86), pp. 760–3.
78 'Report from the Committee appointed to re-consider the several Returns of the Felons and Vagabonds, ordered for Transportation these seven Years last past, and to inquire how many Persons were actually transported, how many died or escaped before Transportation, how much Money hath been raised for those Purposes, and to whom paid', *JIHC*, vol. IV, Appendix, pp. cciii et seq. Apart from the minutes of interviews with officials and merchants, the report consists entirely of county by county lists of the names of prisoners ordered for transportation at the various assizes, the presentments of money made, the names of prisoners actually transported and the names of those who died in Dublin's Newgate prison while awaiting transportation. There are also details of the sale of twenty convicts as indentured servants in Philadelphia in 1740.
79 See Chapter 15.
80 Lockhart, *Some Aspects of Emigration*, p. 88.
81 *Freeman's Journal*, 13–15 May 1788.
82 Lockhart, *Some Aspects of Emigration*, p. 96. According to Lockhart, Grandall was believed to have been a Presbyterian.
83 A.R. Ekirch, *Bound for America: The Transportation of British Convicts to the Colonies 1718–1775*, Oxford: Clarendon Press, 1987, pp. 25, 46–7. Smith,

Colonists in Bondage, p. 134, had earlier estimated that at least 10,000 Irish were transported to the American colonies between 1703 and 1775.

84 Lockhart, *Some Aspects of Emigration*, p. 89.
85 *Ibid.*, p. 31.
86 J.W. Hammond, 'George's Quay and Rogerson's Quay in the Eighteenth Century', *Dublin Historical Record*, vol. v, no. 2, pp. 48–9.
87 Lockhart, *Some Aspects of Emigration*, p. 92.
88 17 Geo II, c. 4, *Irish Statutes*, vol. vi (1733–47), pp. 654–5.
89 As far as I am aware, this difference in practice has not been remarked upon by the historians of transportation. This may be because it was not spelled out in the relevant legislation. After the Home Office took over responsibility for Irish transportation in early 1791, however, the British system was observed in New South Wales.
90 The relevant legislation was 24 Geo. III, c. 56. See Alan Atkinson, 'The Free-Born Englishman Transported: Convict Rights as a Measure of Eighteenth Century Empire', *Past and Present*, no. 144 (August 1994), p. 95, and John Howard, *The State of the Prisons ...*, Warrington: William Eyre, 1776, p. 426.
91 Truxes, *Irish-American Trade*, p. 129.
92 Lockhart, *Some Aspects of Emigration*, p. 85.
93 'A Return of twenty Servants from on Board the Ship Hibernia, Nathaniel Sears Master, for Account of Mr. Thomas Cooke, Merchant, in Dublin', *JIHC*, vol. iv, Appendix, p. ccxxix.
94 Lockhart, *Some Apects of Emigration*, p. 86.
95 George Bryan's commercial activities are referred to briefly by Truxes, *Irish-American Trade*, pp. 120–1. Subsequently a judge and a leading figure in the Presbyterian Irish community, his political career has been recounted in detail in Joseph G. Foster, *In Pursuit of Equal Liberty: George Bryan and the Revolution in Pennsylvania*, Philadelphia: University of Pennsylvania Press, 1994.
96 For details of the ships, see 'Ship Registers for the Port of Philadelphia, 1726–1776', *Philadelphia Magazine of History and Biography*, vol. xxiv (1900), p. 510; vol. xxv (1901), pp. 269, 275; vol. xxvii (1903), pp. 96, 239, 243.
97 Edward W. Neill, *Terra Mariae*, Philadelphia, 1867, p. 213, cited by J.D. Butler, 'British Convicts Shipped to American Colonies', *American Historical Review*, vol. ii, no. 1 (October 1896), p. 27.
98 Cited by Butler, 'British Convicts', p. 22.
99 Ekirch, *Bound for America*, p. 114.
100 Lockhart, *Aspects of Emnigration*, p. 85.
101 Schmidt, 'Sold and Driven', p. 17. This article provides a detailed account of the method of disposing of convicts on arrival in Virginia.
102 Ekirch, *Bound for America*, p. 128.
103 Margaret M.R. Kellow, 'Indentured Servitude in Eighteenth-Century Maryland', *Histoire Sociale-Social History*, vol. xvii, no. 34 (November 1984), p. 237.
104 Lockhart, *Some Aspects of Emigration*, p. 93.
105 *Ibid.*, p. 95.
106 Ekirch, *Bound for America*, p. 191. For contemporary accounts of the conspiracy, see K. Colman and M. Ready, eds., *The Colonial Records of*

the State of Georgia ..., vol. 20, Athens: University of Georgia Press, 1982, pp. 246–7, 258–9, 270–3, 462–3.

107 Cited by Kenneth Morgan, 'English and American Attitudes Towards Convict Transportation 1718–1775', *History*, no. 72 (1987), p. 417.

108 Kenneth Morgan, 'The Organization of the Convict Trade to Maryland: Stevenson, Randolph & Cheston, 1768–1775', *William and Mary Quarterly*, 3rd series, vol. XLII (1985), p. 226; Ekirch, *Bound for America*, p. 124.

109 Smith, *White Servitude*, p. 39.; Ekirch, *Bound for America*, pp. 138–9; Lockhart, *Some Aspects of Emigration*, pp. 86–7.

110 Kellow, 'Indentured Servitude', p. 239.

111 Ekirch, *Bound for America*, p. 138.

112 William Eddis, *Letters from America*, ed. by Aubrey C. Land, Cambridge, Mass.: Belknap Press, 1969, p. 36.

113 *Virginia Gazette*, 25 April 1776, cited by Peter Wilson Coldham, *Emigrants in Chains* ..., Baltimore: Genealogical Publishing Co. Inc., 1992, p. 151.

114 For a useful summary of the debate, see Morgan, 'The Organization of the Convict Trade', pp. 418–24.

115 William Eden, *Principles of Penal Law*, 2nd edn., London: B. White & T. Cadell, 1771, p. 33.

116 Cited by Eden, *Principles of Penal Law*, p. 35.

117 For a discussion of Eden's influence on penal policy and practice, see G.C. Bolton, 'William Eden and the Convicts', *Australian Journal of Politics and History*, vol. 26, no. 1 (1980), pp. 30–44.

118 Dan Byrnes, '"Emptying the Hulks": Duncan Campbell and the First Three Fleets to Australia', *The Push from the Bush*, no. 24 (April 1987), pp. 2–23, revised and updated on disc, 1996.

119 Anon., *Animadversions on the Street Robberies in Dublin; Together with a Proposal of a Scheme to Prevent them for the Future in a Letter to a Member of Parliament*, Dublin: George Faulkner, 1765, 22pp. The pamphlet was re-printed in its entirety in the *Irish Jurist*, vol. XXIII (New Series), pt. 2 (Winter 1988), pp. 437–356, with an introduction by Dr Brian Henry. I am indebted to Dr Henry for bringing the pamphlet to my notice. Subsequent quotations are from this source.

120 See Stanley H. Palmer, *Police and Protest in England and Ireland 1780–1850*, Cambridge: Cambridge University Press, 1988, p. 81.

121 The last shipment of British convicts on the *Jenny* was landed at George-Town in April 1776. *Virginia Gazette*, 25 April 1776, cited by Coldham, *Emigrants in Chains*, p. 151. It is not known when the last Irish shipment took place.

122 *PP* 1731–1800, vol. IX, no. 286.

123 17 & 18 Geo. III, c. 9, *Irish Statutes*, vol. XI (1776–1783), pp. 73–83.

124 *Ibid.*, p. 73.

125 Starr, 'Irish Police and Prisons', p. 447.

126 *Hibernian Journal*, 8–10 September 1783: letter from 'Citizen'.

127 *Hibernian Journal*, 19 February and 24 March 1783.

128 See Chapter 7.

129 *JIHC*, vol. XI, Appendix, p. dxxxi, cited by Starr, 'Irish Police and Prisons', p. 447.

130 *Ibid.*

131 See Cormac O Grada, *Ireland: A New Economic History 1780–1939*, Oxford: Clarendon Press, 1994, p. 19.
132 *Hibernian Journal*, 8–10 January 1783.
133 *Freeman's Journal*, 4–6 February 1783.
134 *Hibernian Journal*, 17–19 February 1783.
135 *Hibernian Journal*, 19–21 February 1783.
136 *Freeman's Journal*, 6–8 February 1783.
137 *Hibernian Journal*, 28–30 April 1783.
138 *Hibernian Journal*, 22–24 January 1783.
139 *Ibid.*
140 Rutland to Treasury, 20 February 1784, *T/1/610/183–5*; Rutland to Treasury, 7 April 1784, *T/1/610/131–2*.

Chapter 2

1 *Hibernian Journal*, 23 July 1784.
2 *Ibid.*
3 *Hibernian Journal*, 19 July 1784.
4 *Hibernian Journal*, 23 July 1784.
5 McKinley (or McKenly) was a grocer and dye-stuff merchant on Dublin's Coombe who took advantage of the 1772 Act for the relief of insolvent debtors and was appointed gaoler by Sir George Ribton, Sheriff of Co. Dublin, in 1773. He died in 1801 (*Hibernian Journal*, 19 July 1773, 29 April 1774).
6 *Hibernian Journal*, 23 June 1784.
7 *Hibernian Journal*, 19 July 1784.
8 *Walker's Hibernian Magazine*, October 1785, p. 559.
9 *Walker's Hibernian Magazine*, December 1784, p. 742.
10 *Hibernian Journal*, 19 May 1790.
11 *Walker's Hibernian Magazine* of September 1789 described this ruse:

> a poor mariner, as is likewise a stranger, was tricked out of a guinea by a sharper who dropped a small bag containing a ring, wrapped carefully in cotton, and enclosed in the following letter:
>
> > 'Dublin, September the 8th, 1789
> > Madam, I send you the enclosed gold ring according to your direction, which I hope will please you better than the last one I sent you. The price of it is two pounds five shillings and fivepence sterling. So no more at present from your humble servant,
> > > 'Thomas Carroll'
>
> The villain, on the sailor's taking up the bag, claimed, in the usual way, a share of the prize as an immemorial right, unluckily the seaman, wishing perhaps to present it to a sweetheart, gave the sharper a guinea, but afterwards on examination, found the ring base metal, although marked in the accustomed manner, and superficially gilt ....

12 *Walker's Hibernian Magazine*, February 1790, p. 190.

13   *Hibernian Journal*, 16 January 1784.
14   *Walker's Hibernian Magazine*, April 1787, p. 224.
15   *Dublin Chronicle*, 31 July 1790.
16   *Hibernian Journal*, 13–15 May 1783.
17   *Freeman's Journal*, 2–23 October 1788.
18   26 Geo. III, c. 43, *Irish Statutes*, vol. xiii (1785–86), pp. 884–909.
19   *Freeman's Journal*, 2–4 January 1787, 22–24 March and 31 March–2 April 1791. The 1788 Act was 28 Geo. III, c. 49, *Irish Statutes*, vol. vol. xiv (1787–89), pp. 731–2.
20   *Walker's Hibernian Magazine*, March 1785, p. 167.
21   *Hibernian Journal*, 5–7 September 1783.
22   *Freeman's Journal*, 11–13 February, 2–4 October and 30 October–1 November 1787; *Hibernian Journal*, 15 September 1786, 2 November 1787. For an account of McGowran's career, see Henry, *Dublin Hanged*, pp. 104.
23   Trinity College seems to have particularly prone to this form of theft. *Walker's Hibernian Magazine*, November 1790, p. 479.
24   5 George II, c. X, *Irish Statutes*, vol. v; 27 Geo. III, c. 52, *ibid.*, vol. xiii, pp. 361–67.
25   *Walker's Hibernian Magazine*, October 1787, p. 558.
26   *Walker's Hibernian Magazine*, January 1789, p. 53 and February 1789, p. 110.
27   *Walker's Hibernian Magazine*, April 1788, p. 221.
28   *Hibernian Journal*, 15–17 September 1783; *Dublin Evening Post*, 16 September 1783.
29   *Dublin Journal*, 30 November 1784.
30   Jaroslav Hasek, *The Good Soldier Svejk and His Fortunes in the World War*, London: Penguin Books, 1974.
31   *Freeman's Journal*, 13–16 January 1787.
32   17 & 18 Geo III, c. 21, *Irish Statutes*, vol. xi (1776–80), pp. 196–7.
33   *Walker's Hibernian Magazine*, September 1787, pp. 502–3, October 1787, p. 559; *Freeman's Journal*, 4–6 and 6–9 October 1787.
34   *Dublin Chronicle*, 8 July and 9 September 1788, 6 March and 6 April 1790.
35   *Dublin Chronicle*, 25 October 1788.
36   *Hibernian Journal*, 17 December 1784.
37   *Ibid.*
38   *Hibernian Journal*, 4 October 1786.
39   *Freeman's Journal*, 28–31 October 1786.
40   *Hibernian Journal*, 23 July 1783; *Freeman's Journal*, 4–6 October 1787 and 3–5 May 1791.
41   *Dublin Chronicle*, 5 July 1788.
42   *Hibernian Journal*, 29 September–1 October 1783.
43. *Hibernian Journal*, 4–7 and 14–16 April 1783.
44   The following account of Barrington is based on an anonymous 44pp. pamphlet, *The Genuine Life and Trial of George Barrington, From his Birth, in June 1755, to the Time of his Conviction at the Old-Bailey in September, 1790, for Robbing Henry Hare Townsend, Esq. of his Gold Watch, Seals, etc.*, London: Robert Barker, 1792. This was used extensively by Richard S. Lambert, *The Prince of Pickpockets: A Study of George Barrington Who Left His Country For His Country's Good*, London: Faber, 1930. There is a useful list of Barrington's writings, real and attributed, by J.A. Ferguson in the Royal Australian

Historical Society, *Journal and Proceedings*, vol. XVI (1930), pp. 51–80. A new biography is long overdue.

45 *Ibid.*

46 These were depicted in *The Memoirs of George Barrington*. See Plate 5.

47 *Hibernian Journal*, 20 September 1784.

48 *Freeman's Journal*, 7–9 February 1788. (Original emphasis.)

49 According to the *Dublin Chronicle* of 27 February 1790, Barrington was extremely fortunate to have escaped prosecution for a theft of money from a woman passenger whom he had befriended on the packet-boat from Holyhead to Dublin.

50 See H.D. Miles, *Pugilistica: the History of British Boxing ...* 3 vols., Edinburgh: J. Grant, 1906, I, p. 71. Mendoza's daughter, Sophia, was transported to Van Diemen's Land in 1828 for larceny. (P. Tardiff, *Notorious Strumpets and Dangerous Girls: Convict Women in Van Diemen's Land 1803–1829*, Sydney: Angus & Robertson, 1990, pp. 1576–9.)

51 *Morning Post*, 11 March 1790.

52 *Dublin Morning Post*, 16 September 1790. See also, *Freeman's Journal*, 8–11 and 15–18 May 1790.

53 Lambert. *The Prince of Pickpockets*, p. 169.

54 *Freeman's Journal*, 11–13 March 1790; *Morning Post*, 9 and 16 March 1790.

55 *Dublin Chronicle*, 15 April 1790.

56 Joseph Holt, *A Rum Story: The Adventures of Joseph Holt Thirteen Years in New South Wales (1800–12)*, ed. by Peter O'Shaughnessy, Sydney: Kangaroo Press, 1988, pp. 51–2.

57 Barrington's time in New South Wales has been described by Lambert, *The Prince of Pickpockets*, and by Frank Clune in *Rascals, Ruffians and Rebels of Early Australia*, Sydney: Angus & Roberston, 1987, pp. 1–14. See also, *Australian Dictionary of Biography*, vol. I, pp. 62–3.

58 The prologue, now known to have been written by Henry Carter of Leicester, was first published in the *Annual Register* for 1801. Attribution to Barrington derives from its publication in *The History of New South Wales* under his name in 1802. (*Australian Encyclopaedia*, vol. I, Sydney: Angus & Robertson, 1958, pp. 438–9.)

59 *Freeman's Journal*, 3–5 October 1786.

60 *Walker's Hibernian Magazine*, August 1790, p. 191.

61 *Hibernian Journal*, 24 November 1784. See also, *Hibernian Journal*, 15 December 1784.

62 *Hibernian Journal*, 5 November 1784.

63 *Ibid.*

64 *Freeman's Journal*, 15–18 September, 20–22 September and 20–23 October 1787.

65 *Hibernian Journal*, 8 December 1784.

66 *Freeman's Journal*, 16–19 December 1786. The relevant Act was 23 & 24 Geo. III, c. 57. For further details, see Patrick Meehan, 'Early Dublin Public Lighting', *Dublin Historical Record*, vol. V, no. 4 (June–August 1943), pp. 130–136.

67 *Walker's Hibernian Magazine*, June 1787, p. 334.

68 *Dublin Evening Post*, 9 September 1783.

69 *Hibernian Journal*, 23–25 April 1783.

70   26 Geo. III, c. 24, *Irish Statutes*, vol. XIII (1785–86), p. 751.
71   *Freeman's Journal*, 15–18 September 1787.
72   *Walker's Hibernian Magazine*, November 1786, p. 615.
73   *Walker's Hibernian Magazine*, October 1788, pp. 557–8.
74   *Walker's Hibernian Magazine*, October 1788, p. 559; *Dublin Chronicle*, 9–11 October 1788.
75   *Morning Post*, 23 April 1791.
76   *Morning Post*, 6 August 1789; *Freeman's Journal*, 23–26 April 1791.
77   *Hibernian Journal*, 10 December 1784.
78   *Hibernian Journal*, 2–4 August 1784.
79   *Hibernian Journal*, 30 October 1786. For other examples, see *Walker's Hibernian Magazine*, January 1790, p. 95 (Gort, Co. Clare). For the significance of the attack, see M. Elliott,*Wolfe Tone: Prophet of Irish Independence*, Yale University Press, 1989, pp. 38–9.
80   *Walker's Hibernian Magazine*, December 1789, p. 670.
81   *Morning Post*, 5 April 1791
82   *Ibid.*

Chapter 3

1   *Hibernian Journal*, 26 July 1784.
2   *Dublin Journal*, 12–14 October 1784.
3   *Hibernian Journal*, 30 July 1784.
4   Lady Gilbert, ed., *Calendar of Ancient Records of Dublin in the Possession of the Municipal Corporation of that City*, vol. XIV, Dublin: Dollard Ltd., 1909, pp. 148–9.
5   17 and 18 Geo. III, c. 11, *Irish Statutes*, vol. XI (1776–80), pp. 13–29
6   *Morning Post*, 15 March 1783. See also, B. Henry, 'Machine in the Gallows', *Alumnus*, 1991, p. 43.
7   A good deal of the available information about Newgate has been digested from Bernadette Doorley in her chapter in David Dickson, ed., *The Gorgeous Mask: Dublin 1700–1850*, pp. 121–31. Apart frm the various parliamentary reports published in *JIHC*, other sources which can be consulted are J. Warburton, J. Whitelaw and R. Walsh, *History of the City of Dublin* ... , 2 vols., Dublin, 1818, and Maurice Craig, *Dublin 1660–1860*, Dublin: Allen Figgis Ltd., 1952, pp. 197–9.
8   *Hibernian Journal*, 27 September 1780.
9   Gilbert, *Calendar of Ancient Records of Dublin*, vol. XIII, pp. 224–5.
10   In early October 1784, Lord Mayor Thomas Greene ordered the market to be transferred 'to some convenient place near the Merchant's-quay or Old-bridge ...', but nothing seems to have come of this. *Freeman's Journal*, 12–14 October 1784.
11   For information on Cooley, see Craig, *Dublin 1660–1860*, pp. 195–99.
12   Dublin, 1780, p. 58.
13   John Howard, *The State of the Prisons in England and Wales, with Some Preliminary Observations, and an Account of Some Foreign Prisons*, Warrington: William Eyres, 1776.

14 Thos. King Moylan, 'The Little Green', Part I, *Dublin Historical Record*, vol. VIII, no. 3 (June–August 1946), p. 90.

15 Joseph P. Starr, 'The enforcing of law and order in eighteenth century Ireland: A Study of Irish Police and Prisons from 1665 to 1800', Ph.D. Thesis, Trinity College, Dublin, 1968, p. 465.

16 'Report of the Committee appointed to enquire into the State of the Gaols and Prisons in this Kingdom', 15 June 1782, *JIHC*, vol. XII (1788), p. dxxxiii. Howard's detailed report of his observations on Irish prisons was published posthumously in *Account of the Principal Lazarettos in Europe and ... Those in Great Britain and Ireland*, London, 1791.

17 Craig, *Dublin 1660–1860*, p. 198.

18 Warburton, Whitelaw and Walsh, *History of the City of Dublin*, vol. I, p. 1047. See also, G.N. Wright, *An Historical Guide to Ancient and Modern Dublin*, 2nd edn., London, 1825, p. 112.

19 Gilbert, *Calendar of the Ancient Records of Dublin*, vol. XIII, p. 383.

20 *Freeman's Journal*, 6–8 February 1787.

21 *Freeman's Journal*, 24–27 July 1790.

22 'Report of the Committee', 15 June 1782, p. dxxxiii.

23 Starr, 'The enforcing of law and order', pp. 489–91.

24 *Freeman's Journal*, 14–17 May 1785.

25 Gilbert, *Calendar of the Ancient Records of Dublin*, vol. XIII, p. 350.

26 *Ibid.*, p. 126.

27 *Dublin Chronicle*, 17 May 1788.

28 Warburton, Whitelaw and Walsh, *History of the City of Dublin ...*, vol. I, pp. 1048–9.

29 *Hibernian Journal*, 30 July–1 August 1783.

30 *Hibernian Journal*, 12 July 1784.

31 *Hibernian Journal*, 17 July 1784; *Dublin Journal*, 15–17 July 1784.

32 *Hibernian Journal*, 19 July 1784.

33 *Hibernian Journal*, 6 August 1784.

34 *Ibid.*

35 *Hibernian Journal*, 28 February 1785.

36 *Hibernian Journal*, 7 January 1786.

37 *Freeman's Journal*, 19–22 June 1784. See also, *Hibernian Journal*, 23 June 1784.

38 Freida Kelly, *A History of Kilmainham Gaol: The Dismal House of Little Ease*, Dublin: Mercier Press, 1988, p. 17. This is the best available published summary of the history of the two Kilmainhams.

39 *Walker's Hibernian Magazine*, February 1784, p. 111.

40 *Hibernian Journal*, 23 June 1784.

41 *Ibid.*

42 *Hibernian Journal*, 23 June 1784.

43 *Hibernian Journal*, 22 October 1784.

44 *Walker's Hibernian Magazine*, July 1787, p. 389.

45 Cited by A.J. Nowlan, 'Kilmainham Jail', *Dublin Historical Record*, vol. XV (1958), p. 106.

46 *Hibernian Journal*, 11 June 1787.

47 *Hibernian Journal*, 8 June 1785.

48 *Freeman's Journal*, 26–28 April 1787.

49 Nowlan, 'Kilmainham Jail', p. 106.
50 *Hibernian Journal*, 31 August 1789.
51 *Walker's Hibernian Magazine*, March 1786, p. 166; *Freeman's Journal*, 18–21 March 1786.
52 Cited by Kelly, *Kilmainham Gaol*, p. 20. Howard's 1787 visit to Dublin was widely reported (see, e.g., *Hibernian Journal*, 11 June 1787).
53 *Hibernian Journal*, 5–7 September 1783.
54 *Hibernian Journal*, 7 July 1784.
55 *Hibernian Journal*, 1 December 1784.
56 'Report from the Committee appointed to inquire into the present State, Situation, and Management of the public Prisons, Jails, and Bridewells, of this Kingdom', *JIHC*, vol. vii (1783), p. cxxxi.
57 *Dublin Journal*, 4–6 January 1787; *Freeman's Journal*, 4–6 January 1787.
58 'Report from the Committee appointed to enquire into the present State, Situation and Management of the public Prisons, Gaols and Bridewells of this Kingdom', *JIHC*, vol. xi (1787), p. dxxx.
59 *Hibernian Journal*, 9 May 1787.
60 *Walker's Hibernian Magazine*, May 1787, p. 279.
61 *Hibernian Journal*, 29 May 1786. For a detailed study of Fitzpatrick's career as a social reformer, see Oliver MacDonagh, *The Inspector-General: Sir Jeremiah Fitzpatrick and the Politics of Social Reform, 1783–1802*, London: Croom Helm, 1981.
62 Jeremiah Fitzpatrick, *An Essay on Gaol-Abuses, and on the Means of Redressing Them: Together with the General Method of Treating Disorders to which Prisoners are Most Incident*, Dublin: P. Byrne & C. Brown, 1784.
63 27 Geo. III, c. 39, *Irish Statutes*, vol. xiv (1787–89), pp. 334–338.
64 'Report on the State of Gaols and Prisons', *JIHC*, vol. xii (1788), pp. dccxxxii–dccxxxvi.
65 *Irish Statutes*, vol. xi (1776–80), pp. 124–25.
66 Howard, *An Account of the Principal Lazarettos*.
67 'Report of the Committee appointed to inquire into the present State and Situation of the Public Gaols and Prisons throughout this Kingdom', 11 July 1793, *JIHC*, vol. xvii (1793), p. ccccviii.
68 *Hibernian Journal*, 20 August 1788.
69 *Hibernian Journal*, 4 April, 14 May and 25 July 1783.
70 *Hibernian Journal*, 5 January 1784.
71 *Hibernian Journal*, 10 May 1784.
72 *Hibernian Journal*, 28 June 1784.
73 *Hibernian Journal*, 1 October 1784.
74 *Hibernian Journal*, 18 October 1784.
75 *Hibernian Journal*, 8 December 1784.
76 *Hibernian Journal*, 11 February 1785.
77 *Hibernian Journal*, 2 March 1785.
78 *Hibernian Journal*, 18 and 23 May 1785.
79 *Hibernian Journal*, 17 August 1785.
80 *Hibernian Journal*, 28 November 1785.
81 17 and 18 Geo. III, c. 11 , *Irish Statutes*, vol. xi (1776–80), pp. 13–29.
82 These figures are based on the list for the period 1780–95 made by Brian Henry, *Dublin Hanged*, pp. 173–84. The list is by no means a complete one, however.

83 *Hibernian Journal*, 8–10 August 1783.
84 *Hibernian Journal*, 4–6 August 1783.
85 *Hibernian Journal*, 8–9 August 1783.
86 *Hibernian Journal*, 26 July 1784.
87 *Hibernian Journal*, 2 December 1785.
88 *Maryland Gazette*, 12 May 1785.
89 *Walker's Hibernian Magazine*, June 1785, p. 336.
90 *Freeman's Journal*, 4–6 November 1788.
91 *Freeman's Journal*, 4–6 November 1788.
92 Eden, *Principles of Penal Law*, p. 28.
93 *Walker's Hibernian Magazine*, January 1783, p. 53; *Hibernian Journal*, 20 January 1783. See Brian Henry, 'The Machine in the Gallows', *Alumnus*, 1991, pp. 43–8.
94 *Walker's Hibernian Magazine*, August 1783, p. 448. For other bungled hangings, see *ibid.*, March 1784, p. 166 and July 1789, p. 591.
95 Henry, *Dublin Hanged*, p. 85.
96 *Hibernian Journal*, 22 March 1784.
97 *Freeman's Journal*, 7–10 August 1790.
98 J.E. Walsh, *Rakes and Ruffians: The Underworld of Georgian Dublin*, Dublin: Four Courts Press, 1979, pp. 73–4. (Originally published in 1847 as *Ireland Sixty Years Ago*.)
99 *Ibid.*, p. 70. Lambert is discussed in Chapter 4.
100 For the full texts of these songs, see Donal O'Sullivan, ed., 'Dublin Slang Songs, with Music', *Dublin Historical Record*, vol. I (1933), pp. 78–93.
101. *Walker's Hibernian Magazine,* September 1788, p. 446.
102. O'Sullivan, 'Dublin Slang Songs', p. 85.

Chapter 4

1 *JHC*, vol. xl, p. 1161. (Original emphasis.)
2 E. Herrick Cheeseman, *White Servitude in Pennsylvania*, Philadelphia, 1926, p. 254.
3 'Estimate of a Contract to be Entered into between W.H. for receiving on Board a Ship in the River Thames, such Convicts as may be sent from the Different Gaols, Transporting the same to a Port in N. America', n.d., T/1/581, f. 135; 'W.H.' appears to have been William Hamilton, not William Hurford as assumed by Frost. Campbell to Treasury, 27 December 1782, *ibid.*, f. 137.
4 Frost, *Botany Bay Mirages*, p. 18, suggests that the contractor William Hurford may have taken them to Nova Scotia. If this can be established, it may explain the mysterious report by Nova Scotia historian, Beamish Murdoch, of the attempted landing of convicts at Halifax on 1 November 1784 (*History of Nova Scotia*, vol. iii, p. 37).
5 A detailed account of Moore's initiatives and their outcome can be found in A.R. Ekirch, 'Great Britain's Secret Convict Trade to America, 1783–1784', *American Historical Review*, vol. lxxxix (1984), pp. 1285–91, upon which the present work has drawn. Salmon's original letters to Moore can be found in the Peter Forge Collection, ser. 8D, Woolsey and Salmon Letterbook, Library of Congress, Washington D.C. According to Ekirch (p. 1287),

Salmon did not know Moore but was given his name by his (Moore's) brother Phillip who was a merchant in Philadelphia.

6 North to George III, 11 July 1783, Sir John Fortescue, ed., *The Correspondence of King George The Third from 1760 to December 1783 ...*, 6 vols., London: Macmillan & Co., 1928, vol. vi, p. 415.

7 George III to North, 12 July 1783, *ibid.*, p. 416.

8 North to George III, 18 July 1783, *ibid.*, p. 418. A search of the records of the Continental Congress has not revealed any resolution of this kind. Roscoe R. Hill, ed., *Journals of the Continental Congress 1774–1789*, 34 vols., Washington D.C.: Government Printer, 1937, xxiv [1 January–29 August 1783].

9 George III to North, 18 July 1783, *The Correspondence of King George the Third*, vol. vi, p. 419.

10 Salmon to Moore, 30 April 1783, Woolsey and Salmon letterbook.

11 Salmon to Moore, 3 October 1783, *ibid.*

12 Salmon to Moore, 22 November 1783, *ibid.*

13 Salmon to Moore, 20 December 1783, *ibid.*

14 *Archives of Maryland xlviii: Journal and Correspondence of the State Council of Maryland 1781–1784*, Baltimore: Maryland Historical Society, 1931, p. 484. According to Ekirch, 'Great Britain's Secret Convict Trade', p. 1289, note 15, Ridley had received the information in a letter from Jay who was then in Paris for the peace negotiations. Jay had in turn been informed by a London merchant, Joshua Johnson. I am grateful to Dan Byrnes for pointing out to me that Ridley had been Duncan Campbell's agent since 1770. Personal communication, 22 August 1996.

15 Gillen, 'His Majesty's Mercy', pp. 84–6. For official correspondence over the outcome of the voyage, see Moore to Nepean, 21 April 1786, *FO* 72/7 and Nepean to Moore, 5 June 1786, *FO* 72/8.

16 Nepean to Colonel Despard, 15 September 1785, *FO* 72/6, f. 902.

17 *Ibid.*, pp. 86–7. For Moore's own account of the third voyage, see his letter to Nepean of 21 April 1786, *FO* 72/7 and his undated petition to the Commissioners of the Treasury seeking compensation, *HO* 42/9, ff. 565–6.

18 Cited by Martin, 'Alternatives to Botany Bay', p. 158.

19 Cited by Gillen, 'His Majesty's Mercy', p. 86.

20 For the earlier despatch of convicts to Cape Coast Castle, see Oldham, *Britain's Convicts*, pp. 68–81; for the Lemain and Das Voltas Bay plans, see *ibid.*, pp. 95–6.

21 Shaw, *Convicts and the Colonies*, p. 48.

22 *Daily Universal Register*, 9 December 1786, cited by Martin, 'A London Newspaper', p. 176.

23 See below, Chapter 11, p. 216.

24 Shaw, *Convicts and the Colonies*, p. 138.

25 North to Parr, 12 August 1783, *CO* 218/25, f. 403, cited by Gillen, 'His Majesty's Mercy', p. 62.

26 Beamish Murdoch, *History of Nova Scotia ...*, 3 vols., Halifax [Nova Scotia]: Barnes, 1865–67, vol. i, pp. 6–7. The twelve survivors were rescued by the original pilot, Chedotel, who was sent back for the purpose by King Henry IV.

27 Shaw, *Convicts and the Colonies*, p. 43.

28 Mackay, *A Place of Exile*, pp. 38–9.
29 Murdoch, *History of Nova Scotia*, vol. III, pp. 34–5. Oddly enough, there is no mention of the *Sally* and her passengers in James W. St. G. Walker, *The Black Loyalists: The Search for a Promised Land in Nova Scotia and Sierra Leone 1783–1870*, New York: Dalhousie University Press, 1976. However, they are dealt with briefly by Allan Everett Marble, *Surgeons, Smallpox, and the Poor: A History of Medicine and Social Conditions in Nova Scotia, 1749–1799*, Montreal: McGill-Queen's University Press, 1993, pp. 147, 148, 151, 157.
30 'List of the Americans now in Bridewell who wish to be transported to Nova Scotia', 6 May 1784, *CO* 217/35, f. 186.
31 Peckham to Sydney, n.d. [May 1784], *CO* 217/35, f. 186.
32 Marble, *Surgeons*, p. 157.
33 Parr to Sydney, 1 September 1784, *CO* 217/56, f. 218. For Sydney's disingenuous reply of 5 October 1784, see *ibid.*, pp. 227–8.
34 Parr to Sydney ('private'), 26 July 1784, *CO* 217/59, f. 192.
35 Parr to Nepean ('private'), 9 October 1784, *CO* 217/59, f. 208.
36 Murdoch, *History of Nova Scotia*, vol. III, pp. 34–5.
37 See Frost, *Botany Bay Mirages*, pp. 17–18. Mackay, *A Place of Exile*, p. 29, refers to a failed attempt to land felons in Newfoundland but unfortunately provides no details.
38 *JHC*, vol. XL, London, 1803, p. 954. (Original emphasis.)
39 See Ged Martin, 'A London Newspaper and the Founding of Botany Bay, August 1786–May 1787', in Martin, *The Founding of Australia*, p. 176.
40 Frost, *Botany Bay Mirages*, pp. 17–18.
41 *Hibernian Journal*, 9 July 1784.
42 *Hibernian Journal*, 13 August 1784.
43 *Ibid.*
44 *Hibernian Journal*, 6–8 August 1783.
45 Eden, *Principles of Penal Law*, p. 34. The principle was accepted in 1785 by the Beauchamp Committee, which was also no doubt aware of Nepean's confidential inquiry of October 1784 as to whether the Portuguese government would be interested in taking British convicts. See *JHC*, vol. XL, p. 1162; Mackay, *A Place of Exile*, p. 42.
46 *Dublin Evening Post*, 23 August 1783; *Hibernian Journal*, 25 August 1783. It is possible that the correspondent was John Meloney, an Irish-born Loyalist who was the first settler at Sydney. See McKinnon, *Old Sydney*, pp. 5–8.
47 *Hibernian Journal*, 16 January 1784. I can find no evidence that Lord North's government in fact had such a scheme in mind, but it is certainly plausible.
48 Richard Brown, *A History of the Island of Cape Breton ...*, London: Sampson Low, Son, & Marston, 1869, p. 392.
49 J.G. MacKinnon, *Old Sydney: Sketches of the Town and its People in Days Gone By*, Sydney [Cape Breton], 1918, pp. 31–2.
50 Anon. to anon., 5 August 1789, *Dominion of Canada. Report of the Department of Public Archives for the Year 1944*, Ottawa: Government Printer, 1945, p. xxxvii.
51 *Hibernian Journal*, 8–10 September 1783.
52 *Ibid.*
53 *Hibernian Journal*, 10–12 September 1783.
54 *Hibernian Journal*, 8 January 1783 and 1 September 1784.

55 *Hibernian Journal*, 29 September 1784.
56 *Hibernian Journal*, 3 January 1785.
57 For the details of this extraordinarily makeshift scheme, see Oldham, *Britain's Convicts*, pp. 95–108 and Alan Atkinson, 'The Convict Republic', *The Push from the Bush*, no. 18 (October 1984), pp. 66–84.
58 *Hibernian Journal*, 27 April 1785.
59 *Ibid.*
60 *Hibernian Journal*, 20 June 1787.
61 William Eden, *A History of New Holland from its first Discovery in 1616 ...*, London, 1787. Oldham, *Britain's Convicts*, p. 229, n.515, confuses this with George Barrington's later attributed book.
62 *Walker's Hibernian Magazine*, February 1786, pp. 57–8 (subsequent quotation from this source).
63 *Freeman's Journal*, 13–16 January 1787.
64 R.R. Hill, ed., *Journals of the Continental Congress 1774–1789, Vol. XXXIV, 1788–1789*, Washington D.C.: United States Government Printing Office, 1937, pp. 494–5, 528; *Archives of Maryland*, vol. XLVIII, p. 484.

Chapter 5

1 *Hibernian Journal*, 8 May 1783. For different estimates of Irish emigration to North America and the Caribbean, see Truxes, *Irish-American Trade*, p. 129–30.
2 According to R.C. Nash, by the mid-1790s Irish exports to the United States had reached eight times the level achieved before the Revolutionary War. 'Irish Atlantic Trade in the Seventeenth and Eighteenth Centuries', *William and Mary Quarterly*, vol. XLII (1985), p. 340.
3 Buckingham to Townshend, 2 February 1783, BM Add. MSS 40177.
4 *Hibernian Journal*, 12–14 and 14–17 March 1783.
5 *Freeman's Journal*, 18–20 February 1783.
6 *Freeman's Journal*, 6–8 February 1783.
7 *Freeman's Journal*, 20–22 February 1783; *Hibernian Journal*, 21 February 1783.
8 *Hibernian Journal*, 14–17 March 1783.
9 *Hibernian Journal*, 23–25 April 1783.
10 Built in 1777, the *Duke of Leinster* had been bought by Bryan in the same year for £4,270.10.2 and he had subsequently spent about £500 fitting her out in Dublin. The ship's history and specifications were set out in the certificate of registration for the British plantation trade issued at the Customs House in Dublin on 20 March 1788. *CO* 152/70.
11 *Hibernian Journal*, 2–7 May 1783
12 *Hibernian Journal*, 30 June–2 July 1783.
13 *Hibernian Journal*, 19–21 September 1783.
14 *Ibid.*
15 *Hibernian Journal*, 22–24 September 1783.
16 *Hibernian Journal*, 20–11 October 1783.
17 *Hibernian Journal*, 24–26 October 1783.
18 *Dublin Journal*, 30 November 1784.
19 *Freeman's Journal*, 19–21 October 1786.

20 *Dublin Journal*, 18 November 1784.
21 *Walker's Hibernian Magazine*, March 1784, p. 166.
22 Phineas Bond to the Duke of Leeds, 3 January 1790, in J.F. Jamison, ed., 'Letters of Phineas Bond, British Consul at Philadelphia, to the Foreign Office of Great Britain, 1790–1794', *Annual Report of the American Historical Association for the Year 1897*, Washington D.C., 1898, p. 455.
23 25 Geo. III, c. 17, *Irish Statutes*, vol. XIII (1785–86), pp. 118–122.
24 *Freeman's Journal*, 27–29 May 1788; *Walker's Hibernian Magazine*, June 1788, pp. 334–5.
25 D.W. Galenson, *White Servitude in Colonial America: An Economic Analysis*, Cambridge: Cambridge University Press, 1981, p. 179.
26 Bond to Carmarthen, 16 November 1788, in J.F. Jamison, ed., 'Letters of Phineas Bond, British Consul at Philadelphia, to the Foreign Office of Great Britain, 1787, 1788, 1789', *Annual Report of the American Historical Association for the Year 1896*, Washington D.C., 1897, pp. 582–3. For a detailed discussion of Bond and his time in the United States, see Joanne Loewe Neel, *Phineas Bond: A Study in Anglo-American Relations, 1786–1812*, Philadelphia: University of Pennsylvania Press, 1968.
27 Bond to Carmarthen, 16 November 1788, in Jamison, 'Letters of Phineas Bond ... 1787, 1788, 1789', p. 583.
28 *Ibid.*, p. 582.
29 Neel, *Phineas Bond*, p. 75; Bond to Leeds, 10 November 1789, in Jamison, 'Letters ... 1787, 1788, 1789', p. 644.
30 Bond to Leeds, 1 November 1790 and 3 January 1791, in Jamison, 'Letters ... 1790–1794', pp. 464–5, 472–3.
31 Bond to Leeds, 16 November 1788 and 10 November 1789, in Jamison, 'Letters ... 1787, 1788, 1789', pp. 581–3, 642–5.
32 Bond to Leeds, 3 January 1790, in Jamison, 'Letters ... 1790–1794', p. 455.
33 Bond to Leeds, 15 August 1789, in Jamison, 'Letters ... 1787, 1788, 1789', p. 613.
34 Bond to Leeds, 3 January 1790, in Jamison, 'Letters ... 1790–1794', p. 455.
35 Bond to Carmarthen, 2 July 1787, in Jamison, 'Letters ... 1787, 1788, 1789', p. 545. See also, Bond to Carmarthen, 20 November 1788, *ibid.*, p. 554.
36 Bond to Carmarthen, 17 May 1787, *ibid.*, p. 537.
37 *Maryland Gazette, or Baltimore General Advertiser*, 14 November 1783.
38 *Maryland Gazette, or Baltimore General Advertiser*, 21 November 1783.
39 *Maryland Gazette: or, The Baltimore General Advertiser*, 12 March 1784.
40 *Maryland Gazette: or, The Baltimore General Advertiser*, 26 March 1784.
41 *Maryland Journal and Baltimore Advertiser*, 10 February 1786.
42 *Hibernian Journal*, 12 September 1787.
43 *Freeman's Journal*, 4–6 October 1787.
44 *Freeman's Journal*, 22–25 October 1788.
45 *Hibernian Journal*, 21 January 1788.
46 *Freeman's Journal*, 2–5 October 1787; *Walker's Hibernian Magazine*, July 1786, p. 391.
47 *Hibernian Chronicle*, 20 December 1787.
48 *Hibernian Journal*, 21 January 1788.
49 *Hibernian Journal*, 21 January 1789.

50 *Hibernian Journal*, 13 October 1788, 21 January 1789.
51 *Morning Post*, 7 April 1789.
52 *Hibernian Journal*, 22 June 1789.
53 It is not the case, as asserted by Henry, *Dublin Hanged*, pp. 85–6, that Cunningham and Ellis were members of the group of convicts returned from Newfoundland to Dublin in January 1790. Their names were not on the list of the convicts embarked at St John's for Spithead on the *Elizabeth and Mary* on 24 October 1789. (See Appendix II.)
54 *Morning Post*, 9 July 1789.
55 *Hibernian Journal*, 21 February 1790.
56. *Dublin Chronicle*, 22 July 1790. See below, p.
57 For the exploits of the gang and details of their prosecution, see Henry, *Dublin Hanged*, pp. 86–9.
58 *Morning Post*, 1 January 1791; *Hibernian Journal*, 1 January 1791.
59 *Morning Post*, 30 September 1790. It is not clear whether this was the same Laurence Lynch who was convicted for robbery in April 1791 and hanged at Newgate later that month. (See Henry, *Dublin Hanged*, p. 29.)
60 *Walker's Hibernian Magazine*, January 1791, p. 95.
61 *Morning Post*, 18 February 1790.
62 *Hibernian Journal*, 26 October 1791.
63 *Walker's Hibernian Magazine*, July 1786, p. 391; *Hibernian Journal*, 13 June 1788. There is no report of when and where Lambert was transported but it was probably on the *Nancy* to St Kitt's in the Leewards in November 1784.
64 *Hibernian Journal*, 25 July 1788; *Walker's Hibernian Magazine*, July 1788, p. 446.
65 An account of Lambert's life was printed in *Freeman's Journal*, 30 September–1 October 1788.
66 *Hibernian Journal*, 10 September 1788, 12 September 1788; *Walker's Hibernian Magazine*, September 1788, pp. 502–3.
67 *PPC* 1/21; *Hibernian Journal*, 12 June 1789.
68 *Dublin Chronicle*, 6–9 September 1788.
69 *Walker's Hibernian Magazine*, November 1786, p. 615.
70 *Freeman's Journal*, 17–19 April 1787. (Original emphasis.)
71 *Freeman's Journal*, 30 November–2 December 1786.
72 *Freeman's Journal*, 20–22 May 1788.
73 *Walker's Hibernian Magazine*, September 1788, p. 503; *Dublin Chronicle*, 6–9 September 1788.
74 *Dublin Chronicle*, 23–25 April 1789.
75 K. Grose, '"A Strange Compound of Good and Ill": Laurence Hynes Halloran', in B. Reece, ed., *Exiles from Erin: Convict Lives in Ireland and Australia*, London: Macmillan, 1991, pp. 85–111.
76 *Hibernian Journal*, 12 June 1789. (Original emphasis.) For the Lewellin case and its ramifications, see Henry, *Dublin Hanged*, pp. 42–3.
77 *Hibernian Journal*, 17 June 1789.
78 *Freeman's Journal*, 25–27 June 1789.
79 Deposition of Richard Robinson in the Court of Vice-Admiralty, St John's, 21 July 1789, *HO* 28/6, ff. 281–2; *Hibernian Journal*, 10 August 1789.
80 *Morning Post*, 30 January 1790.
81 *Freeman's Journal*, 10–12 December 1789.

82 It seems unlikely that Fay became very successful in Bordeaux. L.M. Cullen makes no reference to him in 'The Irish Merchant Communities of Bordeaux, La Rochelle and Cognac in the Eighteenth Century', in L.M. Cullen and P. Butel, eds., *Negoce et Industries en France et en Irlande aux XVIIIe et XIXe Siecles*, Paris: Editions du Centre National du Recherche Scientifique, 1980, pp. 51–63.

83 *Walker's Hibernian Magazine*, December 1788, p. 671.

84 *Morning Post*, 16 July 1789.

85 Sir Jeremiah Fitzpatrick, *Thoughts on Penitentiaries*, Dublin: H. Fitzpatrick, 1790, p. 12.

Chapter 6

1   *Hibernian Journal*, 13 October 1784.

2   *Hibernian Journal*, 25 October 1784; *Freeman's Journal*, 23–26 October 1784.

3   *Freeman's Journal*, 16–18 November 1784.

4   *Ibid.*

5   P.H. Bruce, *Memoirs...*, London, 1782. For some background information on Bruce, see Michael Craton, *A History of the Bahamas*, 2nd. edn., London: Collins, 1968, pp. 137–141.

6   *Hibernian Journal*, 19 November 1784. In fact, the poor soil and arid climate of the Bahamas could not support plantation agriculture and the experiment was given up after a few years.

7   *Ibid.*

8   *Ibid.*

9   The *David* was wrecked at the entrance to Nassau harbour on or about 17 May 1784. Sandra Riley, *Homeward Bound: A History of the Bahamas Islands to 1850 with a definitive Study of Abaco in the American Loyalist Plantation Period*, Miami: Island Research, 1983, p. 160.

10 *Hibernian Journal*, 1 September 1784; *Dublin Journal*, 31 August–2 September 1784.

11 *Hibernian Journal*, 17 September 1784.

12 *Dublin Journal*, 9–11 November 1784; *Hibernian Journal*, 10 November 1784.

13 *Freeman's Journal*, 11–13 November 1784.

14 *Dublin Journal*, 12–14 October 1784.

15 *Dublin Journal*, 16 November 1784; *Hibernian Journal*, 17 November 1784.

16 *Dublin Journal*, 20 November 1784.

17 *Hibernian Journal*, 19 September 1788.

18 *Hibernian Journal*, 19 November 1784.

19 *Freeman's Journal*, 16–18 November 1784.

20 Truxes, *Anglo-American Trade*, pp. 99–100.

21 CO 241/18.

22 *Cal. S. P. Colonial: America and the West Indies (1696–97)*, p. 559, cited by Beattie, *Crime and the Courts*, p. 483.

23 Extract of a Letter from St. Eustatia, dated January 30th, 1785, *Maryland Gazette*, 7 April 1785.

24 *Maryland Gazette*, 28 April 1785. This report was reprinted in *Freeman's Journal*, 21–24 May 1785.

25 Liston to Carmarthen, 31 January 1784 [*sic*], FO 72/4, ff. 127–8.

26 *Ibid.*

27 *Hibernian Journal*, 23 May 1785; *Freeman's Journal*, 17–19 May 1785.

28 *Hibernian Journal*, 23 May 1785, 19 September 1788.

29 *Dublin Journal*, 27 November 1784.

30 *Hibernian Journal*, 22 November 1784.

31 *Hibernian Journal*, 2 May 1785. See also, *Freeman's Journal*, 12–14 May 1785.

32 *Freeman's Journal*, 20–22 September 1785.

33 *Hibernian Journal*, 26 September 1785.

34 *Freeman's Journal*, 24–27 September 1785.

35 Truxes, *Irish-American Trade*, makes no mention of this firm.

36 William Deakins Senior had come to George Town from Ireland in December 1772 and dealt in Irish indentured servants before the war. By December 1786 his son, Col. William Deakins, was running the business.

37 R.J. Brugger, *Maryland: A Middle Temperament 1634–1980*, Baltimore: Johns Hopkins University Press, 1989, pp. 156–7. A detailed history of the Company can be found in Walter S. Sanderlin, *The Great National Project: A History of the Chesapeake and Ohio Canal*, Johns Hopkins University Studies in Historical and Political Science, Series LXIV, No. 1, 1946. Some discussion of the Company's labour problems in 1785 can be found in Peter Way, *Common Labour: Workers and the Digging of North American Canals 1780–1860*, Cambridge: Cambridge University Press, 1993, pp. 37–8. However, Way appears to be unaware of the convict origins of some of the Irish workers at Seneca Falls. A useful popular account of the canal project, indicating its topography, is Wilbur E. Garrett, 'George Washington's Patowmack Canal', *National Geographic*, vol. 171, no. 6 (June 1987), pp. 716–53.

38 See John Pickell, *A New Chapter in the Early Life of Washington in Connection with the Narrative History of the Potomac Company*, New York: Burt Franklin, 1858, and Michael J.O. O'Brien, *George Washington's Association with the Irish*, New York: P.J. Kennedy & Sons, 1937, pp. 190–3.

39 Way, *Common Labour*, pp. 39–40.

40 Records of the Potomac Company, National Archives, Washington [NAW], Proceedings. 1785–1828, RG 79, Box 2, ff. 10, 14.

41 Plunket was a Dubliner and Nesbitt was from Co. Down. For a brief profile of Nesbitt's American career, see E.R.R. Green, 'The Irish in American Business and Professions', in D.N. Doyle and O. Dudley Edwards, eds., *America and Ireland, 1776–1976: The American Identity and the Irish Connection*, London: Greenwood Press, 1980, p. 195.

42 Records of the Potomac Company, 'Waste Book'. 1785–1800. NAW RG79/167, vol. 1, f. 10. It is not clear exactly how many were purchased but as Fitzgerald paid £100.5.0 and the market price for an unskilled servants was £10, it was probably about ten. See also, *Maryland Gazette*, 7 July 1786; *Hibernian Journal*, 19 July 1788. Fitzgerald had come to Alexandria in 1769 where he developed a successful import–export business, trading with Britain and the West Indies. Wounded at the battle of

Monmouth, New Jersey, in June 1778, he retired from the Revolutionary Army at the rank of colonel. He was elected as a director of the Potowmack Company in May 1785 and Mayor of Alexandria in June 1786.

43 Way, *Common Labour*, pp. 32–3.

44 *Virginia Journal*, 23 March 1786.

45 *Maryland Gazette*, 10 August 1786, cited by Way, *Common Labour*, p. 33.

46 Cited by Thomas F. Hahn, *George Washington's Canal at Great Falls, Virginia*, Shepherdstown [West Virginia]: American Canal and Transportation Center, 1976, p. 18.

47 *Virginia Journal and Alexandria Advertiser*, 26 January 1786. The report was reprinted in the *Maryland Gazette*, 16 February 1786. Nevertheless, escapes continued.

48 *Virginia Journal and Alexandria Advertiser*, 2 March 1786.

49 *Virginia Journal and Alexandria Advertiser*, 11 and 18 May, 15 June, 24 July, 3, 13, 17 and 24 August, 7 September, 16 November 1786.

50 *Virginia Journal and Alexandria Advertiser*, 24 August 1786. For an account of the shocking injuries sustained by another Irish worker in a blasting accident, see the *Virginia Journal and Alexandria Advertiser*, 3 August 1786.

51 *Virginia Journal*, 13 July 1786.

52 Records of the Potomac Company, 'Waste Book'. 1785–1800. NAW, RG 79/167, vol. I, ff. 24–5.

53 Records of the Potomac Company, NAW, RG 79/160, Proceedings 1785–1828, Box 2.

54 *Virginia Journal and Maryland Advertiser*, 13 July 1786.

55 *Maryland Gazette*, 7 September 1786. The report was copied from a New York report dated 29 July 1786 but the original newspaper in which it was published cannot be identified. (Subsequent quotations from this source.)

56 *Ibid.*

57 *Ibid.* (Original emphasis.)

58 *Hibernian Journal*, 26 May 1786.

59 *Ibid.*

60 *Hibernian Journal*, 2 June 1786.

61 *Freeman's Journal*, 13–15 June 1786.

62 *Hibernian Journal*, 19 June 1786.

63 *Freeman's Journal*, 20–22 June 1786.

64 *Hibernian Journal*, 19 June 1786.

65 *Freeman's Journal*, 27–29 March 1787; *Hibernian Journal*, 19 September 1788; *Dublin Chronicle*, 16 September 1788.

66 NAW, RG 79/167, vol. I, f. 28. Robert Townshend Hooe was a partner with Richard Harrison in the merchant firm of Hooe and Harrison which seems to have been involved in trade with the West Indies. He was also a sheriff of Fairfax County where John Fitzgerald was a Justice of the Peace.

67 Way, *Common Labour*, p. 38.

68 See, e.g., the *Maryland Journal* advertisements for Michael Welch and Robert McCann on 8 January 1788 and for Dennis Holland on 8 August.

69 *Hibernian Journal*, 19 June 1786.

70 For the payments made to Alcock for these shipments, see Appendix I.

71 *Hibernian Journal*, 4 May 1787.

72   *Hibernian Journal*, 9 May 1787; *Freeman's Journal*, 8–10 May 1787.

73   *Hibernian Chronicle*, 19 May 1788; *Freeman's Journal*, 15–17 May 1788.

74   *Hibernian Journal*, 21 January 1788.

75   *Hibernian Journal*, 19 September 1788; *Dublin Chronicle*, 16 September 1788.

76   As we have already noted, Murdoch, *History of Nova Scotia*, vol. III, p. 37, reported the attempted landing of convicts at Halifax on 1 November 1784 and this may have been the shipment William Hamilton was supposed to have arranged in 1783 There is no other record of an Irish or British shipment arriving in Nova Scotia in 1787, although the *Chance* which left Dublin in October 1787 was originally reported as being bound there (amongst other places). It is possible that the Irish newspaper report was based on the November 1784 incident.

77   R.R. Hill, ed., *Journals of the Continental Congress, 1774–1789*, vol. XXXIII, 1787, p. 511.

78   The *Dublin Chronicle* of 16 September 1788 reported that Irish convicts had been landed at Massachusetts.

79   *Freeman's Journal*, 6–8 May 1787.

80   *Hibernian Journal*, 15 October 1787; *Freeman's Journal*, 11–13 October 1787, 23–25 October 1787. According to the *Maryland Gazette* of 8 August 1787, there were 106 men and 24 women shipped.

81   Deposition made by James Hamilton to Chief Justice, New Providence, 14 January 1788, CO 23/27, ff. 106–7. The following account of the voyage is based on this source, together with reports published in the *Kingstown General Advertiser*, 19 April 1788; *Hibernian Journal*, 19 September 1788; and *Dublin Chronicle*, 16 September 1788. According to the latter, there were only 44 survivors.

82   [William Wylly], *A Short Account of the Bahama Islands, Their Climate, Productions, &c. ...*, London, 1789, p. 42.

83   *Ibid.*, pp. 42–3. The names of the convicts were given as: Walter Gibbons, John Waylin, Mary Thornton, Judith Kelly, Mary Holmes, Thomas Dawson, Esther Daniel, Walter Mooney, Edward Short, Biddy Ferguson, Nicholas Basky, James Neil, James Burns, Bernard Doyle, Mary Burke, Mary Galvin, Nell Connor, Jane Mooney, Mary Cork, Mary Fairlie, Betsey McGowan, Thomas Daniel, Bridget Stacey and Thomas Glynn.

84   Craton, *A History of the Bahamas*, p. 176.

85   Dunmore to Grenville, 1 March 1790, CO 23/30, f. 192.

86   Riley, *Homeward Bound*, p. 174. See also, J. Leitch Wright Jr., *William Augustus Bowles: Director General of the Creek Nation*, Athens [Georgia]: University of Georgia Press, 1967, p. 32.

87   CO 23/30, f. 143.

88   *Maryland Gazette*, 8 August 1788.

89   *Ibid.*

90   *Maryland Journal, and Baltimore Advertiser*, 5 September 1788.

91   Wylly, *A Short Account*, p. 42. (Original emphasis.) For detailed accounts of Dunmore's troubles, including his conflict with Wylly, see Craton, *A History of the Bahamas*, pp. 173–6; Riley, *Homeward Bound*, pp. 170–9.

92   Smallwood to Samuel Chase, John Neale, Thomas Russell and Llyde [sic] Goodwin, 7 August 1788, Maryland State Papers, Series A, 6636–66–27.

93 *Ibid.*, 6636–66–251
94 Son of Sir William Temple, 6th Baronet of Stowe, Sir John Temple (c.1730–1800) had been appointed surveyor-general of customs in North America in 1760 and was one of the five original members of the Board of Customs. After his removal from this appointment he returned to England in 1772 where he became surveyor-general of customs. He was appointed Consul-General to the United States in 1785.
95 Outerbridge's original deposition, together with the other relevant papers, can be found in Papers of the Continental Congress, Record Group 360, National Archives, Washington, D.C. (microfilm group M427). With the exception of the deposition, all have been published in R.R. Hill, ed., *Journals of the Continental Congress 1774–1789*, vol. xxxiv. 1788–1789, Washington, D.C. Government Printing Office, 1937, pp. 494–5
96 *Maryland Journal, and Baltimore Advertiser*, 1 February 1788.
97 *Maryland Gazette*, 8 August 1788.
98 Dunmore to Sydney, 29 February 1788, CO 23/27
99 *Ibid.*
100 *Maryland Journal, and Baltimore Advertiser*, 5 September 1788; Wylly Memorandum, CO 23/29, f. 148.
101 Memorandum, [?] October 1789, HO 100/27, f. 323; Sydney to Dunmore, 21 June 1788, CO 23/27, f. 130.
102 Sydney to Buckingham, 16 August 1788, HO 100/23, ff. 319–20.
103 S. Douglas to J. King, 24 October 1794 (private), HO 100/52, f. 234.
104 *Kingstown General Advertiser*, 19 April 1788.
105 *Freeman's Journal*, 16–18 October 1788.
106 *Ibid.*
107 Jay to President of Congress, 3 September 1788, in Hill, *Journals of the Continental Congress*, vol. xxxiv, pp. 494–5.
108 *Ibid.*, p. 530.
109 *Ibid.*, p. 528. It is not altogether clear why Williamson and Baldwin took this initiative, although Williamson was a long-time friend of Benjamin Franklin and may well have been influenced by his anti-transportation views. Williamson's father was also an Irish Presbyterian immigrant to America in 1730 and his wife's parents were from Derry (*Dictionary of American Biography*, vol. 10, New York: Charles Scribner & Sons, 1964, pp. 298–300).
110 William Waller Hening, ed., *The Statutes at Large; Being a Collection of all the Laws of Virginia* ... , vol. xii, Richmond [Virginia]: George Cochrane, 1823, pp. 668–9 [facsimile edition, Charlottesville: University Press of Virginia, 1969]. See Appendix iii for the full text of the statute.
111 *The Papers of James Madison* ..., ed. by H.D. Gilpin, 3 vols., Washington, D.C.: Langtree & O'Sullivan, 1840. iii, p. 1430; Ballagh, *White Servitude*, p. 38.
112 This important despatch can not be found in the HO 100 series but was referred to by Grenville in his letter to Hobart of 14 December 1789, BM Add MS 59251, ff. 138–9. Hobart subsequently reported to Grenville on 22 December 1789 that the despatch could not be found in the Lord Lieutenant's office. (*Ibid.*, ff. 142–3.)

Chapter 7

1 Orde to Nepean, 17 May 1785, *HO* 100/16, f. 378.
2 For Burke's stinging attack on the Gambia proposal, see Cobbett's *Parliamentary History*, vol. XXV, London, 1815, pp. 391–2.
3 See L.M. Cullen, *An Economic History of Ireland Since 1660*, London: B.T. Bathsford Ltd., 1972, pp. 97–8.
4 Orde to Pitt, 15 November 1785, cited by Palmer, *Police and Protest*, p. 97.
5 Rutland to Pitt, 15 August 1784, *Correspondence between the Right Honble. William Pitt and Charles Duke of Rutland ... 1781–1787*, Edinburgh: John Blackwood & Sons, 1890, p. 37.
6 Draft of a letter to Rutland, 1 January 1786, *HO* 100/18, f. 5, cited by Palmer, *Police and Protest*, p. 97.
7 Henry, *Dublin Hanged*, p. 135.
8 For an account of the 1784 disturbances, see Henry, *Dublin Hanged*, pp. 66–68.
9 J.J. Donnelly, 'The Rightboy Movement, 1785–88', *Studia Hibernica*, 17 and 18 (1977–78), pp. 120–202.
10 27 Geo. III, c. 15, *Irish Statutes*, vol. XIV (1787–89), pp. 165–70; 27 Geo. III, c. 40, *ibid.*, pp. 338–45. In his discussion of the Police Act, Kevin Boyle makes no mention of its transportation provisions. ('Police in Ireland Before the Union', *Irish Jurist*, vol. VII (new series), 1972, pp. 115–37; vol. VIII (new series), pt. 1, 1973, pp. 90–116; vol. VIII (new series), no. 2, 1972, pp. 323–48.) For a more detailed discussion of the Police Act, the Riot Act and the Country Police Act, see Palmer, *Police and Protest*, pp. 96–115. For a discussion of the political context of the Riot Act, see J. Kelly, 'The Genesis of 'Protestant Ascendancy': The Rightboy Disturbances of the 1780's and their Impact upon Protestant Opinion', in G. O'Brien, ed., *Parliament, Politics and People: Essays in Eighteenth Century Irish History*, Dublin: Irish Academic Press, 1989, pp. 119–21.
11 26 Geo. III, c. 24, *Irish Statutes*, vol. XIII (1785–86), p. 758.
12 *Ibid.*, p. 760.
13 24 Geo. III, c. 56. See Shaw, *Convicts and the Colonies*, p. 49.
14 *Ibid.*
15 *Freeman's Journal*, 18–21 March 1786.
16 Cited by Palmer, *Police and Protest*, p. 101.
17 *Parliamentary Register*, vol. VI, pp. 340–1, cited by O'Brien, *Anglo-Irish Politics*, p. 111.
18 *Freeman's Journal*, 21–22 March 1786.
19 *Ibid.*
20 *Hibernian Journal*, 26 May 1786.
21 *Hibernian Journal*, 31 January 1787.
22 *Freemans's Journal*, 23–26 September 1786.
23 *Hibernian Journal*, 27 and 29 September 1786. There is no record of anyone called Crewis on board the *Endeavour* in April 1770 (J.C. Beaglehole, ed., *The Voyage of The Endeavour 1768–1771*, London: Hakluyt Society, 1968, Appendix V, pp. 588–601). It is difficult to avoid the conclusion that Crewis was a fraud.
24 *Hibernian Journal*, 4 October 1786.

25 *Freeman's Journal*, 10–12 October 1786.
26 *Freeman's Journal*, 10–12 October 1786.
27 *Hibernian Journal*, 27 September 1786.
28 *Hibernian Journal*, 27 October 1786. (Original emphasis.)
29 *Hibernian Journal*, 17 November 1786.
30 *Hibernian Journal*, 8 November 1786.
31 See A. Atkinson, 'The Ethics of Conquest, 1786', *Aboriginal History*, vol. 6, pt. 2 (1982), pp. 82–91 and Ged Martin, 'A London newspaper on the founding of Botany Bay, August 1786–May 1787', in Ged Martin, ed., *The Founding of Australia*, Sydney: Hale & Iremonger, 1978, pp. 169–84.
32 *Hibernian Journal*, 19 June 1789.
33 *Hibernian Journal*, 17 November 1786.
34 *Freeman's Journal*, 6–9 January 1787; *Dublin Journal*, 9–11 January 1787.
35 *Freeman's Journal*, 9–11 November 1786.
36 *Ibid.*
37 Elliott, *Wolfe Tone*, pp. 55–8. It is possible that Tone was also the correspondent to the *Freeman's Journal*.
38 *Hibernian Journal*, 20 April 1787.
39 *Dublin Journal*, 4–6, 9–11 January 1787.
40 *Freeman's Journal*, 6–9 January 1787.
41 Hamilton to Nepean, 29 September 1786, *HO* 100/18, f. 342.
42 Nepean to Hamilton, 24 October 1786, *HO* 100/18, ff. 369–72. The significance of the omission has been remarked on by Michael Roe, 'Motives for Australian Settlement: a document', *Tasmanian Historical Research Association, Papers and Proceedings*, 2 (1952), pp. 18–19 and by Alan Atkinson, 'Whigs and Tories and Botany Bay', in Martin, *The Founding of Australia*, p. 199.
43 Hamilton to Nepean, 1 November 1786, *HO* 100/18, f. 391.
44 Orde to Nepean, 11 November 1786, *HO* 100/18, f. 395. (Original emphasis.) The suggestion is an interesting echo of Henry Cromwell's 1657 letter to Secretary Thurloe about the proposal to send 2,000 Irish children to Barbados (see Chapter 1).
45 *Irish Parliamentary Debates*, vol. XI (1791), p. 226, cited (with some errors) by R. McDowell, *Irish Public Opinion 1750–1800*, London: Faber, 1944, p. 135.
46 *Irish Parliamentary Debates*, vol. XI (1791), pp. 225–6.
47 For a discussion of the issue, see O'Brien, *Anglo-Irish Politics*, pp. 125–6.
48 Rutland to Sydney, 16 December 1786, *HO* 100/18, f. 417.
49 *Ibid.*
50 *Freeman's Journal*, 5–7 December 1786.
51 George had been elected to this position by Dublin Corporation in November 1785 in place of Dudley Hussey, who had died in office. He resigned in May 1794 after being appointed one of the barons of His Majesty's Court of Exchequer in Ireland and William Walker was elected to replace him.
52 *Hibernian Journal*, 13 December 1786.
53 *Freeman's Journal*, 16–19 December 1786.
54 *Freeman's Journal*, 30 September–3 October 1786, 26–28 October 1786; *Hibernian Journal*, 13 November 1786, 15 November 1786.

55 *Freeman's Journal*, 30 September–3 October and 9–11 November 1786.

56 *Freeman's Journal*, 26–28 October 1786; *Hibernian Journal*, 1 November 1786.

57 *Freeman's Journal*, 30 September–3 October 1786.

58 *Hibernian Journal*, 15 November 1786; *Walker's Hibernian Magazine*, November 1786, p. 616.

59 See Appendix III for the 7 November 1789 listing which includes a James Cunningham.

60 'List of Prisoners under Sentence or Order of Transportation as received from the different parts of the Country & transported from Cork in the Queen Transport', National Maritime Museum, Greenwich, MS MKH/9.

61 For an account of this popular institution, see Walsh, *Rakes and Ruffians*, pp. 107–19. For the coronation of the 'King of Dalkey' for 1789, see the *Morning Post*, 7 July 1789 and *Hibernian Journal*, 10 July 1789.

62 *Freeman's Journal*, 30 November–2 December 1786. Not all the identities of those listed can be easily established.

63 *Freeman's Journal*, 2–4 January 1787.

64 *Ibid.*

65 *Walker's Hibernian Magazine*, December 1786, opp. p. 685.

66 The British Library's copy of the cartoon has the date '1784' clearly inscribed on the right hand corner of the print, together with the names of Burke, Fox and North. Interestingly, the version in *Walker's Hibernian Magazine* is a reversed image without annotation except for the identical title. I am grateful to Professor Michael Bennett of the University of Tasmania for information on the earlier provenance and political significance of the anonymous cartoon which he suggests may be by Rowlandson (personal communication, April 1996). Reproduced by Jonathan King, *The Other Side of the Coin: A Cartoon History of Australia*, Sydney: Angus & Robertson, 1976, p. 18, and by J. Hirst, *Convict Society and Its Enemies ...*, Sydney: Allen & Unwin, 1983, pp. 189–90, the cartoon has been seen by Australian historians more as 'the beginning of a stock joke' about 'law-breakers becoming law-makers' than as a satirical representation of contemporary British politics. See Michael Bennett, 'A Botany Bay Mirage: Australia's First Political Cartoon', *Tasmanian Historical Studies*, vol. 5, no. 1 (1995–96), pp. 16–18.

67 See W.J. McCormack, *The Dublin Paper War of 1786–1788: A Bibliographical and Critical Inquiry ...*, Dublin: Irish Academic Press, 1993, and Kelly, 'The genesis', p. 115.

68 *Walker's Hibernian Magazine*, December 1786, pp. 685–7.

69 See O'Brien, *Anglo-Irish Politics*, pp. 39–42.

70 For a brief but comprehensive discussion of this event, see Palmer, *Police and Protest*, pp. 84–9.

71 *Walker's Hibernian Magazine*, February 1787, p. 90.

72 *Hibernian Journal*, 26 May 1786.

73 *Ibid.*

74 *Hibernian Journal*, 2 June 1786.

75 26 Geo. III, c. 27, *Irish Statutes*, vol. XIII (1785–86), pp. 767–82.

76 *Freeman's Journal*, 9–11 February 1787.

77 *Freeman's Journal*, 20–23 January 1787.

78 *Freeman's Journal,* 6 September 1787.
79 *Dublin Journal,* 4–6 January 1787; *Freeman's Journal,* 4–6 January 1787.
80 *Hibernian Journal,* 9 May 1787.
81 *Walker's Hibernian Magazine,* May 1787, p. 279.
82 *Hibernian Journal,* 17 September 1787, *Walker's Hibernian Magazine,* September 1787, p. 593.
83 *Freeman's Journal,* 15–18 September 1787.
84 *Hibernian Journal,* 25 August 1788.
85 *Hibernian Journal,* 27 August 1788. The story of the extraordinary Frederick Lambert has been briefly outlined by Henry, *Dublin Hanged,* pp. 161–2.
86 *Hibernian Journal,* 12 May 1788.
87 *Freeman's Journal,* 12–14 October 1786.
88 *Freeman's Journal,* 28 April–1 May 1787.
89 *Hibernian Journal,* 2 May 1787.
90 Pitt to Orde, 31 March 1787, NLI MS 15905/3.
91 *Walker's Hibernian Magazine,* September 1787, p. 501.
92 *Dublin Journal,* 22 May 1788.
93 'Report from the Commssioners of Police of the present State of the several Gaols and Prisons within the District of the Metropolis ...', *JIHC,* vol. XI (1788), p. DXLIII.
94 *Hibernian Journal,* 12 May 1788.
95 For an account of this voyage, see Chapter 8.
96 *Hibernian Journal,* 23, 26 May 1788. See also, *Freeman's Journal,* 17–29 May 1788.
97 *Ibid.*
98 *Freeman's Journal,* 20–22 May 1788.
99 Buckingham to Sydney, 8 October 1788, Sydney Papers D8, NLI MS. 52.
100 For the voyage of the *Providence,* see Chapter 8.
101 *Annual Register,* 1788, vol. XXX, Chron. p. 223.
102 *The Times,* 5 December 1788, cited by Martin, 'Convict Transportation to Newfoundland', p. 86.
103 Grenville to Buckingham, 27 July 1789, *HO* 100/27, ff. 216–19.
104 Buckingham to Grenville, 11 July 1789, *Dropmore Papers,* p. 483.
105 Buckingham to Lords Justices, 11 July 1789, BL Add MS 59251.
106 Accounts of the number of convicts transported 1787–89 and the costs involved were duly published in *JIHC,* vol. XIII (1790), p. cccli.(See Appendix I.) Details for the years 1785–1787 were apparently unavailable.

Chapter 8

1 Martin, 'The Alternatives to Botany Bay', in his *The Founding of Australia,* p. 155, mistakenly describes the first of these as a British shipment.
2 *Dublin Chronicle,* 15 May 1788.
3 *Freeman's Journal,* 10–13, 15–17 and 17–20 May 1788; *Dublin Chronicle,* 15 May 1788.
4 *Freeman's Journal,* 15–17 May 1788.
5 *Freeman's Journal,* 22–24 May 1788.
6 *Freeman's Journal,* 10–13 May 1788.

7 *Ibid.*

8 *Freeman's Journal*, 13–15 May 1788. (Original emphasis.)

9 *Freeman's Journal*, 15–17 May 1788.

10 *Hibernian Journal*, 19 May 1788.

11 *Freeman's Journal*, 20–22 May 1788.

12 *Hibernian Chronicle*, 22 May 1788.

13 *Freeman's Journal*, 15–17 May 1788.

14 *Freeman's Journal*, 24–27 May 1788. (Original emphasis.)

15 *Hibernian Journal*, 19 May 1788; *Freeman's Journal*, 15–17 May 1788.

16 *Freeman's Journal*, 17–20, 20–22 and 22–24 May 1788.

17 *Hibernian Journal*, 19 May 1788; *Hibernian Chronicle*, 22 May 1788.

18 *Ibid.*

19 *Hibernian Chronicle*, 19 May 1788.

20 *Hibernian Journal*, 29 October 1787; *Freeman's Journal*, 25–27 October 1787.

21 *Freeman's Journal*, 22–24 May 1788.

22 *Walker's Hibernian Magazine*, December 1787, pp. 668–9.

23 *Walker's Hibernian Magazine*, March 1788, p. 162.

24 *Ibid.*, p. 163; *Freeman's Journal*, 15–17 May 1788.

25 *Hibernian Journal*, 9 September 1788; *Dublin Chronicle*, 9 September 1788.

26 The issue of the *Centinel* containing the original report cannot be found. However, it was copied in the *Providence Gazette and Country Journal* [Rhode Island] of 12 July 1788 and the *Salem Mercury* of 15 July 1788.

27 *Hibernian Journal*, 19 September 1791.

28 *Providence Gazette and Country Journal*, 12 July 1788; *Freeman's Journal*, 26–28 May 1789.

29 *Freeman's Journal*, 26–28 May 1789.

30 *Hibernian Journal*, 6 October 1788.

31 *Dublin Chronicle*, 14 October 1788.

32 *Hibernian Journal*, 22 October 1788.

33 *Dublin Chronicle*, 18 September 1788.

34 *Ibid.*

35 *Hibernian Journal*, 21 January 1789, 19 June 1789.

36 *Dublin Chronicle*, 16–18 October 1788.

37 *Walker's Hibernian Magazine*, September 1788, p. 503; *Dublin Chronicle*, 9 September 1788.

38 *Freeman's Journal*, 21–23 October 1788.

39 *Freeman's Journal*, 28–30 October 1788.

40 *Ibid.*

41 *Freeman's Journal*, 21–23 October 1788.

42 *Dublin Chronicle*, 18–21 October 1788.

43 *Dublin Chronicle*, 4–7 October 1788.

44 *Ibid.*

45 *Freeman's Journal*, 8–11 November 1788.

46 The most complete published account, consisting of a selection from the original documents in the *CO 217* series, can be found in *Report of the Board of Trustees of the Public Archives of Nova Scotia for the Year 1950* [*Report of the Board*], Halifax: King's Printer, 1951, pp. 14–38. Accounts by Richard Brown (*A History of the Island of Cape Breton ...*, London: Sampson Low, Son, & Marston, 1869, pp. 399–401), Elva E. Jackson ('The Day The Convicts

Landed: A True Account of the Forced Emigration of Convicted Prisoners to Cape Breton Island', *Weekly Cape Bretoner*, 13 October 1956, p. 3) and Albert W. Almon ('Unwelcome Guests at Cape Breton', Beaton Institute, University College of Cape Breton, MG 12, 11A) have all been closely based on *CO 217*. A transcription of material in the *CO 217* series relating to Cape Breton Island, known as 'Cape Breton A', can also be found in the Beaton Institute. This, together with *Report of the Board*, are the primary sources used here. For a detailed account of the political context, see Robert J. Morgan, 'Orphan Outpost: Cape Breton Colony 1784–1820', Ph.D. thesis, University of Ottawa, 1972, pp. 28–66. The story of the convicts passed into the oral tradition of Cape Breton and was well known as late as the 1940s. See the scrapbook of Mrs MacNeil, n.d., Beaton Institute, T–49.

47 *Hibernian Journal*, 19 July 1789; *Dublin Chronicle*, 20 June 1789.

48 Deposition of Francis Dixon, 15 December 1788, *Report of the Board*, p. 18.

49 This account is based on Lieut.-Governor Macarmick's summary of the evidence given at the trial of McDonald and Prendergast at Sydney on 12 March 1789. Macarmick to Grenville, 16 May 1790, Cape Breton A, vol. 66, p. 379.

50 Deposition of William Campbell, 18 December 1788, *Report of the Board*, pp. 23–4.

51 Macarmick to Grenville, 18 December 1788, *Report of the Board*, p. 22.

52 Taitt to Grenville, 9 March 1790, Cape Breton A, vol. 73, p. 1.

53 MacKinnon, *Old Sydney*, p. 87.

54 Mathews to Macarmick, 14 March 1789, enclosure no. 5, Macarmick to Grenville, 30 March 1789, Cape Breton A, vol. 73. Mathews was the former Mayor of New York.

55 See Robert J. Morgan, 'Orphan Outpost: Cape Breton Colony, 1784–1820', Ph.D. Thesis, University of Ottawa, 1972, p. 57. For a brief published account of politics during the governorships of des Barres and Macarmick, see Robert Morgan, 'The Loyalists of Cape Breton', in Don Macgillivray and Brian Tennyson, eds., *Cape Breton Historical Essays*, Sydney [Cape Breton]: College of Cape Breton Press, 1980, pp. 18–23.

56 Morgan, 'Orphan Outpost', p. 59.

57 Macarmick to Sydney, 18 April 1789, *BT* 6/32, f. 97.

58 Murdoch, *History of Nova Scotia*, vol. III, p. 74.

59 Parr to Nepean ('private'), 20 April 1789, CO 217/61, f. 73.

60 ? to ?, 5 August 1789, *Dominion of Canada. Report of the Department of Public Archives for the Year 1944*, p. XXXVII.

61 Grenville to Macarmick, 20 October 1789, Cape Breton A.

62 *Ibid.*

63 Grenville to Buckingham, 27 July 1789, *HO* 100/27, ff. 216–9.

64 *Ibid.*, f. 217.

65 Fitzgibbon to Buckingham, 20 July 1789, Letter-Book of 1st Marquis of Buckingham. 1782–1789. vol. IV, BM Add. MS. 40180, ff. 138–9.

66 *Ibid.*

67 S. Bernard to Hobart, 7 February 1792, *HO* 100/36, f. 208.

68 *Hibernian Journal*, 10 August 1789.

Chapter 9

1 *Hibernian Journal*, 17 June 1789. A detailed account of the specifications of the *Duke of Leinster* can be found in its Dublin Customs House registration certificate at *CO* 152/70.

2 *Hibernian Journal*, 20 May 1789.

3 *Freeman's Journal*, 16–18 June 1789.

4 *Freeman's Journal*, 13–16 June 1789, 16–18 June 1789.

5 *Freeman's Journal*, 16–18 June 1789.

6 *Hibernian Journal*, 22 June 1789.

7 *Dublin Chronicle*, 13 June 1789.

8 *Hibernian Journal*, 13 June 1789.

9 *Dublin Chronicle*, 11 June 1789.

10 See Appendix III. Contrary to the claim made by Henry (*Dublin Hanged*, p. 163) that the Newfoundland list was an indent which had been sent with the convicts on the ship, it was in fact prepared at St John's and included only those 65 convicts who had been rounded up by the magistrates and placed in the Winter house. The list of convicts for the voyage to Barbuda may have been prepared in Dublin, although its omission of any details other than age makes it a passenger list rather than a convict indent in the accepted sense.

11 *Freeman's Journal*, 11–13 June 1789.

12 'Deposition of Richard Robinson in the Court of Vice-Admiralty, St John's, 21 July 1789', *HO* 28/6, f. 281.

13 *Ibid.*

14 'Examination of James Maguire and Mathew Demsey [*sic*]', *CO* 194/38, ff. 91–4.

15 This is the modern name. In 1789 it was called Bay of Bulls.

16 'Deposition of Richard Robinson'.

17 'Extract of a letter from Portsmouth, November 14 [1789]', *Nova Scotia Gazette*, 30 March 1790. I am indebted to Dr Jerry Bannister for this reference.

18 In its issue for 6 June 1789, the *Dublin Chronicle* reported that fifteen English and eleven Irish vessels had recently sailed from Waterford for Placentia and Bay Bulls.

19 Osborn to Popple, 28 July 1731, *CSP (CS)*, vol. 38 (1731), p. 205. I am indebted to Dr Jerry Bannister for this reference.

20 Anon., *A Short Review of the Political State of Great Britain at the Commencement of the Year One Thousand Seven Hundred and Eighty-seven ...*, London, 6th edn., 1787, p. 80, cited by Martin, 'Convict Transportation to Newfoundland', p. 85.

21 *The Times*, 5 December 1788, cited by Martin, 'Convict Transportation to Newfoundland', p. 86.

22 Truxes, *Irish-American Trade*, p. 137. For a contemporary description, see Arthur Young, *A Tour in Ireland*, 2 vols., Dublin: Whitestone, 1780, vol. II, pp. 184–5.

23 See John Mannion, 'The Waterford Merchants and the Irish–Newfoundland Provisions Trade, 1770–1820', in L.M. Cullen and P. Butel, eds., *Negoce et Industrie en France et en Irlande aux XVIIIe et XIXe Siècles*,

Paris: Editions du Centre National du Recherche Scientifique, 1980, pp. 27–43.

24 *CO* 1/47, f. 115, cited by Head, *Eighteenth Century Newfoundland*, p. 97.

25 See George Casey, 'Irish Culture in Newfoundland', in Cyril J. Byrne and Margaret Harry, eds., *Talamh An Eisc: Canadian and Irish Essays*, Halifax: Nimbus Publishing Ltd., 1986, p. 203.

26 *Ibid.*, p. 209.

27 'Examination of James Maguire and Mathew Demsey'.

28 'Extract of a letter from Portsmouth'.

29 *Freeman's Journal*, 24–26 September 1789.

30 *Ibid.*

31 For a contemporary reference to the likely results of a fire at St John's, see Paul O'Neill, *The Oldest City: The Story of St John's, Newfoundland*, Erin [Ontario]: Press Porcepic, 1975, p. 50.

32 'Extract of a Letter from Newfoundland [St John's] and dated 21st August [1789]', *CO* 194/38, f. 282.

33 *Freeman's Journal*, 24–26 September 1789.

34 Petition to St John's magistrates, *CO* 194/38, f. 91. For Milbanke, see *DNB*, vol. XIII, pp. 369–70 and J. Charnock, *Biographia Navalis ...*, 6 vols., London: R. Faulder, 1794–98, VI, pp. 81–2. Milbanke was made Admiral of the Blue in 1793.

35 'Examination of James Maguire and Mathew Demsey'.

36 'Extract from a Letter from Portsmouth'.

37 *CO* 194/38, f. 97. See also, Elford to Milbanke, 9 September 1789, *ADM* 1/472, 334.

38 Elford to Milbanke, 9 September 1789, *ADM* 1/472, f. 334.

39 'Extract of a Letter from Newfoundland'.

40 *Ibid.*

41 *Ibid.*

42 There had been an outbreak of the disease at Trinity Harbour before the arrival of the *Duke of Leinster*. See *SPG Journal*, vol. 25 (1787–92), mfm. 567, p. 228. According to the census conducted for Milbanke in September 1789, the wintering population of Petty Harbour, St John's and Torbay was 4,420. 'General return of the Newfoundland Fishery for the Year 1789', *CO* 194/38, f. 264. However, the Revd Walter Price estimated in November 1789 that the population of St John's alone was 4,200. Price to Revd W. Morice, 14 November 1789, SPG Journal, vol. 25 (1787–92), mfm. 567, p. 231.

43 O Donel to Troy, 24 December 1789, in C.J. Byrne, ed., *Gentlemen-Bishops and Faction Fighters: The Letters of Bishops O'Donel, Lambert, Scallan and Other Irish Missionaries*, St John's [Newfoundland]: Jesperson Press, 1984, p. 100.

44 Price to Dr W. Morice, 14 November 1789, SPG Journal, vol. 25 (1787–92), mfm. 567, p. 231.

45 Anglican Church Burials, St John's 1752–90. He seems to have been confused with James Reily of Cootehill in the list made on 7 September 1789.

46 *CO* 194/3, f. 424, cited by Head, *Eighteenth Century Newfoundland*, p. 98.

47 *Calendar of State Papers (Colonial)*, 1714, pp. 54–5, cited *ibid.*

48 Raymond J. Lahey, *James Louis O'Donel in Newfoundland 1784–1807: The Establishment of the Roman Catholic Church*, Newfoundland Historical Society Pamphlet No. 8, 1984, p. 5.

49 Capt. Griffith Williams, *An Account of the Island of Newfoundland, With the Nature of its Trade, and Methods of carrying on the Fishery ...*, London: printed for Capt. Thomas Cole, 1765, pp. 8–9.

50 O' Neill, *The Oldest City*, p. 49.

51 *Ibid.*, p. 16.

52 Cited by Michael J. McCarthy, *The Irish in Newfoundland 1623–1800*, St John's [Newfoundland]: Henry Cuff Publications Ltd., 1982, p. 28.

53 Lahey, *James Louis O'Donel*, p. 5.

54 Cited, *ibid.*, p. 5.

55 John Mannion, 'Irish Merchants Abroad: The Newfoundland Experience, 1750–1850', *Newfoundland Studies*, vol. 2, no. 2 (1986), p. 151.

56 Cited by Lahey, *James Louis O'Donel*, p. 6.

57 To take one example, at the trial Michael Bushell for the murder of John Bryan in 1789, the witness Daniel Moroney, 'Shoreman Servant', had to be examined in Irish. *CO* 194/38, f. 154.

58 Langdon to Elliot, 6 September 1786, *ADM* 1/472, p. 296.

59 A.H. McLintock in *The Establishment of Constitutional Government in Newfoundland, 1783–1832: A Study of Retarded Colonisation*, London: Longmans, Green & Co., 1941, p. 59.

60 The following account is largely based on Hans Rollman, 'Prince William Henry at Placentia', *The Newfoundland Ancestor*, vol. 9, no. 1 (May 1993), pp. 19–27.

61 *Ibid.*, pp. 60–1.

62 Prince William Henry to King George III, 21 September 1786, in A. Aspinall, ed., *The Later Correspondence of George III ...* , 5 volumes, Cambridge: Cambridge University Press, 1962, i, p. 249.

63 *Ibid.*

64 Clarence to Elliot, 22 August 1786, cited by Lahey, *James Louis O'Donel*, pp. 12–13.

65 O Donel to Troy, 30 November 1786, in Byrne, *Gentlemen-Bishops*, pp. 59–60. Gleeson's identity is not clear. According to Byrne, p. 58, it was probably Martin Gleeson whose name appeared on the St John's Grand Jury list for 1788. However, it may also have been the John Gleeson who signed the petition to the magistrates about the convicts in August 1789.

66 For the most detailed published accounts of the abortive rebellion, see McCarthy, *The Irish in Newfoundland*, pp. 47–51. See also, C.J. Byrne, 'Ireland and Newfoundland: The United Irish Rising of 1798 and the Fencible's [*sic*] Mutiny in St John's, 1799', paper read to the Newfoundland Historical Society, St John's, 5 November 1977, 8pp. typescript, Queen Elizabeth II Library, Memorial University of Newfoundland.

67 O Donel to Bishop Joseph-Octave Plessis, 14 May 1800, in Byrne, *Gentlemen-Bishops*, pp. 171–2; Lahey, *James Louis O'Donel*, pp. 24–8.

68 Enclosures, Buckingham to Sydney, 17 July 1788, *HO* 100/23, f. 298.

69 Buckingham to Sydney, 17 July 1788, *ibid.*

70 See P. O'Donnell, *The Irish Faction Fighters of the 19th Century*, Dublin: Anvil Books, 1975.

71 Ronald J. Fitzpatrick, '"An Emissary from Hell": Father Patrick Power and the 1788 Riot at Ferryland', *The Newfoundland Ancestor*, vol. 9, issue 1 (May 1993), pp. 28–33.

72 See Lahey, *James Louis O'Donel*, pp. 14–16 and Byrne, *Gentlemen-Bishops*, pp. 69–76.

73 O Donel to Troy, 16 November 1788, in Byrne, *Gentlemen-Bishops*, p. 74.

74 Elliot to Ferryland magistates, 24 October 1788, Governors' Letter Books, G.N. 2/1/1, vol. 12, p. 437.

75 O Donel to Troy, 16 November 1788, in Byrne, *Gentlemen-Bishops*, p. 75.

76 O Donel to Elliot, n.d., 1788, *ibid.*, p. 70.

77 This must be one of the earliest references to the export of the traditional game to north America.

78 *Ibid.*, p. 71.

79 McLintock, *Constitutional Government in Newfoundland*, pp. 58–60.

80 *Hibernian Journal*, 2 December 1790.

81 Milbanke to magistrates of St John's, 10 September 1789, Governors' Letter Books, G.N. 2/1/a, vol. 11.

82 *Ibid.*

83 Milbanke's order of 14 September 1789, *ibid.*, f. 100.

84 Milbanke to magistrates of St John's, 16 September 1789, *ibid.*, f. 99.

85 Oddly enough, the incident is not mentioned by McLintock in his classic study of the Newfoundland constitution.

86 See Appendix III.

87 *Walker's Hibernian Magazine*, October 1788, p. 559.

88 *Dublin Evening Herald*, 16 January 1789.

89 *Hibernian Journal*, 3 November 1788.

90 Report of assizes at St John's, 30 September 1789, *CO* 194/38, ff. 168–75.

91 *Ibid.*, ff. 177–8. The convict listing of 7 September 1789 (see Appendix III) mistakenly described Reiley as having died on 13 August. He was probably confused with John Reiley, 28, also of Cavan.

92 Milbanke's order of 13 September 1789, Governors' Letter Books, G.N. 2/1/a, vol. 12, f. 8.

93 Milbanke's order of 13 October 1789, *ibid.*, f. 37. The escapees were Santy Hame [*sic*], Thomas Walsh, James Ryan, John Kiernan, Patrick Lawler and Abraham Pallett.

94 *Ibid.*

95 Milbanke to Grenville, 20 September 1789, *ibid.*, ff. 86–7.

96 *Ibid.*

97 C. Grant Head, *Eighteenth Century Newfoundland: A Geographer's Perspective*, Toronto: McLelland & Stewart, 1976, pp. 203–4.

98 Mannion, 'Irish Merchants Abroad', p. 160; 'General return of the Newfoundland Fishery for the Year 1789', *CO* 194/38, f. 264.

99 Mannion, 'Irish Merchants Abroad', p. 160.

100 Milbanke to Rose, 17 September 1789, Governors' Letter Books, G.N. 2/1/a, vol. 12, f. 14.

101 Milbanke's order of 13 October 1789, *ibid.*, f. 41.

102 Milbanke to O Donel, 2 November 1790, cited by Lahey, *James Louis O'Donel*, p. 19.

103 Milbanke to Harris, 12 September 1789, Governors' Letter Books, G.N. 2/1/a, vol. 12, f. 4. Harris' report is not extant.
104 Milbanke to Admiralty, 4 September 1789, *HO* 28/6, f. 369.
105 *CO* 194/38, f. 101.
106 Milbanke to John Lees, Barrack Master, 24 October 1789, Governor's Letter Books, G.N. 2/1/a, vol. 12, f. 54.
107 Milbanke to Philip Stevens, 24 October 1789, *ADM* 1/472, p. 340. See also, 'An Account of the Expense of maintaining, and sending to England in the Brig Elizabeth and Clare, a number of Irish Convicts, who were landed upon the island of Newfoundland in the Year 1789', enclosure, Milbanke to Grenville, 8 December 1789, *CO* 194/38, f. 182.
108 *Hampshire Chronicle*, 4 January 1790.
109 Milbanke to Coyshe, 24 October 1789, *ibid.*, f. 118.
110 I am grateful to Jed Martin ('Convict Transportation to Newfoundland', p. 93, n. 51) for this point.
111 Milbanke to magistrates of Harbour Grace, 7 October 1789, Governors' Letter Books, G.N. 2/1/a, vol. 12, f. 30.
112 Milbanke to magistrates of Harbour Grace, 20 October 1789, *ibid.*, f. 48.
113 Milbanke to Grenville, 5 December 1789, *CO* 194/38, f. 180.
114 *ADM* 1/472.
115 Enclosure in Milbanke to Grenville, 24 October 1789, *ibid.*, f. 112.
116 See Appendix III.
117 *Hampshire Chronicle*, 7 December 1789.
118 Report of sheriffs to Milbanke, 29 October 1791, *CO* 195/14.
119 See E.R. Seary, *Family Names of the Island of Newfoundland*, Memorial University: St John's [Newfoundland], 1976; John Mannion, 'Tracing the Irish: A Geographical Guide', *The Newfoundland Ancestor*, vol. 9, no. 1 (May 1993), pp. 12–17.

Chapter 10

1 Grenville to Thurlow, 17 November 1789, *Dropmore Papers*, pp. 539–40.
2 Thurlow to Grenville, 17 November 1789, *ibid.*, p. 540.
3 Grenville to Thurlow, 18 November 1789, *ibid.*
4 Thurlow to Grenville, 18 November 1789, *ibid.*, pp. 540–41. (Original emphasis.)
5 Privy Council Registers, vol. 134, 2 May 1789 to 31 March 1790, *PC* 2/134, ff. 301–5.
6 Thurlow to Grenville, [?] November 1789, *ibid.*, p. 542.
7 Home Office to Lords of the Admiralty, 23 November 1789, *HO* 28/6, f. 376.
8 Grenville to Hobart, 25 November 1789, *Dropmore Papers*, p. 542.
9 *Ibid.*, p. 543.
10 Onslow to Home Office, 20 December 1789, *HO* 28/6.
11 Report by R. Sheppard, M.D. and T. Trotter, M.D., 21 December 1789, *ibid.*
12 *Faulkner's Dublin Journal*, 14 January 1790.
13 *Hampshire Chronicle*, 4 January 1790.
14 *Hampshire Chronicle*, 11 January 1790.

15 Nepean to Lords Justices of Ireland, 23 November 1790, *HO* 100/27, f. 287.
16 Fitzgibbon to Grenville, 28 November 1789, *ibid.*, p. 544.
17 *Ibid.*
18 Lords Chief Justices to Grenville, 1 December 1789, *ibid.*, ff. 293–4. For the instructions to the Revenue Commissioners made at the Lords Justices' direction, see Hamilton to John Draper, 1 December 1789, BM Add MS 59521, f. 105.
19 Hobart to Grenville, 1 December 1789, *Dropmore Papers*, p. 545.
20 *Ibid.*
21 For Buckingham's assessment of the strength of feeling on this issue, see his despatch to Sydney of 18 November 1788, *HO* 100/23, ff. 380–1.
22 Peter Jupp, *Lord Grenville 1759–1834*, Oxford: Clarendon Press, 1985, pp. 21–9.
23 I am grateful to Dr James Kelly for making this point to me.
24 *Dictionary of National Biography*, vol. XVII, p. 982. See also, H. Boylan, *A Dictionary of Irish Biography*, Dublin: Gill & Macmillan, 1978, p. 322.
25 Hobart to Grenville, 1 December 1789, *Dropmore Papers*, p. 545.
26 *Ibid.*
27 Fitzgibbon to Grenville, 2 December 1789, *ibid.*, p. 548.
28 *Ibid.*, p. 548.
29 *Ibid.*, p. 548.
30 Grenville to Fitzgibbon, 2 December 1789, *ibid.* p. 548.
31 Grenville to Westmorland, 5 December 1789, *ibid.*, p. 550.
32 Grenville to Hobart, 5 December 1789, *ibid.*, p. 550.
33 *Ibid.*, p. 551.
34 Jupp, *Lord Grenville*, pp. 91–2.
35 Grenville to Fitzgibbon, 2 December 1789, *Dropmore Papers*, p. 549.
36 *Ibid.*, p. 549.
37 Fitzgibbon to Grenville, 14 December 1789, *ibid.*, p. 554.
38 *Ibid.*, p. 554.
39 Grenville to Fitzgibbon, 9 December 1789, *ibid.*, p. 552.
40 *Ibid.*, p. 552.
41 *Ibid.*, p. 552.
42 Hobart to Grenville, 9 December 1789, *ibid.*, p. 531.
43 *Ibid.*
44 Grenville to Hobart, 14 December 1789, BM Add MS 59251.
45 Hobart to Grenville, 22 January 1790, *Dropmore Papers*, p. 560.
46 Hobart to Barnard, 2 February 1790, *HO* 100/29, f. 39.
47 Kavanaugh, 'John Fitzgibbon', vol. II, p. 295.
48 *Freemans's Journal*, 19–21 November 1789.
49 *Ibid.*
50 *Freeman's Journal*, 10–12 December 1789.
51 *Ibid.*
52 *Freeman's Journal*, 28–29 January 1790.
53 *Dublin Chronicle*, 2 February 1790; *Freeman's Journal*, 30 January–2 February 1790.
54 *Morning Post*, 2 February 1790.
55 *Morning Post*, 15 December 1789; *Dublin Chronicle*, 12 December 1789; *Freeman's Journal*, 10–12 December 1789.

Chapter 11

1　For a full list of these, see Appendix III.
2　*HO* 100/29, ff. 194–5. The full text of the contract can be found at Appendix III.
3　This firm was no doubt the successor to Samuel & Arthur Bryan & Co. of Dublin. We have already seen that Samuel Bryan had arranged for his son George to become a partner in a merchant firm with James Wallace in Philadelphia in 1751. George Bryan in Dublin seems very likely to have been his son, sent back in turn to the family business.
4　*HO* 100/24, f. 196. For the full text, see Appendix III.
5　Hobart to Grenville, 22 December 1789, BM Add MS 59251, ff. 142–3.
6　*Ibid.*
7　Bryan to Christian, 4 November 1789, *CO* 152/70. Subsequent quotations from this source.
8　*Hibernian Journal*, 11 November 1789.
9　*Ibid.*
10　See Desmond V. Nicholson, *Antigua, Barbuda and Redonda: A Historical Sketch*, St John: Museum of Antigua and Barbuda, 1991, p. 22.
11　Extract of letter from Lovell to Codrington, 18 January 1790, enclosure in Nepean to Hobart, 18 March 1790, *HO* 100/29, f. 149.
12　Shirley to Grenville, 12 March 1790, *CO* 152/69, ff. 34–5.
13　Bryan and Freeman to Shirley, 22 January 1790, *ibid.*, f. 164.
14　*Ibid.*
15　*Ibid.*
16　Hutchinson to Nepean, 19 February 1794, *CO* 7/1.
17　Truxes, *Irish-American Trade*, pp. 98–9.
18　E.V. Goveia, *Slave Society in The British Leeward Island...*, Westport [Conn.]: Greenwood Press, 1980, p. 227.
19　Gibbes to Shirley, 7 February 1790, *CO* 152/69, ff. 167–8.
20　Parker to Shirley, 13 February 1790, *CO* 152/69, f. 172.
21　*Ibid.*
22　Resolution of the House of Assembly, n.d., *ibid.*
23　Council to Assembly, 18 February 1790, *ibid.*, f. 174.
24　'Extract of A Letter from St. John's [*sic*], Antigua, dated March 4, 1790', *Walker's Hibernian Magazine*, May 1790, p. 479.
25　Lovell to Codrington, 16 March 1790, *CO* 152/70.
26　*Ibid.*
27　Antigua Magistrates to Shirley, 26 February 1790, *ibid.*
28　Shirley to Grenville, 12 March 1790, *ibid.*, f. 35.
29　Grenville to Shirley, 22 May 1790, *ibid.*, ff. 38–9.
30　*Ibid.*
31　Goveia, *Slave Society*, p. 265n, See also, p. 69.
32　Shirley to Hutchinson, 13 November 1790, *CO* 152/70. It is not clear what connection Shirley or his nephew had with Thomas 1st Earl of Ailesbury (1729–1814).
33　'Resolution of Legislative Assembly', n.d., *ibid.*
34　Shirley to Dundas, 24 January 1792, *ibid.*
35　Codrington to Grenville, 16 March 1790, *ibid.*

36 'Extract from a Letter from St. John's, Antigua, dated March 4, 1790', *Walker's Hibernian Magazine*, May 1790, p. 479.
37 Codrington to Nepean, 3 October 1790, *CO* 152/70.
38 *Ibid.*
39 Nepean to Hobart, 18 March 1790, *HO* 100/29, ff. 147–8.
40 Hobart to Nepean, 25 March 1790, *ibid.*, ff. 192–3.
41 *Ibid.*
42 Grenville to Westmorland, 17 March 1790, *ibid.*, p. 567. (Original emphasis.)
43 Hamilton to Nepean, 11 June 1790, *HO* 100/30, ff. 77–8.
44 V.L. Oliver, *The History of the Island of Antigua*, 3 vols., London, 1894–1899, *I*, p. cxxxix.
45 Hamilton to Nepean, 11 June 1790, *HO* 100/30, ff. 77–8.

Chapter 12

1 *Freeman's Journal*, 3–5 June 1790.
2 *Freeman's Journal*, 29 May–1 June 1790.
3 *Morning Post*, 20 March 1790. Also, *Freeman's Journal*, 16–18 March 1790.
4 *Morning Post*, 1 June 1790.
5 *Morning Post*, 10 June 1790.
6 *Morning Post*, 10 July 1790.
7 *Freeman's Journal*, 15–17 July 1790.
8 *Hibernian Journal*, 9 July 1790; *Hibernian Chronicle*, 19 July 1790.
9 There was no report to this effect, but it was said to have been the cause of another serious riot at Newgate in August 1792. *Hibernian Journal*, 28 September 1792.
10 *Morning Post*, 8 April 1790.
11 *Freeman's Journal*, 24–26 June 1790.
12 *Freeman's Journal*, 1–3 June 1790.
13 *Freeman's Journal*, 6–8 July 1790; *Hibernian Journal*, 9 July 1790; *Walker's Hibernian Magazine*, July 1790, p. 95. For the amended Chalking Act, see 17 and 18 Geo. III, c. 11, *Irish Statutes*, vol. xi (1776–80), pp. 100–101.
14 *Morning Post*, 10 July 1790; *Hibernian Journal*, 19 July 1790.
15 Henry, *Dublin Hanged*, p. 164.
16 Miraculously, only one prisoner was wounded in the day-long battle. The fullest account of the riot was published in the *Morning Post*, 10 July 1790.
17 *Walker's Hibernian Magazine*, July 1790, p. 95.
18 *Hibernian Journal*, 6 July 1790.
19 *Dublin Chronicle*, 20 July 1790.
20 *Dublin Chronicle*, 20 July 1790, p. 280.
21 *Dublin Chronicle*, 22 July 1790.
22 *Hibernian Journal*, 21 July 1790.
23 *Dublin Chronicle*, 22 July 1790, p. 288; *Walker's Hibernian Magazine*, July 1790, p. 96.
24 *Ibid.*
25 *Hibernian Journal*, 21 July 1790.
26 *Morning Post*, 20 July 1790.

27 Lady Gilbert, ed., *Calendar of the Ancient Records of Dublin* ..., vol. XIV, Dublin: Dollard Ltd., 1909, pp. 173–4.
28 *Morning Post*, 18 February 1790.
29 *Hibernian Journal*, 13 September 1790.
30 *Ibid*.
31 *Dublin Chronicle*, 14 September 1790, p. 472.
32 *Hibernian Journal*, 17 December 1790.
33 *Freeman's Journal*, 11–13 January 1787; *Hibernian Journal*, 1 October 1788, 5 September 1788, 29 September 1788.
34 *Hibernian Journal*, 1 October 1788.
35 Warburton, Whitelaw and Walsh, *History of the City of Dublin*, i, pp. 534–5.
36 *Hibernian Journal*, 27 and 30 March 1789; *Dublin Chronicle*, 8 and 24 October 1789, p. 608.
37 *Morning Post*, 2 October 1790. See also, *Dublin Chronicle*, 9 July, 30 September and 2 October 1790 and *Walker's Hibernian Magazine*, September 1790, p. 287.
38 *Morning Post*, 2 October 1790; *Dublin Chronicle*, 2 October 1790.
39 *Dublin Chronicle*, 21 October 1790.
40 *Morning Post*, 2 October 1790.
41 Starr, 'The Enforcing of Law and Order', p. 448.
42 *Morning Post*, 13 March 1790.
43 *Freeman's Journal*, 20–22 May 1790.
44 *Ibid*. (Original emphasis.)
45 Gilbert, *Calendar*, vol. XIV, pp. 148–9.
46 *Freeman's Journal*, 22–24 June 1790. (Original emphasis.)
47 *Ibid*.
48 *Morning Post*, 17 July 1790; *Hibernian Journal*, 19 July 1790.
49 Brief accounts of the James-street penitentiary can be found in Starr, 'The enforcing of law and order', pp. 448–51, and MacDonagh, *The Inspector General*, pp. 138–141. For further discussion, see Chapter 15.
50 *Dublin Chronicle*, 21 October 1790.
51 *Freeman's Journal*, 11–13 January 1791.
52 *Freeman's Journal*, 21–23 April 1791. (Original emphasis.)
53 Starr, 'The enforcing of law and order', p. 449.
54 MacDonagh, *The Inspector General*, p. 140. See also, Henry Heaney, 'Ireland's Penitentiary 1820–1831: An Experiment that failed', *Studia Hibernica*, vol. 14 (1974), p. 29.
55 *Irish Statutes*, vol. XVI (1792–93), pp. 294–5.

Chapter 13

1 Hobart to Nepean, 8 January 1790, HO 100/29, f.5.
2 Nepean to Buckingham, 27 July 1789, HO 100/27, f. 217; see also, Grenville to Lord Justices of Ireland, 25 November 1789, *ibid*., f. 289.
3 Fitzpatrick, *Thoughts on Penitentiaries*, p. 18.
4 *Ibid*., pp. 19–20.
5 *Ibid*., p. 20.

6   This account is based on *Dublin Chronicle,* 18 February 1790, p. 1003 and *Parliamentary Record,* Dublin: P. Byrne & J. Moore, vol. x, 1791, pp. 226–7. All quotations are from these two sources.

7   23 and 24 Geo. III, c. 41, *Irish Statutes,* vol. xii (1781–84), pp. 709–15

8   *Freeman's Journal,* 4–6 March 1790.

9   *Irish Statutes,* vol. xv (1790–91), pp. 226–7.

10 This point has been well made by Martin, 'Convict Transportation to Newfoundland', p. 97, n. 81.

11 Hobart to Nepean, 25 March 1790, *HO* 100/29, f. 202. Subsequent quotations from this source.

12 Westmorland to Grenville, 6 March 1790, BM Add MS 59251, f. 172. Subsequent quotations from this source.

13 Hamilton to Nepean, 11 June 1790, *HO* 100/30, ff. 77–8.

14 Hobart to Nepean, 15 July 1790, *ibid.,* f. 128.

15 Hobart to Nepean, 28 July 1790, *ibid.,* f.151.

16 Hobart to Nepean ('Private'), 10 August 1790, *HO* 100/30, f. 159.

17 Hobart to Nepean ('Private'), 22 September 1790, *ibid.*

18 Grenville to Westmorland, 31 October 1790, *ibid.,* ff. 212–13.

19 *Ibid.*

20 Richards to Hobart, 2 November 1790, *ibid.,* ff. 232–3.

21 Nepean to Hobart, 5 January 1791, *HO* 100/32.

22 *Morning Post,* 1 February 1791.

23 Hobart to Nepean, 18 January 1791, *HO* 100/32, f. 25; Hobart to Scrope Bernard, 14 February 1791, *ibid.,* f. 59.

24 Mollie Gillen, 'Lemain Island', *The Push,* no. 30 (1992), p. 3. For details of the firm's slave-trading activities, see Roger Anstey, *The Atlantic Slave Trade and British Abolition 1780–1810,* London: Macmillan, 1975, and Herbert S. Klein, 'The English Slave Trade to Jamaica', *Economic History Review,* Series 2, vol. 31, no. 1 (February 1978), pp. 24–45. For the text of Anthony Calvert's February 1785 tender, see Atkinson, 'The Convict Republic', pp. 72–3. Anthony Calvert was a member of the Africa Committee of merchants which was attempting to maintain a monopoly of trade with Ghana and the Gambia.

25 See Michael Flynn, *The Second Fleet: Britain's Grim Convict Armada of 1790,* Sydney: Library of Australian History, 1993, pp. 65–76.

26 *Ibid.,* p. 27.

27 Nepean to Hobart, 4 March 1791, *HO* 100/32, ff. 141–4.

28 *Ibid.,* f. 146.

29 A number of these letters from Hobart can be found in Musters and Papers, AONSW 2/8274.

30 *Dublin Evening Post,* 20 January 1791.

31 *Public Register,* 26 February to 1 March 1791.

32 *Morning Post,* 8 February 1791. (Emphasis added.)

33 See Appendix III for these.

34 *Ibid.*

35 See Appendix III.

36 The following account is substantially drawn from Johnson and Flynn, 'Convicts of the *Queen',* which I gratefully acknowledge.

37 Musters and Papers, AONSW 2/8274, f. 325.

38 *Ibid*, ff. 333–4.
39 *Hibernian Journal*, 14 July 1790.
40 *Freeman's Journal*, 11–13 January 1791; *Morning Post*, 13 January 1791.
41 *Freeman's Journal*, 19–21 October 1790.
42 *Freeman's Journal*, 28–30 October 1790.
43 *Freeman's Journal*, 28–30 October 1790.
44 *Hibernian Journal*, 16–18 July 1790.
45 *Morning Post*, 18 July 1789.
46 *Walker's Hibernian Magazine*, April 1789, p. 222.
47 *Hibernian Journal*, 26 May 1786.
48 *Hibernian Journal*, 4 August 1788.
49 *Hibernian Journal*, 12 December 1788.
50 *Hibernian Journal*, 14 July 1790; *Freeman's Journal*, 7–10 August 1790.
51 *Hibernian Journal*, 6–8 October 1789: *Walker's Hibernian Magazine*, October 1789, p. 559.
52 *Hibernian Journal*, 12 April 1790.
53 PPC, f. 25.
54 T.J. Kiernan, *Transportation from Ireland to Sydney, 1791–1816*, Canberra: The author), 1954, p. 36.
55 Musters and Papers, AONSW 2/8274, ff. 307–8.
56 *Ibid*, ff. 333–4.
57 *Ibid*, ff. 323–4.
58 *Ibid*, ff. 261.
59 *Hibernian Journal*, 12 December 1788.
60 *Hibernian Journal*, 21 April 1790.
61 *Morning Post*, 10 February 1791; *Public Register*, 22–24 February 1791; *Walker's Hibernian Magazine*, February 1791, p. 191.
62 *Dublin Chronicle*, 19–21 March 1789.
63 *Freeman's Journal*, 28–30 May 1789.
64 *Walker's Hibernian Magazine*, May 1789, pp. 252–6; 1790, pt. 2, pp. 260–63.
65 *Morning Post*, 11 April 1789.
66 *Hibernian Journal*, 16 December 1789.
67 *Hibernian Journal*, 1 April 1789.
68 *Hibernian Journal*, 3 April 1789.
69 *Ibid*. This reference was to the small outcrop in Sydney Harbour known as 'Rock Island' or 'Pinchgut' which was being used as a place of punishment for convicts within two weeks of the first settlement at Sydney Cove.
70 *Hibernian Journal*, 6 May 1789.
71 *Morning Post*, 30 May 1789.
72 *Magee's Weekly Packet*, 19 March 1791; *Hibernian Chronicle*, 31 March 1790.
73 *Hibernian Journal*, 12 January 1791.
74 *Morning Post*, 13 January 1791.
75 *Hibernian Journal*, 12 June 1789.
76 *Hibernian Journal*, 19 June 1789.
77 *Dublin Chronicle*, 2–5 May 1789.
78 *Dublin Chronicle*, 19 February 1791.
79 *Morning Post,* 19 February 1791.
80 *Hibernian Journal*, 18 February 1791.
81 *Hibernian Journal*, 2 March 1791.

82 *Magee's Weekly Packet*, 5 March 1791; *Morning Post*, 1 March 1791.
83 *Dublin Chronicle*, 11–13 March, 20 April 1790; *Dublin Morning Post*, 13 March 1790.
84 *Dublin Evening Post*, 1 March 1791.
85 *Hibernian Chronicle*, 10 March 1791.
86 *Hibernian Chronicle*, 6 May 1790.
87 *Ibid.*
88 Hobart to Nepean, 8 March 1791, *HO* 100/32.
89 *Hibernian Journal*, 18 March 1791; *Magee's Weekly Packet*, 19 March 1791.
90 *Evening Post*, 1 March 1791.
91 *Freeman's Journal*, 30 April–3 May 1791. For an earlier proposal of this kind, see *Hibernian Journal*, 20 June 1787.
92 *Ibid.* (Original emphasis.)
93 Walsh, *Rakes and Ruffians*, p. 117.

Chapter 14

1 PRO *BT* 107/8 and 9. After her return from New South Wales via India, the *Queen* made voyages to the West Indies in 1794 and 1796, but from that time her name ceased to appear in the annual lists. It is possible, of course, that her name was changed once more.
2 See J.F. Millar, *A Handbook on the Founding of Australia* ..., Williamsburg [Va.], Thirteen Colonies Press, 1988, pp. 38–42. Alternatively, the *Queen* may have resembled in appearance the *Aston Hall*, a three-masted West Indiaman of 300 tons built in Maryland for T. Curtis in 1773 and used in the Halifax–London trade before being chartered as a transport by the British government in 1778. See J.F. Millar, *Early American Ships*, Williamsburg [Va.]: Thirteen Colonies Press, 1986, p. 52.
3 C. Bateson, *The Convict Ships 1787–1868*, Sydney: Library of Australian History, 1983, p. 131.
4 Navy Board to Blow, 25 January 1791, Mackinnon Hood Papers, NMM MKH/9, MS68/099.
5 Contract dated 18 November 1790, *ibid.* Subsequent quotations from this source.
6 *Hibernian Journal*, 18 March 1791; *Magee's Weekly Packet*, 19 March 1791.
7 'List of Prisoners under Sentence or Order of Transportation received from the different Parts of the Country & Transported from Cork in the Queen Transport', Appendix VI.
8 AONSW 4/4003A. The copy is dated March 1798. For the court documents, see AONSW 2/8274, pp. 257–346. As all Irish court records and transportation registers up to 1836 were destroyed in the Four Courts fire of 1922, these documents are unique. I wish to thank Perry McIntyre for bringing them to my attention.
9 *Historical Records of New South Wales*, cited by Johnson and Flynn, 'Convicts of the Queen', p. 17.
10 NMM MKH/9.
11 Cummings to Hood, 9 April 1791, *ibid.*
12 Tyler to Cummings, n.d., *ibid.* Subsequent quotations from this letter.

13 Hayes was himself to be transported to New South Wales on the *Atlas* from Cork in November 1801 after being convicted of abducting a Quaker heiress. For the most recent account of Hayes and his Australian experience, see Hugh Anderson, 'The Hard Case of Sir Henry' in Reece, *Exiles from Erin*, pp. 52–79.

14 I am indebted to Dan Byrnes for this information.

15 Phillip to Grenville, 8 November 1791, *HRA*, vol. 1, p. 294.

16 Hood to Navy Board, n.d. [14 April 1791], NMM MKH/9.

17 'Copy of a Protest against Lieut. Blow', [6 April 1791], *ibid*. Nicholson's report, if he in fact made one, is not with Hood's papers at NMM MKH/9.

18 Hood to Navy Board, n.d., *ibid*.

19 Hood to Lords of the Admiralty, 16 April 1791, *ibid*.

20 *ADM* 106/2637.

21 Hood to Hood, 21 April 1791, NMM MKH/9.

22 Blow, Cummings and Owen to Hood, n.d., *ibid*.

23 Undated and unsigned statement, *ibid*.

24 'List of Prisoners under Sentence or Order of Transportation ...', *ibid*.

25 Bateson, for example, described the *Queen* as sailing 'at the beginning of April' (p. 132).

26 *Hibernian Chronicle*, 21 April 1791.

Chapter 15

1 Hobart to Nepean, 4 June 1791, *HO* 100/33, f. 33.

2 Nepean to Hobart, 20 June 1791, *ibid*., f. 53.

3 Bernard to Hamilton, 13 December 1791, *ibid*., f. 203.

4 Hamilton to Bernard, 23 December 1791, *ibid*., ff. 215–17; Hamilton to Bernard, 29 December 1791, *HO* 100/36, f. 8.

5 Hobart to Bernard, 13 March 1792, *HO* 100/37, f. 11.

6 See Bernard to Hobart, 7 February 1792, *HO* 100/36, f. 208; Bernard to Hobart, 7 February 1792, *ibid*., f. 210; J. King to S. Douglas, 10 July 1794, *HO* 100/52, f. 144.

7 Westmorland to Dundas, 4 August 1792, *ibid*., f. 200.

8 Westmorland to Dundas, 28 August 1792, *ibid*., f. 234.

9 Sankey to Hobart, 1 September 1792, *ibid*., ff. 238–9.

10 Sankey to Hobart, 3 September 1792, *ibid*., f. 242.

11 By 1793, Freetown in Sierra Leone was an established settlement and the centre of British trading and other interests in West Africa. There had been earlier talk of cotton cultivation there.

12 Hobart to Nepean, 2 September 1792, *HO* 100/52, f. 240.

13 *Hibernian Journal*, 9 September 1792. For a subsequent escape, see *Freeman's Journal*, 1–4 October 1792.

14 Hobart to Nepean, 28 September 1792, *HO* 100/52, f. 281.

15 Abercorn to Dundas, 4 October 1792, *HO* 100/39, ff. 6–7.

16 Hobart to Nepean, 22 October 1792, *ibid*., f. 48.

17 Nepean to Hobart, 13 October 1792, *ibid*., f. 28.

18 Nepean to Hobart, 20 October 1792, *ibid*., f. 35.

19 Hamilton to Hobart, 24 and 25 October 1792, *ibid*., ff. 48, 51–2.

20 Hobart to Nepean, 27 November 1792, *ibid.*, f. 103.
21 Hobart to Nepean, 3 December 1792, *ibid.*, f. 113. Nepean's letter of 28 November is missing.
22 Bateson, *The Convict Ships*, p. 146.
23 32 Geo. III, c. 27, *Irish Statutes*, vol. XVI (1792–93), pp. 294–5.
24 'Report of the Committee appointed to inquire into the Present State and Situation of the Public Gaols and Prisons throughout this Kingdom', *JIHC*, vol. XV (1793), Appendix, p. ccccviii. Subsequent quotations from this source.
25 Starr, 'Irish Police and Prisons', p. 451.
26 MacDonagh, *The Inspector General*, p. 141.
27 Hamilton to Nepean, n.d., *HO* 100/52, f. 88.
28 Douglas to Nepean, 9 May 1794, *HO* 100/51, ff. 274–5.
29 Hamilton to Nepean, 9 May 1794, *HO* 100/52 [n.f.]; Hamilton to Nepean, 30 June 1794, *ibid.*, f. 136.
30 Westmorland to Portland, 8 October 1794, *ibid.*, f. 220.
31 *Hibernian Journal*, 1 May 1795.
32 Bateson, *The Convict Ships*, pp. 148–50.

Bibliography

Calendars, Guides and Bibliographies

Blessing, P.J., *The Irish in America: A Guide to the Literature and the Manuscript Collections*, Washington, D.C.: Catholic University of America Press, [c. 1992].

'Calendar of Papers relating to Nova Scotia', in Douglas Brymner, *Report on Canadian Archives, 1894*, Ottawa, 1895.

Knight, R.B., *Guide to the Manuscripts in the National Maritime Museum*, 2 vols., London: Mansell, 1977.

O'Dea, A., *Bibliography of Newfoundland*, 2 vols., Toronto: University of Toronto Press, 1986.

Public Archives of Nova Scotia, *Inventory of Manuscripts in the Public Archives of Nova Scotia*, Halifax, 1976.

Report on Canadian Archives 1895, Ottawa: Government Printer, 1896.

Walne, Peter, ed., *A Guide to Manuscript Sources for the History of Latin America and the Caribbean in the British Isles*, London: Oxford University Press, 1973.

Manuscript Sources

Public Record Office, London:

ADM 1	Admiralty: Correspondence and Papers
ADM 106	Navy Boards: Records
BT 6	Miscellanea
BT 107	Registrar General of Shipping and Seamen, Transcripts and Transactions, Series I
CO 7	Antigua and Montserrat: Original Correspondence
CO 23	Bahamas: Original Correspondence
CO 28	Newfoundland: Original Correspondence
CO 152	Leeward Islands: Original Correspondence
CO 194	Newfoundland: Original Correspondence
CO 195	Newfoundland: Entry Books
CO 217	Nova Scotia and Cape Breton: Original Correspondence
CO 218	Nova Scotia and Cape Breton: Entry Books
FO 72	General Correspondence before 1906: Spain
HO 42	Domestic Correspondence, George III
HO 100	Ireland: Correspondence and Papers
PC 2	Registers
T 1	Papers

British Library:

Add MSS 40177–40180, 40733 Letter-Books of George Nugent-Temple-Grenville, Earl Temple 1779, 1st Marquis Buckingham 1784, chiefly during his two periods as Lord Lieutenant of Ireland (1782–1783, 1787–1789)
Add MS 58914   Grenville–Dundas Correspondence
Add MS 58938   Grenville–Thurlow Correspondence
Add MS 59251
Add MS 59252

National Maritime Museum, Greenwich:

NMM MKH/9   Mackinnon Hood Papers

National Archives of Ireland:

PPC 1   Prisoners' Petitions and Correspondence

National Library of Ireland:

NLI MS 52 D8   Sydney Papers
NLI MS 15905/3

Provincial Archives of Newfoundland and Labrador, St John's, Newfoundland:

G. N. 2/1/a   Governors' Letter-Books

Beaton Institute, University College of Cape Breton, Sydney, Cape Breton:

Cape Breton Papers A
T49   Scrapbook of Mrs MacNeil
MG 12, 11A   Albert W. Almon, ' Unwelcome Guests at Cape Breton'

Library Of Congress:

Peter Forge Collection ser. 8D Woolsey and Salmon Letterbook

National Archives, Washington:

RG 79   Records of the Potomac Company
RG 360   Papers of the Continental Congress

Maryland Record Office, Annapolis:

Maryland State Papers, Series A, 6636–66–27, 6636–66–251

Archives Office of New South Wales, Sydney:

AONSW 2/8274   Musters and Papers
AONSW 4/4003A   Ships' Indents

Published collections of documents

Archives of Maryland XLVIII: *Journal and Correspondence of the State Council of Maryland 1781–1784*, Baltimore: Maryland Historical Society, 1931.

Aspinall, A., ed., *The Later Correspondence of George III ...*, vol. I (December 1783–January 1793), Cambridge: Cambridge University Press, 1962.

Colman, K. and M. Ready, eds., *The Colonial Records of the State of Georgia: Original papers, Correspondence to the Trustees, James Oglethorpe, and Others 1732–1735*, vol. 20, Athens: University of Georgia Press, 1982.

Dominion of Canada. Report of the Department of Public Archives for the Year 1944, Ottawa: Government Printer, 1945.

Fortescue, Sir John, ed., *The Correspondence of King George The Third from 1760 to December 1783 ...*, 6 vols., London: Macmillan & Co., 1928.

Gilbert, Lady, ed., *Calendar of Ancient Records of Dublin in the Possession of the Municipal Corporation of that City*, vol. XIII, Dublin: Dollard Ltd., 1907.

—— *Calendar of Ancient Records of Dublin in the Possession of the Municipal Corporation of that City*, vol. XIV, Dublin: Dollard Ltd., 1909.

Gwynn, Fr Aubrey, 'Documents Relating to the Irish in the West Indies', *Analecta Hibernica*, no. 4 (October 1932), pp. 139–286.

Hening, William Waller, ed., *The Statutes at Large; Being a Collection of all the Laws of Virginia, from the First Session of the Legislature, in the Year 1619*, vol. XII, Richmond: George Cochran.

Hill, Roscoe R., ed., *Journals of the Continental Congress 1774–1789*, 34 vols., Washington: United States Government Printing Office, 1936–37.

Historical Manuscripts Commission, *Tenth Report, Appendix. Part V. The Manuscripts of the Marquis of Ormonde, The Earl of Fingall, the Corporations of Waterford, Galway., &c*, London: HMSO, 1885.

Historical Manuscripts Commission, *Thirteenth Report, Appendix, Part III. The Dropmore Papers ...*, London: HMSO, 1892.

Historical Manuscripts Commission, *Fourteenth Report, Appendix, Part I. The Manuscripts of ... The Duke of Rutland, K.G., Preserved at Belvoir Castle*, vol. III, London: H.M.S.O., 1894.

Historical Records of Australia. Series i. Governor's Despatches to and from England, ed. by F. Watson, 26 vols., Sydney: Government Printer for the Library Committee of the Commonwealth Parliament, 1914–1925.

Historical Records of New South Wales, ed. by F.M. Bladen, 7 vols., Sydney: Government Printer, 1893–1901.

Jamison, J. Franklin, ed., 'Letters of Phineas Bond, British Consul at Philadelphia, to the Foreign Office of Great Britain, 1787, 1788, 1789', *Annual Report of the American Historical Association for the Year 1896*, Washington, D.C., 1897.

——, 'Letters of Phineas Bond, British Consul at Philadelphia, to the Foreign Office of Great Britain, 1790–1794', *Annual Report of the American Historical Association for the Year 1897*, Washington, D.C. 1898.

Report of the Board of Trustees of the Public Archives Authority of Nova Scotia For the Year 1950, Halifax: King's Printer, 1951.

Stock, Leo Francis, *Proceedings and Debates of the British Parliaments respecting North America*, 7 vols., Washington D.C.: Carnegie Institution, 1941.

The Papers of James Madison ..., ed. by H.D. Gilpin, 3 vols., Washington D.C.:
Langtree & O'Sullivan, 1840.
The Statues at Large, Passed in the Parliaments held in Ireland ... [Irish Statues]
20 vols., Dublin, 1786–1801.

Contemporary works

Anon., *Animadversions on the Street Robberies in Dublin; Together with a Proposal of
a Scheme to Prevent them for the Future in a Letter to a Member of Parliament*,
Dublin: George Faulkner, 1765.
Anon., *The Genuine Life and Trial of George Barrington, From His Birth, in June
1755 , to the Time of his Conviction at the Old-Bailey in September, 1790, for
Robbing Henry Hare Townshend, Esq. of his Gold Watch, Seals, etc.*, London:
Robert Barker, 1792.
Bruce, P.H., *Memoirs* ..., London, 1782.
Eden, William [Lord Auckland], *Principles of Penal Law*, 2nd edn, London:
B. White & T. Cadell, 1771.
———, *The History of New Holland from its First Discovery in 1616 to the present
time, with a particular account of its produce and inhabitants; and a description
of Botany Bay; also a List of the Naval, Marine, Military, and Civil Establishent.
To which is prefixed an Introductory Discourse on Banishment by the
Rt. Hon. William Eden*, London, 1787. (Reprinted, with an introduction by
J.J. Auchmuty, Sydney: Royal Australian Historical Society, 1970.)
Fitzpatrick, J., *An Essay on Gaol-Abuses, and on the Means of Redressing Them:
Together with the General Method of Treating Disorders to which Prisoners are Most
Incident*, Dublin: P. Byrne & C. Brown, 1784.
———, *Thoughts on Penitentiaries*, Dublin: H. Fitzpatrick, 1790.
Howard, John, *The State of the Prisons in England and Wales, with Some
Preliminary Observations, and an Account of Some Foreign Prisons*, Warrington:
William Eyres, 1776. [Bicentennial facsimile edition, with a Preface by Martin
Wright, Abingdon [United Kingdom]: Professional Books, 1977.
———, *An Account of the Principal Lazarettos in Europe ... and ... and Additional
Remarks on the Present State of Those in Great Britain and Ireland*, London:
William Eyres, 1789.
———, *The State of the Prisons*, London: Dent, 1929.
Hull, Charles Henry, ed., *The Economic Writings of Sir William Petty*, 2 vols., New
York: Augustus M. Kelley, 1963.
Ligon, Richard, *A True and Exact History of the Island of Barbados* ..., London:
Humphrey Moseley, 1657.
Luffman, John, *A Brief Account of the Island of Antigua, Together with the Customs
and Manners of Its Inhabitants* ..., London, 1789.
Pool, Robert, and John Cash, *Views of the Most Remarkable Public Buildings,
Monuments and Other Edifices in ... Dublin*, Dublin, 1780.
*The Voyage of Governor Phillip to Botany Bay: With Contributions by Other Officers
of the First Fleet and Observations on Affairs of the Time* by Lord Auckland, ed.
by J.J. Auuchmuty, Sydney: Angus & Robertson, 1970.
Walsh, John Edward, *Rakes and Ruffians: The Underworld of Georgian Dublin*,
Dublin: Four Courts Press, 1979 (originally published in 1847 as *Sketches of
Ireland Sixty Years Ago*).

Warburton, J., J. Whitelaw and R. Walsh, *History of the City of Dublin* ..., 2 vols., London: T. Cadell and W. Davies, 1818.

[Wylly, William], *A Short Account of the Bahama Islands, Their Climate, Productions, &c. To Which are Added Some Strictures upon their relative and political Situation, the Defects of their present Government, &c. &c.*, London, 1789.

[Young, Arthur], *Political Essays Concerning the Present State of the British Empire particularly respecting I. Natural Advantages and Disadvantages. II. Constitution. III. Agriculture. IV. Manufacture. V. The Colonies. And VI. Commerce*, London: W. Strachan & T. Cadell, 1772.

Newspaper, magazines, etc.

Ireland:

Dublin Chronicle
Dublin Evening Herald
Dublin Evening Post
Dublin Journal
Faulkner's Dublin Journal
Freeman's Journal [Dublin]
Hibernian Chronicle [Cork]
Hibernian Journal [Dublin]
Magee's Weekly Packet [Dublin]
Morning Post [Dublin]
Public Register [Dublin]
Walker's Hebernian Magazine [Dublin]

Britain:

Hampshire Chronicle
The Times
The Annual Register

United States:

Maryland Gazette [Annapolis]
Maryland Journal, and Baltimore Advertiser
Providence Gazette and Country Journal [Rhode Island]
Virginia Journal and Alexandria Advertiser

Later works

Akenson, D.A., *The Irish Diaspora: A Primer*, Toronto: P.S. Meany Co. Inc., 1993.

Anon., 'Historical Notes and Queries', *William and Mary College Quarterly*, Ser. 1, vol. 8, p. 273.

Atkinson, A., 'The Ethics of Conquest, 1786' *Aboriginal History*, vol. 6, pt. 2 (1982), pp. 82–91.

———, 'The Convict Republic', *The Push from the Bush*, no. 18 (October 1984), pp. 66–84.

————, 'The First Plans for Governing New South Wales, 1786–87, *Australian Historical Studies,* no. 94 (April 1990), pp. 22–40

————, 'Beating the Bounds with Lord Sydney, Evan Nepeam and Others', *Australian Historical Studiesm,* no. 99 (October 1992), pp. 217–9

————, 'The Free-Born Englishman Transported: Convict Rights as a Measure of Eighteenth Century Empire', *Past and Present,* no. 144 (August 1994), pp. 88–115.

Ballagh, James Curtis, *White Servitude in the Colony of Virginia: A Story of the System of Indentured Labour in the American Colonies,* New York: Burt Franklin, 1969.

Bateson, C., *The Convict Ships 1787–1868,* Sydney: Library of Australian History, 1983.

Beaglehole, J.C., ed., *The Voyage of the Endeavour 1768–1771,* London: Hakluyt Society, 1968.

Beattie, J.M., *Crime and the Courts in England 1660–1800,* Princeton University Press, 1986.

Beckles, Hilary McD., 'A "riotous and unruly lot": Irish Indentured Servants and Freemen in the English West Indies, 1644–1713', *William and Mary Quarterly,* 3rd Series, vol. XLVII (October 1990), pp. 503–23.

Bennett, Michael, 'A Botany Bay Mirage: Australia's First Political Cartoon', *Tasmanian Historical Studies,* vol. 5, no. 1 (1995–96), pp. 16 –18.

Blake, J.W., 'Transportation from Ireland to America, 1653–60', *Irish Historical Studies,* vol. III, no. 10 (September 1942), pp. 267–281.

Bolton, G.C., 'William Eden and the Convicts, 1771–1787', *Australian Journal of Politics and History,* vol. 26, no. 1 (1980), pp. 30–44.

Boylan, Henry, *A Dictionary of Irish Biography,* Dublin: Gill & Macmillan, 1978.

Boyle, Kevin, 'Police In Ireland Before The Union: I', *The Irish Jurist,* vol. VII, New Series (1972), pp. 115–137; II and III, vol. VIII, New Series (1973), pp. 90–116, 323–348.

Bridenbaugh, Carl and Roberta, *No Peace Beyond the Line: The English in the Caribbean 1624–1690,* New York: Oxford University Press, 1972.

Brown, Richard, *A History of the Island of Cape Breton ...,* London: Sampson Low, Son, & Marston, 1869.

Bruchey, S., ed., *The Colonial Merchant: Sources and Readings,* New York: Harper, 1966.

Brugger, Robert J., *Maryland: A Middle Temperament 1634–1980,* Baltimore: Johns Hopkins University Press, 1989.

Butler, J.D., 'British Convicts Shipped to American Colonies', *American Historical Review,* vol. II, no. 1 (October 1896), pp. 12–33.

Byrne, C.J., *Gentlemen-Bishops and Faction Fighters: The Letters of Bishops O Donel, Lambert, Scallan and Other Irish Missionaries,* St John's [Newfoundland]: Jesperson Press, 1984.

Byrne, C.J., and M. Harry, eds., *Talamh An Eisc: Canadian and Irish Essays,* Halifax: Nimbus Publishing Ltd., 1986.

Byrnes, D., '"Emptying the Hulks": Duncan Campbell and the First Three Fleets to Australia', *The Push from the Bush,* no. 24 (April 1987), pp. 2–23. (Revised and updated on disc, 1996.)

————, 'The Blackheath Connection: London Local History and the Settlement of New South Wales, 1786–1806', revised and updated on disc, 1996.

Cadigan, S.T., 'Artisans in a Merchant Town: St. John's, Newfoundland, 1775–1816', *Journal of the Canadian Historical Association*, New Series, no. 4 (1993), pp. 95–119.

————, *Hope and Deception in Conception Bay: Merchant–Settler Relations in Newfoundland 1785–1855*, University of Toronto Press, 1995.

Carr, Lois G., et al., eds., *Colonial Chesapeake Society*, Chapel Hill: University of North Carolina Press, 1988.

Casey, G., 'Irish Culture in Newfoundland', in C.J. Byrne and M. Harry, eds., *Talamh An Eisc: Canadian and Irish Essays*, Halifax: Nimbus Publishing Ltd., 1986, pp. 203–27.

Cheeseman, E. Herrick, *White Servitude in Pennsylvania*, Philadelphia, 1926.

Cobley, J., comp., *The Crimes of the First Fleet Convicts*, Sydney: Angus & Robertson, 1971.

Coldham, P.W., *Emigrants in Chains: A Social History of Forced Emigration to the Americas of Felons, Destitute Children, Political and Religious Non-Comformists, Vagabonds, Beggars and other Undesirables 1607–1776*, Baltimore: Genealogical Publishing Co., Inc., 1992.

Costello, C., *Botany Bay: The Story of the Convicts Transported from Ireland to Australia, 1791–1853*, Dublin: Mercier Press, 1987.

Craton, Michael, *A History of the Bahamas*, London: Collins, 1968.

Crone, J.S., *A Concise History of Irish Biography*, Dublin: The Talbot Press, 1928.

Cuff, R.H., et al., eds., *Dictionary of Newfoundland and Labrador Biography*, St John's: Harry Cuff Publications Ltd., 1990.

Cullen, L.M., *An Economic History of Ireland since 1660*, London: B.T. Batsford Ltd., 1972.

————, 'The Dublin Merchant Community in the Eighteenth Century', in P. Butel and L.M. Cullen, eds., *Cities and Merchants: French and Irish Perspectives on Urban Development, 1500–1900*, Dublin, 1986.

————, 'The Irish Diaspora in the Seventeenth and Eighteenth Centuries', in N. Canny, ed., *Europeans on the move: Studies on European Migration, 1500–1800*, Oxford: Clarendon Press, 1994, pp. 113–149.

D'Alton, Revd A.E., *History of Ireland from the Earliest Times to the Present Day*, London, 1911.

Dickson, D., ed., *The Gorgeous Mask: Dublin 1700–1850*, Dublin: Trinity History Workshop, 1987.

Donnelly, J.J., 'The Rightboy Movement, 1785–88', *Studia Hibernica*, 17 & 18 (1977–78), pp. 120–202.

Donohoe, J., *The Catholics of New South Wales 1788–1820 And Their Families*, Sydney: Archives Authority of NSW, 1988.

Doyle, D.N. and O. Dudley Edwards, eds., *America and Ireland, 1776–1976: The American Identity and the Irish Connection*, London: Greenwood Press, 1980.

Eddis, William, *Letters from America*, ed., by Aubrey C. Land, Cambridge [Mass.]: Belknap Press, 1969.

Ekirch, A.R., 'Great Britain's Secret Convict Trade to America, 1783–1784', *American Historical Review*, vol. LXXXLX, no. 5 (1984), pp. 1285–91.

——, *Bound for America: The Transportation of British Convicts to the Colonies, 1718–1775*, Oxford: Clarendon Press, 1987.

Fergus, Howard A., *Montserrat: History of the Caribbean Colony*, London: Macmillan, 1994.

Flynn, M., *The Second Fleet: Britain's Grim Convict Armada of 1790*, Sydney: Library of Australian History, 1993.

Frost, A., *Convicts and Empire: A Naval Question 1776–1811*, Melbourne: Oxford University Press, 1980.

——, 'Botany Bay: An Imperial Venture of the 1780's', *English Historical Review*, 100 (April 1985), pp. 309–327.

—— 'Historians, Handling Documents, Transgressions and Transportable Offences', *Australian Historical Studies*, no. 99 (October 1992) pp. 192–213.

——, *Botany Bay Mirages: Illusions of Australia's Convict Beginnings*, Melbourne University Press, 1994.

Galenson, D.W., 'British Servants and the Colonial Indenture System in the Eighteenth Century', *Journal of Southern History*, vol. XLIV (1978), pp. 59–66.

——, *White Servitude in Colonial America: An Economic Analysis*, Cambridge: Cambridge University Press, 1981.

Gillen, M., 'The Botany Bay Decision, 1786: Convicts, not Empire', *English Historical Review*, 99 (October 1982), pp. 740–66.

——, 'His Majesty's Mercy: The Circumstances of the First Fleet', *The Push*, no. 29 (1991), pp. 47–109.

——, 'Lemain Island', *The Push*, no. 30 (1992), pp. 3–9.

Goodbody, D., 'The Walls of Dublin', *Dublin Historical Record*, vol. XVII, no. 4 (September 1962), pp. 126–142.

Goveia, E.V., *Slave Society in the British Leeward Islands at the End of the Eighteenth Century*, Westport [Conn.]: Greenwood Press, 1980.

Green, Jack P., 'Society and Economy in the British Caribbean During the Seventeenth and Eighteenth Centuries', *American Historical Review*, vol. LXXIX (December 1974), pp. 1499–1517.

Gwynn, Fr Aubrey, 'Cromwell's Policy of Transportation', Part I, *Studies*, vol. XIX (December 1930), pp. 607–623; Part II, *Studies*, vol. XX (June 1931), pp. 291–305.

Hahn, T.F., *George Washington's Canal at Great Falls, Virginia*, Shepherdstown [W.V.]: American Canal and Transportation Center, 1976.

Halton, J., and Revd M. Harvey, *Newfoundland The Oldest British Colony ...*, London: Chapman & Hall, 1883.

Hammond, J.W., 'George's Quay and Rogerson's Quay in the eighteenth century', *Dublin Historical Record*, vol. V, no. 2, pp. 48–9.

Handcock, W.G., *Soe Long as there comes noe women: Origins of English Settlement in Newfoundland*, St John's [Newfoundland]: Breakwater Books, 1989.

Harrison, F., 'When The Convicts Came: A Chapter from "Land Marks of Old Prince William"', *Virginia Historical Magazine*, vol. XXX, no. 3 (July 1922), pp. 250–61.

Head, C.G., *Eighteenth Century Newfoundland: A Geographer's Perspective*, Toronto: McLelland & Stewart Ltd., 1976.

Heaney, Henry, 'Ireland's Penitentiary 1820–1831: An Experiment that Failed', *Studia Hibernica*, vol. 14 (1974), pp. 28–39.

Heath, James, ed., *Eighteenth Century Penal Theory*, London: Oxford University Press, 1963.

Henry, Brian, *Dublin Hanged: Crime, Law Enforcement and Punishment in Late Eighteenth-Century Dublin*, Dublin: Irish Academic Press, 1994.

——, 'The Machine in the Gallows', *Alumnus*, 1991, pp. 43–8.

——, 'Which Transportation: Irish or English, 1784–1791', *Alumnus*, 1992, pp. 1–12.

Hirst, J.B., *Convict Society and Its Enemies: A History of Early New South Wales*, Sydney: Allen & Unwin, 1983.

Holt, Joseph, *A Rum Story: The Adventures of Joseph Holt Thirteen Years in New South Wales (1800–12)*, ed. by Peter O'Shaughnessy, Sydney: Kangaroo Press, 1988.

Hood, Dorothy, *The Admirals Hood*, London: Hutchinson & Co, n.d.

Hornsby, S.J., *Nineteenth Century Cape Breton: A Historical Geography*, Montreal: McGill-Queen's University Press, 1992.

Howard, D.L., *John Howard: Prison Reformer*, London: Christopher Johnson, 1958.

Hughes, J.L.J., 'A Tour Through Dublin City in 1782', *Dublin Historical Record*, vol. XVII, no. 1 (December 1961), pp. 1–12.

Inglis, Brian, *The Freedom of the Press in Ireland 1784–1841*, London: Faber, 1954.

Johnson, K. and M. Flynn, 'Convicts of the *Queen*', in Bob Reece, ed., *Exiles from Erin: Convict Lives in Ireland and Australia*, London: Macmillan, 1991, pp. 10–26.

Johnston, Edith M., *Great Britain and Ireland 1760–1800: A Study in Political Administration*, Edinburgh: Oliver and Bond, 1963.

——, *Ireland in the Eighteenth Century*, Dublin: Gill & Macmillan, 1974.

Jupp, Peter, *Lord Grenville 1759–1834*, Oxford: Clarendon Press, 1985.

Kellow, Margaret M.R., 'Indentured Servitude in Eighteenth-Century Maryland', *Histoire Sociale-Social History*, vol. XVII (1984), pp. 229–55.

Kelly, Freida, *A History of Kilmainham Gaol: The Dismal House of Little Ease*, Dublin: Mercier Press, 1988.

Kelly, James, 'The Genesis of "Protestant Ascendancy": The Rightboy Disturbances of the 1780's and their Impact upon Protestant Opinion', in G. O'Brien, ed., *Parliament, Politics and People: Essays in Eighteenth Century Irish History*, Dublin: Irish Academic Press, 1989, pp. 93–127.

——, *Prelude to Union: Anglo-Irish Politics in the 1780's*, Cork: Cork University Press, 1992.

Kiernan, T.J., *Transportation from Ireland to Sydney: 1791–1816*, Canberra: the author, 1954.

King, Jonathan, *The Other Side of the Coin: A Cartoon History of Australia*, Sydney: Angus & Robertson, 1976.

Lahey, R.J., *James Louis O'Donel in Newfoundland 1784–1807: The Establishment of the Roman Catholic Church*, Newfoundland Historical Society Pamphlet No. 8 [St John's, Newfoundland], 1984.

Lambert, R.S., *The Prince of Pickpockets: A Study of George Barrington Who Left His Country For His Country's Good*, London: Faber & Faber, 1930.

Land, A.C., ed., *Letters from America of William Eddis*, Cambridge [Mass.]: Harvard University Press, 1969.

Linebaugh, Peter, *The London Hanged: Crime and Civil Society in the Eighteenth Century*, London: Allen Lane, 1991.

Lockhart, A., *Some Aspects of Emigration from Ireland to the North American Colonies between 1660 and 1775*, New York: Arno Press, 1976.

McCaffrey, L., *The Irish Diaspora in America*, Bloomington: Indiana University Press, 1976.

McCarthy, M.J., *The Irish in Newfoundland 1623–1800*, St John's [Newfoundland]: Harry Cuff Publications Ltd., 1982.

McCormack, E.I., *White Servitude in Maryland 1634–1820*, Baltimore: Johns Hopkins Press, 1904.

McCormack, W.J., *The Dublin Paper War 1786–1788*, Dublin: Irish Academic Press, 1993.

McCusker, John J. and Russell R. Menard, *The Economy of British America, 1607–1789*, Chapel Hill [N.C.]: University of North Carolina Press, 1985.

MacDonagh, O., *The Inspector General: Sir Jeremiah Fitzpatrick and the Politics of Social Reform, 1783–1802*, London: Croom Helm, 1981.

McDowell, R.B., 'The Personnel of the Dublin Society of United Irishmen 1791–4', *Irish Historical Studies*, vol. II (1940–1), pp. 12–53.

———, *Irish Public Opinion 1750–1800*, London: Faber, 1944.

———, *Ireland in the Age of Imperialism and Revolution*, 1760–1801, Oxford: Clarendon Press, 1979.

McGinn, Brian, 'Virginia's Lost Irish Colonists', *Irish Roots*, 1993, no. 4, pp. 21–4.

———, 'How Irish is Montserrat?', *Irish Roots*, 1994, no. 1, pp. 20–23, no. 2, pp. 15–17, no. 4, pp. 20–21.

Mackay, D., *A Place of Exile: The European Settlement of New South Wales*, Melbourne: Oxford University Press, 1985.

———, '"Banished to Botany Bay": The Fate of the Relentless Historian', *Australian Historical Studies*, no. 99 (October 1992), pp. 214–16.

MacKinnon, J.G., *Old Sydney: Sketches of the Town and its People in Days Gone By*, Sydney: Don McKinnon, 1918.

McLintock, A.H., *The Establishment of Constitutional Government in Newfoundland, 1783–1832: A Study of Retarded Colonisation*, London: Longmans, Green & Co., 1941.

MacNutt, Q.S., *The Atlantic Provinces: The Emergence of Colonial Society*, Toronto: McLelland & Stewart, 1965.

Malcomson, A.P.W., *John Foster: The Politics of the Anglo-Irish Ascendancy*, Oxford: Oxford University Press, 1978.

Mannion, John, 'The Waterford Merchants and the Irish–Newfoundland Provisions Trade, 1770–1820', in L.M. Cullen and P. Butel, eds., *Negoce et Industrie en France et en Irlande aux XVIIIe et XIXe Sicles*, Paris: Editions du Centre National du Recherche Scientifique, 1980, pp. 27–43.

———, 'Irish Merchants Abroad: The Newfoundland Experience, 1750–1850', *Newfoundland Studies* 2, 2 (1986), pp. 127–90.

———, 'Tracing the Irish: A Geographical Guide', *The Newfoundland Ancestor*, vol. 9, no. 1 (May 1993), pp. 4–18.

Marble, Allan Everett, *Surgeons, Smallpox, and the Poor: A History of Medicine and Social Conditions in Nova Scotia, 1749–1799*, Montreal: McGill-Queen's University Press, 1993.

Martin, G., ed., *The Founding of Australia: The Argument About Australia's Origins*, Sydney: Hale & Iremonger, 1978.

Martin, J., 'Convict Transportation to Newfoundland in 1789', *Acadiensis*, vol. 5 (1975), pp. 84–99.

Meehan, Patrick, 'Early Dublin Public Lighting', *Dublin Historical Record*, vol. v, no. 4 (June-August 1943), pp. 130–36.

Miles, H.D., *Pugilistica: The History of British Boxing ...*, 3 vols., Edinburgh: J. Grant, 1906.

Millar, J.F., *Early American Ships*, Williamsburg [Va.]: Thirteen Counties Press, 1986.

———, *A Handbook on the Founding of Australia, 1788: history, clothing patterns, ship plans, architecture, songs, dances*, Williamsburg [Va.]: Thirteen Colonies Press, 1988.

Moody, T.W., F.X. Martin and F.J. Byrne, eds., *A New History of Ireland*, vol. III, Oxford: Clarendon Press, 1978.

Morgan, K., 'The Organization of the Convict Trade to Maryland: Stevenson, Randolph & Cheston, 1768–1775', *William and Mary Quarterly*, vol. XLII (1985), pp. 201–27.

———, 'English and American Attitudes Towards Convict Transportation 1718–1775', *History*, 72 (1987), pp. 416–31.

Morgan, R.J., 'The Loyalists of Cape Breton', in Don Macgillivray and Brian Tennyson, eds., *Cape Breton Historical Essays*, Sydney [Cape Breton]: College of Cape Breton Press, 1980, pp. 18–25.

Moylan, Thor. King, 'The Little Green', Part I, *Dublin Historical Record*, vol. VIII, no. 3 (June–August 1946), pp. 81–91.

Murdoch, Beamish, *History of Nova Scotia, or Acadie*, 3 vols., Halifax [Nova Scotia]: Barnes, 1865–67.

Murphy, Sean, 'The Corporation of Dublin 1660–1760', *Dublin Historical Records*, vol. XXXVIII, no. 1 (December 1984), pp. 22–35.

Nash, R.C., 'Irish Atlantic Trade in the Seventeenth and Eighteenth Centuries', *William and Mary Quarterly*, vol. XLII (1985), pp. 328–56.

Neel, J.L., *Phineas Bond: A Study in Anglo-American Relations, 1786–1812*, Philadelphia: University of Pennsylvania Press, 1968.

Nicholson, Desmond, *Antigua, Barbuda and Redona: A Historical Sketch*, St John: Museum of Antigua and Barbuda, 1991.

O'Brien, Eris, *The Foundation of Australia (1786–1800)*, London: Sheed & Ward, 1937.

O'Brien, Gerard, *Anglo-Irish Politics in the Age of Grattan and Pitt*, Dublin: Irish Academic Press, 1987.

———, ext, *Parliament, Politics and People: Essays in Eighteeth Century Irish History*, Dublin: Irish Academic Press, 1989.

O'Donnell, Elliott, *The Irish Abroad: A Record of the Achievements of Wanderers from Ireland*, London: Isaac Pitman & Sons Ltd., 1915.

O Grada, Cormac, *Ireland: A New Economic History 1780–1939*, Oxford: Clarendon Press, 1994.

Oldham, W., *Britain's Convicts to the Colonies*, Sydney: Library of Australian History, 1990.

Oliver, V.L., *The History of the Island of Antigua ...*, 3 vols., London, 1894–99.

O'Neill, P., *The Oldest City: The Story of St John's, Newfoundland*, Erin [Ontario]: Press Porcepic, 1975.

———, *Upon This Rock: The Story of the Roman Catholic Church in Newfoundland and Labrador*, St John's [Newfoundland]: Breakwater Books, 1984.

O'Sullivan, Donal, 'Dublin Slang Songs, with Music', *Dublin Historical Record*, vol. I (1943), pp. 75–93.

Palmer, Stanley H., *Police and Protest in England and Ireland 1780–1850*, Cambridge: Cambridge University Press, 1988.

Panter, G.W., 'Eighteenth Century Dublin Street Cries', *Royal Society of Antiquaries of Ireland*, pp. 68–86.

Pedley, Charles, *The History of Newfoundland*, London: Longman, Green, Longman, Roberts & Green, 1863.

Perkins, H., *The Convict Priests*, Melbourne: [the author], 1984.

Pickell, John, *A New Chapter in the Early Life of Washington in Connection with the Narrative History of the Potomac Company*, New York: Burt Franklin, 1858.

Prendergast, John P., *The Cromwellian Settlement in Ireland ...*, London: Longmans, Green, Reaber & Dyer, 1865.

Prowse, D.W., *A History of Newfoundland from the English, Colonial, and Foreign Records*, London: Macmillan, 1895.

Reece, Bob, ed., *Exiles from Erin: Convict Lives in Ireland and Australia*, London: Macmillan, 1991.

———, '"Such a Banditti": Irish Convicts in Newfoundland, 1789', Part I, *Newfoundland Studies*, vol. 13, no. 1 (1997), pp. 1–29; Part II, vol. 13, no. 2 (1997), pp. 127–41.

———, 'Irish Anticipations of Botany Bay', *Eighteenth-Century Ireland*, vol. 12 (1997), pp. 116–36.

Riley, Sandra, *Homeward Bound: A History of the Bahama Islands to 1850 with a Definitive Study of Abaco in the American Loyalist Plantation Period*, Miami: Island Research, 1983.

Roe, Michael, 'Motives for Australian Settlement: a document', *Tasmanian Historical Research Association, Papers and Proceedings*, 2 (1952), pp. 18–19.

Rollman, Hans, 'Prince William Henry in Placentia', *The Newfoundland Ancestor*, vol. 9, no. 1 (May 1993), pp. 19–27.

Sanderlin, Walter S., *The Great National Project: A History of the Chesapeake and Ohio Canal*, Johns Hopkins University Studies in Historical and Political Sciences, series LXIV, no. 1, 1946.

Schmidt, F.H., 'Sold and Driven: Assignment of Convicts in Eighteenth-Century Virginia', *The Push from the Bush*, no. 23 (October 1986), pp. 1–27.

Shaw, A.G.L., *Convicts and the Colonies: A Study of Penal Transportation from Great Britain and Ireland to Australia and other parts of the British Empire*, London: Faber, 1966.

Smee, C.J., comp., *Third Fleet Families of Australia ...'* Artarmon [N.S.W.]: Third Fleet Families of Australia, 1991.

Smith, A.E., *Colonists in Bondage: White Servitude and Convict Labor in America 1607–1776*, Chapel Hill: University of North Carolina Press, 1947.

Smith, Warren B., *White Servitude in Colonial South Carolina*, Columbia University of South Carolina Press, 1961.

Sollers, B., 'Transported Convict Laborers in Maryland During the Colonial Period', *Maryland Historical Magazine*, vol. II, no. 1 (March 1907), pp. 17–47.

Southwood, Martin, *John Howard Prison Reformer: An account of his life and travels*, London: Independent Press Ltd., 1958.

Story, G.M., et al., eds., *Dictionary of Newfoundland English*, 2nd edn, Toronto: University of Toronto Press, 1990.

Tardiff, P., *Notorious Strumpets and Dangerous Girls: Convict Women in Van Diemen's Land 1803–1829*, Sydney: Angus & Robertson, 1990.

Truxes, T.M., *Irish-American Trade, 1660–1783*, Cambridge: Cambridge University Press, 1988.

Walker, James W. St. G., *The Black Loyalists: The Search for a Promised Land in Nova Scotia and Sierra Leone 1783–1870*, New York: Dalhousie University Press, 1976.

Way, Peter, *Common Labour: Workers and the Digging of North American Canals 1780–1860*, Cambridge: Cambridge University Press, 1993.

Williams, Fr. J.J., S.J., *Whence The 'Black Irish' of Jamaica?*, New York: Dial Press, 1932.

Wright, J. Leitch, Jr., *William Augustus Bowles: Director General of the Creek Nation*, Athens [Ga.]: University of Georgia Press, 1967.

Unpublished theses and papers

Byrne, C.L., 'Ireland and Newfoundland: The United Irish Rising of 1798 and the Fencible's [*sic*] Mutiny in St. John's, 1799', address to the Newfoundland Historical Society, St John's, 9 November 1977, 8pp. typescript, Queen Elizabeth II Library, Memorial University of Newfoundland.

Kavanaugh, A.C., 'John Fitzgibbon, Earl of Clare: A Study in Politics and Personality', Ph.D. thesis, Trinity College, Dublin, 2 vols., 1992.

Morgan, Robert, 'Orphan Outpost: Cape Breton Colony 1784–1820', Ph.D. thesis, University of Ottawa, 1972.

Refausse, R., 'The Economic Crisis in Ireland in the early 1780's', Ph.D. thesis, Trinity College, Dublin, 1982.

Schmidt, Frederick Hall, 'British Convict Servant Labour in Colonial Virginia', Ph.D., College of William and Mary, 1976.

Starr, Joseph P., 'The Enforcing of Law and Order in Eighteenth Century Ireland: A Study of Irish Police and Prisons from 1665 to 1800', Ph.D. thesis, Trinity College, Dublin, 1968.

Index

Note: all general references, e.g. to convict transportation, are to Ireland unless otherwise specified.

_____

Abaco (Bahamas), 71, 99
Abercorn, Marquess of, *see* Hamilton, John
Act of Union, 205
Admiralty, 194, 249
Africa, 70, 73, 74, 76, 79, 98, 100, 117, 126, 127, 133, 225, 267
Africa Company, 70, 73
Ailesbury, Lord, 216
Aix la Chapelle, Treaty of, 174
Albico, *see* Abaco
Alboy, Captain, 118
Alcock, Lord Mayor George, 113, 115, 274
Alexander, Lord Mayor William, 152, 165, 202, 203, 274
Alexandria (Va.), 107, 113, 268
Algeria, 74
Algiers, 74
American Loyalists, *see* Loyalists, American
American (Revolutionary) War, xvii, 1, 23, 126, 127, 176
Andrews, Richard, 245
Anguilla (Leeward Is.), 212, 219, 231
Annapolis, 14, 16, 18, 69, 112, 119, 121
Antigua (Leeward Is.), 2, 5, 83, 209, 211, 212
Archer, John, 10–11
Astley, Young, 249
Aston, Sir William, 8–9
Atkins, Governor Jonathan, 6
Auckland, Lord, *see* Eden, William
Avalon Peninsula (Newfoundland), 168

Bahamas, 71, 98, 99, 117–18, 119, 121–3, 150–1, 221
Baldwin, Abraham, 124
Ballad-singers, 61
Baltimore, xvi, 13, 68, 69, 81, 82, 85, 110, 111–12, 116, 117, 119, 123, 166, 121, 209
Banks, Sir Joseph, 175
Barbados, xvi, 2, 4, 5, 7, 99
Barbuda (Leeward Is.), 92, 209, 210–11
Barres, Major F.W. des, 75
Barrington, F., 5
Barrington, George, 35–7, 222
Basseterre (St Kitt's), 102
Bastille, 48, 53
Batavia, 228
Bateson, Charles, 257
Bathurst, Francis, 93
Bay Bulls (Newfoundland), 168, 169, 183, 190
Bay Settlement, *see* Honduras
Beauchamp Committee, 66, 73, 125, 133
Beaufort (Carolina), 256
Beccaria, Cesare, 56, 232
Belfast, 16, 121, 183
Belize, *see* Honduras
Bentham, Jeremy, 57, 230, 232
Bermuda, 70
Bernard, Scrope, 267, 268
Bethesda Chapel (Dublin), 94
Black-dog Prison, 55
Blake, John, xvi
Blandford, 121
Blow, Lieut. Samuel, 258, 263, 264–5, 302, 303

Board of Trade, 8, 85, 176
Bodenstown (Co. Kildare), 42
Bond, Phineas, 85–7
Bonfoy, Governor, 175
Bordeaux, 96
Botany Bay, *see* New South Wales
Botany Bay Parliament, 140–2,
    Appendix V
Botany Bay scheme, 63, 70, 115, 116,
    127, 146, 149, 152, 168, 169,
    218
  cost to Irish government of, 231,
    233, 241
  delays in shipping for, 267–71
  first Irish responses to, 129–32
  Irish attempts to join, 135, 148,
    231, 235–6, 238–9
  Irish legislation enabling
    participation in, 235
  Irish official interest in joining,
    133–4
  Irish participation in, 240
  satirical anticipations of, 137–42
  reduced Irish interest in, 249–52
Bourbon Is., 94
Bourgchier, Sir Arthur, 1
Bourke, Sir Richard, 142
Bowles, William Augustus, 118
Braniforte, Governor de, 101, 103
Break O'Day Boys, 245
Breda, Treaty of, 7
Bridenbaugh, Carl and Roberta, 2
Bridewell, St James St, Dublin, 23, 39,
    45–6, 56, 229–30, 144
Bristol merchants, 2, 4, 5
British Treasury, 25
Broderick, 31
Brooks, Captain Henry, 181–2
Bruce, Captain Peter, 93
Bryan, Arthur, 83, 165, 167–8, 208,
    209, 217, 221, 285, 286–7
Bryan, Edward, 83
Bryan, Edward, 211
Bryan, George, 83, 165, 167–8, 209,
    221, 285
Buckingham, Marquis of, *see*
    Grenville, George Nugent-
    Temple
Burgen, Christopher, 62

Burgess, 24
Burk, Captain, 214
Burke, Edmund, 125, 139
Burke, Fr Edmund, 177, 178
Burke, John, 245
Butler, James (Duke of Ormonde), 8,
    10
Byrne, Dermont, 225

Caffrey, Luke, 64
Camden, Calvert and King, 240, 256,
    258–61, 271, 292–6
Campbell, Duncan, 66, 71
Campbell, Vice Admiral John, 176,
    177
Campbell, Captain William, 160
Canada, *see* Nova Scotia, Cape Breton
    Island, Newfoundland, New
    Brunswick
Canary Is., 101–4, 125
Cannaday, Richard, 9
Cape Breton Is., 73, 74–6, 91, 136,
    158–65, 208, 268
Cape Coast Castle (Ghana), 73, 79,
    240
Cape Spear (Newfoundland), 168
Capital punishment, *see* executions
Carleton, Lord, 197
Carlisle, Lord Lieutenant, 20
Carmarthen, Marquis of (Duke of
    Leeds), 85–7, 103–4, 123–4
Carrickfergus, 247
Carroll, Fr Keane, 10
Cartagena (Colombia), 268–9
Cash, John, 47
Cavan grand jury, 228
Censor hulk, 66
Chalking Act (1778), 46, 59–60, 93,
    223
Chambers, John, 244
Charlemont, Lady, 37
Charlemont, Lord, 32, 253
Charleston, 117, 209, 212
Chesapeake Bay, 106
Chichester plantation (Wexford), 1
China, 94, 129, 132, 251
Christian, Captain William, 208–11,
    284–7
Clanwilliam, Earl of, 92

Clare, Co., 3
Clare, Earl of, *see* Fitzgibbon, John
Clarence, Duke of, 176–9
Clonmel, Lord (Chief Justice), 193,
    197, 198, 199, 202, 203, 204,
    235
Coal-quay (Dublin), 37
Codrington, Sir Christopher, 7
Codrington, Sir William, 211, 215,
    217–18, 219
Codrington family, 210
Coke, Thomas d'Ewes, 140, 192
Colchester, 3
Condron, William, 180
Commerford, Nicholas, 10
Commission of Oyer and Terminer,
    27, 93, 94, 184, 227, 244
Condy and Bryan, 209, 212
Conception Bay (Newfoundland),
    169, 175, 186
Congress, *see* Continental Congress
Connaught, 3
Connecticut, 146, 150, 153, 168
Connery, Elinor, 180
Connolle (Connome), Catherine, 243
Connolly, Catherine, 247
Connolly, Thomas, 247
Connor, 117–18
Connor, John, 74
Conolly, Sarah, 38
Continental Congress, 67, 116, 1
    23–4
convict returnees, xviii, 89–97, 227
    Cunningham, John, 136–7
    Dalton, John, 63
    Dalton, William, 91, 137
    Davis, Obadiah, 137
    Davis, Obigal, 91
    Ellis, 91
    Lambert, Frederick, 11, 63–4, 90–1,
        92–3
    Moran, 115
    Lynch, Lawrence, 92
    O Neal, 227
    Thompson, 92
convict transportation
    American legislation limiting, 3–4,
        18, 80, 112, 119–21, 124, 268,
        282

American objections to, 17, 112,
    123–4
criticism of, 18–21
Cromwellian, 2–5
cost of, 233, 274
early history of, 1–2, 8–11
legislation enabling, 11–12, 15, 23,
    126–8, 234–5
organisation of, 14–15, 127–9
returnees from, *see* convict
    returnees
statistics of, 14–16
substitution of hard labour for,
    21–2, 79
support for, 25
use by courts of, 14
Convict transports
    Albemarle, 37
    Alexander, 257 (convicts of: Rea,
        William, 104)
    Anne-Mary, 105–7, 110, 112;
        convicts of: Stevens, Thomas,
        104
    Chance, 116–18 (convicts of:
        Cauldfield, Patrick, 117, 122;
        Hamilton, James, 117, 121,
        122)
    Boddington's, 271
    Charming Nancy, 150–4
    Dispatch, 90, 115–16 (convicts of:
        Moran, 115)
    Dispatch, 112–13, 152
    Duke of Leinster, 83, 87, 92, 96, 165,
        166, 167, 168, 208, 211–3, 217,
        218, 221, 274; Newfoundland
        voyage, convicts of [*see also*
        Appendix II]: Brosnahan,
        Cornelius, 183; Byrne, John,
        183; Coyle, John, 183; Delaney,
        Michael, 184; Dempsey,
        Matthew, 172, 189; Ellis,
        Samuel, 183; Farrell, John, 184;
        Gibbeons, William, 184;
        Keeley, John, 174; Keough,
        John, 183; Lacey, Francis, 183;
        Leonard, Patrick, 183, 185;
        McAleese, Daniel, 184, 185;
        McDermot, Thomas, 183;
        McGuire, James, 172, 189;

Convict transports, Duke of Leinster
(*cont.*)
   Myler, James, 183, 189; O Neal,
      John, 183, 184, 185; Reily,
      James, 184–5, 186, 190);
   Barbuda voyage (convicts of
      [*see also Appendix IV*]:
      Cunningham, James, 137;
      Dalton, William, 215; Kean,
      Peter, 215; Mooney, Michael,
      215; Tyrrell, Francis, 215)
   Elizabeth and Clare, 188, 190, 191
      (convicts of, *see Appendix II*)
   Fair American, 69, 70
   Four Brothers, 268
   George, 67–9, 80
   Kitty, 268
   Marquis Cornwallis, 273
   Mercury, 69, 70, 80
   Nancy, 101–4, 274 (convicts of:
      Bennett, John, 102; Farrel,
      Mary, 102; Sands, James, 102)
   Prince William Henry, 119, 121, 123
   Providence, 155–9, 274 (convicts of:
      Kirkpatrick, John, 159;
      McDonald, Joseph, 159,
      161–2; Prendergast, Laurence,
      156, 159, 161–2)
   Queen, see separate listing
   Sugar Cane, 271; *Swift, see George*
Cook, Captain James, 130, 131, 132,
   248–9
Cooley, Thomas, 47
Cork, 8, 59, 99, 105, 107, 113, 133,
   144–5, 146, 147
Cotter, Sir James Laurence, 247
Council of State for Ireland, 3
Council for Trade and Plantations, 4
Countess, Captain, 194
County gaols
   building programme for, 59
   conditions at, 57, 59
   escape attempts from, 59
Country Police Act, 126
Court of King's Bench (Irish), 193,
   248
Court of Vice-Admiralty, 171, 256
Cove of Cork, xviii, 254, 260, 265,
   271, 273

Cowes, 194
Cox, Gaoler Richard, 226, 227
Cox's Museum (Dublin), 248
Coyshe, Captain Robert, 188, 189,
   190, 191, 281
Craig, Maurice, 48
Creek Nation, 118
Crewis, 130
Crime
   in the countryside, 41–2
   in Dublin, 26–40
   1790 statistics for, 43–4
Cromwell, Lord Henry, 5
Cromwell, Oliver, 2, 3
Cummings, Ensign William, 258,
   262–3, 265
Cunnin, Captain Michael, 101–4
Cunningham, Anthony, 136–7
Cunningham, John, 91, 136–7
Cunningham, Thomas, 136
Curragh (Co. Kildare), 145
Curtis, Timothy, 256
Customs House (Dublin), 34
Cuyler, Abraham, 75, 161, 162

Dalkey, 78
Dalkey Island (Dublin Bay), xv, 78,
   254–5
Dalkey, King of, 139, 255
Dalkey, Kingdom of, 137, 139
Daly, 14
Dampier, Captain William, 131
Dartmouth, 175
Das Voltas Bay (Namibia), 70, 133
Deakins, Col. William, 106, 107
Debenham, Captain Thomas, 91, 148,
   155, 157–8, 163–5
Defenders, 245
Deficiency law, 7
Defoe, Daniel, 28
Delany, Michael, 227
Delaware R., 86
Dempsey, Charles, 153
Deptford, HMS, 192, 204
Despard, Col., 70
Devereux, Catherine, 244–5
Dickinson, John, 17
Dixon, Francis, 158–9
Dolphin tender, 253

Domett, Captain, 188
Dorrill, Governor, 175
Douglas, Sylvester, 273
Dowling, Sylvester, 211, 212, 217
Doyle, Edward, 53
Drake, HMS, 192
Drogheda, 3, 74, 234
Dublin Castle government, xvii, 123, 149, 208, 219, 255
Dublin Corporation, xvii, 12-3, 22, 23, 39, 46-7, 57, 128, 149, 225-6, 229
Dublin police, 20, 40, 126
Dublin Volunteers, 139
Dundalk, 9
Dundas, Henry, 217, 268, 269
Dunmore, Earl of, *see* Murray, John
Dun Laoghaire, 117

Earlsfort, Lord Chief Justice, 56, 94, 143-4
East India Company
  assignment of convicts to, 23, 77
  monopoly of trade by, 134
  proposed transportation of convicts by, 129, 270
East Indies, 132
Easton, William, 189
Eden, William, 19-20, 21, 56, 62, 74, 77, 79, 232
Eddis, William, 18
Edgeworth, Robert, 96-7
Egan, John, 31
Ekirch, R., xvi, 34
Elford, Major James, 172-3
Elliot, Governor, 176, 180-1
Emigrant ships (to America)
  Conyngham, 86
  Havannah, 86
  Liberty, 84
  Nancy, 86
  Olive Branch, 69
  Sarah and Rebecca, 16
  St James, 86
Emigration (to America)
  abuses in, 85-6
  legislation discouraging, 85
  rate of, 81-2, 85

  see also indenture system, redemptioners, runaway servants
English Harbour (Antigua), 219
Etches, Alexander, 256
Executions
  bungling of, 62, 93
  celebration of, 61, 63-5
  criticism of, 79
  deterrent value of, 60-1
  at Kilmainham, 91
  rate of, 60
  reactions to, 60
  reprieves from, 63
  at Newgate, 60, 61, 62, 63, 64, 93, 223-4, 227
  at St Stephen's Green, 63, 136
Exshaw, Lord Mayor John, 223

Fane, John (Earl of Westmorland), 192, 218, 219, 231, 235, 237, 239, 246, 268, 269, 270, 273
Far East, xvii
Faulkner, Sir Riggs, 247
Fay, Patrick, 61, 93-7, 137, 166, 205, 206
Feeny, Hugh, 63
Ferguson, Sheriff Charles, 264
Ferra, *see* Hierra
Ferryland Harbour (Newfoundland), 169, 187, 188, 189, 179-81
Ferryland 'riots', 179-81
First Fleet, xvi, 115, 131-3, 146, 188, 257
Fisher's Bay (Baltimore), 119
Fitzgerald, Col. John, 107, 113
Fitzgibbon, John (Earl of Clare), xvii, 126, 128, 165, 193, 195-7, 199-200, 201-2, 203, 204, 207
Fitzpatrick, Sir Jeremiah, xvii, 50, 58, 97, 168, 228, 230
  accounts of prison conditions by, 50, 57, 59
  analysis of 1790 crime by, 42-4
  influences on, 56-7
  Inspector-General of Prisons, 56
  and prison building programme, 59
  and prison reform legislation, 57

Fitzpatrick, Sir Jeremiah (*cont.*)
  recommends penitentiary system, 45–6
  supervision of Dublin penitentiary by, 271, 272–3
  and transportation to Botany Bay, 232
  writings of, 56, 232
flax, 133
Flood, Dr Francis, 153
Florida, 99
Florida, Spanish, 118
Forbes, John, 234
Fort Camden (Cork), 264
Fort Charlotte (New Providence), 118
Fort George (St Eustatia), 101–2
Fort Townshend (Newfoundland), 173, 179, 186, 188
Fortaventura (Canary Is.), 101
Foster, John, 195, 197, 200
Four Courts (Dublin), 12, 34
Fox, Brazil, 34–5
Fox, Charles James, 139–40
France, 90, 115, 229
Franklin, Benjamin, 17
Fraser & Co., 256
Freeman, Thomas, 211
French
  expedition to Nova Scotia, 71
  invasion of St Kitt's, 6
  invasion of Montserrat, 7
  invasion of Newfoundland, 174–5
French, Oliver, 3
Frost, Alan, xvi
Fulham, Patrick, 93

Galenson, D.W., 85
Gallows-hill, *see* Kilmainham
Galway, 5
Gambia R., 78, 125, 240
Gamble, Revd, 93, 223
Gardiner, Luke, 141
George, Denis, 135–48
George's Quay (Dublin), 15
George-Town (Maryland), 13, 106, 107, 111, 113, 209
Georgia, Irish convicts in, 17, 124, 268
German Palatines, 87

Gibbes, Governor Johannes, 212
Gibbons, Chief Justice Richard, 162
Giles, James, 88
Gillen, Mollie, xvi
Gleeson, John, 171, 178–9
Godfrey, Patrick, 62
Golden Grove store ship, 248
Goodwin, Peter, 10
Gookin, Daniel, 2
Gordon, George, 141
Gordon riots, 141
Graham, Aaron, 188
Grand Canal, 92
Grandall, Samuel, 14
Grattan, Henry, 128, 234
'Grattan's Parliament', xvii, 198
Great Heneaga, *see* Inagua
Greene, Godfrey, 128
Greene, Lord Mayor Thomas, 25, 80
Grenville, George Nugent-Temple-(Marquis of Buckingham), 46, 95, 122, 124, 146, 147–9, 164–5, 168, 180, 198, 211
Grenville, William, 124, 148, 163–4, 191–4, 197, 199–204, 218, 219, 231, 240
Griffith, Richard, 128, 233
Guernsey, 175
Guinea, 205
Gwynn, Fr Aubrey, xvi

Hacket, William, 90
Halifax (Nova Scotia), 72, 75, 105, 151
Halloran, Lawrence Hines, 95
Hamilton, Captain, 113
Hamilton, James Sackville, 126, 133, 137, 219, 267, 270–1, 272–3
Hamilton, John (Marquess of Abercorn), 269–270
Hamilton, William, 66, 67
Hancock, Governor John, 116
Hanging, *see* Executions
Hanging-ballads, 61, 63–5
Harbour Grace (Newfoundland), 188–9
Hard Labour Act, 21–3, 45, 74, 80, 98
Harris, Lord Mayor Richard, 260, 254, 302

Harris, Revd Richard, 187
Harrison, Captain Richard, 96, 166, 168–9, 205
Hasek, Jaroslav, 32
Hatch, John, 243
Hatton, Lady, 27
Havard, Rice, 8–9
Hawaii, 132
Hayes, Sheriff Sir Henry Brown, 264–302
Hazard tender, 253
'Heads of a Plan', 133
Hebe, HMS, 262
Heneaga, *see* Inagua
Henry, Brian, xvii
Hibernia tender, 271
Hierra (Canary Islands), 101–4, 125
Hobart, Major Robert (Government Secretary), 193, 197–8, 199, 200, 203–4, 207, 208, 211, 218, 241, 267, 268, 269, 270, 271
Hogan, Captain Michael, 273
Hogarth, William, 28
Holland, 228
Holmes, Peter, 57, 228, 233–4, 271
Holt, General Joseph, 37
Home Office, British, xvii, 122, 129, 146, 165, 273
Honduras (Belize), xv, xvi, 69–70, 104
Hood, Captain Alexander, 262–3, 264–5
Hood, Admiral Sir Thomas, 256, 265
Hooe, Robert Townshend, 113
Hooe and Harrison, 113
House of Commons, Irish, 126, 128, 231–4
House of Industry, Dublin, 39
Howard, John, 47–9, 54, 55, 57, 232
Howard Society, 272
Hughes, Patrick, 227
Hulks Act (British), 20, 21, 71
Hulk system (British), xvi, 22–3
Humphrey, William, 185
Hunter, Governor Robert, 8
Hurford, William, 73
Hutchings, Richard, 170
Hutchinson, William, 212, 216

Inagua (Bahamas), 117–18
Indenture system
 for convicts, 13–14, 111
 for free emigrants, 83, 84, 85
Indentured servants, 83–7
India, 132
Indians, American, 84, 118
Inspector-General of Prisons, *see* Fitzpatrick, Sir Jeremiah
'Irishtown', Antigua, 212
Italy, 229

'Jack-a-boy', 145
Jackson, Charles, 245
Jackson, Eyre, 245
James R., 18
Japan, 251
Jamaica, 5, 7, 11, 70, 99
Jay, Foreign Secretary John, 69, 116, 123–4
Jenkin, Sheriff, 101
Jersey, 175, 200
Jones, Capt. William, 54
Jupiter, HMS, 213

Kavanaugh, Ann, xvii, 204
Keegan, Luke, 159–60
Keen, William, 175
Keenan, John, 26–7, 28, 53, 60, 64
Kelso, John, 119, 121
Kenyon, Lord, 204
Kiernan, T.J., 245
Killet, Sir Richard, 248
Kilmainham (New), 54–5
Kilmainham (Old), xviii, 27, 46, 53–5, 62
 conditions at, 53, 54, 55
 escape attempts from, 53, 55, 143, 144, 226
Kilmainham (Gallows-hill), executions at, 26, 34, 60–1, 90, 91–2,
King George III, xv, 66, 67, 124, 129, 144, 198
King James I, 1
King William IV, 177
King, Governor Philip Gidley, 260
Kinsale, 5

Labrador, 155
Langdon, Magistrate, 176
Larry, 63–4
Leeds, Duke of, *see* Carmarthen,
    Marquis of
Leeward Is., 2, 5, 6, 7, 96, 99, 209–217
Lemain Is. (Gambia R.), 70, 78, 125,
    240
Lester, Benjamin, 173
Lewellin, Maria, 61, 95, 96–7
Liberties (Dublin), 25, 91, 172
Ligon, Richard, 5–6
Limerick, 14
Linen Hall (Dublin), 32, 34, 244
Liston, Robert, 103–4
Litle, Margaret, 9
Little, Charles, 248
Little-green (Dublin), 46, 223, 227
Lockhart, Audrey, xvi, 14
Londonderry, 86–7
Long Island (Bahamas), 118
Long Island (New York), 121
Lovell, Langford, 211, 215, 217, 218
Loyalists, American, 71–3, 99

Macarmick, Lieut.-Col. William, 75,
    160–5
MacConmara, Donnchadh Ruadh,
    170
MacCurdy, John, 184, 185
MacDonagh, Oliver, xvii
McEnnallan, Catherine, 244
Machias, Bay of, 116, 190
Mackay, David, xvi
Madrid, 103
Mahony, Timothy, 91
Main à Dieu Harbour (Cape Breton
    Is.), 158–9, 161
Maine, 116
Marsh, Capt., 139
Marshalseas, 54, 55–6, 143–4
Martell, Charles, 158–159, 160
Martin, Ged, xvi
Maryborough (Portlaoise), 226
Maryland, xvi, 1, 8, 17, 67–9, 89,
    119–20, 268
Maryland General Assembly, 69
Mason, George, 124
Massachusetts, 4, 116

Mathew, Lieut.-General, 219
Mathews, David, 161
Maxwell, Governor John, 99
Maxwell, Lieut., 249
May, William, 153
McDaniel, Patrick, 244
McDermot, Anthony, 223
McDowell, R.B., xvii
McGowran, Hugh ('Morning Star'),
    32, 90–1
McKinley, John, 27, 46, 53, 55, 62,
    143, 253
McVeagh, Terence, 247
Mendoza, Daniel, 36–7
Mescouez, Troilus de (Marquis de la
    Roche), 71
Micmac Indians, 75
Milbanke, Vice Admiral Sir Mark, 171,
    183–4, 185, 190, 191, 192, 197,
    199–200, 202, 205, 213, 281
'Mocatasaney', 28
Molloy, Anthony, 91, 156, 157,
    166–7
Montserrat (Leeward Is.), 2, 5, 7,
    212
Moore, George, 66–70, 71, 200
Moore, Samuel, 152–3
Moore, Thomas, 255
Mosquito Shore (Nicaragua), 20
Mountmorres, Lord, 137
Murdoch, Beamish, 73
Murphy, John, 63
Murphy, William, 88
Murray, John (Earl of Dunmore),
    118–20
Muskitta (Newfoundland), 169

Nairne, Lieut., 265
Napper, Captain, 115
Nassau (Bahamas), 119, 121
Navy Board, 240, 258, 264, 265
Nepean, Evan, 73, 125, 133–4, 135,
    218, 219, 231, 267, 270, 271,
    272
Nesbitt, John Maxwell, 107
Nevin, Captain Duncan, 105, 112,
    113
Nevis (Leeward Is.), 7
New Brunswick, 116, 149

Newenham, Denis, 189
Newenham, Sir Edward, 54, 137
Newfoundland, xvi, 148
  attitudes to Catholic Irish in,
    174–6, 177–9
  constitutional status of, 183,
    201–2
  emigration to, 169, 170
  trade with, 169
  workers in, 178, 181
Newfoundland Fencibles Regiment,
  179
Newfoundland Station, 177, 201,
  213
Newgate, xviii, 11, 23, 37, 46, 61
  conditions at, 45–53
  construction of, 47–8
  executions at, 60, 61, 62, 64, 93,
    227
  governance of, 48–9
  riots at, 147, 222–3
  epidemics at, 100, 142
  escapes and escape attempts at, 48,
    52, 100, 142–3, 144, 147, 227,
    269
Newgate (London), 37
New Holland, 131
  see also, New South Wales
New Jersey, 17
New London (Mass.), 146, 150, 153,
  168
New Prison, *see* Newgate
New Providence (Bahamas), 99,
  118–9, 151, 221
New South Wales, xvii, 141, 148, 131,
  220, 235, 241, 251, 260, 263, 267,
  270, 271
  early reports from, 248
  later reports from, 249–50
New South Wales Corps, 191, 258,
  270, 273
New York, 71, 99, 111, 121
Newport News (Va.), 2
Newspapers, 27
Nicholson, Lieut., 264
Nootka Sound, 221
North, Lord, 20, 66, 67, 71, 139–42,
  200
North Carolina, 112, 124, 268

North Wall (Dublin), 91, 96, 101,
  105, 113, 115, 155, 206, 210,
  253
Northington, Lord Lieut., 198
Nova Scotia, 69, 71–3, 76, 105, 115,
  127, 136, 148, 149, 155, 200, 204,
  208
Nowlan, Bridget, 244, 253
Nulty, Matthew, 37, 223

O'Brien, Eris, xvi
O Donel, Fr James Louis, 173–4, 176,
  177, 178–9, 180–1
Oldham, W., xvi
Old New Gate, 46
Oliver, V.L., 219
O'Neile, Henry More, 9
Onslow, Captain, 194
Orde, Chief Secretary Thomas
  interest in Beauchamp Committee,
    125
  knowledge of the India Trade,
    134–5
  and the Police Bill (1786), 125–9,
    133
  response to Botany Bay scheme,
    134, 135
  retirement of, 146
Ormonde, Duke of, *see* Butler, James
Osborn, Captain Henry, 169
Outerbridge, Leonard White, 121,
  123
Owen, Captain Richard, 256, 258,
  262, 263–5, 266

Paca, Governor William, 69
Pacific Islands, xvii, 131–2
Palliser, Governor, 175
Pamp, Captain Thomas, 67
Parker, Commander William, 213–4,
  217
Parliament, 201
  see also, House of Commons
Parliament, British, 198
Parnell, Sir John (Chancellor of the
  Exchequer), 228, 230, 231, 232–3,
  234, 241
Parr, Governor John, 71–3, 160,
  162–3, 208

Patowmack Canal Company, 106–10, 113–15
Patriot opposition, 198, 199, 201, 234, 235
Patriots, *see* Patriot opposition
Pawnbroking Act (1786), 31
Peckham, Lord Mayor Robert, 72
Peeble's gang, 42
Pegasus, HMS, 177
Pellew, Captain Edward, 181, 187
Penelope, 87
Penitentiary Act, British (1779), 20, 77
penitentiary system
   British example cited, 233–4
   debated in Irish Parliament, 232–4
   Dublin Corporation and, 46, 271
   Irish judges questioned on, 236
   Irish legislation for, 271
   operation of, 270–1
   proposed by Sir J. Fitzpatrick, 45–6
   Smithfield penitentiary, 272
Penitentiary system (British), 233–4
Pennsylvania, 1, 17
Petty, Sir William, 3
Philadelphia, 8, 13, 16, 17, 81, 82, 83, 84, 85, 86, 87, 88, 207
Phillip, Governor Sir Arthur, 130, 250
Phoenix Park, 27
Pickpockets, Prince of, *see* Barrington, George
'Pinkindindies', 33
Pitt, William, 70, 126, 132, 200, 269
Pitt, General Sir William, 145
Pitt government, xvi, xvii, 70, 78
Placentia (Newfoundland), 176, 177, 178, 187
Police, *see* Dublin police
Police Act (1778), 21
Police Act (1786), 12, 23, 27, 39, 77, 112, 125–9, 133, 135, 197, 199, 201, 233, 231, 234
Pool, Robert, 47
Poolbeg Fort, 204, 205
Poole (Dorset), 173, 175
Port Roseway (Nova Scotia), 73, 115, 148, 155
Portland, Duke of, 273
Portsmouth, 188, 190, 194, 195, 236, 249, 267

Potomac R., 106
Power, Fr Patrick, 180–1
Prague, 32
Prendergast, J.P., 3, 4
Preston, battle of, 3
Preston, John, 8
Price, Revd Walter, 174, 177, 184–5
Prince William Henry, *see* Clarence, Duke of
Prince of Wales, 198
Pringle and Ridley, 69
Prisons, *see* Newgate, Kilmainham, Black-dog Prison, Marshalseas, county gaols
Prison reform, 51, 57
   see also Fitzpatrick, Sir Jeremiah; Holmes, Peter; Parnell, Sir John; Griffith, Richard
Prisons Act (1784), 233
Pritchard, William, 88–9
Privy Council, 192
prostitution (Dublin), 39–40
public executions, *see* executions

Queen transport, xv, xviii, 137, 189, 240, 241, 267, 271
   contract for, 258–60, 292–6
   convicts embarked on, 36, 137, 189, 242–8, 296–303
   delayed departure from Cork of, 262–5
   origins of, 256
   ownership of, 256–7
   specifications of, 256–7
   convicts embarked on 36, 137, 189, 242–8, 296–303
   (for full list, see Appendix VI: Berrall, Andrew, 243; Blake, James, 243; Brazil, Sarah, 242; Cahir, James, 243; Carr, George, 247–8; Clark, Ann, 242; Cunningham, John, 243; Dwyer, Thomas, 245; Ennis, Mary, 244; Fay, David, 242; Fitzgerald, Patrick, 245; Grant, James, 244; Jackson, Charles, 245; Jackson, Eyre, 245; Kennedy, Edmund, 245; Kirwin, Garrat (Kirwan,

George), 63, 244; Leonard, Patrick, 244; Lynch, Hugh, 244; McClernan, Francis, 245; McDaniel, Terence, 243; McKelvey, James, 247; McMahon, Christopher, 243; Marshall, Charles, 243; Mullen, Thomas, 247; Nulty, Mathew, 37, 223; Owen, Felix, 247; Regan, Thomas, 247; Rieley, William, 247; Stephenson, Margaret, 242; Whelan, Mary, 244)

Queen Charlotte, see Queen transport

Rapahanok R., 121
Rapparees, 11
Read, John, 223
Redemptioners, 85–6
Red string plot (1735), 17
Redmond, John, 37, 222
Regency Crisis, 148, 198–9, 231
Reilly, 24
Relief brig, 160
'Renunciation Act' (1783), 198
Returnees, *see* convict returnees
Revolutionary War, 14, 21
Richards, William Jr, 239, 270–1
Ridley, Matthew, 69
Riely, William, 242
Rightboys, 41, 126, 127
Rhode Is., 14
Riot Act, 126
Robinson, Judge, 27
Robinson, George, 92, 137
Robinson, Richard, 167–8, 171, 190, 192
Roche, Marquis de la, *see* Mescouez, Troilus de
Rodney, Governor, 174
Roe, Gaoler George, 50–2, 57, 91, 147
Roe, Gaoler Henry, 49
Rogerson's Quay (Dublin), 15
Rose, Lord Mayor John, 146, 148, 167, 168, 208, 274, 284–5
Rose, Captain Walter, 186
Rotunda, Dublin, 32
Rowlandson, Thomas, 139
Royal Exchange, Dublin, 34, 47, 227

Royal Hospital, Kilmainham, 94
Royal Navy
    American Loyalists serving in, 72
    recruitment of Irish prisoners by, 23, 24, 222, 231
    timber from Newfoundland for, 169
Rumsey, James, 108, 110
Runaways, *see* servants, runaway
Rutland, Duke of, 25, 26, 56, 125, 126, 133, 135, 146

Sable Is. (Nova Scotia), 71
Salisbury, HMS, 182, 190
Sally transport, 72, 73
Salmon, George, 66, 67–9, 71
Sandy Hook (New Jersey), 154
Sankey, Lord Mayor Henry-Gore, 268–9
Scarborough transport, 257
Scott, John, 6
Searle, Governor Daniel, 6
Second Fleet, 70, 188
Seduction of Artisans Act, 85
Seneca Falls, 106
Senegamba, 205
Sharp, Captain, 248
Shaw, A.G.L., xvi, xvii
Shea, Daniel, 256
Shea, William, 93
Sheil, Patrick, 247
Shelburne, Lord, 134
Shelburne (Nova Scotia), 115
Shenandoah Falls, 106, 108
Sheridan, Charles Francis, 141
Shirley, Governor Sir Thomas, 211–17
Shirley Heights (Antigua), 219
Slaves, negro, 5–6, 109, 115
St Augustine, 72–3, 118
St Christopher's, *see* St Kitt's
St Eustatia (Leeward Is.), 101, 102
St George, Christopher, 245
St Jago de la Naga, 256
St John (Antigua), 211, 212, 215
St John's (Newfoundland),
St John's Quay (Dublin), 83
St Kitt's (Leeward Is.), 2, 5, 6, 7, 101, 102, 104, 212
St Martin's (Leeward Is.), 212, 214, 217

St Vincent's (Leeward Is.), 96
Servants, runaway (in America),
 114–15
  Crowley, John, 109
  Joyce, Edward, 88
  Keating, Andrew, 109
  Lewis, Richard, 88
  Maloan, Hugh, 109
  Meaghan, Robert, 109
  O'Neil, 88–9
  Ready, Patrick, 109
Sierra Leone, 73, 268
Slane Castle, 253
Slaves, negro, 17, 215
Smallwood, Governor William,
 119–21
Smith, A.E., xvi
Society for the Propagation of the
 Gospel, 187
Society of United Irishmen, 179, 273
South Carolina, 112, 268
South Seas, 248–9
Southern Shore (Newfoundland), 169,
 174
Spain, 6, 104, 222, 229
Spithead, 186, 188, 191
Stafford, Captain Patrick, 116–17,
 122, 170
Stamp Act, 14
Starr, J.P., 22
Stevens, Jack, 139
Stewart and Plunkett, 87, 88, 106, 107
Stockden, William, 105
Stoke's Bay (Cowes), 194
Stott, Robert, 262
Stout, Keith, 160
Stuart, Richardson, 108, 110
Sudley, Lord, 27
Surinam, 228
Sydney (Cape Breton Is.), 75–6, 160–5
Sydney (New South Wales), 260, 262
Sydney Cove, xv
Sydney, Lord, *see* Townshend,
 Thomas

Taitt, Provost Marshall David, 160,
 161
Tandy, J. Napper, 139
Temple, Sir John, 121, 123

Tench, Capt. Watkin, 248
Third Fleet, 240, 257, 258
Tholsel, 39, 49, 93, 135
Thompson, Captain William, 119–21
Thurloe, Secretary, 5
Thurlow, Lord Chancellor Edward,
 191–2, 204
Tippin, Gawen, 9
Toler, Serjeant, 143
Tone, Theobald Wolfe, 42, 132
Tories, 11
Tortola (Virgin Is.), 214
Townshend, Thomas (Lord Sydney),
 70, 71, 72, 74–5, 121, 122, 148,
 169, 180, 200, 240
trade
  with North America, xvii, 67, 87,
   132
  with the West Indies, xvii, 132
  with Europe, xvi, 132
  with New South Wales, xvi
  with the Far East, xvii, 134–5
  with the Pacific Islands, xvii
Traile, John, 54
Transportation, *see* convict
 transportation
Transportation (British), 127
Trinidad, 117
Troy, Archbishop John, 173, 178–9
Tunis, 74
Tyler, Corporal Thomas, 263
Tyrone, 245

Vagabond Act, 11, 12, 39
Vagabonds, 15, 23, 244
Virginia, xvi, 1, 8, 13, 17, 89, 112,
 119, 124, 282
Virginia Capes, 106
Virginia Company, 2

Wallace, James, 16
Wallace and Bryan, 16
Walsh, Deputy Gaoler, 51
Warner, Sir Thomas, 2
Washington, George, 106, 107,
 108
Waterford, 169–70, 181, 190
Weir, John, 245
Welsh, Margaret, 184–5

West Indies, 1, 2–8, 9, 251, 99–102, 117–19, 121–3, 210–19, 251
Westmorland, Earl of, *see* Fane, John
White, Surgeon John, 248
Whiteboys, 41, 126, 127, 273
Whitehaven, 96
Wicklow Head, 96, 206
Wild, Jonathan, 30
Wilde, George ('Ree-raw'), 34
William of Orange, 7
Williams, Capt. Griffith, 174–5
Williams, Fr J.J., xvi

Williamson, Hugh, 124
Willoughby, Governor William, 6
Winter, James, 172
Winthrop, Captain Robert, 150, 152, 153–4, 155, 209
Withers, Capt., 27
Wolfe, Attorney-General Arthur, 219, 235
Woodward, Richard, 140
Wylly, William, 119, 122
Wymondham (Norfolk), 233

York, Duke of, 37